Windows® Networking Basics

Kenneth Gregg

IDG Books Worldwide, Inc.
An International Data Group Company

Foster City, CA ◆ Chicago, IL ◆ Indianapolis, IN ◆ New York, NY

IDG BOOKS WORLDWIDE™

Windows® Networking Basics

Published by
IDG Books Worldwide, Inc.
An International Data Group Company
919 E. Hillsdale Blvd., Suite 400
Foster City, CA 94404
www.idgbooks.com (IDG Books Worldwide Web site)

Library of Congress Catalog Card Number: 98-73338

ISBN: 0-7645-3214-6

Printed in the United States of America

10 9 8 7 6 5 4 3 2 1

1B/RW/QZ/ZY/FC

Distributed in the United States by IDG Books Worldwide, Inc.

Distributed by Macmillan Canada for Canada; by Transworld Publishers Limited in the United Kingdom; by IDG Norge Books for Norway; by IDG Sweden Books for Sweden; by Woodslane Pty. Ltd. for Australia; by Woodslane (NZ) Ltd. for New Zealand; by Addison Wesley Longman Singapore Pte Ltd. for Singapore, Malaysia, Thailand, Indonesia, and Korea; by Norma Comunicaciones S.A. for Colombia; by Intersoft for South Africa; by International Thomson Publishing for Germany, Austria, and Switzerland; by Toppan Company Ltd. for Japan; by Distribuidora Cuspide for Argentina; by Livraria Cultura for Brazil; by Ediciencia S.A. for Ecuador; by Ediciones ZETA S.C.R. Ltda. for Peru; by WS Computer Publishing Corporation, Inc., for the Philippines; by Unalis Corporation for Taiwan; by Contemporanea de Ediciones for Venezuela; by Computer Book & Magazine Store for Puerto Rico; by Express Computer Distributors for the Caribbean and West Indies. Authorized Sales Agent: Anthony Rudkin Associates for the Middle East and North Africa.

For general information on IDG Books Worldwide's books in the U.S., please call our Consumer Customer Service department at 800-762-2974. For reseller information, including discounts and premium sales, please call our Reseller Customer Service department at 800-434-3422.

For information on where to purchase IDG Books Worldwide's books outside the U.S., please contact our International Sales department at 650-655-3200 or fax 650-655-3297.

For information on foreign language translations, please contact our Foreign & Subsidiary Rights department at 650-655-3021 or fax 650-655-3281.

For sales inquiries and special prices for bulk quantities, please contact our Sales department at 650-655-3200 or write to the address above.

For information on using IDG Books Worldwide's books in the classroom or for ordering examination copies, please contact our Educational Sales department at 800-434-2086 or fax 317-596-5499.

For press review copies, author interviews, or other publicity information, please contact our Public Relations department at 650-655-3000 or fax 650-655-3299.

For authorization to photocopy items for corporate, personal, or educational use, please contact Copyright Clearance Center, 222 Rosewood Drive, Danvers, MA 01923, or fax 978-750-4470.

ABOUT IDG BOOKS WORLDWIDE

Welcome to the world of IDG Books Worldwide.

IDG Books Worldwide, Inc., is a subsidiary of International Data Group, the world's largest publisher of computer-related information and the leading global provider of information services on information technology. IDG was founded more than 25 years ago and now employs more than 8,500 people worldwide. IDG publishes more than 275 computer publications in over 75 countries (see listing below). More than 90 million people read one or more IDG publications each month.

Launched in 1990, IDG Books Worldwide is today the #1 publisher of best-selling computer books in the United States. We are proud to have received eight awards from the Computer Press Association in recognition of editorial excellence and three from *Computer Currents'* First Annual Readers' Choice Awards. Our best-selling *...For Dummies®* series has more than 50 million copies in print with translations in 38 languages. IDG Books Worldwide, through a joint venture with IDG's Hi-Tech Beijing, became the first U.S. publisher to publish a computer book in the People's Republic of China. In record time, IDG Books Worldwide has become the first choice for millions of readers around the world who want to learn how to better manage their businesses.

Our mission is simple: Every one of our books is designed to bring extra value and skill-building instructions to the reader. Our books are written by experts who understand and care about our readers. The knowledge base of our editorial staff comes from years of experience in publishing, education, and journalism — experience we use to produce books for the '90s. In short, we care about books, so we attract the best people. We devote special attention to details such as audience, interior design, use of icons, and illustrations. And because we use an efficient process of authoring, editing, and desktop publishing our books electronically, we can spend more time ensuring superior content and spend less time on the technicalities of making books.

You can count on our commitment to deliver high-quality books at competitive prices on topics you want to read about. At IDG Books Worldwide, we continue in the IDG tradition of delivering quality for more than 25 years. You'll find no better book on a subject than one from IDG Books Worldwide.

IDG BOOKS WORLDWIDE

John Kilcullen
CEO
IDG Books Worldwide, Inc.

Steven Berkowitz
President and Publisher
IDG Books Worldwide, Inc.

VIII WINNER

Eighth Annual Computer Press Awards 1992

IX WINNER

Ninth Annual Computer Press Awards 1993

1994 COMPUTER CURRENTS READERS' CHOICE 1995

X WINNER

Tenth Annual Computer Press Awards 1994

XI WINNER

Eleventh Annual Computer Press Awards 1995

IDG Books Worldwide, Inc., is a subsidiary of International Data Group, the world's largest publisher of computer-related information and the leading global provider of information services on information technology. International Data Group publishes over 275 computer publications in over 75 countries. More than 90 million people read one or more International Data Group publications each month. International Data Group's publications include: **ARGENTINA:** Buyer's Guide, Computerworld Argentina, PC World Argentina; **AUSTRALIA:** Australian Macworld, Australian PC World, Australian Reseller News, Computerworld, IT Casebook, Network World, Publish, Webmaster; **AUSTRIA:** Computerwelt Osterreich, Networks Austria, PC Tip Austria; **BANGLADESH:** PC World Bangladesh; **BELARUS:** PC World Belarus; **BELGIUM:** Data News; **BRAZIL:** Annuário de Informática, Computerworld, Connections, Macworld, PC Player, PC World, Publish, Reseller News, Supergamepower; **BULGARIA:** Computerworld Bulgaria, Network World Bulgaria, PC & MacWorld Bulgaria; **CANADA:** CIO Canada, Client/Server World, ComputerWorld Canada, InfoWorld Canada, NetworkWorld Canada, WebWorld; **CHILE:** Computerworld Chile, PC World Chile; **COLOMBIA:** Computerworld Colombia, PC World Colombia; **COSTA RICA:** PC World Centro America; **THE CZECH AND SLOVAK REPUBLICS:** Computerworld Czechoslovakia, Macworld Czech Republic, PC World Czechoslovakia; **DENMARK:** Communications World Danmark, Computerworld Danmark, Macworld Danmark, PC World Danmark, Techworld Denmark; **DOMINICAN REPUBLIC:** PC World Republica Dominicana; **ECUADOR:** PC World Ecuador; **EGYPT:** Computerworld Middle East, PC World Middle East; **EL SALVADOR:** PC World Centro America; **FINLAND:** MikroPC, Tietoverkko, Tietoviikko; **FRANCE:** Distributique, Hebdo, Info PC, Le Monde Informatique, Macworld, Reseaux & Telecoms, WebMaster France; **GERMANY:** Computer Partner, Computerwoche, Computerwoche Extra, Computerwoche FOCUS, Global Online, Macwelt, PC Welt; **GREECE:** Amiga Computing, GamePro Greece, Multimedia World; **GUATEMALA:** PC World Centro America; **HONDURAS:** PC World Centro America; **HONG KONG:** Computerworld Hong Kong, PC World Hong Kong, Publish in Asia; **HUNGARY:** ABCD CD-ROM, Computerworld Szamitastechnika, Internetto online Magazine, PC World Hungary, PC-X Magazin Hungary; **ICELAND:** Tolvuheimur PC World Island; **INDIA:** Information Communications World, Information Systems Computerworld, PC World India, Publish in Asia; **INDONESIA:** InfoKomputer PC World, Komputek Computerworld, Publish in Asia; **IRELAND:** ComputerScope, PC Live!; **ISRAEL:** Macworld Israel, People & Computers/Computerworld; **ITALY:** Computerworld Italia, Macworld Italia, Networking Italia, PC World Italia; **JAPAN:** DTP World, Macworld Japan, Nikkei Personal Computing, OS/2 World Japan, SunWorld Japan, Windows NT World, Windows World Japan; **KENYA:** PC World East African; **KOREA:** Hi-Tech Information, Macworld Korea, PC World Korea; **MACEDONIA:** PC World Macedonia; **MALAYSIA:** Computerworld Malaysia, PC World Malaysia, Publish in Asia; **MALTA:** PC World Malta; **MEXICO:** Computerworld Mexico, PC World Mexico; **MYANMAR:** PC World Myanmar; **NETHERLANDS:** Computer! Totaal, LAN Internetworking Magazine, LAN World Buyers Guide, Macworld Netherlands, Net, WebWereld; **NEW ZEALAND:** Absolute Beginners Guide and Plain & Simple Series, Computer Buyer, Computer Industry Directory, Computerworld New Zealand, MTB, Network World, PC World New Zealand; **NICARAGUA:** PC World Centro America; **NORWAY:** Computerworld Norge, CW Rapport, Datamagasinet, Financial Rapport, Kursguide Norge, Macworld Norge, Multimediaworld Norge, PC World Ekspress Norge, PC World Nettverk, PC World Norge, PC World ProduktGuide Norge; **PAKISTAN:** Computerworld Pakistan; **PANAMA:** PC World Panama; **PEOPLE'S REPUBLIC OF CHINA:** China Computer Users, China Computerworld, China InfoWorld, China Telecom World Weekly, Computer & Communication, Electronic Design China, Electronics Today, Electronics Weekly, Game Software, PC World China, Popular Computer Week, Software Weekly, Software World, Telecom World; **PERU:** Computerworld Peru, PC World Profesional Peru, PC World SoHo Peru; **PHILIPPINES:** Click!, Computerworld Philippines, PC World Philippines, Publish in Asia; **POLAND:** Computerworld Poland, Computerworld Special Report Poland, Cyber, Macworld Poland, Networld Poland, PC World Komputer; **PORTUGAL:** Cerebro/PC World, Computerworld/Correio Informático, Dealer World Portugal, Mac*In/PC*In Portugal, Multimedia World; **PUERTO RICO:** PC World Puerto Rico; **ROMANIA:** Computerworld Romania, PC World Romania, Telecom Romania; **RUSSIA:** Computerworld Russia, Mir PK, Publish, Seti; **SINGAPORE:** Computerworld Singapore, PC World Singapore, Publish in Asia; **SLOVENIA:** Monitor; **SOUTH AFRICA:** Computing SA, Network World SA, Software World SA; **SPAIN:** Communicaciones World España, Computerworld España, Dealer World España, Macworld España, PC World España; **SRI LANKA:** Infolink PC World; **SWEDEN:** CAP&Design, Computer Sweden, Corporate Computing Sweden, Internetworld Sweden, it.branschen, Macworld Sweden, MaxiData Sweden, MikroDatorn, Nätverk & Kommunikation, PC World Sweden, PCaktiv, Windows World Sweden; **SWITZERLAND:** Computerworld Schweiz, Macworld Schweiz, PCtip; **TAIWAN:** Computerworld Taiwan, Macworld Taiwan, NEW ViSiON/Publish, PC World Taiwan, Windows World Taiwan; **THAILAND:** Publish in Asia, Thai Computerworld; **TURKEY:** Computerworld Turkiye, Macworld Turkiye, Network World Turkiye, PC World Turkiye; **UKRAINE:** Computerworld Kiev, Multimedia World Ukraine, PC World Ukraine; **UNITED KINGDOM:** Acorn User UK, Amiga Action UK, Amiga Computing UK, Apple Talk UK, Computing, Macworld, Parents and Computers UK, PC Advisor, PC Home, PSX Pro, The WEB; **UNITED STATES:** Cable in the Classroom, CIO Magazine, Computerworld, DOS World, Federal Computer Week, GamePro Magazine, InfoWorld, I-Way, Macworld, Network World, PC Games, PC World, Publish, Video Event, THE WEB Magazine, and WebMaster; online webzines: JavaWorld, NetscapeWorld, and SunWorld Online; **URUGUAY:** InfoWorld Uruguay; **VENEZUELA:** Computerworld Venezuela, PC World Venezuela; and **VIETNAM:** PC World Vietnam.

5/7/98

Credits

ACQUISITIONS EDITOR
Tracy Thomsic

DEVELOPMENT EDITORS
Alex Miloradovich
Stefan Grünwedel

TECHNICAL EDITOR
Mark Cooper

COPY EDITOR
Larisa North

PROJECT COORDINATOR
Susan Parini

COVER COORDINATOR
Andreas Schueller

GRAPHICS & PRODUCTION SPECIALISTS
Vincent F. Burns
Mary Penn
Hector Mendoza
E. A. Pauw

QUALITY CONTROL SPECIALISTS
Mick Arellano
Mark Schumann

PROOFREADER
Laura Bowman

INDEXER
Richard Shrout

About the Author

Kenneth Gregg has over 21 years of experience working with computers as a consultant, software engineer, and manager. For five years, he was an engineer and manager in the Windows NT product group at Microsoft. He is the author of the *Windows NT Server 4.0 Administrator's Bible* (IDG Books Worldwide), and owns Digital Intelligence, a computer consulting and training firm. Ken develops and teaches courses covering computer networking, Windows NT, Windows 9*x*, hardware, and the Internet. He also serves as a beta tester for all Windows operating systems and BackOffice products. Ken holds a B.S. in computer science from Michigan State University, and an M.S. in computer science from the University of Texas.

To my wife, Theresa, who once again let me enter my own little world to write a computer book by "tippy-tapping on the 'puter" for months on end. Her sacrifice has not gone unnoticed.

Preface

Even if you have only two computers, establishing a computer network can help your organization run more efficiently. Today's networks involve many hardware, software, and configuration choices, however, and can be difficult to design, install, and maintain. The array of alternatives is mind-boggling, and there always seems to be someone ready to offer advice – both good and bad. Although navigating around the potential tar pits and making the right choices can take some time and effort, the benefits of networking are well worth the investment. The fact that you've picked up this book says you already realize this.

Why You Should Read This Book

In this book, you'll discover the key concepts, terminology, techniques, and issues associated with establishing and maintaining a successful computer network using Microsoft Windows 98 and other Windows products. Whether you're a computer professional, a business professional, or a "power user" who needs to get up to speed quickly – whether you plan to build and maintain the network yourself or hire an expert – this book is for you. It gives you all the essential information you need to make informed decisions.

Getting Started

You don't need to know anything about computer networks before tackling this book – but to succeed, you do need some experience with personal computers (PCs) and Microsoft Windows operating systems (Windows 98, Windows 95, Windows for Workgroups 3.11, Windows 3.1, or any version of Windows NT). You need to have mastered basic Windows mouse and keyboard skills to follow the step-by-step instructions, and have a fundamental understanding of personal computer hardware components (processors, memory, hard disks, CD-ROMs, and so forth). You don't have to know how all these components work. You just need to understand which functions they perform for you.

Armed with these knowledge prerequisites, you shouldn't have any trouble on your journey through computer networking.

Up and Running

It's perfectly all right to plow through this book without spending a penny on hardware, software, or network consultants. In theory, you can learn about computer networks without a network and even without a computer. However, I strongly recommend you have at least one computer running the Microsoft Windows 98 operating system.

With a Windows 98 computer available, you can follow the step-by-step instructions, and explore the tools and techniques presented throughout this book. And if you're putting a network together, you can see practical applications of the networking concepts you're learning.

How to Use This Book

One of the primary goals of this book is to help you plan your network thoroughly—before spending (and perhaps wasting) lots of time and money. As you progress in your network education, you may also decide that you need to enlist the help of an experienced network professional to install cabling, connect and test computers, or configure the network hardware and software. This book helps you make these critical planning decisions along the way, and covers the specifics of selecting and installing the components you need.

Describing the Parts

You'll find that each part of this book logically builds on the knowledge you gain in previous parts. Here's how it works:

- **Part I: Understanding Computer Networks**—Here, you learn the basic networking concepts: the benefits of networking, a brief historical view of the evolution and use of computer networks, and background information on the Internet and intranets. By the end of Part I, you'll know enough to determine whether a computer network would benefit your organization. You'll also have the background required for the next part, which covers the details of network implementation.
- **Part II: Creating a Computer Network**—This part of the book focuses on understanding, selecting, and installing the infrastructure (cabling, connections, and so forth), and the computer systems required to implement a reliable and efficient Windows 98 network. It provides a practical overview of each aspect of networking technology—including the choices available, relative costs, pros and cons, and specific recommendations. This prepares you for Part III, where you learn how to deal with life as a network administrator after installation.

- **Part III: Administering Your Network** – This part of the book starts with an overview of the responsibilities of a network administrator and the tools required to accomplish these tasks. Then, it delves into the specific areas that require the most attention: administering resources, implementing security, planning for disasters, troubleshooting, and achieving the best performance possible. Along the way, you'll encounter concrete, step-by-step procedures that illustrate key tasks. By the end of Part III, you'll understand the requirements of a network administrator – and if your network is operational, you'll be able to perform several important administrative tasks just by following the examples.
- **Appendixes** – To make your networking experience even more complete and to further your quest for knowledge, two appendixes are included at the back of the book. These appendixes cover network software installation on various operating systems and provide a thorough list of other Windows 98 and networking resources.

Conventional Wisdom

This book uses certain conventions and styles to make your reading experience more enjoyable and informative. Here's what to look for:

- Whenever a new term is introduced, it appears in *italics* and is followed by a definition.
- To make life easier, a shorthand notation is used to guide you quickly through a series of actions. For example, if you see "Click Start → Programs → Accessories → Notepad," this means you should click the Start button, point to the Programs menu item, point to the Accessories menu, and finally click the Notepad menu item.
- Shaded sidebars (like the "Getting Started" and "Up and Running" sidebars earlier in this preface) provide optional topics, anecdotes, or stories that complement or expand the main text.

TIP

Sections marked with the Tip icon contain additional insight, practical techniques, and hints to save you time and effort. Tips often include specific recommendations and advice to help you become a better network administrator.

When the text refers you to another chapter or an appendix in the book, look for the Cross-Reference icon.

When you see a Caution icon, beware of possible pitfalls that could cost you unnecessary time, effort, or money. You'll be warned about potential problems, and how and why to avoid them.

Sections marked with a Note icon highlight supplementary information and additional details. Notes are also used to offer advice and reassurance along the way.

Summary

Every chapter in this book concludes with a summary, just like this one. It briefly recaps the information you just absorbed and points you on your way to the next step in the process.

If you've gotten this far, it's time to turn the page and begin your networking journey. I think you'll find that the valuable knowledge contained in this book will start you on your way to many years of productive and enjoyable networking with Windows 98. I welcome your comments and any suggestions you may have for future editions of this book. You can contact me at `kengr@acm.org`.

Acknowledgments

Thanks to the folks at IDG Books Worldwide for giving me the opportunity to write this book. Their team put a great deal of effort into making this book a reality. Specifically, I want to express deep gratitude to development editors Stefan Grünwedel and Alex Miloradovich, who worked diligently to keep everything on track and running smoothly throughout the entire publishing process. Their professionalism, humor, and patience were assets to the project. Also, thanks to Claire Keaveney for her editorial contributions. Many thanks go to Mark Cooper for his thoroughness as technical editor – he made several good catches, and helped make some of the technical concepts more understandable and complete. Thanks also to Larisa North for her expert copy editing of the final manuscript.

In addition, I would like to thank Tracy Thomsic, acquisitions editor, for helping to move the project from outline to manuscript, and for helping us all cope with a changing landscape along the way. I would also like to express my gratitude to John Read, executive acquisitions editor, and Anne Hamilton, acquisitions editor, for their involvement in the initial concept and in getting the project kicked off.

Many thanks go to the hard-working members of the Windows 98 and Windows NT development and test teams at Microsoft Corporation, who continue to create and improve world-class network operating system products. Special thanks go to the Windows 98 test team for making sure that the beta releases and final product were reliable. I know exactly what it takes to turn out stable operating system products – so your colossal efforts are much appreciated. Now, get some well-deserved sleep.

Finally, I would like to extend my thanks to you, the reader, for the time you invest in this book. I hope it will prove useful as you commence your journey into the world of Windows networking.

Contents at a Glance

Contents

Part I

Understanding Computer Networks

Chapter 1

Why Do You Need a Network?

IN THIS CHAPTER

- Computer network basics: what and why
- Types of networks
- Evolution of networks
- How Windows 98 fits into the networking picture
- Network uses, costs, and benefits

THE FACT THAT you've picked up this book says that you already know a computer network may benefit your organization. You may also know that Microsoft Windows 98 plays an important role in today's PC networks. And you're absolutely correct on both counts. But just what is a computer network, why would you want one, and how do Windows 98 and other Microsoft Windows products fit into the picture?

In this chapter, you'll learn about the basics of a computer network, why you may need one, how networks have evolved to their current forms, and how networks are used in organizations today. You'll also learn how to justify installing a computer network to improve your organization's bottom line. By the end of this chapter, you'll have the background you need to proceed with your Windows networking education.

Now, let's start answering the question posed by this chapter – "Why do you need a network?" – by answering some other important, fundamental questions.

What Is a Computer Network?

If you've ever used a telephone, you've already used a computer network. Armed with a telephone, you can connect to just about any other telephone in the world and share information (for example, the status of Uncle Louie's recovery from bunion surgery). From your perspective, a wire (or radio waves, if you have a cellular phone) connects your telephone directly to the other party, enabling you to communicate with each other. In reality, several computer systems and other communication devices lie between you and the other party. The unseen portion of the telephone network is actually a complex computer network.

In its simplest form, a *computer network* is really just two or more computers connected together so they can exchange information. A network is made up of the collection of computers and the connections between them that allow this information exchange to take place. While most networks connect computers using some form of cable, the connections can also be wireless (for example, radio waves, infrared signals, and so forth). To simplify the discussion, I typically refer to the connection between networked computers as if it were a physical cable, unless I'm specifically discussing wireless networks. Later in this chapter, I provide a bit more detail on what constitutes a computer network, but for now this definition will do the job.

NOTE

As you progress in your network education, you may be overwhelmed by myriad terms and acronyms used to describe networking concepts and technologies. But fear not. You can ground yourself in the knowledge that even the most sophisticated computer networks are really based on the simplest network — two computers with a connection between them. You can boil down and understand many networking concepts by applying them to this simple case.

Why Network Your Computers?

Why are computer networks important? What motivates people to go to the trouble of connecting computers together? These are good questions, and you'll find the answers in a lesson your parents and teachers hopefully taught you early in life – that *sharing* is a good thing to do. Indeed, sharing is the chief motivation for networking computers. A network enables you to share resources such as files, devices (hard disks, printers, modems, and so forth), and software applications. You'll see this concept of sharing come up repeatedly in this book and in your real-world experience with networks.

Problem – Sharing Without a Network

If your organization already has computers, but they aren't yet connected to each other on a network, how do you give a copy of your spreadsheet to Fred down the hall? And how do you print your weekly report on the manager's fancy laser printer? Without a network, you probably resort to copying your files to a floppy disk, walking the disk to the appropriate destination computer, and copying the files from the floppy disk onto the destination computer's hard disk. (This low-tech approach to sharing information has come to be known as *SneakerNet*, because you have to walk the files physically from one place to another. If the humor of this term isn't immediately apparent to you, don't worry. I'll bring it up later and tell you when it's appropriate to laugh.)

How does your organization schedule meetings? If your group consists of more than a handful of people, this activity can be one of your biggest time drains and sources of frustration. You may coordinate nearly everyone's individual schedules, only to find that Ernie has a dentist appointment that conflicts with the meeting. Or perhaps everyone can make it, but the conference room isn't available. Maybe your manager is called out of town at the last minute, and you have to go through the entire process again to reschedule the meeting. The more people, rooms, and meetings you have to juggle, the worse the scheduling problem becomes.

Solution – Sharing with a Network

In all of these situations, installing a computer network can make your life much easier – and make your organization more productive. Without leaving your desk, you can accomplish each of these tasks: Give a copy of your spreadsheet to Fred by sharing the spreadsheet file with him over the network; print your weekly report on your manager's printer by sending it over the network to her shared printer; and schedule that important meeting using a shared group scheduling software application.

No, the network doesn't do *all* the work for you – you still have to perform these activities. But with a network, they take much less time and energy, allowing you to concentrate on doing the job you were hired to do. As you'll see later in this chapter, having a network also enables you to work, cooperate, and communicate in new ways that offer even greater efficiency for your organization. Figure 1-1 shows a conceptual view of a network that allows sharing of files, printers, and applications.

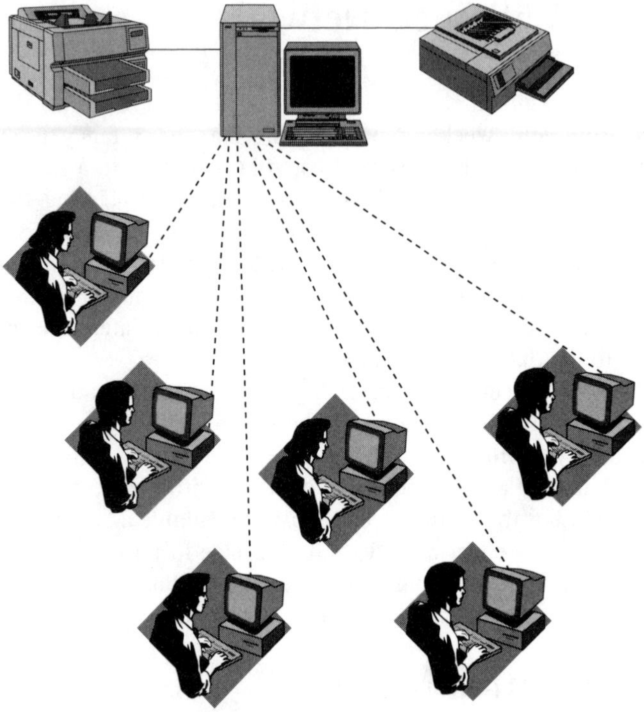

Figure 1-1: A computer network enables many users to conveniently share files, applications, printers, and other devices.

What Makes Up a Network?

Now that you know why networks are important, it's time to dig just a little deeper into the question of what constitutes a computer network. Networks consist of computers and other devices, the physical connections between them, and the additional hardware and software required to enable them to communicate with each other. In the chapters to come, I'll delve into the details of each of these components. For now, though, let's focus on the roles played by the computers, the basic types of networks, and the software that makes it all work.

Network Role-Playing

Step back for a moment from the friendly concept of sharing, and consider a computer network analogy in business terms. A business provides products or services (or some combination thereof) to its customers. Even if a business is primarily product-driven, it provides a set of services to its customers, who are sometimes called clients. So you could say that a business *serves its clients*.

On a network, computers usually play one of two roles. They either offer resources for other computers to use, or they access resources that have been shared by other computers. If a computer on the network shares resources for others to use, it's called a *server computer* or simply a *server.* (Think of the server taking on the role of the business providing services.) If a computer on the network accesses resources that are shared by other computers, it's called a *client computer* or *client.* (Again, in business terms, the client is the customer who accesses the services offered.)

NOTE You'll also see client computers sometimes referred to as *workstations.* They're really the same thing. The idea behind this term is that a client computer usually has someone sitting in front of it, whereas a server computer is often locked away in seclusion. Computers that are on (or next to) people's desks have come to be known as workstations.

In theory, there's really no difference between a server and a client. Only their roles on the network differ. In practice, however, servers are often more powerful computers (with faster processors, more memory, more disk space, and so forth) because of the extra demands placed on them by multiple users. A server must provide service to many users on the network, whereas a client usually needs to keep only one user happy. But servers aren't always more powerful than clients. Depending on what a client computer is asked to do, it may be just as powerful as a server or it may contain components that a server lacks. So you really can't tell the difference between clients and servers without understanding the role they play on the network.

Dedicated Server Networks

In many computer networks, there's a crystal clear distinction between server computers and client computers. Each computer on the network acts as either a server or a client. This type of network is called a *dedicated server network*, and each server computer on the network is called a *dedicated server.*

Computers that are cast in the role of servers have *dedicated* their lives to being servers – they aren't used as client computers. Figure 1-1 illustrates how a dedicated server network might be designed. The computer at the top of the figure is the dedicated server, sharing printers, files, and applications. The remaining computers in the illustration are clients that access resources shared by the server. Likewise, in a dedicated server network, client computers never act as servers – all shared resources on the network are shared by the servers and accessed by the clients.

You may see this type of network referred to as a client-server network in other books. Unfortunately, the term "client-server" has other meanings, which I explain later in this chapter. So I'll consistently use the term *dedicated server network* to refer to this type of network with well-defined roles.

Peer-to-Peer Networks

Now it's time to muddy the waters a bit. Some networks don't distinguish between servers and clients at all. In these networks, every computer is treated as an equal citizen, capable of playing the role of client, server, or both at the same time. This type of network is called a *peer-to-peer network*, and each computer on the network is referred to as a *peer*. In a peer-to-peer network, a peer computer acts as both a server and a client at the same time. So the peer computer on your desktop can (acting as a server) share files and printers with other computers, and it can simultaneously access (acting as a client) other shared resources on the network. Figure 1-2 shows a conceptual view of a peer-to-peer network.

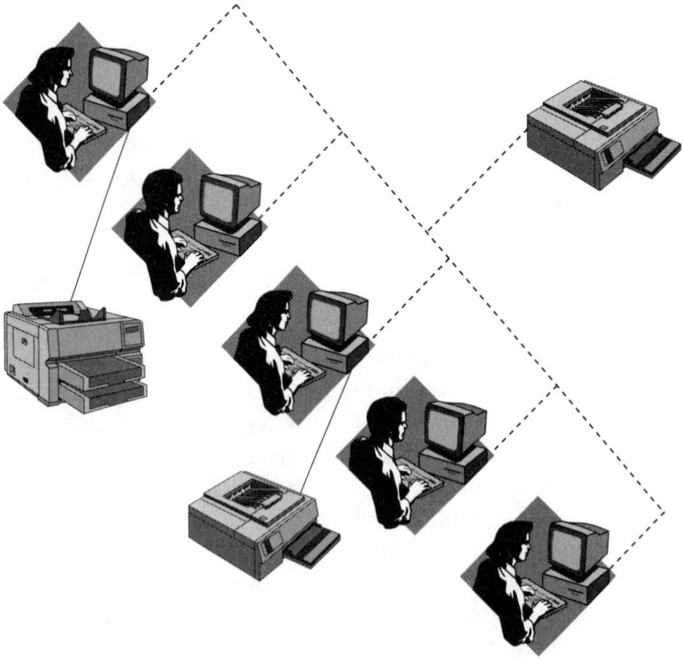

Figure 1-2: A peer-to-peer network enables all computers on the network to share resources with one another.

For example, if your manager has a laser printer attached to the computer in her office, her computer acts as a server when it shares the printer over the network for your group to use. On the same computer, your manager may frequently access files that are shared by her assistant's computer. In this situation, your manager's computer acts as a client when she accesses this shared information. So her computer acts as both a server and a client, depending on the task it's performing. She doesn't have to reboot the computer to change its role – her computer is both a server and a client at all times. This is the essence of peer-to-peer networking. At least for the computers involved, peer-to-peer networking provides the ultimate in democratic freedom – any computer can be anything it aspires to be.

NOTE: As you might guess, both dedicated server and peer-to-peer networks have their pros and cons. How you plan to use your network and what hardware and software you intend to use will influence your choice. In some situations, a hybrid combination of dedicated server and peer-to-peer networks is the best approach. In Chapter 2, I discuss the process of choosing the right approach for your network.

A collection of computers (or users) participating in a peer-to-peer network is sometimes called a *workgroup*. This term sprang from the concept of a small group of users assigned to work together on a common project. The group's productivity can be enhanced by a peer-to-peer network, in which all members of the group can freely share resources with one another. The workgroup concept illustrates the underlying philosophy of peer-to-peer networks, as shown in Figure 1-2.

Networking Software

Computer networks require a combination of both hardware and software. Once you have your network hardware in place, you need a *network operating system*, or *NOS*, to make it all work. A NOS is either a standalone operating system with built-in networking features (for example, Microsoft Windows 98 or Windows NT), or a network software layer that runs on top of an existing operating system (similar to Windows 3.1 running on top of MS-DOS). Either way, the NOS provides all the features required to communicate over the network with other computers, to access network resources, and to share them.

As your network grows in the number of computers (both servers and clients), users, and shared resources, the complexity of planning and maintaining your network increases quickly. Keeping track of user accounts, passwords, and the physical locations of computers, printers, and shared information can become a daunting task. Fortunately, the same software that makes basic networking possible – the NOS – also provides the tools you need to handle these network management tasks.

Throughout this book, you'll learn about these tools and how to use them to your advantage.

Local Area Networks

You can find several different types of computer networks in use today, depending primarily on the size of the physical area they cover. The most common type of network is the *local area network*, or *LAN*. It's a network that spans a fairly limited physical area, usually ranging from a small office to a campus of buildings. A LAN typically uses high-speed wired connections between the computers.

Although a LAN, by definition, covers a small physical area, don't assume that all LANs are small. A single LAN can range in size from two computers to many thousands. For example, the network in my office that connects three computers together is a LAN. It includes one server and two clients. Likewise, the 12,000-computer network on Microsoft's corporate campus is a LAN. It's made up of hundreds of servers and thousands of clients.

LANs emerged in the early days of personal computers, and were originally designed to share expensive printers and hard disks within an organization. Since then, organizations have started sharing other devices including CD-ROM drives, modems, and scanners. LANs are also used today for sharing applications, group scheduling, e-mail, project tracking, and other tasks.

Wide Area Networks

When a network covers a larger area, making it impractical to wire computers together with high-speed communication lines, it becomes a *wide area network*, or *WAN*. A WAN spans a large physical area, connecting several sites of an organization across cities, counties, states, countries, continents, and (perhaps in the future) planets. Because of the longer distances involved, WANs are sometimes referred to as *long-haul networks*.

In theory, the concepts and purposes of WANs are identical to those of LANs. In practice, WANs present additional challenges, because they typically rely on slower long-distance connections between sites using leased lines or even satellite links. As a result, WANs raise their own sets of issues involving additional fixed and recurring costs, reliability, speed, and maintenance.

A WAN is often made up of two or more LANs connected together. For example, you might have a LAN at each site of your organization, and each of those LANs might be connected together to form a WAN. A WAN made up of LANs is essentially a network of interconnected networks, and this is called an *internetwork*, or simply an *internet*. The term *internet* (with a small *i*) refers to any large network made up of interconnected smaller networks.

Name That Network

The acronyms *LAN* and *WAN* are commonly used, but it seems that just about everyone who writes about networking nowadays wants to coin his or her own new network acronyms. Here are a few you may encounter in your travels: MAN (metropolitan area network), CAN (campus area network), GAN (global area network), TAN (tiny area network), FAN (family area network), SAN (storage area network).

Each acronym is designed (and I use that term loosely) to describe a very specific scope of networking. While I'm all for precision, I recommend that you stick to using LAN and WAN when discussing networks. Otherwise, you'll be in danger of getting blank stares or laughter. Or even worse, someone might mistake you for Dr. Seuss when you start spouting "Is a CAN bigger than a FAN? Does the MAN GAN have a TAN? Yes, sir. Yes, sir. GAN is a TAN MAN."

How Have Networks Evolved?

To give you a better understanding of computer networks, it's important to visit their roots. You'll gain valuable perspective to help you understand the reasons for many of the features included in today's computer networks. You'll also understand and appreciate how Microsoft Windows 98 fits in as a key network component.

Computer Network Forerunners

In the days when computer mainframes ruled the earth (the Jurassic period of digital history), computing was highly centralized. A single *central processing unit* (*CPU*), shared by all users, performed all processing. Likewise, all disk storage, printers, tape drives, and other devices were attached to the central mainframe. Users interacted with the mainframe via remote terminals. In those days, computers were physically large, extremely expensive, and very difficult to use and maintain. Companies employed large staffs of experts to manage the centralized system and schedule work on it.

In the 1970s, minicomputers arrived on the scene. They were designed to serve smaller departments or workgroups. Minicomputers were physically smaller, less expensive, and usually less powerful than their mainframe big brothers. But otherwise, they were based on the same approach to computing. Users accessed everything through terminals connected to a central computer.

These models of centralized computing weren't true computer networks, at least not by our definition today. They did, however, accomplish the task of sharing resources exceptionally well. Because all resources were centralized on a single computer, users were able to share everything, including files, printers, and applications. But with the arrival of the *personal computer* (*PC*) in the early 1980s, sharing would become a new problem in need of a solution.

Personal Computer Chaos

When the low-cost PC arrived in 1981, the computing model began to change dramatically. By giving users access to their own desktop computers, organizations were able to decentralize much of the computing workload. With appropriate software applications, users could do a large percentage of their work without having to interact with a terminal attached to a central mainframe or minicomputer. An individual user could even have his or her own printer. The PC represented a cost-effective way to free up the expensive centralized resources, and offered users quick turnaround on the tasks they could accomplish on their desktop PCs.

On one hand, this new era offered tremendous power and freedom to individual users. On the other hand, it was the start of a data processing nightmare, as information began to collect on individual computers. Sometimes, many different versions of the same information lived on many different computers – and there was no convenient or controlled way of sharing or coordinating the information.

What's more, expensive devices such as printers and large hard disks were now distributed to individual offices, no longer sharable by groups of users. It just wasn't cost-effective to equip every user with a printer or large storage device. The pundits who predicted that PCs would put data processing departments out of business were wrong – the greatest challenge was just beginning. PCs sent the well-ordered data processing world spinning out of control.

Early Network Solutions

It didn't take long for solutions to emerge. Within a year of the IBM PC's arrival, several companies began developing and delivering networking hardware and software that would enable users to share information and hardware resources.

Unfortunately, these early products were complex, unreliable, difficult to install and maintain, and not standardized. Some solutions were downright dangerous, with poorly wired networks resulting in computer components dying in a puff of smoke. Even the smallest configuration errors could render the entire network inoperable. Technicians had to learn on the job through trial and error. Lack of standards meant that customers couldn't change vendors to get better quality – that is, not without replacing all their expensive network components.

In 1982 and 1983, several companies began to advance and standardize PC networking communication and software technology. Four of them – Microsoft, Novell, Banyan, and Artisoft – would become dominant players in the PC networking industry for several years to come. At this point, I'll focus on Microsoft's approach to PC networking. I discuss Novell, Banyan, and Artisoft in Chapter 7.

Microsoft's Networking Evolution

Microsoft has taken several approaches to networking, and its products today support both peer-to-peer and dedicated server networks. Over the years, Microsoft has created networking products that either run under standalone operating systems or are integrated directly into the OS. To help you understand Microsoft's networking philosophy and how Windows 98 fits into the picture, let's explore some of the details of its product evolution.

MS-DOS NETWORKING

As far back as 1983, teams at Microsoft and IBM were putting the finishing touches on the MS-DOS 3.0 operating system, which would run on IBM's upcoming offering – the PC/AT computer. By the middle of 1984, IBM had shipped the PC/AT and introduced a *network adapter* for it. A network adapter is an expansion card that plugs into your computer to enable it to communicate on the network. It provides the physical connection between the computer and network cabling.

Soon afterward, Microsoft shipped MS-DOS 3.1, which contained all the basic elements required to share files on a dedicated server computer with client computers. This version of MS-DOS also included features that coordinated file access, enabling more than one client to access shared files at the same time. Although much has changed since then, this product marked the birth of Microsoft networking. As you'll see in later chapters, many of the basic concepts and components live on today in other Microsoft networking products.

IBM engineers added a couple of key features to the MS-DOS network software, and sold the resulting product under the name PC-LAN. With this product, users could share their printers over the network, and for the first time, server computers could also act as clients. PC-LAN was the starting point for Microsoft's peer-to-peer network offerings.

LAN MANAGER NETWORKING

IBM's PC-LAN product supported only IBM hardware. Microsoft jumped in with a similar product called MS-NET, adding support for a wide variety of non-IBM PCs and network adapters. Nearly two years later, Microsoft created MS-NET 2.0, which enabled true peer-to-peer networking for a wide variety of PC and network hardware.

While Microsoft and IBM cooperated on developing the OS/2 operating system, they both worked with 3Com to create a series of products under the name LAN Manager. Microsoft released LAN Manager 2.0 in 1990. It was fully compatible with PC-LAN and MS-NET, but offered faster performance and easier maintenance. That same year, Microsoft released Windows 3.0, setting the stage for the historic Windows success story – which continued with Windows 3.1 in 1992, and still continues to this day.

> **NOTE** Some folks refer to LAN Manager as LANMAN. But LANMAN has always sounded to me like some sort of superhero. "What's that? Lois needs to share that printer? This sounds like a job for ... LANMAN!"

WINDOWS BUILT-IN NETWORKING

In 1993, Microsoft shipped Windows for Workgroups. With probably the least fanfare of any Microsoft product release, it sold so slowly that many insiders started calling it "Windows for Warehouses." Nevertheless, for the first time, a Microsoft operating system included built-in peer-to-peer networking. Microsoft soon offered add-ons for customers of both Windows 3.1 and MS-DOS, to bring similar networking capabilities to these environments. Since then, each successive version of Windows, including both Windows 95 and Windows 98, has contained peer-to-peer networking capabilities.

Windows 95, which appeared on the scene in August of 1995, provided a (mostly) 32-bit operating system that maintained a high degree of compatibility with 16-bit Windows and MS-DOS applications. It was a more complete operating system, because it no longer required an underlying copy of MS-DOS to be present beforehand. Windows 95 included its own well-hidden version of MS-DOS running underneath. Because of its relative ease of use, the availability of affordable hardware to run it, and the biggest software marketing blitz in history, Windows 95 has become the desktop operating system standard, both at home and at work. Estimates put the number of systems running Windows 95 at over 130 million and growing. Prior to the introduction of Windows 98, nearly every PC sold offered at least the option of including a preloaded version of Windows 95.

Windows 95 included essentially the same underlying peer-to-peer networking capabilities as Windows for Workgroups. With Windows 95, however, networking became easier – primarily because of the introduction of Plug and Play technology. When used with the latest hardware, this feature enabled the operating system to configure devices (including network adapters) automatically. It saved the time, effort, and training required to install and configure network hardware. Coupled with the new, easier-to-use graphical interface, Windows 95 made peer-to-peer networking easier than ever.

What Is Windows 98?

Windows 98 is Microsoft's latest mainstream version of Windows, designed for both the home and business markets. It essentially builds on the foundations of Windows 95, extends it to make Internet access easier and more tightly integrated, provides support for emerging hardware technologies, and improves performance and reliability. At the user's option, Windows 98 can also make the graphical user interface and desktop act more like a set of interactive Internet Web pages. I discuss the Internet later in this chapter and in Chapter 4.

NOTE: Like Windows 95, Windows 98 is a 32-bit operating system that maintains a high degree of compatibility with 16-bit MS-DOS and Windows software. Like its older brother, Windows 98 doesn't require a preexisting copy of MS-DOS running beneath it — it includes its own version of MS-DOS. Contrary to some industry reports, Windows 98 still includes a considerable amount of 16-bit code.

The most significant improvements of Windows 98 over Windows 95 include faster program loading, more efficient use of disk space, tighter Internet integration, a navigational interface that looks more like a set of Internet Web pages, and broader hardware device support. On the hardware front, Windows 98 supports the latest device technologies that enable true plug-and-play configuration and efficient power management. I discuss Windows 98 hardware support in Chapter 8.

From a networking perspective, Windows 98 makes a great participant in a peer-to-peer network, or a great desktop client in a dedicated server environment. With appropriate discipline, Windows 98 can be cast in the role of a dedicated server, as well. Networking capabilities are built into nearly every corner of the operating system, making the use of network capabilities consistent and easy. To support the needs of mobile users, Windows 98 includes support for dial-up remote access and laptop-specific hardware features. (If you've been exposed to Windows 95 networking, Windows 98 networking features will look familiar. Tight integration with the Internet is the most visible change you'll notice.)

Throughout this book, you'll see how Windows 98 plays a role in both peer-to-peer and dedicated server networks, how it integrates with other network operating systems, and how you can take advantage of its features to enhance your organization's productivity. If you're already familiar with Windows 95, look for the differences and new features I point out along the way.

How Are Networks Used?

Now that I've discussed the basic networking components, including the Windows 98 network operating system, let's explore in more detail the practical uses of networks. The fundamental purpose of networks – sharing resources – has evolved over the years to encompass many diverse tasks, and new applications for networking are being developed all the time. In this section, I discuss the more popular uses for today's computer networks.

File Sharing

The oldest and most ubiquitous use for networks is sharing data files. One approach to sharing files involves placing the file in a shared location on one computer (acting as a server), and making it available to other computers (acting as clients) on the network. Other users who want access to the file can either open the shared copy directly or copy it over the network to their own local hard disks.

Some database applications use file sharing to store a centralized database file on a server, allowing many users to view and update the file simultaneously. To accommodate this type of application, most NOSs provide functions that enable the application to lock the shared data at the file or data record level. The application can then coordinate access to the data and prevent database updates from stepping on each other.

Printer Sharing

Traditionally, printers are relatively expensive devices. No matter what era of personal computing you look at, high-end printers can cost more than two or three client computers. (Of course, what constitutes a high-end printer has changed over time.) As a result, sharing printers became a primary use of networks early on – a tradition that survives today.

To share a printer, you physically connect the printer to a computer acting as a server. (Printers are usually connected directly to the computer's *printer port*, also called a *parallel port*.) Using the NOS, you share the printer over the network. Users can then print to your shared printer as easily as if the printer were directly connected to their own local PCs. Rather than going out the local printer port, the user's data to be printed travels across the network to the server, and the server sends the data directly to its attached printer.

NOTE: Printer sharing is so pervasive that some printer manufacturers (for example, Hewlett-Packard) have developed printers that you can directly attach to the network — no server computer required. These printers are sometimes called *network printers*, because they include a built-in interface to the network. From a user's perspective, network printers appear and behave just like printers shared by servers on the network. The printer in Figure 1-2 that's directly attached to the network illustrates this approach.

Drive Sharing

When large hard disks and CD-ROM drives were relatively expensive devices, network users attached them to servers and shared them over the network. Users could access the contents of one or more shared CD-ROMs, or store and retrieve their own data in a directory on the server's hard disk. A single hard disk might accommodate many users, each with his or her own private directory. This approach kept the cost of individual PCs lower, and the extra cost of server hardware was spread across many users.

As prices of hard disks and CD-ROM drives fell, the tide shifted in the direction of equipping each client computer with plenty of local storage and its own CD-ROM drive. However, more recent trends in cost reduction in some organizations have begun to push the storage devices back to the server, allowing the use of very inexpensive client PCs. Some low-cost client computers don't even contain hard disks; they rely entirely on storage space supplied by network servers. These low-cost clients are sometimes called *diskless workstations*.

NOTE: In addition to drives and printers, you can share other devices. All you need is the right device and the right software. For example, intelligent fax machines, modems, scanners, and other devices have been shared over computer networks. I won't go into the details of each device here. Just remember that the device-sharing concept can reach beyond printers and drives. In Chapter 2, I discuss these devices in more detail.

Application Sharing

In its simplest form, application sharing is nothing more than file sharing, where the files just happen to be the executable application files themselves. Instead of installing and running an application on a local hard disk, you place the application once on a server. Users then load and run the application over the network. Keep in mind that not all software vendors design their applications to run in this type of shared environment.

Another aspect of application sharing involves placing a data file on a server and sharing it among several applications running on the network. (The application files themselves may or may not be shared.) In this environment, the application's role includes coordinating all access to the shared data file. For example, a group scheduling application running on several networked PCs might store all scheduling data in a single shared file on a server. Likewise, some e-mail applications store all e-mail messages in a set of shared files on a single server computer.

Some applications have two distinct parts – a client portion and a server portion. The two parts play specific roles in performing the application's function. This approach is known as the *client-server application model*, or simply *client-server*. A server application lives on a server computer and runs there exclusively. The client side of the application resides on a client computer and provides the user interface to the server part. The two parts of the application coordinate and exchange data over the network.

A good example of this approach is Microsoft SQL Server, a client-server database application that runs on Windows NT Server. One piece of the application runs on a Windows NT Server computer and provides all access to the contents of a database. The client piece runs on each client computer, and makes requests to the server over the network.

Even if you can install and share an application successfully over the network, you must be sure that your application's license agreement covers this type of shared usage. Some software vendors sell special networked versions of their applications, explicitly stating the maximum number of users who can legally run the program. Other vendors expect you to purchase individual copies of the software for each user, even if you only install one copy on a server. Still other vendors offer license packages that include one copy of the software package and the appropriate number of licenses to cover your users. Make sure you stay legal by having appropriate licenses for all users of your networked applications, or you might make some new friends — from the FBI.

Front-to-Back Networking

Client-server computing has its own set of terminology. The client side of an application is often called its *front end*, referring to the user interface portion with which a user interacts. In other words, the front end is the face of the application that the user sees. Conversely, the server side of a client-server application is sometimes called its *back end*. The back end, which typically performs the bulk of the actual work, is typically hidden from the user — perhaps in a back room where the server computer resides.

You may see these terms used frequently as you learn about client-server computing. The Microsoft BackOffice family of software products is an example of a set of client-server back end applications.

Remote Access

More and more users these days are hitting the road with their laptop PCs in hand. At the same time, many other users are opting to skip the long commute and work from home while staying in touch with the office. (Working at home and communicating with the office electronically has become known as telecommuting.) As all of these users become increasingly dependent on their networks at the office, the need to connect their computers from remote locations has become significantly more important over the last few years.

Remote access is a generic term that actually refers to several alternative approaches. In the following sections, I discuss the most popular remote access techniques.

REMOTE E-MAIL ACCESS

If users need only to send and receive *electronic mail* (*e-mail*, which I discuss further in Chapter 3) messages, they can use a modem to dial in to an e-mail server at the office. Once connected, they can pick up their e-mail messages and compose and send messages to other users. This is a fairly straightforward task, but doesn't give the user access to any other shared network resources.

REMOTE CONTROL

If users need remote access to files on their desktop PCs at the office, they can implement an approach called *remote control*. This approach to remote access requires a special software package that runs on both the remote computer and on the user's office PC. The software enables the user to take remote control of the office PC. The remote user's keyboard, mouse, and video display act as if they're directly attached to the PC at the office.

The remote control software sends keyboard and mouse actions to the office PC, and receives changes in the display from the office PC. Each remote user takes control of exactly one PC on the office LAN, so each remotely controlled PC requires its own modem and copy of the remote control software. PC AnyWhere from Symantec, Carbon Copy from Microcom, and CoSession Remote from Artisoft are all examples of remote control software.

REMOTE NODE

Users who need full access to shared resources on the LAN at the office must use a remote access approach called *remote node*. (A *node* refers to a computer or other device that's directly attached to the network.) Most modern NOSs, including Windows 98, provide some form of remote node capability.

With this approach, users can dial in to a remote access server at the office. Once they're connected, they have complete access to the network – just as if their remote PC were directly connected to the network. Users can remotely access whatever shared resources they would normally be able to access at work. Remote nodes (remote access clients) can dial in to a single remote access server and have a virtual connection to the LAN. In contrast to remote control, the remote node approach funnels all remote users through a single server on the network.

In the Microsoft world, remote node is referred to alternatively as *RAS* (*Remote Access Service*) and *DUN* (*Dial-Up Networking*). Windows 95 included remote access client software, and the Microsoft Plus! pack added a single-modem remote access server. Windows 98 includes both the client and server components, as does Windows NT Workstation. Windows NT Server includes the complete form of RAS, which can handle up to 256 simultaneous remote nodes (that is, when it's equipped with up to 256 modems).

The Internet

Unless you've been living in a cave for the past few years (no offense intended to cave-dwellers), you're probably already familiar with – if not overwhelmed by – the *Internet*. The Internet (with a capital *I*, this time) is the global interconnected network consisting of thousands of smaller networks and millions of individual computers. Recall that the term *internet* (with a small *i*) refers to any large network made up of interconnected smaller networks. The *Internet* (with a capital *I*) is one example – the biggest example – of an internet.

The Internet supports several global communication services. They include e-mail, real-time chatting and conferences, secure (and not so secure) business transactions, running discussion groups covering myriad topics, and even voice and video conferencing. But perhaps its most significant service is the *World Wide Web*, *WWW*, or *Web*. The Web is a huge collection of documents that contain text, graphics, videos, sounds, and other types of information. These documents include links to each other, enabling users to choose their own path through the material by browsing and jumping directly to further details or to other points of interest.

Organizations can present themselves and their products or services by establishing a *Web site* – a collection of documents that offers information to anyone who wants it. The best Web sites provide some sort of service to their customers, while saving the organization time or money in the process. For example, some publishers offer electronic versions of their periodicals, saving subscription costs for consumers and printing costs for publishers. Another good example is the Federal Express Web site. There, a customer can type a package tracking number and instantly see where in the world the package is. Customers don't have to wait on hold to get this information, and the company saves money by reducing the number of incoming phone calls.

You can connect individual computers or your entire LAN to the Internet. You can set up a limited Web server using Personal Web Server on Windows 98, which can provide up to ten connections. (Because each user session typically takes up two or more connections, only a handful of users can be served.) Or, if you want to build a world-class Web server, you can use Windows NT Server and Microsoft *IIS* (Internet Information Server). Either way, you can publish your own Web site within your organization or on the Internet directly from your LAN. (There are, of course, security concerns to address when you connect your LAN to the Internet. I address these issues in Chapter 4 and in Chapter 12.)

Intranets

As standards and tools have emerged for use on the Internet, organizations have come to realize that they can apply these same techniques to their internal LANs. Organizations publish lots of information to their employees – handbooks, newsletters, training materials, annual reports, executive profiles, and a host of other documents. Moreover, many organizations rely on central databases, which are constantly accessed and updated by staff members. You can implement these documents and applications using the tools and techniques originally designed for the Internet.

An *intranet* is nothing more than a LAN or WAN that uses Internet tools and techniques to offer services to a single organization. Rather than using many different applications to publish, view, and interact with information, an intranet enables users to employ Internet software to access everything.

Extranets

Some organizations have realized increased productivity and cost savings by selectively providing external access to their intranets. For example, if you open up your intranet to major suppliers, key customers, and strategic allies, you can streamline both communication and commerce activities with them. An intranet that's available to selective external organizations is called an *extranet.*

The term extranet is also sometimes used to describe a relatively new phenomenon – the virtual private network, or VPN. Using the public Internet as a link between sites, you can create a WAN that connects LANs at multiple physical sites within your organization. With security features such as data encryption enabled, you can end up with a company-wide network whose individual LANs are tied together into a single virtual network via low-cost Internet connections. Windows 98 includes support for creating a VPN. I discuss VPNs further in Chapter 5.

How Do You Justify a Network?

If computer networks didn't provide measurable benefits to organizations, everyone would still use SneakerNet (that is, their feet) to share, print, and move information. But because networks increase user productivity and reduce costs, installation of a LAN is becoming as much of a requirement of doing business as installation of a copier, fax machine, or phone system. Some organizations have abandoned network cost justification altogether, accepting the need for a LAN as a given in today's business environment. In the following sections, I discuss both the benefits and costs of networking to assist you in your analysis.

Networking Benefits

In this section, I discuss the measurable benefits to your organization of networking your computers together. They include increased productivity, lowered costs, smaller storage requirements, and reduced effort.

INCREASING PRODUCTIVITY

Just as standalone PCs can increase user productivity, networks of PCs enhance that productivity even further. Users can share, access, view, and modify information anywhere on the network without leaving their desks. Users don't have to schlep floppy disks from one place to another, wait to print out information they want to share, and become distracted from their normal work flow. All of this translates to more time available to perform the actual job at hand.

NOTE

The productivity costs of interrupting a user's work flow are often underestimated. Some studies have shown that workers who deal with information require up to 15 minutes to get back into full productivity after each interruption. If they have to interrupt their workflow more frequently than this, some workers never reach their full productive potential.

SAVING MONEY

Sharing expensive devices such as printers, scanners, and large hard disks over a network can save money. The most obvious component of these savings is the total purchase price – you need fewer devices. But don't overlook other savings components. Fewer expensive devices mean fewer maintenance contracts, service calls, and upgrade costs. Over time, these recurring cost savings can dwarf the initial capital investment in the equipment.

SAVING DISK SPACE

Sharing software applications can generate savings in several ways. Perhaps the most obvious cost reduction is in the cost of the software itself. Most networked versions of applications cost less per user than purchasing individual copies for each user. You can also realize savings in your total disk space requirements. Today's applications take up a lot of hard disk real estate. If nearly everyone in your organization uses a word processing program, you may not have to consume all that space on every computer. Instead, install the software only once on a server computer, and let everyone access that single copy. (Don't forget what I said about software licenses earlier in this chapter. Stay legal.)

SAVING EFFORT

Another less obvious benefit of application sharing involves the time saved during software installation and configuration. If you install the software only once on a server, and configure it in a standard way, you'll spend much less time than if you had to install it on multiple client computers. What's more, this approach is less prone to errors and easier to troubleshoot, because you only perform the operation once, and every user has access to the same copy of the software. Finally, when it's time to upgrade, many software applications let you apply the upgrade once on the server – you don't have to visit every computer on the network.

In addition, networks can save a lot of effort by enabling users to view and maintain a single centralized copy of important documents and other data files. Without a network, it's easy to end up with multiple copies and versions of files on various computers. Invariably, users waste surprising amounts of time discussing and resolving the issue of whose version is the most up-to-date. With a network and appropriate user discipline, you can eliminate this time-wasting activity.

SEIZING OPPORTUNITIES

Once you have a network in place, additional opportunities for increased productivity and reduced costs become available to you. For example, if you have a tape backup drive installed on your server, you may want to start backing up data on individual client PCs as well. With the right software, you can easily do this over the network. As your network grows, you may want to automate the cumbersome and endless task of keeping an accurate inventory of the hardware and software installed in each PC. Software products such as Microsoft Systems Management Server (SMS) enable you to gather, update, analyze, and report this information automatically over the network.

Networking Costs

You're only looking at half the picture if you focus only on the benefits of networking. In justifying your need for a network, you must analyze the costs as well. In this section, I discuss some obvious and not-so-obvious networking costs.

INSTALLING A NETWORK

Everyone who participates on the network needs a PC. Although PC prices have come down, they're still the most significant cost factor in most networks. You need to consider the cost of clients and servers, and factor in any special devices you need on your servers (for example, printers, large hard disks, tape drives, scanners, and so forth). Each server and client PC that participates on the network also needs a network adapter and appropriate networking software.

In addition, you need what I call a *network infrastructure* to connect all the computers together. By this, I mean all the cabling and other hardware required to physically connect your computers together. In a very small network, the infrastructure might be a single cable running between two computers. In a large network, it includes cabling installed in walls and ceilings, devices to connect the cabling together, sockets in walls that accept network connections, and other items.

You may decide to install the infrastructure yourself or hire an experienced professional. Either way, you need to consider the cost of the materials and labor to put the infrastructure in place, test it, and maintain it. (Don't worry about the details now. I cover the specifics in later chapters.)

MAINTAINING A NETWORK

If you install and configure a network properly, it's typically very reliable. Even if nothing ever breaks, you need to perform a few administrative tasks that include backing up data, managing print jobs, modifying user accounts and security policies, and adding hardware and software components as your network grows.

Realistically, because a network relies on many hardware and software components working together in harmony, problems can and do creep out of the woodwork. Hardware components can fail, software can manifest bugs, cables can disconnect or break, well-meaning users can alter software configurations, and malicious users can wreak intentional havoc. As a result, you need to plan for the cost of troubleshooting, maintaining, and upgrading your network.

SHARING APPLICATIONS

Sharing applications isn't without its costs. Networked applications can be a bit more difficult to install and configure than their single-user counterparts. Software manufacturers understand networking issues in varying degrees. The number of hoops you must jump through during the installation process usually says a lot about a manufacturer's level of network knowledge. The complexity of the installation process often depends on whether the vendor designed the application for a networked environment or tried to force-fit it to work on a network.

Applications that run over the network sometimes run more slowly than applications installed on a local hard disk. The required pieces of the application must travel from the server to the user's computer before they can run. This performance degradation may or may not be noticeable to users. It depends on the application itself, the number of users accessing it, the level of traffic on your network, the network technology you're using, and the efficiency of your server and client computers. (I cover these topics in later chapters.)

Summary

In this chapter, you've learned about the basics of computer networks, where they came from, and how your organization can benefit from them. You've also been introduced to Microsoft Windows 98, and learned about the role it plays in your network. In Chapter 2, I show you how a network fits together, how a network shares resources, and the pros and cons of peer-to-peer and dedicated server networks.

Chapter 2

Sharing Resources on a Network

IN THIS CHAPTER

- Connecting devices to a network
- Sharing networked resources
- Choosing peer-to-peer or dedicated server networks
- Using Windows 98 as a dedicated server

ONCE YOU UNDERSTAND what a network is and how it can benefit your organization, it's logical to ask about the details of how to connect to the network. You may also be wondering how network resources are shared and accessed. Finally, how do you decide on the organization of your network? What are the pros, cons, costs, and benefits of peer-to-peer and dedicated server networks?

In this chapter, I discuss the basic hardware and software requirements for connecting a computer or other device to a network. Then, I cover in more detail how various network resources can be shared. I also discuss the important differences between peer-to-peer networking and dedicated server networking. By the end of this chapter, you'll have enough knowledge to decide which approach (or combination of approaches) is right for your organization.

Connecting Devices to a Network

When you connect devices to a network, those connections must be both physical (via hardware) and logical (via software). In this section, I discuss the basic hardware and software requirements for connecting computers and other devices to your network. These basic requirements include, namely, network adapters and network operating systems.

Network Adapter Hardware

Every device you connect to your LAN must contain a hardware interface to the network. To be network-ready, a computer needs a network adapter to provide the physical connection. Some computers contain built-in network adapters on the motherboard, while others require installation of an optional adapter. Either way, a network adapter is the most basic requirement for physically connecting a computer to your LAN.

In other networking books and articles, you'll sometimes see network adapters referred to as *network interface cards* (*NICs*) and sometimes *network adapter cards* (*NACs*). Since I'm not a huge fan of SMA (so many acronyms), I refer to these devices as network adapters throughout this book. But now you'll at least recognize NIC-NACs when you see them on the bookshelf.

As I mentioned in Chapter 1, computers aren't the only devices you can connect to a network. Any device can be connected, as long as it contains the proper internal hardware and software required to attach it. Network printers, scanners, towers of hard disks, towers of CD-ROM drives, and other devices are available for direct network connection. Some manufacturers of these devices offer the network adapter as an option, while others build it into the devices.

A device that doesn't include a provision for its own network adapter, however, must be connected indirectly through a networked computer or some other device. For example, you typically connect a printer (that doesn't have its own network adapter) to a computer that's already on the network. The computer then acts as an external interface between the printer and the network.

Network adapters, whether they live inside computers or other devices, must be physically compatible with the type of network you've chosen to install. I discuss the details, pros, and cons of different types of networks in Chapters 5 and 6.

Network Operating System Software

In addition to a network adapter, each computer or other networked device requires appropriate NOS software. In the case of network printers and other directly connected devices, manufacturers typically build the software right into the network adapter or into the device itself. In this situation, you don't need to perform any additional software installation or configuration. Computers, however, require installation and configuration of a NOS.

The role of a NOS is similar to that of a traditional operating system. A traditional operating system deals with managing the low-level details of communication with devices attached to the local computer. Similarly, a NOS takes care of all the housekeeping and communication details associated with computers and devices attached to the network. For example, a NOS may announce the availability of shared resources to the network, validate user passwords, and coordinate moving data over the network.

A MATTER OF PROTOCOL

Just as successful human communication requires a language understood by both sender and receiver, successful network communication requires the use of some sort of common language. A network language is called a *protocol.* It's simply a set of rules and conventions used to format and interpret information sent across the network. Both the sender and receiver of the information must speak the same language. In other words, they must use the same network protocol.

Over the years, many different incompatible network protocols have appeared on the scene. (I discuss the more popular surviving ones in Chapter 6.) NOS manufacturers have tended to invent their own unique network protocols, rendering them incompatible with NOSs provided by other manufacturers. As a result, computers and other devices running network software from different manufacturers are often unable to communicate with each other, even if they're physically connected to the same network. This proprietary behavior forced customers to use a single NOS manufacturer throughout the network.

CLIMBING THE TOWER OF BABEL

In the real world, networks grow and technologies change. Network administrators daily find themselves faced with the challenge of making two incompatible networks talk to each other without disrupting service to their users. *Interoperability* refers to the capability of networked computers to interact with each other, even if their NOSs come from different manufacturers. There are three common approaches you can take to solve the interoperability problem for your network:

- **Use the same manufacturer's NOS on each networked computer.** This approach is easy to implement if you're creating a new network from scratch. But if you're expanding an existing network, or trying to get two different networks to talk to each other, it may be totally impractical. (This approach doesn't actually achieve interoperability, because only one manufacturer's NOS is involved.)
- **Use the same network protocol on each networked computer, regardless of what NOS it's running.** This approach relies on each NOS manufacturer to supply an appropriate set of network protocols that are compatible with the protocols offered by other NOSs. Most NOS manufacturers, including Microsoft, have started offering multiple network protocols with their products, to allow network interoperability by standardizing on a single protocol.

- **Run multiple network protocols on your network in parallel.** This has become a popular approach, especially in environments where specific software applications require specific protocols. Unfortunately, this approach imposes an extra overhead of memory and network traffic, because multiple network protocols must operate in parallel over the network.

Fortunately, most NOS manufacturers have now recognized the critical importance of interoperability. They offer multiple industry-standard network protocols, providing lots of flexibility in solving the interoperability problem. For example, Microsoft Windows 98 includes support for network protocols that talk to computers running Microsoft, UNIX, and Novell network software, among others.

In Chapter 6, I discuss the most important network protocols. Then, in Chapter 7, I discuss the attributes of various network operating systems, with particular emphasis on Microsoft Windows 98.

Sharing Networked Resources

Once you've physically attached a computer, printer, or other device to your LAN, and you have the appropriate NOS software in place, you still need to share and access resources on the network. In this section, I discuss in more detail how to go about sharing resources and gaining access to them.

Sharing Files

File sharing is the most frequently used feature of a network. But how do you go about sharing files and then accessing them over the network? To answer this, let's examine how you access files on your local hard disk or CD-ROM. Using your favorite approach to hard disk navigation (for example, an MS-DOS command line, Windows 3.1 File Manager, or Windows Explorer), you begin by identifying the correct hard disk and locating the directory (or folder) where the file is stored. You then use an appropriate application to access the file.

To understand sharing files on the network, it's important first to understand the significance of drive letters on a local computer. Each hard disk, floppy drive, and CD-ROM drive on your computer has a unique alphabetic drive letter associated with it. For example, the first floppy drive is drive A, the second (if any) is drive B, and the first hard disk is drive C. If you have more than one hard disk, or the hard disk is divided into more than one partition, additional drive letters are assigned to each hard disk or partition. A CD-ROM drive is usually designated drive D, E, or F, depending on how many hard disks are present. As new drives are added to the system, an additional drive letter is assigned to each one. When you access a file, you first point to the drive letter, and then navigate through folders to find the right file on that drive. As you're about to discover, drive letters are equally significant in making network connections to access shared files.

Sharing and accessing files over a network isn't much different from dealing with files locally. You use the same navigation tools to perform network operations as you do to manage local files on your hard disk. To share a file, you first identify the hard disk and directory where it lives. You then tell the NOS to share the contents of that directory over the network.

Just as each file and directory on your local hard disk needs a name, each shared resource needs its own name. So you need to select an appropriate name for the resource at the time you share it. This gives users something to refer to when they want to access your shared resource over the network. The name you assign to a shared resource on your server is called a *sharepoint.*

To access a shared file, a user asks the NOS to connect to your shared resource by specifying its location on the network. The user specifies both the name of your server and the sharepoint name of your shared resource on that server. When the user makes this connection request, the NOS automatically assigns an unused drive letter to this connection. This drive letter enables the user to refer to the shared resource as if it were a locally attached hard disk. From then on, the user can access your shared directory using this drive letter.

For example, let's say that the first unused drive letter on the user's computer is E, because C and D are already used by the local hard disk and CD-ROM drive. Therefore, the NOS assigns drive letter E to the user's connection to the shared resource. The user can then run Windows Explorer or other applications to navigate and access files within drive E as if it were just another local hard disk. The contents of drive E, however, are on the server containing the shared files.

TIP

One way to better understand how server names and sharepoint names are used is to think of the network as one huge hard disk. This mythical hard disk contains all the shared files and directories on every server attached to the network. Now imagine that each server stores its shared files in a unique directory on this common hard disk, and each directory is named after its associated server. Beneath that directory are subdirectories representing all the individual shared resources. These subdirectories bear the sharepoint names. So, just as a hard disk letter and directory can pinpoint the location of a file on your local hard disk, a server name and sharepoint name together can pinpoint the location of a file on the network.

Let's look at a specific example. Say you have a server computer called FINANCE that contains a spreadsheet file whose full pathname is C:\TAX\APRIL99.XLS. You want to share that file on the network with other users. Using a command line or graphical file manager such as Windows Explorer, tell the NOS to share the contents of the C:\TAX directory on the network, using a sharepoint name of TAXFILES. That's all there is to it. Figure 2-1 illustrates this example.

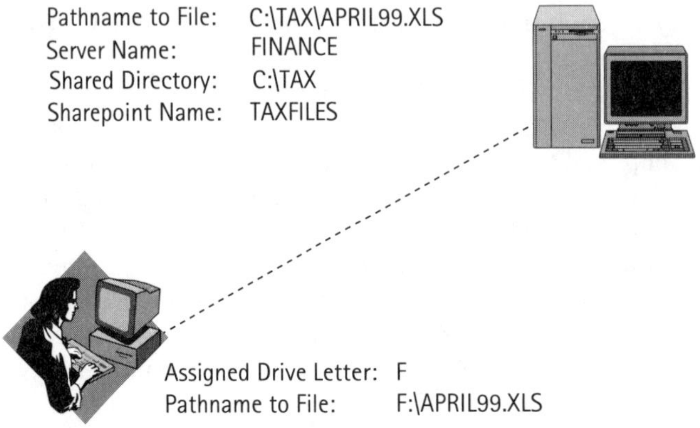

Figure 2-1: Users access shared files by connecting to a sharepoint on the server where the files reside.

To access the file, a user can tell the NOS to assign an unused drive letter, such as F, to the TAXFILES sharepoint on the FINANCE server. (This action is sometimes called *mapping* a drive letter to a sharepoint.) From then on, that user simply accesses the APRIL99.XLS file on drive F. In other words, the user refers to the file using the full pathname F:\APRIL99.XLS. From the user's perspective, drive F acts just like a local hard disk. But it really accesses the C:\TAX directory on the FINANCE server computer, as shown in Figure 2-1.

In future chapters, I fill you in on all the details of how to create, access, and manage shared resources using Windows 98. For now, it's important only that you understand the concepts. We'll deal with the mechanics later.

Sharing Disks

You may be interested in sharing more than just individual files over the network. Sharing the contents of directories or even entire hard disks can be very useful in some work environments. If you have a server with a very large, expensive hard disk, you may want to share that storage space among several users. Or you may want to share the entire contents of a CD-ROM over the network. It turns out that sharing the contents of directories and entire drives is a more general case of sharing files over the network.

In the example in the previous section, you actually saw how to share not only a file, but the contents of an entire directory. By sharing C:\TAX, the server is really sharing the entire contents of the C:\TAX directory, including all files and subdirectories contained within it. If the file MAY99.XLS happens to live in the same directory, users connecting to the TAXFILES sharepoint can access it as well.

To share an entire hard disk, you share its root directory over the network. For example, instead of sharing C:\TAX in the previous example, you share C:\. Figure 2-2 illustrates sharing an entire hard disk.

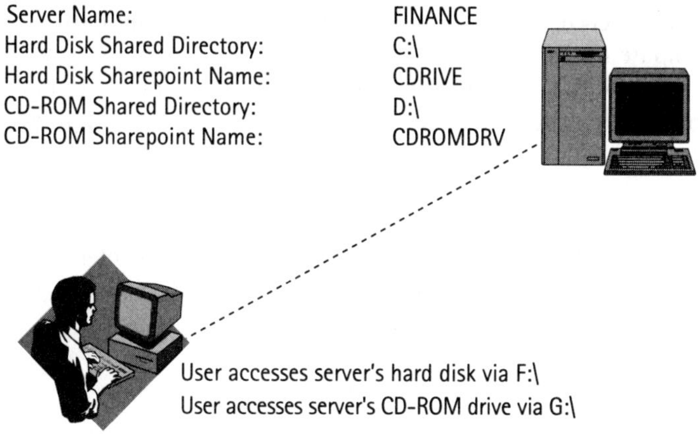

Figure 2-2: You can share the contents of an entire hard disk by sharing its root directory over the network.

For security reasons, it's typically not a good idea to share your entire drive C, because it gives network users access to all of your operating system files. Using password protection helps limit the risk, but it's best to avoid setting yourself up for potential disaster. When you share hard disk space, either share a hard disk that doesn't contain operating system files, or create a subdirectory on drive C and share that. Some network administrators create a separate subdirectory for each user. You can also create a separate subdirectory for each type of data or for each application.

Using the same techniques, you can share CD-ROM drives and other removable storage devices over the network, as shown in Figure 2-2. However, you need to be careful when sharing removable storage. Many users may be relying on the presence of specific data in the drive. You can't remove or replace the media without potentially affecting lots of people and lots of work.

Sharing Tape Drives

Backing up critical data periodically on your network is an important key to avoiding loss of data and time. Because all hard disks eventually fail, a good backup plan is essential. The most common media used for backup today is magnetic tape, although rewritable CD-ROM and magneto-optical drives are becoming more popular over time. A good tape drive, capable of fast backup of network data, is a relatively expensive device. So, rather than equipping each computer on the network with its own tape drive, you can strategically attach one to a selected computer, and then back up all your data over the network.

The most common approach to sharing a tape drive involves creating hard disk sharepoints on the computers you want to back up. The computer equipped with the tape drive then attaches to those share points and copies their contents to tape. Likewise, if you ever need to restore data from tape, you can use the same approach to restore it over the network.

XREF

You'll learn how to select the right tape drive for Windows 98 in Chapter 8. In Chapter 13, I discuss the details of implementing a solid plan for backing up the valuable information on your network.

Sharing Printers

Sharing printers is the most common device sharing activity. It's very cost-effective to share a printer on the network, because printers are relatively expensive devices and are more efficiently utilized by multiple users. A typical single user can keep a printer attached to a standalone PC in an office busy only a small percentage of the time. Multiple users can keep a printer much busier.

With the wide variety of printers available, it's feasible to offer all network users access to several different types of printers by sharing one of each on the network. For example, you may need a high-speed, black-and-white laser printer for general report printing, and a slower color printer for creating slide presentations. By sharing both on the network, users can benefit from each device and select the one that's appropriate to their immediate needs.

To understand sharing printers on the network, it's important to understand the significance of printer device names on a local computer. Each printer port (parallel port) on your computer has a unique device name that starts with the letters LPT and ends with a port number. For example, if a computer has two parallel ports, they are named LPT1 and LPT2. When you decide to send a job to a local printer, you specify which printer you want to use. For example, if you have a high-speed, black-and-white laser printer attached to LPT1, and a color inkjet printer attached to LPT2, you must choose between them before printing. Some printers are designed to be attached to a serial communication port instead of a parallel port. Serial ports and modems have device names that start with COM and end with the port number. So if you have a modem on the first serial port and a printer on the second serial port, they would be named COM1 and COM2, respectively.

The NOS can make a shared printer appear to applications as if it's locally attached to the client computer's printer port. If the client computer has no local printers attached, the user can connect to the shared printer and tell the NOS to assign the LPT1 printer device name to this connection. Then, applications on the client computer can simply send print jobs to the LPT1 device name, as if it's a local printer port. The applications don't need to be aware that the printer is actually attached to another computer and is accessed over the network. Figure 2-3 illustrates this concept.

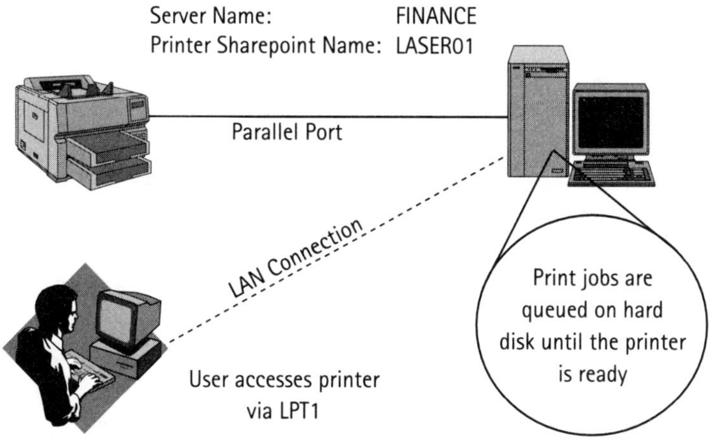

Figure 2-3: A server can share a printer over the network, and a client application can use the printer as if it were attached to a local printer port.

Even if your computer has its own printer attached locally, you can still connect to other printers over the network and choose which printer to use for a particular print job. For example, if your local printer is attached to LPT1, you can have the NOS connect to a shared printer over the network and assign the LPT2 device name to it. Then, when it's time to print, you can select which printer you want to use – the local LPT1 printer, or the remote LPT2 printer.

PRINTING QUEUES (AND OTHER LETTERS)

Recall that you can attach a printer to a networked computer via its parallel or serial port, or you can attach it directly to the network using a built-in network adapter. Regardless of how a printer is connected to the network, it needs a mechanism for storing print jobs and managing those jobs before the printer is ready to receive them. This mechanism is called a *print queue* (or sometimes *printer queue*).

A print queue contains print jobs that are waiting to be sent to a specific printer. The print queue also provides a list of all the waiting print jobs, enabling users to view their status and manage them. While the relatively slow printer device is busy printing one job, new jobs are *queued* for later printing. A component of the NOS called the *spooler* stores new print jobs on the hard disk until the printer is ready to receive them, as shown in Figure 2-3. This internal activity is called *spooling*. (Imagine that – a spooler is responsible for spooling!)

When the printer is ready for its next job, the spooler sends the next queued job to the printer at whatever speed the printer can receive it. From the application's point of view, the print job has gone to an extremely fast printer – it seems to the application as though the job prints instantly. In reality, the job is only queued to the hard disk for later printing. Because the application doesn't have to wait for actual printing to complete, you can use it to perform other tasks almost immediately. In reality, it may be quite awhile before your job is printed, depending on the speed of the printer and the number of other print jobs waiting in the queue.

NOTE

Why is this activity called spooling? Consider a spool of wire. You store wire on a spool until you need it later. If you get more wire than you can use right away, you can add it to the spool. Then, when you finally need wire, you remove what you can use and leave the rest on the spool. Now, think of the hard disk as the spool and the print jobs as pieces of wire that you can't use right away.

MINDING YOUR QUEUES

Print queues and spoolers aren't network-specific phenomena. Traditional operating systems on standalone computers have them, too. In a networked environment, however, multiple users can send jobs to your shared printers, taking maximum advantage of these powerful features.

Users can submit jobs remotely and manage those jobs from their desktops. Print job management includes deleting jobs in the queue, rearranging jobs by changing their priorities, placing them on hold for later printing, and other operations. Some NOSs provide security features to limit what individual users can do to print queues, especially when their actions may affect other users' print jobs.

TAKING THE DIRECT APPROACH

You can connect a printer to a parallel port or serial port on a networked computer, or attach it directly to the network via a built-in network adapter. Hewlett-Packard (HP), Lexmark, and Epson, among others, offer network printers with built-in or optional internal adapters.

If your printer doesn't have a built-in network adapter, but you want to attach it directly to the network, you're not completely out of luck. External devices called *print servers* can attach one or more printers to the network. Print servers have parallel ports for printer connections and a network port for attachment to the LAN. At the time of writing, these devices can run between $250 and $500, depending on features. The HP JetDirect series of external print servers is a good example of this type of device.

Location, Location, Location

Even if you connect a printer directly to the network, you usually have to assign a computer to manage its print queue. (Some self-contained printer devices don't require this, but most do.) One computer can control many print queues, but the point is that there's still a computer involved. As a result, I'm often asked the question "Why would anyone want to connect a printer directly to the network?" The answer for most organizations is another question — "Where do you want to put the printer?"

Let's look at an example. Say you want to put three printers into a small room that you've dedicated to them. In the room, you place the printers, paper and toner supplies, output storage bins, recycling bins, and so forth. You decide that you don't want to place a computer in the same room for two reasons. First, there's no space for a computer. Second, you don't want your users to play with the print queues, cancel each others' jobs, or do anything else malicious or accidental that could shut down all the printers. (You could resolve the second issue with security features in the NOS, but the most effective security measure is cutting off all physical access to the computer.)

By directly connecting the printers to the network, you eliminate the need for a computer in the same physical location. The computer that you assign to manage the print queues can live anywhere on the network.

JUMPING IN THE PRINTER POOL

If you need a lot of printing capacity on a specific type of printer, you can take advantage of an operating system feature called *printer pooling*. It enables you to define a single print queue that actually feeds print jobs to more than one identical printer. (The collection of identical printers itself is called a *printer pool*.) From user and application viewpoints, there's just one printer and one print queue that services it. In reality, the single print queue feeds jobs to whatever printer is available to take the next job. This approach can dramatically increase print job throughput. Figure 2-4 illustrates the concept of printer pooling.

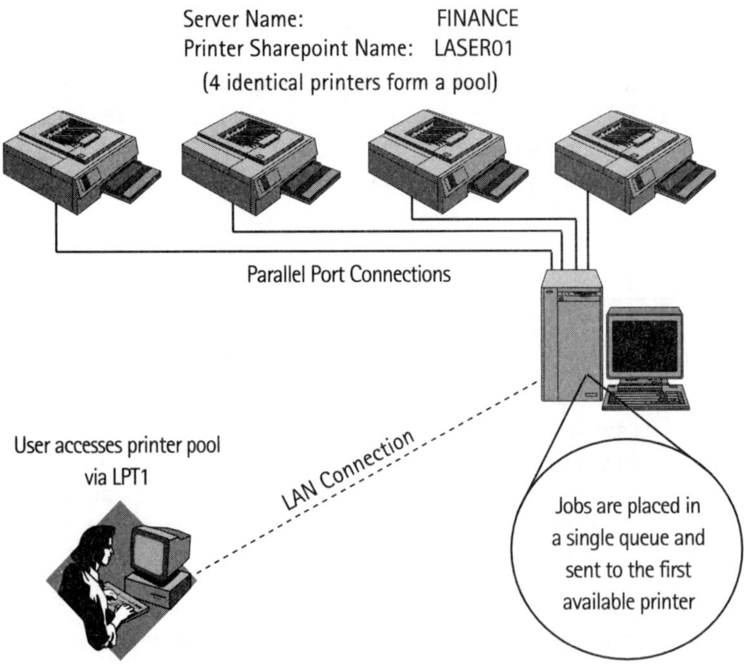

Figure 2-4: In printer pooling, a single print queue feeds multiple printers with print jobs.

CAUTION

The printers that participate in a printer pool must be identical in every way. They must use the same printer driver and be essentially interchangeable. Why? When you send a job to a printer that's part of a printer pool, the user has no way of telling the NOS which printer to use. The client only sees a single print queue. The server's NOS is responsible for selecting an available printer from the pool to print the job.

Sharing Fax Devices

It's amazing how often you see a person print a copy of a report, hand-carry it to a fax machine, manually complete a cover page, wait for the transmission to finish, file the fax confirmation page, and throw away the original printed document. And it's even more amazing when the person has a fax/modem in his or her desktop computer. Does it really make sense to convert the electronic document to paper, convert the paper document into electronic form for fax transmission, and then trash the paper document? Of course not. Leaving the document in electronic form saves both time and paper.

Does this mean you should equip every computer with a fax-capable modem? Not necessarily. In many offices, the community fax machine has its own dedicated phone line. Users know that they can count on being able to send a paper copy if someone isn't already using the fax machine. But offices with many PCs and modems often share one or a small number of phone lines between these modems. At any given time, a user may or may not be able to grab control of the phone line to send an urgent fax. So, users spend time and paper the old-fashioned way – they burn it.

A fax server acts a lot like a shared printer – accepting documents, placing them in a queue, and sending them out as faxes whenever the fax/modem device becomes available. Some fax server software packages automatically attach standard cover pages and send electronic confirmation messages to the user who originated the fax. Others accept incoming faxes from the outside world, and store them on the server's hard disk for later distribution.

Sharing Modems

Although modems may be inexpensive enough to add one to every computer, separate phone lines are still relatively expensive commodities. Organizations with many PCs and modems sometimes have to share one or a very small number of phone lines. As a result, users may not be able to establish a modem connection while a shared phone line is in use.

The good news is that, in most environments, not all users need to access the outside world at the same time – so you can get away with fewer modems and fewer phone lines. By installing these modems (and their phone lines) on a server computer, you can use the network to share them with all your users.

If everyone on the LAN requires Internet access, you can achieve even greater savings through modem and phone-line sharing. By using a single modem and establishing one connection to the Internet, all users can operate on the Internet through the LAN. Of course, many users generating traffic on a single Internet connection can make the process painfully slow, so you can use additional modems and phone lines to improve performance.

Sharing Scanners

Sharing an expensive scanner device on your network can save money in a couple of ways. First, it can amortize the cost of the device over multiple users. Second, it can reduce the need for creating paper copies or printouts by storing and distributing the information exclusively in electronic form. This approach not only saves on paper and other consumables, it also reduces the need for physical storage of paper copies. Incoming postal mail, faxes, journal articles, and paper memos are all candidates for electronic distribution using a shared scanner.

Scanners are inherently manual devices in that someone has to feed them with physical documents. With appropriate software, however, you can arrange to deliver scanned documents directly to users, fax them to external recipients, store them on servers, and even distribute them to customers through a Web site on the Internet.

Some manufacturers now offer network scanners, which include a network adapter inside the scanner device. The concept is identical to network printers, except the scanner is used for input rather than output. This approach enables you to place the scanner anywhere on the network. Although they're more expensive than basic scanners, network scanners can also act as copiers and fax machines by sending scanned documents to printers or fax/modems, respectively. Use of all the features across your network typically requires that you install driver software on all networked computers. The HP Network ScanJet 5 is a good example of this product category.

Choosing Peer-to-Peer or Dedicated Server Networks

Once you've determined what resources you intend to share on your network, you can turn your attention to another important decision. Should you implement a peer-to-peer network or a dedicated server network? Although you can share resources in either environment, the type of network you select will have an impact on costs, security, ease of use, and other factors. In this section, I discuss both environments and provide you with the information you need to decide which one is best for your organization.

> NOTE: Although Windows 98 is a peer-to-peer network operating system, you can still use it in a dedicated server network environment. One approach involves using Windows 98 as a client NOS and Windows NT Server as a dedicated server. But even without Windows NT Server in the picture, you can still implement a dedicated server network using Windows 98. It just takes a little more planning and discipline for you and your users. I'll show you what you need to do in this and subsequent chapters.

Establishing Selection Criteria

Before digging into the details of each type of network, it's a good idea to analyze your situation and understand the following factors in your organization.

USER NEEDS

Ultimately, you should design your network to serve your users efficiently. If users simply need to share files and printers, and no other needs are on the horizon, satisfying them is fairly straightforward. However, if your users also need several client-server applications, e-mail, and Internet access, your task becomes more complex. Don't forget to consider future user needs.

ORGANIZATION AND BUDGET SIZE

Small networks generally require less attention to security and less centralized administration. Larger networks require tighter security and more centralization of administrative functions. Understand both the number of users and the number of computers you expect to participate in your network, now and in the foreseeable future.

Of course, the financial bottom line may restrict your choices of network implementation. For money reasons, you may not be able to implement the ideal network right away. But understanding the path to growing your network is important to its long-term success.

BUSINESS NATURE

The type of business you're in may dictate certain requirements and expectations of your network. Will your business grind to a halt if your network goes down, or if a particular computer crashes? Will the network be used primarily as a productivity tool to share resources, or will it be a vital component of daily business operations? Will the nature of your business change in the foreseeable future, and will this affect the requirements placed on your network design?

SECURITY REQUIREMENTS

The reasons for keeping your data and other resources secure can range from avoiding accidental data loss to preventing international espionage. The level of security you require depends on the type of business you're in, the value of your data, who has access to your computers, the expertise of your users, and so forth. And if you're designing weapons systems, for example, the government may impose certain security requirements on your network. Don't forget to consider future security needs as your network expands.

EXPECTED TRAFFIC LEVEL

Even with a small number of users, the amount of traffic on your network can vary widely. Your users may need to move large amounts of data around, or run large applications across the network. If so, you'll need to consider supplying additional hardware horsepower – and you'll need to carefully plan where the data is going, to avoid performance bottlenecks. On the other hand, if users only occasionally print reports and update small data files over the network, traffic levels will be more modest. Be sure to look down the road toward probable future traffic levels.

ADMINISTRATIVE SUPPORT REQUIREMENTS

All networks require some amount of administration effort. It must be done – whether one person, a central group, or individual users are responsible for this function. If you don't already have one or more people ready to support the network, you'll need to assign this responsibility. If you don't plan to centralize network administration, consider the costs of training individual users so they can administer their own nodes on the network.

In the following sections, I discuss the details of peer-to-peer networking, dedicated server networking, and a combination of the two.

Understanding Peer-to-Peer Networking

In a typical peer-to-peer network (or workgroup), no single person is assigned to administer the resources of the entire network. Because each user's computer is a potential server, individual users completely control which resources their computers share with the rest of the network. Users are responsible for making shared resources available, maintaining applications and data on their own computers, installing and upgrading applications, and deciding who gets access to their shared resources. Individual users control their own security policies, selecting and assigning passwords to individual resources they share with others. Assigning individual passwords to each shared resource is known as *share-level access control.*

Peer-to-peer networks tend to be relatively small. Most of these networks fall in the range between two and ten nodes. Larger peer-to-peer networks become difficult to manage, because so many network administrators (that is, users) control sharing, securing, and maintaining shared resources. Networks of more than ten nodes typically use a dedicated server approach, or they combine peer-to-peer and dedicated server approaches. I discuss this in more detail later in this chapter.

UP-FRONT COSTS

The overall cost of a peer-to-peer network tends to be less than that of a dedicated server network, because you don't have to invest in one or more powerful central server computers. On the other hand, keep in mind that because peer-to-peer computers act as both clients and servers, individual computers may be more expensive than typical client computers in a dedicated server network. Not only does each computer support its local user, it must also use some hardware resources to support remote users.

For example, let's say your computer needs to act as a print server because you're lucky enough to have the fancy color laser printer in your office. As a result, you may need more free hard disk space to store other users' print jobs before they're printed. Likewise, if your group's customer database file lives on your hard disk, you may need a more powerful CPU, a faster network adapter, and a faster hard disk to handle the extra traffic that everyone else generates on your computer.

The cost of peer-to-peer network operating system software is usually lower than that of a dedicated server NOS. This cost difference shows up both in the cost of the software itself and in the cost of the hardware required to run it. Dedicated server software often requires a more expensive hardware platform on which to run.

PASSWORD PANDEMONIUM

The control by individual users over resources and their passwords in peer-to-peer networks leads to what I like to call *peer-to-peer password pandemonium.* Because each resource can be assigned its own unique password, users are forced to remember (or record on sticky notes in their desk drawers) many passwords. As the network grows and the number of shared resources grows, the list of required passwords can become quite long. In the real world, this unfortunate situation leads to several possible outcomes:

- **Written password lists** – Users individually keep lists of resources and their passwords on paper in their desk drawers or in electronic files on their computers. This practice makes the list of passwords easily accessible to people who shouldn't have access. Security is compromised.
- **Distributed password lists** – Users publish lists of resources and their passwords, sending them in e-mail and even posting them on office walls. Security is compromised.
- **Standard passwords** – Users begin to assign the same standard password to many different resources. Once you know one password, you can access many different resources with it. This approach is equally insecure, and defeats the purpose of being able to assign unique passwords to each resource. Security is compromised.

- **No passwords** – Users stop assigning resource passwords altogether, because it's such a hassle to communicate the password to everyone and keep the list of passwords up-to-date. Security is compromised.

I've seen combinations of these practices used to varying degrees in real peer-to-peer networks. Typically, some users are very concerned about security, assigning unique passwords to all their shared resources, changing the passwords often, and communicating those changes only to those users who really need access. Other network users see security as an annoyance, so they don't assign any passwords and they try to encourage others to follow them.

NETWORK DISCIPLINE

The resulting lack of security caused by these activities is one of the primary arguments against peer-to-peer networking. However, the problem isn't completely insurmountable. If you can train your users to set, change, communicate, and properly protect passwords, your network can be just as secure as a dedicated server network. Success in making a network secure rests with the network administrator. In other words, in a peer-to-peer network, the responsibility rests with the individual users and with whomever is responsible for training them.

Speaking of training, don't forget to consider the cost of additional user training when implementing a peer-to-peer network. Because peer-to-peer users must act as both users and administrators of their own computers, they usually require more training than dedicated server network users. Users who have a printer that they want to share must learn how to share and maintain it on the network. Those who want to share files from their desktop computers will have to learn the appropriate techniques. And, of course, everyone will need to understand the importance of security.

SELECTING PEER-TO-PEER NETWORKING

Peer-to-peer networks make the most sense if all the following conditions are true of your network environment:

- You plan to have ten or fewer computers participate in the network.
- You have no plans to expand your network significantly in the foreseeable future.
- You're not concerned with securing access to shared resources, or you're confident you can train your users to implement an appropriate security policy.
- Your computers are located in the same general physical area (for example, on a LAN in an office suite).

Even if a peer-to-peer network meets your needs today, you can always convert it to a dedicated server network later. However, the added centralized control and security imposed in a dedicated server environment can make former peer-to-peer users feel as though their basic liberties are threatened. People accustomed to the free-wheeling world of peer-to-peer networks often complain when it goes away. (Just as in management, it's easier to start with more restrictions and perhaps relax them later than to start with no restrictions and impose them later.) If you think you'll need a dedicated server network in the foreseeable future, it's best to start with one.

Understanding Dedicated Server Networking

A dedicated server network (sometimes called a *server-based network* or *client-server network*) includes one or more computers that are dedicated to acting as servers. The servers are optimized to provide quick access to shared network resources. Dedicated servers also provide centralized security to ensure that resources aren't accessed by unauthorized users.

Because the dedicated server approach centralizes control of data and other shared resources, one person or group is typically responsible for administering the network. Unlike the peer-to-peer environment, dedicated server networking doesn't allow individual users to share resources, assign passwords, and perform other administrative tasks that affect the network. Users are users, and administrators are administrators.

Dedicated server networks tend to be larger than peer-to-peer networks. They can be as small as two nodes, but can support hundreds or even thousands of users. A peer-to-peer network with thousands of nodes would be impossible to manage, but dedicated server NOS software provides the capacity and tools to manage huge collections of computers.

Because many users rely on these central servers, the NOSs provide redundancy features that keep resources available even if certain hardware components fail. This concept is known as *fault tolerance*—the ability to tolerate a hardware fault and still continue to operate. I discuss fault tolerance in Chapter 13.

As a network increases in both size and traffic, you can add more servers to handle the extra load. Spreading many tasks across different server computers can balance the load and improve overall network performance.

NOTE: Centralizing critical data on one or a few servers makes the task of backing up the data easier. If critical information is scattered all over the network, as is typical in a peer-to-peer network, you can back it up, but you must pinpoint where the critical data is and make sure it doesn't move over time.

MANAGEABLE SECURITY

Dedicated server networks offer a much more structured approach to securing network resources. Recall the Password Pandemonium section earlier in this chapter. Each resource in a peer-to-peer network can have its own unique password, forcing users to remember or record a large number of passwords. In a dedicated server network, an administrator sets security policies that apply to all network users. Each user is assigned an account with a unique password that grants the user access to the network. The network administrator can then grant the user specific types of access to individual shared resources on the network. The dedicated server NOS is responsible for authenticating the user once, and then permitting or preventing access to individual resources. This approach to security is called *user-level access control.*

NOTE

In the Windows networking world, this approach to security requires a user account on a Windows NT Server computer. Windows NT Server performs authentication when the user logs on to the network. Windows 98 cannot be used to authenticate user accounts.

Once a user logs on with his or her password, no other passwords are needed to access individual resources. This approach is much easier on users — they don't have to remember long lists of passwords. User-level access control is also more secure. Users can (and should) keep their own passwords secret, and no password ever has to be published to anyone else.

NOTE

It may seem as though dedicated server networking is always the way to go, considering its approach to managing passwords and security. Indeed, many network administrators choose to implement dedicated server networks based on this one criteria. However, peer-to-peer networks perform just fine in some situations. You'll need to weigh the costs and benefits for your particular organization and needs. Just keep this in mind as you progress through this section.

Let's look at an example. Eight peer-to-peer network users each share three resources on the network. Because all eight users believe in tight security, the users assign a unique password to each shared resource. As a user on this peer-to-peer network, you must remember or write down 24 different passwords and their associated resources. What's more, each user must communicate any password changes to you and to all other network users.'

In contrast, a dedicated server network enables you to access all the shared resources by remembering and using one unique password assigned to you. You can change it at any time, and it never has to be communicated to anyone. Even the network administrator doesn't need to know your password. And if you're not allowed to access certain resources, the network administrator can set those restrictions so that your single password gives you access to what you should be able to access – nothing more. In this example, you need only one password – not 24 different ones.

SERVER SPECIALIZATION

A dedicated server can perform many diverse functions, or it can be specialized to perform just one specific task on the network. In the following sections, I discuss some examples of specialized dedicated servers.

FILE SERVERS A file server is dedicated to the task of sharing files over the network. High-speed hard disks and network adapters are critical to good file server performance. A file server may share files directly with client applications, or it may act as a distribution point for files that are copied to client computers. File servers can also be used as repositories or transfer points for users to transmit files from one client computer to others. Users can also take advantage of the large hard disk space available on a file server to store data that doesn't fit on their local computers.

PRINT SERVERS A print server acts solely as the interface between the network and one or more shared printers. It contains the print queues for each printer it controls. (I introduced the concept of print queues earlier in this chapter.)

Because printers are relatively slow devices, dedicated print servers usually have large hard disks on which to queue pending print jobs. A print server can typically get away with a slower processor, because it can easily keep up with the task of feeding multiple printers with data. If the server receives a high volume of print job traffic from the network, however, it should be as well-equipped as a file server. High capacity print servers need fast hard disks and high-speed network adapters.

> **NOTE:** Earlier in this chapter, I mentioned a different kind of print server — a device that connects a non-network-ready printer directly to the network. Since that's exactly what a computer does when it shares a printer on the network, the term *print server* is appropriate in both cases. In this book, when you see the term *print server*, it refers to a computer acting as a print server, unless otherwise noted.

APPLICATION SERVERS An application server runs the server portion of one or more client-server applications. The server applications interact with client applications, running on client computers, to respond to requests for service and provide access to data on the server computer. For example, Microsoft SQL Server is a client-server database application. The server portion of SQL Server runs on a computer acting as an application server. It provides all access to the database definition and contents.

The speed of CPUs, hard disks, and network adapters are critical to application server performance. CPU performance is particularly important, because the server portion of the application runs on the server computer, servicing requests in behalf of many clients. The importance of hard disk speed and network adapter performance depend on the volume of data transmitted by your client-server application.

NOTE: Elsewhere, you may see the term *application server* used to describe sharing a single copy of an application over the network. In reality, this activity falls within the file server realm. The files that make up the application are simply shared and loaded over the network. In this book, the term *application server* refers to a server computer that's running the server portion of a client-server application.

MAIL SERVERS A mail server is a specialized form of either a file server or an application server, depending on the type of e-mail application you're using. If e-mail is implemented as a set of shared files accessed directly by client applications, a mail server simply shares those files on the network. In this situation, a mail server acts just like a file server.

If e-mail is implemented as a client-server application, both the server portion of the mail application and the e-mail data itself reside on the server. Client e-mail applications interact with the server application to access and manage the e-mail data. In this case, the mail server is really an application server.

FAX SERVERS A fax server manages incoming and outgoing faxes by sharing one or more fax/modem devices. As I discussed earlier in this chapter, outgoing faxes are treated much like print jobs. They're queued on disk until a fax/modem is available to send them. Incoming faxes are stored on disk for later distribution. A single fax/modem device and a single phone line can use fax server software to make electronic faxing available to all network users.

COMMUNICATION SERVERS A communication server manages the flow of information – such as e-mail and file transfers – between your network and other networks, mainframes, or remote users. Communication servers are sometimes called *routers* or *gateways*, depending on the functions they perform. (I discuss more specifically what routers and gateways do in Chapter 5.) For now, just think of them as translators between a source and destination that aren't compatible with each other. They may perform:

- **Physical conversions** – if the source and destination are physically wired differently,
- **Logical conversions** – if the source and destination speak different network protocols, or
- **Both physical and logical conversions** – if the source and destination are wired differently and use different network protocols.

For example, Microsoft SNA Server, which runs on Windows NT Server, acts as a gateway between PC network clients and IBM mainframe computers. *SNA* stands for *Systems Network Architecture*, the convention used to communicate with IBM mainframes. The computer running SNA Server acts as a communication server by establishing a connection to the mainframe, and then managing a pathway between network clients and the mainframe.

Another good example of a communication server is Microsoft's Remote Access Server (RAS). It provides a link between remote computers and your network. Users dial in to a server running RAS, and the data they send and receive travels through the RAS server to its ultimate destination. RAS lets the remote clients (remote nodes) act as if they're locally attached network nodes. See Chapter 1 for a discussion of the difference between remote control and remote node.

RAS can manage one or more modems and remote nodes simultaneously. Windows 98 includes a scaled-down version of RAS. It has the capability of acting as a remote node client or as a dial-in server with one modem. Windows NT Server includes the complete form of RAS, which can handle up to 256 simultaneous remote nodes.

DIRECTORY SERVERS A directory server provides a means for users to find, store, retrieve, and secure information and other resources on the network. It also provides a convenient way to organize and manage a set of diverse network information. Directory servers typically include NOS-specific databases to manage data about users, user accounts, shared network resources, physical resource locations, security attributes, and other information about the network. These databases might be centralized on a single server, or they might be distributed automatically throughout the network.

Windows NT Server combines computers, users, and shared resources into logical groupings called *domains*. A domain centralizes and organizes the information required to establish and maintain user accounts and access of individual users to individual resources. This information can be copied automatically to other servers on the network, to provide redundancy if the main server goes down. Windows NT Server 5.0 Active Directory takes this concept a step further by organizing all of this information in a hierarchical tree structure and distributing it automatically throughout the network.

A pure Windows 98 network doesn't include directory servers. If you have a Windows NT Server computer on your network, however, Windows 98 can take advantage of the centralized directory information and use it to authenticate users and enforce network security.

SPLIT PERSONALITIES As you may have guessed by now, some dedicated servers in the real world perform multiple server functions at the same time. For example, a Windows 98 computer might share files, printers (managing the queues for one or more printers), hard disk space, and productivity applications. Likewise, a Windows NT Server computer might act as a directory server (managing user accounts, security, and resource information), a print server, and an application server (running the server portion of a client-server application such as Microsoft SQL Server).

If a LAN contains only one or a small number of dedicated servers, chances are they're performing multiple server functions. The larger the number of servers in your network, the more likely they are to perform more specialized functions. For example, in a large network, you might have many dedicated directory servers, one or two mail servers, and a large number of file and print servers.

UP-FRONT COSTS

The initial cost of a dedicated server network tends to be higher than that of a peer-to-peer network. The greatest cost difference lies in the hardware and software requirements of one or more dedicated server computers. Dedicated servers cost more than peer-to-peer nodes because dedicated servers typically need a lot of hard disk space, one or more fast CPUs, a large memory, high-speed network adapters, and perhaps additional devices to improve reliability and prevent data loss. And as I mentioned earlier in this chapter, a dedicated server NOS is usually more expensive than a peer-to-peer NOS.

On the other hand, client computers in a dedicated server network can be less expensive than the average peer-to-peer node. Clients serve only their local users, so they don't need additional hardware to handle demands imposed by other users. At first blush, it may appear that large dedicated server networks are less expensive than peer-to-peer networks with an equivalent number of nodes. As a network grows, however, more (and perhaps more powerful) dedicated servers are required to handle the additional demands created by more users.

SERVER HARDWARE

As the network becomes large and you assign more tasks to a dedicated server, you need to provide the server with more powerful hardware and a powerful NOS to run on it. For example, a database server that provides large amounts of data to many users may require a more powerful CPU and support for very large files. Not all NOSs support these features.

XREF: I compare the features of the Microsoft network operating systems in Chapter 7, and discuss choosing computer hardware in Chapter 8.

Windows 98 supports computers containing a single CPU. Increasing the computing power of a Windows 98 computer requires a faster CPU and perhaps a faster motherboard. A *multiprocessing* (or *MP*) system is a computer that contains more than one CPU. Windows NT supports *symmetric multiprocessing* (*SMP*) computers, which distribute the workload evenly across all CPUs in the computer. Furthermore, NT enables you to create and access huge files containing up to 16 exabytes (EB), or 2^{64} bytes.

SELECTING DEDICATED SERVER NETWORKING

Dedicated server networks make the most sense if one or more of the following conditions are true of your network environment:

- You plan to have more than ten computers participate in the network, or you plan to expand your network to more than ten nodes in the foreseeable future.
- Your computers are located in more than one physical area (for example, on multiple floors of a building, or at multiple sites).
- You need centralized control of network administration, including sharing resources, imposing security, backing up data, and managing who has access to individual resources.
- You need to enforce the security of your data and other resources, and teaching users to implement security themselves isn't an option.

Combining Peer-to-Peer with Dedicated Server Networks

Conceptually, the distinctions between peer-to-peer and dedicated server networks are clear; however, many networks in actual organizations end up combining the two in some way. Although this mixing of network types can be confusing, you'll find that it demonstrates the flexibility provided by network hardware and software.

The typical combination network uses one or more dedicated servers to share the bulk of the critical data, applications, printers, and so forth. Clients on the network run peer-to-peer NOS software, enabling them to act as clients and also share their own resources on the network. Peer-to-peer operating systems such as Windows NT Workstation, Windows 98, and Windows 95 can be configured to share resources and enforce user-level access control provided by a Windows NT Server computer.

This approach provides the best of both worlds – centralized user passwords control access to all resources, and users still have the flexibility of sharing their own resources. A combination like this is very common. In fact, Microsoft's internal network is configured this way. Keep in mind, however, that this type of network requires a lot of planning and user training to ensure that it's implemented correctly and properly secured. Without proper configuration and user training, a combination network can turn into a network administrator's nightmare.

Using Windows 98 as a Dedicated Server

Although Windows 98 is a peer-to-peer NOS, you can cast it in the role of a dedicated server in your network. Doing this requires that you and your network users exercise discipline and control. The Windows 98 software won't enforce the rules for you. Here are a few basic requirements that need to be enforced for implementing a successful Windows 98 dedicated server:

- **Dedicate servers to specific tasks** – Plan and assign specific server tasks to specific computers, and don't burden those computers with interactive user tasks. Ideally, dedicated servers shouldn't be forced into double duty as clients. You want their computing resources focused on serving the rest of the network. This is purely a matter of discipline. It's up to the network administrator to define and enforce these roles.
- **Tune the servers with appropriate hardware** – Be sure to equip your dedicated servers with appropriate hardware to handle their assigned server tasks. Don't treat these computers as though they're clients. It's easy to fall into the trap of underpowering your servers to save costs. Just remember that dedicated servers must provide efficient service to many users. Productivity gains from a well-equipped server far outweigh the additional hardware costs. (I discuss hardware selection in Chapter 8.)

- **Disable file and printer sharing on all client computers** – Shut off the server function on all client computers, and enable it only on computers that play the dedicated server role. This approach begins to centralize control, and information flows through dedicated servers rather than between peers. To enforce this approach, you can prevent users from enabling the server functionality on their client computers. Unfortunately, you can't always prevent a determined user from finding and installing the utility required to turn the server features on again.

Summary

In this chapter, you've discovered how computers are connected to a network, and how resources are then shared and accessed over the network. You've also learned about the key differences between dedicated server networks and peer-to-peer networks. In Chapter 3, I show you how popular applications such as e-mail, group scheduling, and office productivity applications operate in a networked environment. I also provide some advice on how to decide which applications should be networked.

Chapter 3

Using Networked Applications

IN THIS CHAPTER

- Understanding electronic mail and group scheduling
- Implementing groupware
- Using network administration tools
- Using networking productivity applications
- Deciding which applications to network: feasibility, costs, and benefits

WITH A COMPUTER NETWORK in place, it makes business sense to network as many of your computing activities and applications as possible. Not all applications are designed for a networked environment, but some applications make no sense without a network. For example, many organizations consider electronic mail an indispensable tool – the "killer application" on computer networks. Indeed, many organizations depend on e-mail for a hefty portion of their daily communication tasks. Likewise, group scheduling and collaboration software provide ways to increase user productivity both in and out of the workplace.

In this chapter, you'll learn about key types of networked applications including e-mail, group scheduling, and network administration tools. You'll also discover how you can increase the benefits of traditional desktop applications by running them on a network. Finally, I discuss how you can decide whether or not to network individual applications in your organization.

Understanding Electronic Mail

With electronic mail, you can communicate quickly with one or many people – regardless of where they are, whether they're busy, or what time it is. Messages are delivered automatically, and recipients can read and respond at their own convenience. E-mail can cut way down on time-wasting activities such as playing voice mail tag, visiting a colleague's office only to find it empty, and sending a fax or traditional mail. Moreover, compared with more traditional forms of communication, e-mail is essentially free if you already have the network.

Understanding How E-mail Works

Regardless of the type of network you use, most e-mail systems operate on pretty much the same principles. You designate a server computer (either a dedicated server or a peer-to-peer server) to act as the e-mail post office. An e-mail message from a user arrives at the post office server from the network. The message is storedin the central post office until the message recipient decides to download messages. The recipient's messages are then forwarded over the network from the post office to the recipient's computer. This approach to e-mail has become known as the *store and forward* approach. Figure 3-1 illustrates this concept.

E-mail — It's in There!

Because e-mail is such a popular network application, some network operating systems include it as an integral feature. For example, Windows 98 includes the Outlook Express mail client. If you have an existing e-mail server (such as Microsoft Mail on Windows 95 or Windows NT, or Microsoft Exchange Server on Windows NT Server), you can use Outlook Express to send, receive, and manage e-mail within your organization. And if you have access to the Internet, you can use Outlook Express to exchange e-mail with anyone.

If you don't have either, you can set up a workgroup post office using Microsoft Mail, which is available for download free of charge from `ftp://ftp.microsoft.com/bussys/mail/pcmail-public/`. (A *post office* refers to a server where e-mail messages are stored until they're delivered to their recipients.) Or, if you have Windows NT Server on your network, you can purchase Microsoft Exchange Server. Alternatively, if you have a Windows 95 computer on your network, you can set it up as a workgroup post office. The Windows 95 Resource Kit shows you how. (See Appendix B for information on Microsoft Resource Kits.)

With an e-mail client such as Outlook Express, you can browse through the e-mail, sort it, and automatically sift and organize messages by routing them to specific folders based on a set of filter criteria. You can also use Outlook Express as a universal inbox and outbox to send and receive e-mail to and from multiple e-mail accounts (for example, an Internet account, America Online, and CompuServe).

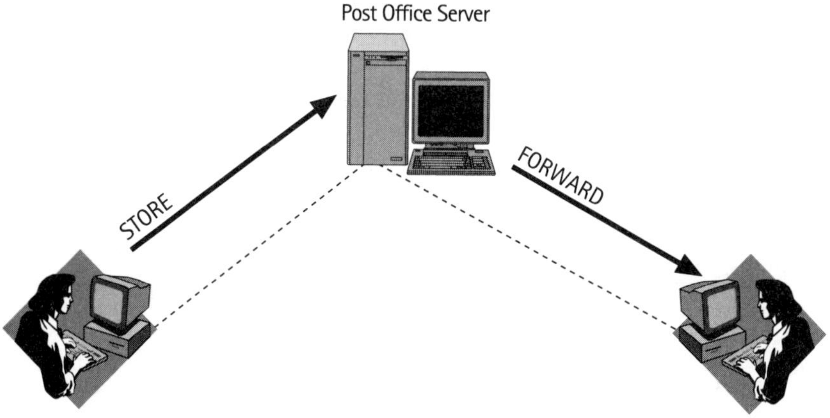

Figure 3-1: E-mail messages are stored on a post office server, and are then forwarded toward their final destinations.

Some e-mail packages consist only of client applications that access a set of shared post office files on a server. More sophisticated client-server e-mail packages include a server application that communicates with e-mail clients and controls all access to the centralized post office data files. Microsoft Mail Postoffice is an example of the shared file approach to e-mail. You can install and run it in a peer-to-peer network, designating one computer as the post office server. In contrast, Microsoft Exchange Server is a true client-server application, and requires Windows NT Server to run it.

Many different e-mail packages are in use today, and few are truly compatible with each other. If you're faced with the task of seamlessly connecting two e-mail systems together, or a LAN e-mail system with the Internet, you'll probably need an *e-mail gateway*. An e-mail gateway performs the translation required between disparate e-mail systems, so users can send and receive messages between them simply by specifying an appropriate e-mail address.

Establishing E-mail Roles

E-mail within a LAN is fairly easy to implement. Once it's set up, its operation is automatic. Messages are stored and forwarded without intervention. You don't have to worry about disgruntled postal workers in your electronic post office. However, you do need to perform a set of basic administrative tasks to ensure that your e-mail system keeps running smoothly. This means that, even in a peer-to-peer network, you need to designate e-mail administration responsibility to a specific person or group.

Is this a full-time job? The answer to that question depends on the number of e-mail users and the level of e-mail traffic. In practice, an e-mail system serving several hundred users can require a full-time administrator. If the number of users is under 40, you can usually perform the tasks in a couple of hours each week. But as more users take advantage of e-mail in your organization, and as they individually send more and more information, the required administrative tasks will grow in scope.

E-mail administration responsibilities include the following tasks:

- Installing the e-mail application and establishing the central post office
- Creating e-mail accounts and assigning passwords
- Training users on e-mail procedures, features, and etiquette
- Updating e-mail account information as users are hired, fired, or transferred
- Backing up post office data files and restoring them when necessary
- Maintaining adequate disk space on the post office server
- Maintaining adequate post office server performance through hardware upgrades and maintenance

Modern e-mail systems offer many useful features, including attachment of files (such as spreadsheets, documents, graphics, and so forth), return receipts, and even voice and video annotations. In other words, e-mail isn't just for text anymore. Yet with all the bells and whistles, many people are hesitant to change their current communication habits. An effective e-mail system requires a bit of behavior modification. Users need to check their e-mail frequently, filter through the extraneous messages, and answer important messages quickly. This behavior modification aspect of using e-mail applications makes training users somewhat more difficult.

TIP

It's important to realize up front that users can quickly become highly dependent on e-mail. They only half-joke about suffering from "e-mail withdrawal," after going on vacation or experiencing an e-mail server crash. So, as time goes on, user tolerance decreases dramatically for e-mail server downtime, lost messages, and other problems. From a network administrator's perspective, that translates to a need for increasing reliability and availability of the e-mail server and its data. Keep this in mind as you plan your e-mail implementation. E-mail dependency is as real as any other addiction — and when users have withdrawal symptoms, they come after the network administrator!

Implementing an E-mail System

Once you decide to implement an e-mail system in your organization, you face several administrative decisions. The most fundamental one involves selecting or equipping a server to handle the post office function. Each e-mail application has unique requirements, so you need to use those requirements as a starting place.

> **NOTE:** Large organizations may need more that one post office server, to spread the heavy e-mail load across multiple servers and multiple portions of the network. Figure 3-2 shows an example of a network with two post offices. If you establish multiple post office servers, they must communicate with each other to forward e-mail sent from a user of one post office to a user of another post office. (This activity is similar to the way the U.S. mail works when a letter is mailed from one city or region to another.) Too many post office servers can bog down a network with traffic between post offices. A good rule of thumb is no more than 200 users on any one post office. Because each e-mail application has different requirements, however, you should refer to your application documentation for recommendations.

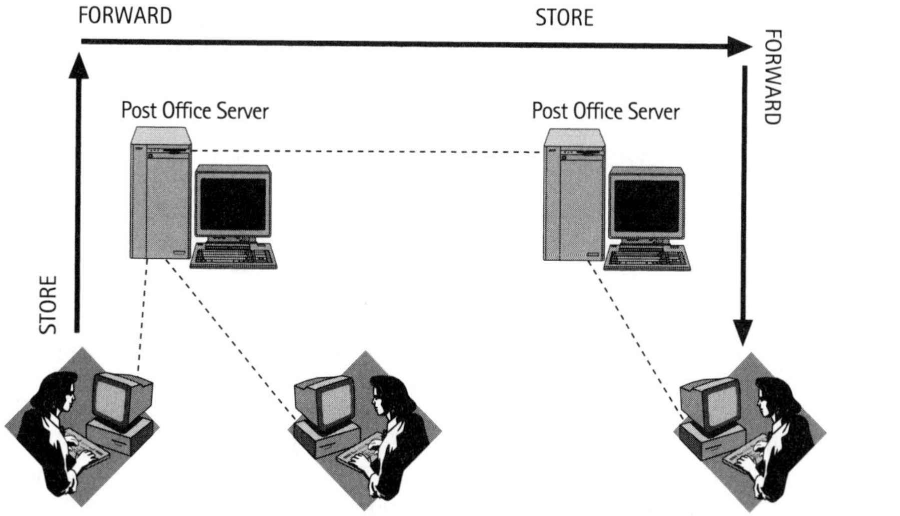

Figure 3-2: E-mail messages may be stored on one post office server, forwarded to and stored on another post office server, and then forwarded to their final destinations.

How do you select an appropriate server to fill the post office role? In an e-mail application, it's critically important to provide sufficient hard disk space for storage of the users' e-mail before it's downloaded to the client computers. E-mail application vendors provide guidelines for the amount of storage to provide each user. Unfortunately, their recommendations too often tend to be on the low side, especially considering the increasing use of attached documents, sound files, videos, and other large chunks of e-mailed data. These items consume a lot of disk space.

My rule of thumb is 15MB per user. Some users consume only 1MB, whereas others require more than 15MB. The average user most likely takes up between 5MB and 10MB of storage. Of course, this may vary from time to time, depending on what they're sending and receiving. The 15MB-per-user rule works well for both Microsoft Mail Postoffice and Microsoft Exchange Server. So, you'll need about 3GB of hard disk space to handle comfortably a post office serving 200 users.

CAUTION

Don't forget to account for the hard disk space required by the network operating system, the e-mail application itself, and any additional disk space requirements imposed by other applications. All of this space is over and above the required per-user post office hard disk space.

If you plan to support a lot of e-mail traffic, be sure your server and network hardware components are up to the task. Fast hard disks, fast network adapters, and (in a client-server e-mail application) fast CPUs can help provide efficient e-mail service to your users. I discuss how to select high-performance hardware for your server computers in Chapter 8.

In most e-mail packages, each user is assigned a mailbox name. In assigning these names, your goal should be to make users' lives (and yours) as simple as possible. If they already have a user name on the network, or an Internet address, do your best to use the same name for their mailbox name in your e-mail system. The fewer names a user has to remember, the better.

When selecting mailbox names (or user names in general), it's best to construct a combination of their first and last names. If you use first names alone or last names alone, you're bound to run into duplicates within the organization. For example, if you have three people named Jeff, and you tack numbers onto their names to differentiate them, Jeff1 might be completely happy with his mailbox name. But Jeff0 and Jeff2 might take offense at being numbered zero and two, respectively. (Don't laugh. This actually happened to three colleagues of mine named Jeff.)

Two conventions for assigning e-mail names predominate:

- **First initial followed by full last name** – For example, Ken Gregg would be *kgregg*. This approach is more commonly used, because last names tend to be more unique than first names (at least in some cultures).
- **First name followed by last initial** – For example, Ken Gregg would be *keng*. This approach is often used in smaller, less formal organizations. Emphasis on the first name yields a more personal flavor.

You can handle duplication by adding letters to the initial. For example, if the organization already had a *keng* (which was the case at Microsoft when I arrived there as a new employee), you could add another letter to the last initial. My assigned e-mail name became *kengr*.

If your e-mail addresses include post office or e-mail gateway names, try to keep them simple as well. If possible, use your company name so users have short, easy-to-remember e-mail addresses. There's nothing more annoying to a user than a lengthy, complicated e-mail address that looks something like `kengr@mrbill.gatewayx.yoda.postoffice0.yourcompany.com`. There's only so much space on a business card for an e-mail address.

NOTE

If you decide to connect two e-mail systems together, or connect your LAN e-mail system to the Internet, you'll need an e-mail gateway. Some are included with the e-mail package, and others must be purchased separately. Gateways are designed for specific e-mail systems. For example, Microsoft Mail Postoffice and Microsoft Exchange Server both support gateways to IBM PROFS, OfficeVision, X.400, SMTP, IBM SNADS, Fax Services, MHS, and AT&T Easylink Services. Whenever you connect e-mail systems together, be sure to consider security. You don't want unauthorized external users to have access to your e-mail system or your network.

As a convenience, most e-mail packages let you define mailing lists (or *aliases*) that you can use to send messages to groups of people using a single e-mail address. For example, you might create an e-mail alias called *Salesgroup* that includes all the individual e-mail addresses of people in the sales organization. When you want to send a message to the entire sales group, simply send it to the Salesgroup alias.

Using and Teaching E-mail Etiquette

Because e-mail is so easy to use, it's typically much less formal than other written business communication. As a result, messages are often short – sometimes they aren't even in complete sentences. Although there's nothing inherently wrong with communicating this way, it can lead to misunderstandings. E-mail lacks the visual and auditory cues that help us humans understand when someone is being funny, sarcastic, angry, and so forth. Serious-sounding e-mail can offend or anger the recipient, even if the sender was only joking.

To facilitate better e-mail communication, users have developed a set of abbreviations that act as a sort of electronic shorthand for common expressions and emotions. For example, BTW stands for "by the way" and IMHO stands for "in my humble opinion." Sequences of characters that simulate facial expressions are called *emoticons*. Table 3-1 lists a few of the many emoticons used in e-mail today. If you tilt your head 90 degrees to the left, you'll see how the characters resemble facial expressions.

TABLE 3-1 EMOTICON EXPRESSIONS USED IN E-MAIL MESSAGES

Emoticon Character Sequence	Facial Expression or Emotion
:-) or :^)	Smile or "don't take this seriously"
:-D or :^D	Big grin or silly grin
:-O or :^O	Yawn or boredom
;-) or ;^)	Wink
:-* or :^*	Kiss
:-(or :^(	Frown, sadness, or disappointment
:-< or :^<	Big frown or extreme sadness
>:-(or >:^(	Anger
:'-(or ;'^(	Tears, crying, extreme sadness
:-o or 8°	Surprise

Spamming is an Internet term that refers to sending unwanted, unsolicited e-mail to a group of e-mail addresses without their prior consent. The unsolicited e-mail itself is referred to as *spam*. (The term sprang from a Monty Python sketch in which the repeated chanting and singing of the word "spam" prevented others from communicating with each other.) Spam e-mail wastes the time of its recipients, wastes network bandwidth, and wastes disk space. Train your users not to spam others within your organization or on the Internet. (Yes, the term *spam* is both a noun and a verb. I sometimes wonder if the good people at Hormel take offense at this.)

Using E-mail Effectively

Electronic mail is certainly a convenient way to communicate, but it isn't always the most appropriate way to communicate. With an e-mail system at their disposal, users can sometimes get caught in one or more e-mail traps that waste time and energy.

Users sometimes hide behind their e-mail, saying things in writing that they wouldn't or shouldn't say in person. I've also known some managers that hide behind e-mail to avoid face-to-face meetings and confrontations. E-mail should be used as a tool for efficient communication, not as a replacement for person-to-person interaction, and certainly not as an electronic shield to hide behind.

Frequently, new users employ e-mail for all their communications, even if the recipient is two steps down the hall. This approach is very inefficient, especially if the recipient needs to respond to or discuss the issue at the moment. E-mail is great if the recipient isn't there, or is too busy to discuss the issue, but a brief face-to-face discussion is often the quickest way to go. (When office intercom systems first showed up, people reacted similarly. They frequently used the intercom to chat with people in the office next door, instead of taking the two extra steps to chat in person.)

E-mail sent to group aliases is a convenient way to communicate quickly with many people at once. When an e-mail discussion starts, though, irrelevant traffic can waste considerable time and bandwidth. The most frustrating phenomenon is a stream of "me, too" messages. One person states an opinion, another agrees with it, and a flood of responses that essentially say "me, too" pour into everyone's mailboxes. (If you extrapolate the "me, too" phenomenon, you get "me, three" and eventually "me, four hundred" messages.) There are more efficient ways to solicit opinions from members of the group.

Universal agreement isn't always the problem either. Sometimes users get into heated discussions and arguments. Frequently, other members of the group e-mail alias are subjected to the unpleasant exchange. I've seen managers compelled to step in and tell the pugilists to "take it offline." Arguing via e-mail, and letting others watch, is a waste of everyone's time.

Although it seems our offices are still buried in paperwork, e-mail can replace much of the paper trail you keep in file cabinets (or on the desk or floor of your office). If you save copies of the e-mail you send and receive, you can easily reconstruct key events, decisions, discussions, and other important communications. It's all neatly filed away on your hard disk, if you ever need it. And even if you delete it, chances are it was backed up while it was on the post office server. I discuss backing up data in Chapter 13.

If you decide to implement an e-mail system, be sure to have good reasons for it. Most important, be sure your users understand the goals of the system and how to use it efficiently. E-mail can generate a big productivity boost – but without the proper training and discipline, it can easily become a huge productivity drain.

Understanding Electronic Group Scheduling

The advent of computer networks has been the key to truly useful electronic group scheduling. With networked scheduling software, you can quickly and automatically check whether all potential meeting attendees are available at a specific time. If some team members can't attend, you can easily look for a time that works for everyone. You can automatically update their schedules with the new appointment, and cancel it just as easily. If multiple people handle one person's schedule, each of them can make updates to a single electronic copy, and no two meetings will ever overlap. For example, for a short time there were four administrative assistants adding meetings to my schedule. Without group scheduling software, I would have been double-booked and triple-booked several times a day. Microsoft Schedule+ and Microsoft Outlook (the full version, included in Microsoft Office Professional) are two good examples of group scheduling applications. Figure 3-3 shows a typical view of a user's Schedule+ calendar.

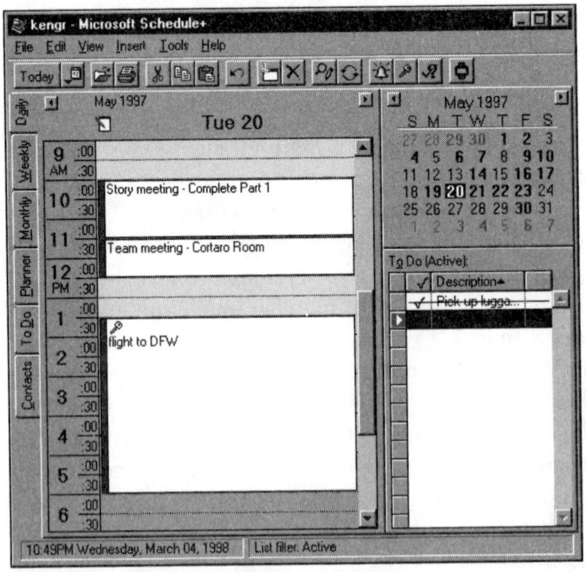

Figure 3-3: Schedule+ installed on a network enables multiple users to coordinate meetings and other events electronically.

Using Electronic Schedules

Modern group scheduling software enables you to access other people's schedules to determine when they're busy and free. You can easily check on the availability of several people at the same time. Another useful feature of group schedulers is the capability to set up a recurring meeting. You can arrange the first meeting, and then specify when and how often to schedule it into the future. This feature really saves time, especially if you have several different periodic meetings to attend. And if you're like me, and you lose track of time during meetings in your office, you can tell the scheduler to sound a chime a few minutes before your next appointment is scheduled.

In most scheduling packages, you can specify how a particular item in your schedule appears to others. You don't have to share all the details of where you'll be, only that you'll be busy at a certain time. In some products, you can assign different levels of schedule access to different members of your organization. For example, the vice president may want to allow his two assistants to have complete access to his schedule. All three people should be able to view the details and set up meetings. But you may not want to grant individual engineers the capability to schedule meetings in the VP's schedule or to see all the details of the VP's existing meetings.

TIP

Some group scheduling packages support a link to various hand-held devices such as pocket computers and wrist watches. You can keep the device in sync with your online schedule by periodically transferring schedule information between your PC and the portable device. It's all very convenient, but if your schedule is volatile, this approach can be just as troublesome as having multiple copies of your schedule floating around. No matter what technology you use, to avoid a stale schedule, you need to synchronize the copies frequently.

As I mentioned in Chapter 1, you aren't limited to using group scheduling software just to schedule people. You can also schedule other resources such as conference rooms, audiovisual equipment, teleconferencing equipment, and even catered meals. Just create a group scheduling account for each of these entities, and train users to include all the appropriate resources when scheduling a meeting or event. By integrating scheduling with e-mail, you can automatically notify the facilities department, food services department, and other organizations to supply what you need for your meeting.

Integrating Scheduling with E-mail

Most of the available group scheduling software packages offer tight integration with your e-mail software. In fact, some products, such as Microsoft Outlook, include e-mail and group scheduling in a single software package. Why is this important? In most organizations, not everyone elects to use scheduling software. Some people still prefer to keep their schedules in a planner, on a calendar, or on a hand-held organizer device. People who do use scheduling software tend to check their schedules at varying frequencies – typically, less often than they check their e-mail.

If you assume that everyone uses e-mail and checks it frequently, you can direct scheduling software to send e-mail invitations to meetings and automatically manage RSVPs via e-mail. You can even tell the software to send one or more e-mail reminders to attendees as the meeting time approaches. And, of course, you can automatically send e-mail the moment a meeting is canceled or postponed.

Group scheduling software that integrates with e-mail often uses the same list of user names and passwords as your e-mail system. This is a big advantage, especially if you have many users on your network. E-mail users can automatically have access to group scheduling – you don't have to create separate scheduling accounts for them.

When you're selecting both an e-mail application and a group scheduling application, make sure that the two can work together. Standardization has enabled applications from different vendors to work well together. However, mixing and matching applications from different vendors may not provide all the features available when applications come from the same source. I recommend, whenever possible, that you choose one manufacturer for both e-mail and scheduling. If that's not practical, use a combination that you know will work, based on a real-world installation.

Implementing Groupware: Beyond E-mail

E-mail is ideal for two-way communication between two individuals, or one-way communication from an individual to a large group. For example, e-mail is a great way for you to discuss an issue with Fred. Making an announcement of an organizational change to a large group of people is also an efficient use of e-mail. But once you start sending copies of an e-mail discussion to several people, you can start an avalanche of frustration and wasted time. Individuals start discussing topics unrelated to the original message, but they continue to copy everyone else on the responses. When others join in with "me too" and "I agree" messages, your organization begins to spend a significant amount of time reviewing and deleting irrelevant and unwanted e-mail.

Organizing Group Discussions and Meetings

E-mail isn't designed for efficient many-to-many discussions, but networks offer an ideal platform for these. That's where groupware discussion software fits in. It acts almost like an electronic bulletin board or an unmoderated meeting. Individual users can post ideas and responses. Other users can observe, respond immediately, or join the discussion at their convenience. Discussions can be organized according to topics, so it's easy for newcomers to catch up with the thinking process that has gone into a particular issue. Lotus Notes is a good example of this type of groupware. Some of today's e-mail packages have evolved to include groupware discussion features.

The latest generation of group discussion software enables you to hold live online meetings across your network. Microsoft NetMeeting is a good example of this software genre. With a microphone on each participating PC, you can collaborate via real-time audio discussions and illustrate your points on a shared electronic whiteboard. (These virtual whiteboards don't have the unsightly dust and odorous markers for which real whiteboards are infamous.) If you can afford to equip all the participants with attached video cameras, your online meetings can include real-time video conferencing as well. Windows 98 includes a version of NetMeeting.

NOTE

Chat programs represent a primitive form of discussion software. They enable you to "call" people by "ringing" their computer. When the called party answers, the two of you can conduct a quick electronic discussion. People either love or hate chat programs — there's no middle ground. Some folks believe it's a great way to contact someone with an urgent message, even if the person is already talking on the telephone. Others think chat programs are annoying, intrusive, and a waste of time. Voice mail, e-mail, and face-to-face discussions are often more appropriate and more effective methods of communicating.

Managing and Collaborating in Teams

Another great use of groupware centers around project-oriented team management and collaboration. If you have users who manage or are members of project teams, software such as Microsoft Team Manager can make life easier for the entire team.

This class of groupware can help coordinate and track project milestones, allowing everyone centralized access to key project information. Each team member can see how his or her part of the project fits into the overall schedule, and can update the project status based on individual progress.

For the team manager, the software can flag potential schedule problems, help record team member achievements, and track project costs. The manager doesn't have to travel around asking for bits of information from each team member – it's all centralized and updated in one place. (Of course, managers still need to walk around and visit their team members occasionally. No software can substitute for that.)

Using Network Administration Tools

The most powerful and useful network applications are those required to control and maintain the network. Some of these tools are integrated into what the average network user sees every day. Others are really only useful to network administrators. Network administration tools enable you to manage shared resources, individual server and client computers, user accounts, passwords, permissions, and other entities on the network. In some cases, you can examine, troubleshoot, and reconfigure computers remotely through the LAN or via a remote access connection over a phone line. (In Part III of this book, I cover network administration tools and techniques in more detail.)

Network features are tightly integrated into almost every utility provided with Windows 98, including Windows Explorer and the desktop itself. Windows 98 includes underlying support and utilities that enable remote management of computers over the network. For example, a utility called Net Watcher enables you to monitor and control users, open files, and share resources on both local and remote PCs. As shown in Figure 3-4, Net Watcher displays the details of each shared resource, along with the computers that are currently connected to it. If other computers on the network are configured for remote administration, you can use the same tool to manage other computers without leaving your desk.

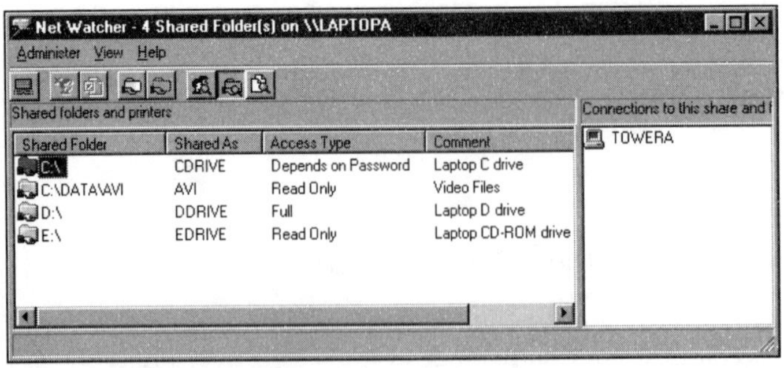

Figure 3-4: Windows 98 Net Watcher enables you to view and manage network resources and connections.

Some network administration capabilities are built directly into familiar Windows applications. Windows Explorer, for example, includes features that enable you to connect to and disconnect from shared resources, start or stop sharing local resources on the network, and browse the network for other shared resources. The Network Neighborhood icon, which appears on the Windows 98 desktop when networking software and hardware are present, provides a convenient and consistent way to view the network and all its shared resources. You'll learn more about using network administration tools and techniques in Part III.

Each Windows 98 computer includes its own internal database, called the *registry*. If you're familiar with MS-DOS and Windows 3.1, you can think of the registry as taking the place of AUTOEXEC.BAT, CONFIG.SYS, and scores of Windows INI initialization files. (Both Windows 95 and Windows NT have registries, too, but their contents aren't identical to the Windows 98 registry.) The registry contains information about the local computer's installed hardware, drivers, software applications, desktop settings, and many other important tidbits.

Knowledgeable network administrators can view and manage the registry on local and remote networked computers using a variety of tools provided in Windows 98. Windows 98 also includes a utility called REGEDIT that enables you to examine and modify the registry directly, but you can change the most important settings with other Windows 98 tools that are easier and safer to use. Many of the applications in Control Panel provide easy and safe access to parts of the registry.

CAUTION

Whenever possible, use standard Windows utilities to alter the registry, and avoid editing it directly with REGEDIT. It's very easy to make a mistake while modifying the registry, and the consequences can range from strange system behavior to a completely unbootable computer. So avoid the registry editor utility like the plague, unless you really know what you're doing and you have a way to recover the system if you misstep.

Networking Productivity Applications

Office productivity software suites are among the most widely used software products in organizations today. These productivity suites usually include at least a word processor, spreadsheet, graphical presentation package, and database. The Microsoft Office suite is a typical example. It comes in several flavors, each including a different combination of productivity applications. In most cases, the manufacturers have designed the applications to be tightly integrated, enabling you to link different types of documents with each other. For example, you can link a presentation slide showing a pie chart with data in a spreadsheet. When data in the underlying spreadsheet changes, the pie chart in the presentation slide is updated automatically.

Documents are meant to be shared. Otherwise, why would you spend time and energy creating them? Most desktop productivity applications were originally designed for use by an individual on a standalone or client computer. But even if your productivity applications aren't designed specifically for installation and execution on a network, you can still share your information electronically by sharing the document files themselves.

> **CAUTION** If you intend to store a document on a server computer and allow more than one user to modify it at the same time, make sure your application is designed to handle this situation. Most databases allow multiple users to access the files by preventing multiple simultaneous updates to a single database record; however, many other document-oriented applications coordinate updates at the file level. This means that whoever updates the document last wins — other users' updates may be completely overwritten and lost.

Now that computer networks have become office staples, many of these suites include support for easy installation and execution on a LAN. What's more, with the explosion of Internet and intranet use, more and more productivity applications include the capability to convert documents into Web pages. This makes it easier than ever to publish and share information over the network, both inside and outside your organization.

In the following sections, I discuss how you can increase the effectiveness of the most common desktop productivity applications in a networked environment. In Chapter 4, I discuss the Internet and intranets in more detail.

Using Word Processing Software

The most obvious way to distribute a word processing document is to share the document file on the network. You can attach it to e-mail instead, if the recipient isn't on your LAN but has the right software to view the document. (Many applications now include viewer software that you can distribute to your recipients free of charge, if they don't have the application you used to create your document.) You can even distribute word processing documents as files from your Web site. Microsoft distributes much of its online documentation as Microsoft Word files at `http://www.microsoft.com`. If you prefer to publish your documents, rather than forcing recipients to download files, you can easily convert most word processing documents into Web pages. Some word processing applications include this conversion capability as a built-in feature. Others require the use of an add-on component or third-party utility software.

In a networked environment, one of the most interesting and useful features of word processing packages is revision editing. If you've ever collaborated with someone else on developing a large or complex document, you probably wanted an easy way to focus in on what the other person changed in his or her latest revision. Knowing exactly what was changed can save lots of time, because you don't have to reread the entire document to review a few small changes. It can also enable you to respond to changes with which you agree or disagree. The revision editing feature enables the word processor to keep track of all the changes made to a document automatically, and includes a detailed record of who made the changes and when they were made.

If several people within an organization need to generate different documents in a standard format, you can place a standard document template file on a server, share it, and point each new document to it. Then, whenever the standard format is revised, all documents based on the template will reflect the changes automatically.

Using Spreadsheet Software

Like word processing documents, spreadsheet files are easily shared and distributed as files on a server, as files attached to e-mail, as files downloadable from a Web site, or as Web pages. If your recipient doesn't have matching spreadsheet software, you can usually provide a spreadsheet viewer for free.

To see how shared spreadsheets work, consider a typical budgeting process. Some organizations use a separate spreadsheet file for each departmental budget. Each file is based on a standard template stored on a server. As department managers turn in their budget files (either by copying the files to a server or e-mailing them), a master budget spreadsheet can automatically reflect the total organizational budget. The budgets are never printed, and managers can easily shuffle funds around to see the effects before finalizing the budget. Later, the same spreadsheets can track budgets versus actual expenses.

Spreadsheet data is often used as the underlying source material for portions of word processing documents and graphical presentations. If your supervisor wants to have the most up-to-date numbers reflected in her presentation to upper management, she can simply link to your spreadsheet (even over the network), and never have to worry about changing the presentation manually. Of course, the success of this approach requires that you keep the contents of your spreadsheet current.

Using Presentation Software

Graphical presentation software has revolutionized the effort, cost, and technique of presenting information to a group of people. Equipped with presentation software and a computer video projector, you no longer need to invest in creating expensive slides or overhead transparencies. What's more, your presentation can immediately reflect last-minute changes, or changes made to the underlying data stored on the network. Today's presentation packages enable you to include multimedia audio and video, as well as complex slide transitions and animation.

You can share and distribute presentation files over a LAN or from a Web site. Most vendors provide free viewer software for recipients who don't have your presentation application. This capability provides a valuable opportunity to distribute training materials to new employees, customers, and people training for new positions. The capability to play a presentation over the network on a user's computer saves additional time and money. Users don't need to attend a live presentation (which may occur at an inconvenient time or at a remote location), reserve a VCR and videotape, or even leave their desks.

Your organization might have a standard presentation slide format, required for all presentations. For example, your company may require the company logo, copyright notice, and confidentiality statement on each slide. You may even have company-wide standards for the size, color, and position of this information on each slide. Once again, users can simply link their presentations to a standard template stored on the network, and see changes in that template reflected the next time they open their presentations.

Microsoft Office includes PowerPoint presentation software, which works well in both a standalone and networked environment. Windows 98 includes the Microsoft NetShow player, which enables you to view audio, video, and other multimedia presentations over the network.

Using Database Software

Database software tends to be the most network-friendly component of productivity application suites. By their very nature, databases are well-suited to handling requests and updates from multiple users simultaneously. Databases allow more complex queries and analysis than most spreadsheets can handle, and it's relatively easy to create forms for data entry and reports for output. The database itself is usually implemented either as a shared file on a server or as the data underlying a client-server application. In either case, users run client database software to access and update the data. Of course, you can share the generated database reports with others on the network who don't run the database software themselves.

Microsoft Access is an example of the shared file approach. Each user runs the Access application on a client computer, accessing a common database file stored on a server. In contrast, Microsoft SQL Server is implemented as a client-server application. The database files themselves live on a server, and the SQL Server application controls all access to the data. On client computers, client database applications extract and update data by communicating with the SQL Server application over the network.

Deciding Which Applications to Network

Should every application in your organization be networked? In a perfect world, the answer would be yes. Every application would understand how to behave properly in a networked environment. Installation, maintenance, and updates would be simplified. Application performance would be acceptable. Cost-effective multi-user licenses would lower your initial investment. In a perfect world, every application would offer all of these benefits. Unfortunately, we don't live in a perfect world.

So how do you decide which applications to network? The answer is that you need to consider each application on a case-by-case basis. Treat each decision to network an application as you would any other business decision – analyze feasibility, costs, and benefits. I discuss these decision criteria in the following sections.

Feasibility

The first and most fundamental hurdle to overcome is determining whether it's even possible to install and operate a specific application in a networked environment. Even though PC networks are now ubiquitous in organizations, some software vendors haven't quite figured out how to network their applications yet. Applications designed from the starting gate as network-friendly are certainly better candidates than standalone programs that have been force-fit into a networked environment.

CAUTION

Some applications are designed to be run only on a network. Applications such as e-mail, group scheduling, and so forth just don't make any sense outside of the network context. While you can be sure this class of applications is network-ready, you still need to determine what the vendor requires for proper installation and execution. For example, one brand of accounting software may require a specific network configuration — one that may not match your network.

When you consider networking an application, it's important to account for two key areas – namely, installation and execution. Application installation is critical. If you can't install an application properly to run over the network, you're going to have a pretty tough time actually running it over the network.

Before investing in a new application, talk with the vendor and discuss the specific requirements for getting it running over the network. If possible, get a copy of the documentation that provides the details of network installation. These documents can speak volumes (and often *are* volumes) about how much trauma you'll have to suffer to properly install and use the application on your network.

If you're already committed to an application and its future versions, talk with your vendor about your plans to implement a network. It's better to jump in with your eyes open, so you'll know what extra work to expect. You may discover that your vendor doesn't support networking. At that point, you'll have to decide whether to switch applications or continue operating your application on individual computers. If the application does support networking, be sure to find out if it's completely compatible with Windows 98 and with your chosen network protocols.

Costs

Assuming it's possible to install and run the application on your network, your next step involves analyzing the costs. The most obvious cost of networking an application is the software itself. Be sure to check with the vendor for network license pricing before you invest in multiple copies of the application. You can sometimes get a significant price break by purchasing one copy of the software (including media and documentation) and the appropriate number of licenses. On a per-user basis, it's usually cheaper to acquire the software using this approach, but some vendors require that you purchase complete packages for each user.

TIP

If you're thinking of networking an application that you already own, your first step should be to read your license agreement. Most agreements detail the number of computers on which you can legally install the software, and whether or not you can install it on a network. Who knows? You may already have a license to network your application and you don't even know it!

As I mentioned in Chapter 1, installation and configuration of networked applications can be more complex than that of non-networked applications. So, expect to spend some additional effort preparing for and installing networked applications. When you install a new application on your network, you're likely to be on the phone at least once to the vendor's technical support staff before you get the application running correctly.

Another potential cost of running an application over the network is decreased performance. Depending on the application's design, it may run more slowly over the network. If the application is designed as a single, monolithic executable file, the initial load time can be high. From the user's point of view, it may appear that the program starts out sluggishly, and then seems to "wake up" and operate normally. Some applications are designed in several modules, which load as needed. They may appear speedier initially, but may slow down when the user invokes certain features for the first time.

NOTE: Some software vendors sell networked applications in packages based on the number of licensed users. If the vendor only sells licenses in increments of, say, ten users at a time, you may end up paying for licenses you're not using. For example, if your organization has 21 users and you can only purchase an application license in increments of ten users, you'll need to purchase 30 licenses, and nine will go to waste — at least until your organization grows. Most vendors offer single-user licenses for situations like this, but you should expect to pay more for them per user.

Benefits

I discussed the major benefits of networking your applications back in Chapter 1. You may be able to save on the cost of the software itself, when viewed from a cost-per-user perspective. In addition, you may be able to simplify future software upgrades by installing them once on your server, rather than on each client computer. (Some applications still require that you take action at each client to upgrade the software, so this may or may not be a benefit.) You may also benefit from smaller disk space requirements on client computers, resulting in potentially lower hardware costs on each user's desktop.

If application data is shared, in addition to the application itself, your organization benefits from a single, centralized copy of information. Confusion over who has the latest version of data, how to merge different versions, and how to arrange for backup of multiple versions may disappear. Error-prone duplication of the same data in multiple places can give way to a cleaner, more centralized approach to managing your information.

Summary

E-mail is clearly the "killer" network application in today's business environment. It is used for a wide range of communication tasks, both inside and outside the organization. Groupware, and especially group scheduling software, is quickly becoming an important force in helping users manage time and coordinate efforts. In this chapter, I presented the issues associated with implementing an effective e-mail system, group scheduling system, and other networked applications.

In Chapter 4, I delve more deeply into leveraging the Internet and intranets in your organization. There, you'll discover how these same networked application concepts can broaden in scope to incorporate an entire organization or an entire planet.

Chapter 4

Understanding the Internet and Intranets

IN THIS CHAPTER

- Understanding the difference between the Internet and intranets
- Hooking up to the Internet
- Choosing your Internet access method, service provider, and browser and server software
- Establishing your Web site
- Boning up on Internet ethics

THE GLOBAL PHENOMENON of the Internet has changed the way businesses and individuals access and use information. As both a powerful communication tool and a comprehensive data repository, the Internet has quickly become a necessity in today's business environment. Therefore, it's important to understand what the Internet offers and how you can connect individual Windows 98 computers or your entire network to it. It's also important to understand how the same tools used for the Internet can be used within organizational intranets.

In this chapter, you'll learn more about how the Internet is put together, the connection options available to you, and the steps required to put your organization on the Internet. By the end of this chapter, you'll understand the decisions, tasks, costs, and issues involved in connecting to this important resource.

Understanding the Internet

The Internet's roots can be traced back to the late 1960s, when the Advanced Research Projects Agency (*ARPA*, under the U.S. Department of Defense) designed a network to safeguard military information stored on computers all over the country. Originally called ARPANET, this network connected strategically located computers so that if one link were destroyed by an attack or natural disaster, surviving computers could continue to communicate with each other. A network protocol called *TCP/IP* (*Transmission Control Protocol/Internet Protocol*) was developed to enable communication across a variety of physical networks including satellite connections, wireless radio, telephone links, and so forth. TCP/IP – along with its advantages and disadvantages – is discussed in Chapter 6.

In 1985, the National Science Foundation (NSF) funded several national supercomputer centers including the Cornell Theory Center at Cornell University, the National Center for Supercomputing Applications (NCSA) at the University of Illinois, the Pittsburgh Supercomputing Center, the San Diego Supercomputer Center at the University of California, and the Jon von Neumann Center at Princeton University. The NSF linked these five supercomputer centers, and enabled regional and university computer centers to connect to them. The initial motivation to connect these was the availability of remote access to these supercomputer resources. This event marked the birth of the Internet as we know it today.

Interconnecting Networks

By 1994, the NSF announced the establishment of four *network access points* (*NAPs*), which would offer high-speed connections between networks on a regional scale. Operated by the private sector, these NAPs were created in San Francisco, Chicago, New Jersey, and Washington, DC.

Over the years, many universities, research facilities, and private companies all over the world have hooked up to this network to exchange information. More recently, millions of organizations and individuals have connected to the Internet to access, publish, and discuss vast amounts of information on just about every topic ever conceived. Some historians and thinkers believe that the Internet is a revolution in communications that is just as significant as the invention of the printing press. Indeed, the concept of having instant access to a global information resource at home, at school, and at work has already changed the way we work with and think about information.

Internet Organization

The top layer of the Internet is made up of a handful of NAPs. However, most organizations don't deal directly with a NAP. (Is all this talk of NAPs making you sleepy?) The Internet has been further subdivided hierarchically into several layers to maintain performance, simplify management, and achieve robustness of the network. The layer of the Internet that businesses and consumers deal with directly is populated by *Internet service providers*, or *ISPs*. For a fee, they provide organizations and individuals with dial-up or dedicated connections to the Internet. Later in this chapter, I fill you in on how to select and work with an ISP to connect your organization to the Internet.

Online services, including MSN (Microsoft Network), AOL (America Online), and CompuServe, also act as ISPs by offering Internet access to their customers in addition to other information services. Most of these organizations provide Internet access at no additional charge beyond their standard monthly fees.

NAPs and ISPs connect to each other using high-speed communication lines. The set of these fast links is called the Internet's *backbone*. *Backbone* is actually a more generic term, referring to any high-speed link between networks. Other lower-speed networks connect to the backbone, much like ribs connect to a person's backbone. (This analogy works well, except for spineless people like me.)

Recall from Chapter 1 that the Internet is a set of interconnected computer networks. Each computer or other device that connects to the Internet is called a *host*. This term is sometimes a bit confusing, because the term *host* has traditionally been used in the industry to refer to computers that provide services. On the Internet, however, a host can be a server or it can simply be a client computer that accesses information.

Each host on the Internet requires a unique address to identify it. Ranges of these addresses are doled out to ISPs by an organization called *InterNIC* (Internet Network Information Center). ISPs, in turn, assign smaller ranges of addresses to individual organizations. Once you're allocated a range of addresses, you can assign them to the individual hosts on your network that require Internet access. (I discuss the significance of these addresses further in Chapter 6.)

Understanding the World Wide Web

The Internet provides only the physical and logical infrastructure that connects millions of computers together. Many believe that the World Wide Web (WWW, or simply the *Web*) provides the killer application for this global network. The Web is considered the content of the Internet, providing all sorts of information by using a rich set of tools that manage and link text, graphics, sound, and video. Providing and viewing information on the Web is accomplished using server applications and client applications.

If you've already explored the Web, you'll recognize the client-side application as the *Web browser*. Netscape Navigator and Microsoft Internet Explorer are the dominant browser applications in the Windows environment. (At the time of writing, Microsoft Internet Explorer is included in the Windows 98 operating system.) A Web browser receives, interprets, and displays pages of information from the Web. The user can navigate within pages, jump to other pages by clicking hypertext links, and point to just about any page on the Web. Figure 4-1 illustrates the Microsoft Internet Explorer browser interface.

Figure 4-1: Microsoft Internet Explorer acts as a Web browser to interpret and display Web pages and interact with the user.

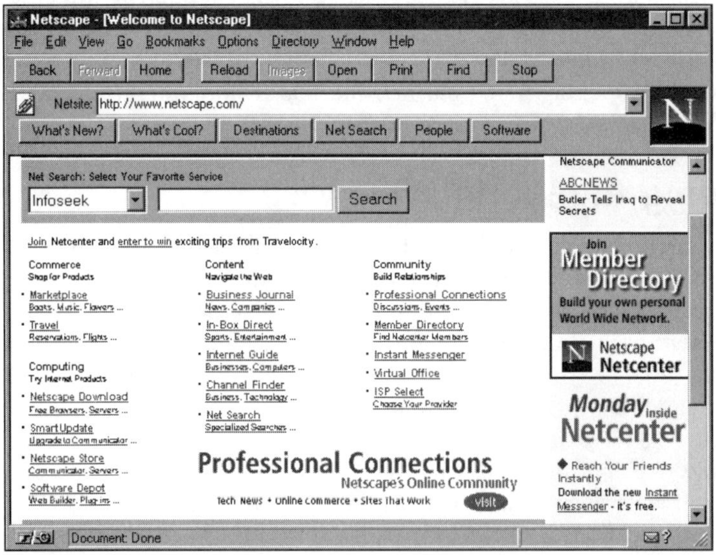

Figure 4-2: Netscape Navigator is one of the two top contenders in the Web browser arena. With appropriate plug-in software, it can process a variety of data types.

Third-party software plug-ins are available for Navigator, to enable the user to see and hear Internet video and audio broadcasts, video conferences, and animation. Similar features are available in Microsoft products. If you go the Internet Explorer route, however, you rely on Microsoft to build these features into its browser. Now that Netscape has made its browser source code widely available to developers, we may see a stream of new innovations in the Navigator product line, or many distinct flavors of the browser floating around. Figure 4-2 illustrates the Netscape Navigator browser interface.

The server-side application is called a *Web server.* It communicates with Web browser clients to deliver the requested Web pages over the Internet. Web server software runs on server-class computers that are typically attached to a high-speed Internet connection. Microsoft Internet Information Server (IIS) is a great example of a powerful Web server. It is used by many organizations and ISPs to offer Web page services. (Actually, IIS provides other services as well, including file transfer and connections to databases. The latter enables users to query and modify databases, place online orders, and see up-to-date information reflected immediately in Web pages.) IIS requires Windows NT Server in order to run. In fact, IIS comes bundled with Windows NT Server.

TIP

Both Windows 98 and Windows NT Workstation include a scaled-down version of IIS, called Microsoft Personal Web Server, or *PWS*. Because of its limitation to no more than a handful of users, I don't recommend it for publishing Web pages to the Internet. (PWS is limited to ten connections, but because each user session typically takes up two or more connections, only a small number of users can be served.) However, you can use it to create a Web site internally for a small workgroup. Or, you can use it as a staging area to test and perfect your Web site before placing it out on the Internet. For detailed instructions on installing PWS on Windows 98, click Start → Programs → Internet Explorer → Personal Web Server. When it's time to set up your own Web server on the Internet, however, you'll need the added power and capacity of IIS. Figure 4-3 illustrates the Personal Web Manager, which provides the user interface to PWS on Windows 98.

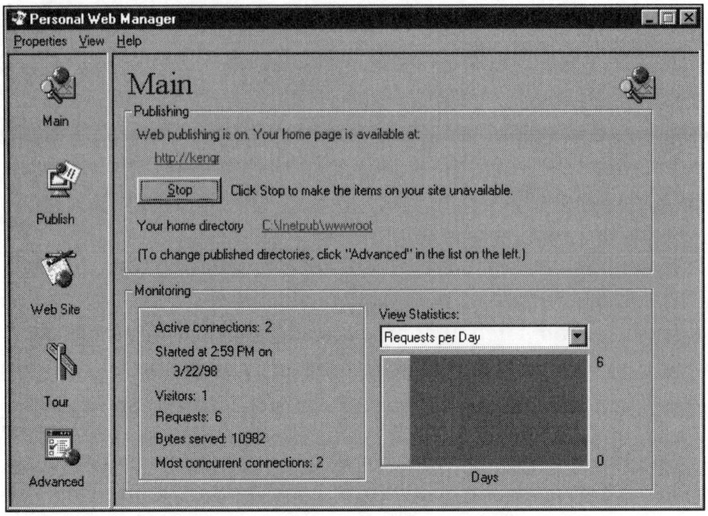

Figure 4-3: Microsoft's Personal Web Manager provides the management interface to the Personal Web Server included in Windows 98.

As you'll see later in this chapter, setting up a Web server and publishing a Web site is fairly straightforward with the tools provided in Windows 98 and other Microsoft products. You no longer have to be a network expert or professional programmer to create compelling Web content. After learning more about the nuts and bolts, however, you may decide to have an ISP handle all the Web server details, while you concentrate on building a great Web site. Your decision will depend on the size of your organization, the costs you're willing to incur, and the level of administrative support available to your Web project.

TIP

If you want to see the HTML program code underlying a specific Web page, you can view the raw source code using your Web browser. In Microsoft Internet Explorer, click View → Source. In Netscape Navigator, click View → Document Source. If you view the HTML source code behind a page with lots of colors, formatting, and graphics, you'll see all sorts of commands that control these attributes.

Ye Olde Text-Based Tools

These days, most of the development activity, document publishing, and browsing on the Internet are performed with graphical tools on the Web. So why bother discussing the old text-based tools that were the heart and soul of the Internet just a few years ago? The answer is simple. Web pages aren't linked to all the available resources out there on the Internet. A knowledge of these text-based tools can help you complete your Internet-based research activities. (You can find copies of most of these tools on the Internet by searching for them using your favorite search engine.) They are described as follows:

- *FTP*, which stands for *File Transfer Protocol*, was the original tool used for transmitting files between computers over the Internet. Now that Web browsers can perform file transfers, standalone FTP tools have lost favor. Some users, however, find that standalone FTP tools are faster performers. To download a file using FTP, you need its filename and the Internet address of an FTP site that offers it.
- *Gopher* is a search capability that enables you to sift through all sorts of information on the Internet by entering a keyword. Unlike Web search engines such as Yahoo! and AltaVista, Gopher searches all Internet resources, not just Web sites.
- *Archie* is a search capability that tracks the content of FTP file download sites all over the Internet, and indexes them by filename. If you know the name of the file you're searching for, you can use Archie to find a set of FTP sites that offer it for download. And *Veronica* is to Gopher what Archie is to FTP. In other words, Veronica keeps track of Gopher sites, and enables you to search many of them at once by entering a single keyword.
- *WAIS*, which stands for *Wide Area Information Server*, is closer in functionality to the Internet search engines in use today. WAIS technology is still used on some Web sites. It enables you to perform keyword searches of databases, and generates a list of files qualified by the relevance of the files to the keywords.

Speaking Web Languages

Web pages are actually small computer programs, written in a computer language understood by Web browsers. The primary language used for Web pages is called *HTML*, which stands for HyperText Markup Language. HTML provides a way of describing exactly how a page will look when it's published on the Web.

HyperText refers to the capability of linking pages together so users can quickly navigate through material based on their own interests. (If you've used the Windows Help system to find the answer to a question, you've probably clicked several hypertext links.) *Markup* refers to the capability to specify position, size, font, color, and other attributes of elements on the page. Therefore, HTML is a programming language that enables you to create and link together pages, and to specify just about every detail of how the page looks when viewed by a Web browser. (In ancient times, before the days of Windows, people used markup languages such as nroff or troff to insert commands in their documents to control how text was printed. In terms of the underlying concept, not much has changed since then.)

On the surface, creating a Web page is as simple as using a text editor (such as Windows Notepad) to write a small HTML program. Unfortunately, if you take this route to Web site creation, you have a bit of a learning curve ahead of you. Although HTML isn't rocket science, it requires study and practice. Because so many millions of organizations and individuals want to create Web sites, but don't want to learn a computer language to do it, a number of visual tools have been created to automate the process.

If your goal is to publish documents on your Web site (either existing ones or new ones), you can create Web pages out of Microsoft Word or Corel WordPerfect documents. Depending on the software version, they either include the ability to save files in HTML format or offer this feature as an add-on component. Either way, you can pour your word processing documents into Web pages with relative ease, maintain most of the formatting characteristics, and avoid learning the ins and outs of HTML.

Armed with the right graphical tools, you can create and maintain an entire Web site without ever seeing a line of HTML code. Microsoft FrontPage is a great example of this type of product. Windows 98 includes a limited version called FrontPage Express. The full version of FrontPage, which adds Web site administration features and more advanced Web page features, is available separately or as part of the Windows NT Server product.

NOTE

HTML isn't the end of the line for markup languages. Development of several new languages is under way, to provide more powerful Web publishing capabilities. One of the most promising is *XML*, or *Extensible Markup Language*. Some experts believe it will replace HTML in the next few years. You can find out more about XML at `http://www.ucc.ie/xml/`.

The Java Cup Runneth Over

No discussion of Internet programming languages would be complete without a shameless coffee pun referring to the Java programming language. Unlike HTML, Java is more like a traditional programming language, similar to C or C++. Rather than just describing how a page looks, Java programs can perform useful work ranging from displaying an animation to updating files, to detecting what sort of browser you're running.

Java programs are downloaded to the Web browser and are executed on the user's client computer. Although they offer tremendous power, they also represent a security risk. Because Java programs can perform tasks outside the confines of the browser, there's potential for malicious mischief on the user's computer. To address this issue, modern browsers provide a way of disabling Java program execution, and virus detection software vendors offer products to scan Java code before it's executed.

Understanding Web Users

Who is using the World Wide Web? If you plan to use it, or plan to create a Web site presence on it, you should understand who's out there browsing this information. Recent surveys have shown the following characteristics of Web users. Of course, with the continued explosive growth of Web usage, statistics like these can quickly become historical footnotes – but the characteristics and trends presented here should provide a baseline you can use in evaluating the Web for your organization. Over time, as Internet access is provided to more and more people, the profile of a Web user will more closely match the profile of an average person. Here are some of the common characteristics (according to the GVU Web User Survey, October 1997):

- **Income** – The median household income of a Web user is $53,000, and has been trending downward over time. Of those using the Web, over 16 percent have an income over $75,000.
- **Commerce** – About 68 percent of Web users have purchased a product or service online. The most frequently cited reason for avoiding electronic commerce is a concern over the secure handling of credit card information. Nevertheless, only two percent of survey respondents reported having a bad purchasing experience.

- **Education** – About 47 percent of Web users have a college degree of some sort. This number is steadily trending downward, because more students and young children are obtaining Web access through schools and libraries. The decreasing cost of PC hardware has also played a role in this trend.
- **Web Experience** – About 38 percent of Web users have between one and three years' experience on the Web, whereas almost 20 percent have less than six months' experience. Nearly 46 percent of Web users have created a Web page. Over 65 percent primarily access the Web from home.
- **Age** – The bulk of users are within the age range of 18 to 46 years old, with about 36 being the average age; however, the distribution is spreading more evenly across younger and older age groups, as more students and seniors gain access to the Web.
- **Gender** – Women now comprise nearly 40 percent of Web users, up from about five percent in 1994. By the year 2000, some experts estimate that 18 million women will use the Web, and that the distribution of male and female users will be about even.

Understanding Intranets

As I mentioned in Chapter 1, an intranet is an internal network that uses Internet tools and protocols to publish information within a single organization. Rather than developing custom applications to tie data together and present it to users, organizations can now use Internet tools to pull everything together and publish it. Web tools are quickly replacing traditional application development in many organizations.

Establishing an Intranet

To establish an intranet, you need to set up an internal Web server, using either PWS (supplied with Windows 98 or Windows NT Workstation), or IIS (supplied with Windows NT Server). If you plan to serve fewer than, say, five users, PWS will suffice. If you plan to serve more than five, however, opt for IIS. On the client side, simply equip each client with an appropriate Web browser.

NOTE

Just about everything I discuss in this and subsequent chapters regarding Internet tools, protocols, and techniques applies to intranets as well. The only element missing from the intranet environment is the requirement to make an external connection to the Internet and deal with an ISP and telecommunications carrier.

Testing with an Intranet

Some network administrators overlook another important use of an intranet – as a testbed for Web sites before they're placed on the Internet. Many organizations implement their initial Web site (and subsequent updates) in two phases. In the first phase they place the Web site on the intranet, where internal users can test it, make any necessary corrections, and incorporate useful feedback. Once the site is working well, they can publish it to the Internet for the world to see.

There's another underlying practical aspect to this approach. Because it often takes time to establish ISP contracts, additional phone lines, high-speed data lines, assigned network addresses, and so forth, you can be developing and testing your Web site internally before your pages ever set foot on the Internet.

Hooking Up to the Internet

You can select one of three ways to connect a computer to the Internet. Windows 98 includes all the support for software, hardware, and network protocols required for Internet access:

- **Online Service Internet Access** – Several online service organizations, such as Microsoft Network (MSN), America Online (AOL), and CompuServe, offer dial-up access to the Internet as one of the set of services they provide. They typically offer full access, including Web, e-mail, and newsgroup services.
- **Individual Dial-Up Access** – You can access the Internet from a single computer by installing Dial-Up Networking (DUN) and the TCP/IP network protocol. By dialing into an account with an ISP, you can use all the Internet services offered by the ISP's computers that are directly connected to the Internet.

- LAN Access – If you connect one of your LAN server computers to the Internet, other computers on your LAN can access the Internet through their network adapter using the TCP/IP network protocol. All Internet traffic goes through the Internet-connected server, providing Internet services to all computers connected to the LAN.

If you're going to set up high-speed data lines, establish a Web site, or access the Internet via multiple computers on your network, it's best to avoid the online services and establish a relationship with an ISP. An ISP has the knowledge and equipment to support your efforts as you connect your organization to the outside world.

NOTE: When you consider hooking up your business to the Internet, it helps to think like a plumber. An ISP provides you with a tap into the main Internet pipeline (the Internet backbone), and your telecommunications carrier provides you with the pipe that runs from that tap to your site. The capacity of both the tap and the pipeline control the bandwidth of your connection to the Internet. I discuss both aspects of Internet plumbing in the next section.

Putting Your Organization on the Internet

Whether you want to provide one or more users with access to the Internet, or set up your own Web server, you face several decisions and a not-so-trivial amount of work. Selecting the right approach to accessing the Internet will depend on your organization's needs, the quality of service you want to achieve, and the amount of money you have to spend. With all the pieces in place and properly configured, and with users trained and ready to take advantage of it, an investment in connecting to the Internet can pay off in many ways.

In this section, I discuss the key decisions and work items you need to plan for in establishing your Internet connection.

Choosing Your Internet Access Method

The method you use to access the Internet depends on two factors: your communication bandwidth requirements, and how much you're willing to pay for access. Because the amount of Internet traffic is steadily increasing, and because much of the traffic (such as video and audio) requires increased speed, it's a good idea to pay for as much bandwidth as you can possibly afford. Dedicated lines, sometimes called *leased lines*, that provide 24-hour access are preferable to dial-up lines that support only occasional access. It all comes down to a tradeoff between bandwidth and cost.

The bandwidth you buy can pay for itself over time. Providing high-speed Internet access to your users can have some ancillary affects on your bottom line. First, users don't need to wait for slow downloads of graphics and other files. Also, users tend to access the Internet for more information, and are more apt to double-check the information they uncover. Of course, if you have users who waste their time browsing areas not related to their work, a high-speed connection enables them to waste their time much faster. That, too, can improve your bottom line.

> NOTE: If you're setting up a Web server for your organization, a high-speed link to the Internet is absolutely essential if you want to minimize customer frustration and maximize retention once customers hit your site. In the past, Web users exercised the virtue of patience when browsing sites, but their tolerance for slow page load times and long delays in server response has worn thin. These days, you're lucky if a user will wait more than 25 seconds to see your Web page take shape before giving up and moving on to another site.

Your ISP may be able to help you select and coordinate installation of your access line, but it usually ends up being your responsibility. In most areas, establishing your access line involves working directly with a local telecommunications carrier – typically your telephone company. Now that the industry is deregulated, you may discover that your phone company offers the services of an ISP as well. Either way, keep in touch with your ISP during the decision process, to ensure that you end up with an access method and equipment that are compatible with the ISP's services.

Several connection options exist, but availability and cost vary widely depending on geographic location and on the telecommunications infrastructure already installed in your area. For example, I ordered one service in Seattle and had it installed and running within a week. When I attempted to order the same service in Tucson, the cost was twice as high, and installation time was estimated to take between two weeks and seven months. The average time required to arrange for installation falls between three and eight weeks, so include this time factor in your plan.

Table 4-1 presents a brief comparison of technologies for connecting to the Internet. (In parts of the world, some of the services listed aren't yet available.) Note that *bps* stands for bits per second, *Kbps* is kilobits (thousand bits) per second, *Mbps* is megabits (million bits) per second, and *Gbps* stands for gigabits (billion bits) per second.

TABLE 4-1 COMPARISON OF INTERNET CONNECTION OPTIONS

Connection Technology	Transmission Speed	Connection Type	Number of Simultaneous Connections
POTS	28.8 to 56Kbps	Dial-up analog line	1–10 clients
ISDN	64 to 128Kbps	Dial-up digital line	10–500
Frame Relay	56Kbps to 1.5Mbps	Dedicated digital line	10–500
SMDS	56Kbps to 34Mbps	Dedicated digital line	10–1000
T1	1.544Mbps	Dedicated digital line	50–500
T3	23 to 44.746Mbps	Dedicated digital line	500–5000+
ATM	155 to 622Mbps to 1.2Gbps+	Dedicated digital line	5000–15,000+

Table 4-1 introduces several new acronyms. *POTS* stands for *Plain Old Telephone Service* – the standard analog phone lines running to most homes and businesses. (Yes, I know – there's an acronym for just about everything in this business.) Notice that the slowest POTS modem I've listed is 28.8Kbps. Although you can still find modems slower than this, I don't recommend them for Internet access. The user's browser experience would just be too painful.

POTS lines are fairly limited in the number of users they can comfortably – and they're definitely the wrong choice if you're connecting a Web server to the Internet. I recommend POTS lines for only a small number of users who need occasional Internet access to send and receive e-mail and perform research on the Web. If your needs go beyond this, look carefully at faster options.

ISDN stands for *Integrated Services Digital Network.* It's the lowest-cost digital solution, and in most locations, requires the least amount of installation time and troubleshooting. *SMDS* stands for *Switched Multimegabit Digital Service,* which at the time of writing is available only in selected telecommunication markets. *ATM* stands for *Asynchronous Transfer Mode.* Depending on the equipment you install, ATM achieves the most promising bandwidth – commonly up to 622Mbps, and even all the way up to 1.2Gbps and beyond! Because ATM can support voice, audio, and data on a single line at very high speeds, some analysts expect it to play a key role in the next generation of the information superhighway. I discuss ISDN and ATM in more detail in Chapters 5 and 6, respectively.

All of these services may or may not be offered in your area. Check with your telecommunications carrier or ISP for details. Costs of Internet connections can vary widely, depending on your region and the level of service you purchase. For example, at the time of writing, in my region, the recurring costs are as follows:

- ISDN can cost $50 to $100 per month and up
- T1 can cost $1,500 to $2,500 per month and up
- T3 can set you back between $65,000 and $85,000 or more per month

Check with your telecommunications carrier for detailed quotes, and be sure that you understand all the charges involved. Some are structured with a flat rate that covers a certain amount of connect time or data transmitted, with additional charges when you exceed these limits. Distance of the communication line is also a factor in the cost. The longer the distance between your site and the carrier's equipment, the higher the cost will be.

Most carriers charge a one-time setup fee that covers the administrative and labor costs associated with establishing the service. Installation charges can vary widely in terms of price and what's included. Some carriers include all the required customer equipment in the installation charge. Others include no equipment, relying on you to obtain and install the appropriate hardware and software at your end of the connection. In this case, the installation charge covers setting up their end of the connection to accommodate you.

TIP

If the carrier doesn't provide the equipment for your end of the connection, it probably offers a list of recommended equipment. It's best to select from this list, to be sure the carrier is familiar with the equipment. When you're establishing high-speed connections, it's unlikely that a connection will just work the first time you fire up all the pieces. You'll probably be on the phone with the carrier to troubleshoot one or more components before you get everything running correctly — and configuring equipment the carrier understands will save a lot of time for both of you.

The Truth About 56K Modems

Watch your step with all the hype about 56Kbps modems. The improved speed is limited to downloading only — that is, moving data from the server to the client. Slower speeds of 33.6Kbps or less prevail when sending data from the client to the server. This approach is great for client browsers downloading Web pages and files. But it doesn't help at all if the computer is transmitting outgoing e-mail, uploading files to the Web, or acting as a Web server to offer information to other Internet clients.

Competing 56K technologies have yielded a single standard that's different from either of the two original approaches. If you purchase a 56K modem, make sure it complies with the latest approved ITU (International Telecommunications Union) 56K standard. If it's an X2- or K56Flex-compatible modem, be sure to ask if it's easily upgradable to the new ITU standard. This ITU standard is commonly referred to as *V.90*.

Also, make sure your ISP has the required digital connection to the telephone network, enabling it to download to you at the higher speed. If your ISP doesn't have the right equipment in place, you won't reap any benefits from the faster modem. (In the United States, the FCC limits the maximum speed of data transmission from the ISP to 53Kbps.) Finally, keep in mind that your actual connection speed will depend on the quality of the signal on your phone lines. Even with a 56K modem and the right ISP, you could end up with an effective speed of 28.8Kbps or less on a noisy phone line.

Selecting an Internet Service Provider

Your selection of an ISP is critical to the success of your connection to the Internet. You need to deal with a reliable organization that provides good support and charges competitive rates. And you certainly want your ISP to be around for the long haul as your requirements grow. For these reasons, I strongly recommend you choose an ISP with national presence, rather than a local outfit. National ISPs are more likely to be there tomorrow, and are more likely to offer round-the-clock customer service.

Beware of local ISPs offering very low monthly rates if you prepay for six or more months in advance. This is a competitive market, and it's difficult for small ISPs to stay in business if their rates are low. I've seen many of these ISPs gather a chunk of change from customers shopping for a low rate, refuse to invest the money to increase their capacity, and then fold up their tents and leave town. Customers have prepaid for a service that no longer exists. Avoid prepaying more than a month or two, until you have some experience with and confidence in your ISP.

How do you find an ISP? If you take my advice and go with a national ISP, you can find their contact information listed in Appendix B. At the time of writing, the major players in the United States include AT&T, NETCOM, Sprint, PSINet, EarthLink, and Concentric. (Your version of Windows 98 may include desktop icons that enable you to sign up easily for one or more of these services.) There's a lot of consolidation in the industry, so names change and some ISPs are being subsumed by others.

If you decide you'd rather select a local ISP, public telecommunications carriers offer a good starting point. They're going to be around for a long time, and they're offering increasingly competitive services and pricing. If you want to explore all your local ISP options, check the local newspaper under "business," the Yellow Pages under "computer bulletin boards and online services" or simply "Internet," computer retail stores, or local universities and colleges.

ORDERING ISP SERVICES

Many ISPs offer only dial-up access to the Internet, one or more e-mail accounts, and perhaps a small chunk of disk space for a personal Web site. Others provide a wide range of services including high-speed dedicated connections, advice on leveraging the Internet, custom authoring of Web pages, subleasing Web site space to other organizations, and other consulting and support services.

> CAUTION: If you're planning to have your ISP host your Web site on its servers, ask if the servers are blocked by any of the "Web censor" software on the market. Occasionally, censor software, which is designed to protect children from viewing certain types of offensive sites, will lock out an entire ISP if only one site hosted by the ISP is objectionable. When this happens, users running the censor software can't get to your legitimate Web site, either. It's a good idea to ask your ISP about its policy of shutting down offensive sites.

For basic dial-up Internet access, including an e-mail account, Web access, and a noncommercial Web page, expect to pay $15–$25 per month. Initial setup fees can run from $25–$300, depending on which services you're buying. If your ISP hosts a full Web site for you, you'll pay more; Web site hosting fees can add $30 or more to your monthly costs. Of course, the high-speed dedicated access lines discussed in the previous section will cost you a lot more. Additional charges can be based on hard disk space used, volume of data transmitted, number of customer hits on your Web site, or some combination of these. Look for a plan that doesn't penalize you financially for having a popular Web site. In other words, I recommend staying away from billing plans that charge based on the amount of data transmitted or the number of Web site hits.

Keep in mind that ISP charges don't typically include the cost of the access line running from your telecommunications carrier to your site. (See the previous section, "Choosing Your Internet Access Method.") These are often called the *local loop* charges, and are typically billed separately by your telecommunications carrier. The recurring ISP charges usually include only the ISP's end of the connection, and it leaves you the responsibility of the physical connection at your end. Some ISPs may quote, install, and bill for the entire link, but most will refer you to your telecommunications carrier.

EVALUATING ISP PERFORMANCE

Ask your ISP for performance statistics, especially in the area of service interruptions and downtime. Even if you're not sure what the numbers mean, this is a great way to filter out the amateur ISPs. If an ISP doesn't maintain these statistics, it's definitely time to walk away. If it maintains them but doesn't want to share them with you, it probably has something to hide about its performance.

It's a good idea to check out your potential ISP's other customers, especially if you plan to invest heavily in its services. At the very least, get a list of references you can contact. Better yet, try to arrange a visit to one or more of them to see how they're set up and how happy they are with the service.

No matter what you read or what an ISP tells you about reliability, you will most definitely experience periodic outages. This is just a fact of life on the Internet. That said, you need to consider your ISP's customer service plan as part of your selection criteria. Be sure it maintains a 24-hour manned network operation center that you can contact in case of a service outage. You need to know that a phone call from you will be answered by a real person who can quickly address the problem. Leaving messages on voice mail or pagers is much less desirable. I know of one ISP (now out of business) that offered support only via e-mail or its Web site – services you can't get to if the problem you're having is the inability to communicate electronically with your ISP.

NOTE

Keep in mind that if you end up with a lemon ISP, you can always switch to a different one. However, it takes some effort, can produce interruption in service, and is generally a pain to do. That's why it's important to strive up front to find an ISP you'll be happy with for the long haul — and one that will be there for that long haul. You're forging an important business relationship, so try your best to select the right ISP the first time.

Deciding on Browser Software

As I mentioned earlier in this chapter, Microsoft Internet Explorer and Netscape Navigator are the top contenders in the browser field. As these two products jockey for position, they leapfrog each other with new versions and functionality. I won't get into which one you should choose. That decision is left up to you.

TIP

While it's all right to let users choose and use their favorite browser, I do recommend that you standardize on a single brand and a single version. Doing this will eliminate possible headaches caused by feature mismatches between your Web tools and individual browsers. For example, if you use Microsoft FrontPage to create your Web site, some versions of Netscape Navigator may not support all the features you decide to use. Moreover, training users will be easier because they'll be equipped to help each other use the standardized browser version.

Deciding on Server Software

If you're not building an intranet and you're letting an ISP host your Web site, you don't need a Web server at all. If you *are* building an intranet or hosting your own Web site, however, your next step involves selecting appropriate server software. On the Microsoft front, you need to decide between PWS and IIS, as I discussed in an earlier section. Alternatively, you could select Netscape's Enterprise Server or another non-Microsoft product. Just be sure that all the browsers, servers, and Web creation tools you select will work well together.

NOTE

If you plan to have your ISP host your Web site, you don't have to select or install Web server software. But you're not completely off the hook, either. It's important to know what features your ISP's Web servers support. Many ISPs offer a choice of UNIX-based or Windows NT-based Web servers. If you plan to use Microsoft tools such as FrontPage to create your Web site content, you should opt for a Windows NT Web server running IIS. Doing this ensures that the ISP's server will support all the features you may use in FrontPage (the light version included in Windows 98 or the full version).

Scheduling Access Line Installation

If you're not using existing phone lines for your Internet connection, order installation of your access lines as soon as possible after you've decided on the access method. Because of the high demand for Internet access, many telecommunications carriers have a huge backlog of installation work. In some areas, they may even need to run additional lines or install new equipment to support digital service to you. So the sooner you get them started on the work, the better.

While you wait for this work to be done, you can proceed with selection and installation of browser software, set up an intranet, create Web site content, and begin testing it internally. Taking this parallel route can help you reach your goals more quickly and efficiently.

TIP

If your LAN is in place, and you're providing user access to the Internet or intranet through your LAN, it may save you time to install the browser software on a server, and let your users install it from there.

Scheduling Connection Equipment Installation

If your telecommunications carrier or ISP doesn't provide the hardware required at your end of the connection, you need to arrange to obtain and install the equipment as soon as your line is installed. Again, it's a good idea to order this equipment when you know how you're connecting. However, you can't really arrange for installation until your lines are installed. As soon as they are, you can get the ball rolling on equipment installation.

Traditionally, the folks responsible for each leg of the connection take responsibility only for their portions, and not for getting everything working together. For example, when you have an ISDN line installed, the phone company will probably verify that the line is working, but won't attempt to test the ISDN equipment at your site. Likewise, the equipment installer will verify that the equipment is working, but won't necessarily get it to work with the newly installed line. Finally, the ISP often takes the position of supporting only your tap into the Internet, and not the pipeline or equipment at your end. To avoid headaches and finger-pointing, it's best to bring in an expert whose goal is to get the whole set of components configured and working together properly.

Establishing Your Web Site

If you plan to establish a Web site for your organization on the Internet, you need to take several steps to reach that goal. Regardless of whether you or your ISP will host the site, a number of tasks are required to achieve a useful and successful Web site. In this section, I discuss the key decisions and work items associated with setting up a Web site.

TIP

If you don't plan to create a Web site for your organization, you can skip this section and refer to it later if you change your mind. If you're outsourcing the task of establishing your Web site (to your ISP or someone else), I recommend that you read this section anyway to understand the issues involved. Once you're armed with this knowledge, you'll be better equipped to ask the right questions and get what you want from your Web site developer.

SELECTING YOUR DOMAIN NAME

Computers on the Internet must be uniquely identified by name. A convention has been developed that organizes these names into a hierarchical tree. This convention is known as the *domain name system*, or *DNS*. It enables you to assign a unique name to a computer that fits into a worldwide hierarchy of computers on the Internet. Your first step involves selecting a *domain name* that uniquely describes your organization. For example, Microsoft's domain name is `microsoft.com`.

The top level of the hierarchy consists of types of organizations or countries. Table 4-2 lists the domain name organization types in use today. (These are sometimes called *domain extensions*, because they look like filename extensions.) In addition to these organization types, a number of countries have top level domain names (for example, .us, .uk, and so forth). The geographic extensions are rarely used in the U.S. – most organizations place their domain names under the appropriate organizational tree.

TABLE 4-2 TOP LEVEL ORGANIZATION TYPES USED IN DOMAIN NAMES

Domain Name	Organization Type
.com	Commercial enterprise – used primarily for businesses and organizations that engage in for-profit commerce
.edu	Educational institution – used primarily for colleges and universities, and other entities that grant degrees
.gov	Government organization – used for all United States federal government agencies (other than the military)
.mil	Military organizations – used for all branches of the United States military
.net	Network support or infrastructure organizations – used for network service providers including ISPs, telecommunications carriers, and so forth
.org	Other organizations – used primarily for non-profit organizations, professional organizations, clubs, and so forth

The top level domain name you select will depend on the type of organization you're representing. By far, the .com name is the most common for businesses. Domain names ending in .com and .org are the easiest to obtain. Obtaining other domain extensions may require proof that your organization falls into these categories. For example, you can't create a .gov domain name unless you're really a part of the U.S. government.

NOTE: Some organizations select more than one organization type (for example, .com, .org, and .net), and create domain names for each of them. This approach makes it easier for customers to find them online. The customer doesn't have to memorize the organization type — any one of them will get the customer to the company's site. As you'll see later in this chapter, however, there are costs associated with creating each domain name.

Because the existing domain names that use the extensions listed in Table 4-2 are getting a bit crowded, a number of new extensions have been proposed. Table 4-3 presents these proposed organization types. At the time of writing, the addition of these extensions is still the subject of debate, so they're not yet available. As you can see, some of these extensions muddy the waters a bit in terms of how customers find organizations. If you're a commercial retail business that performs online commerce to sell information, do you select .com, .firm, .store, .info, or do you create domain names for each of these types?

TABLE 4-3 PROPOSED NEW DOMAIN EXTENSIONS

Domain Name	Organization Type
.firm	Businesses of all types
.store	Online retail businesses that perform electronic commerce
.web	Organizations that offer services or information related to the World Wide Web
.rec	Recreational sites
.info	Information resource services
.nom	Individual people on the Internet
.arts	Organizations that offer services or information related to the arts

The next component of your domain name uniquely describes your organization. Most businesses use their company name or initials for this component. Others use words that identify the organization's line of business. For example, Microsoft uses `microsoft`, AT&T uses `att`, America Online uses `aol`, and the IEEE Computer Society uses `computer`. When considering this component of your domain name, select a name that:

- Is easy to remember and easy to type. Consider it as important as your organization name or logo.
- Doesn't exceed a total of 26 characters (including the domain extension).
- Directly relates to your organization.
- Invokes the proper image of your organization.
- Is not already used by someone else.
- Is not an obviously trademarked name (unless you own the trademark).

The last two points are sticky ones. Because domain names must be unique, and because the Internet is such an impartial entity, domain names are doled out on a first-come, first-served basis. So if someone already has a domain name that's identical to the one you want, you're the one who has to select a different name. Conversely, you can't reserve names that are probably trademarked by large corporations with the hope of selling them rights to the name for big bucks. People have already tried this and have lost cases in court.

Once you've decided on the domain name you want, you need to research whether it has already been taken by another organization. It's a good idea to have a few alternate names at your fingertips, in case your top choices are already taken. The easiest way to do this research is via the Web. Most ISPs will handle domain name checking and registration for you, but if they don't, you can do it yourself. InterNIC maintains a database of assigned domain names at `http://www.internic.net`. As soon as you've settled on a domain name that's available, you need to reserve the name by registering it.

Your domain name isn't the same as your e-mail address or Web site address, but it acts as a component. Your ISP will let you set up one or more e-mail accounts that typically end with the domain name. For example, Fred's e-mail address might be `fredr@digital-intelligence.com`, where `digital-intelligence.com` is the domain name. The *fully qualified domain name*, or *FQDN*, includes both the domain name and the host name. Therefore, a host called `sales` in the `digital-intelligence.com` domain would have an FQDN of `sales.digital-intelligence.com`. Likewise, the Web site address might be `http://www.digital-intelligence.com`. This complete form of the Web site address is known as a *URL*, which stands for *uniform resource locator*.

REGISTERING YOUR DOMAIN NAME

Domain name registration costs $100 to reserve the name for the first two years. After that, you'll pay $50 for each additional year to hold onto the name. Once the name is reserved and paid for, it becomes an asset that you own (much like a trademark is an asset). Most ISPs will take care of administrative tasks for you, but you'll still have to pay your $100 up front to the InterNIC to reserve the name.

When you begin this process with an ISP, make absolutely sure that you end up owning the domain name. If you pay InterNIC directly, and have them bill you directly for subsequent renewal years, you will definitely own the name. But if you pay your ISP and it handles all the details for you, it may end up owning the name. This doesn't sound like a big deal until you decide to change ISPs. Then, if the ISP owns your domain name, it can hold the name hostage and attempt to keep you as a customer. Give yourself the freedom to switch ISPs in the future by ensuring that you own your domain name.

Depending on the backlog of your ISP and the InterNIC, domain name registration may take only a few hours or as long as several days. Once you start the process, however, you're guaranteed that the name is reserved and can't be co-opted by anyone else. Just be sure to pay your InterNIC bills on time to keep it that way.

NOTE: At the time of writing, there are plans to open up domain name registration to more service organizations. As a result, you may or may not deal with InterNIC in registering your domain name. Whichever organization you work with, be sure you end up owning your domain name, regardless of which ISP you use in the future.

PLANNING AND DESIGNING YOUR SITE

Planning the organization and content of your Web site is perhaps the most important step in establishing the site. A typical Web site begins with a *home page* – the default starting point that makes the first impression. Other pages linked to the home page often contain links to organization news and press releases, products and services, feedback and guestbook forms, and search capabilities.

According to surveys of Web users, the best Web sites tend to have certain desirable characteristics. Users say that the most effective Web sites:

- Are updated frequently with new information.
- Include links to other relevant Web sites, including complementary businesses, interest groups, and other related organizations.
- Make it extremely easy to find information by offering clear organization, menus, and search capabilities.
- Make it easy to contact your organization via e-mail or a Web-based form from each page on the site.
- Respond quickly to inquiries made by customers, via e-mail or Web-based forms.
- Download pages quickly, and offer a text-only mode to accommodate slow communication links.
- Make it easy to get back to your home page from each page on the site.

As you design your site, you should use the Web for what it does best. Avoid long text articles that contain no illustrations (unless you're providing a text-only site just for slow browsers). Include links between information wherever possible – even linking topics within the same Web page. Also, do whatever you can to encourage the user to bookmark your pages, so it's easy for them to return to your site.

Creating truly effective Web sites requires knowledge of graphic design, typography, and marketing. Your site represents your organization to the world, and must deliver a clear message to be successful. Too many organizations make the mistake of assigning Web site design to technical people who don't have graphic design or marketing skills. If you have these skills available in-house, take advantage of them. If you don't, consider outsourcing your Web site design project.

CREATING AND TESTING YOUR SITE

As I mentioned before, using a graphical Web page editor such as Microsoft FrontPage can free you from having to learn a new language. Most high-end editors like FrontPage include wizards that walk you through the process of creating an entire Web site. This is a great starting place for your first Web site, because it builds the skeletal framework and enables you to fill in details as needed. Every page in your site should have a link back to the home page, and should provide an easy way for users to contact you via e-mail or a feedback form.

As I mentioned earlier in this chapter, it's best to test your Web site in-house using an intranet. This approach lets you wring out design and technical problems before you go live. In addition to pounding on every link and feature to make sure they all work, you may want to consider using Web site testing software or services. Software products are available that enable you to test the validity of Web pages and Web sites in various environments. Testing services can verify how your site will behave when viewed with various brands and versions of browsers. You can find a list of Web site testing resources in Appendix B.

PROMOTING YOUR SITE

A Web site without visitors is a waste of time, effort, and money. Unfortunately, the phrase "if you build it, they will come" applies only to a certain baseball field in Iowa. If you want people to visit your site, you must actively promote it. Add your Web site URL to all your printed materials, including advertising, stationery, newsletters, business cards, and so forth. Attach your URL to every e-mail your organization sends. Announce your site to your existing customers through a special mailing, and consider issuing a press release to announce your new site to everyone else.

Cross-linking Web sites with business partners is another great way to attract visitors. Look for noncompetitive, complementary organizations and contact the site managers about pointing your Web sites at each other. (This step is critically important. Linking to another site without permission can result in lawsuits these days.) Just make sure it's easy for your customers to get back to your site – you don't want to lead them away from your site forever.

Perhaps the most important way to promote your Web site, however, is to register it with the popular Internet search engines such as Yahoo!, Excite, and Infoseek. Doing this correctly will attract the majority of visitors you get. Users can look up a specific subject or set of keywords, and discover your site in the list of results. In Appendix B, I've included a list of the most popular search engines.

Each search engine requires a slightly different set of information to register your site. You need to be able to accurately and concisely describe your organization and your Web site, second guess how customers will likely search the Web to find you, and craft an appropriate list of keywords and phrases that they'll probably use in their search.

CAUTION

Once you've composed this list of keywords, be sure to use those words in the text of your Web pages. If you don't use them, or you embed them in graphics, some search engines won't find your site. On the other hand, don't overuse the keywords either. Some search engines treat frequent repetition of keywords as an attempt to appear first in the list of results — much like AAAAA Plumbing is obviously trying to appear first in the Yellow Pages under Plumbing. The search engine may penalize you for this behavior. If you must repeat a keyword frequently, embed some of the references in graphics.

Other than your time, there's usually no cost for registration. Register with the top search engines first. This gives you the biggest return on the investment of your time, since the majority of users will select one of these engines to do their online research. You should expect two to three weeks to elapse between the time you register and the time your site begins to show up in search results, so start the process as soon as your site is ready. If you can't afford the time, you can purchase software that enables you to register with several search engines at once.

MAINTAINING YOUR SITE

Web sites are, by definition, living documents. If you let your site become stale with outdated or incorrect information, broken links to other sites, or other problems, you won't attract or retain many customers. Keep the site's information up to date, and if possible, gather as much feedback on the site as you can from visitors. Offering incentives for feedback, such as discounts or freebies, may help. When you incorporate the feedback into your site, you can test new approaches to presenting your organization and its products and services.

It's important to budget time for Web site maintenance in perpetuity. Be sure your organization's management recognizes the site as an ongoing commitment. Updating information, fixing problems, and incorporating customer feedback all take time and effort. You can't just set up your Web site and forget it. It's as alive as those electronic pets that always ask to be fed.

Connecting to the ISP

This part of the process is relatively simple, although it involves some important details. Your ISP will provide you with access phone numbers, Internet addresses for various key servers, and perhaps Internet addresses for the computers on your LAN. You'll need to keep track of this information and use it during the configuration and connection process.

Be prepared to stay in close contact with your ISP during this critical period, as you configure and test your connection to the Internet. During this initial stage, the availability of your ISP is critically important.

Educating Yourself and Your Users

Once you have Internet access (or have your intranet running, for that matter), it's important to get yourself and your users trained to take advantage of this investment. Just as a tree falling in a forest with no one around doesn't make a sound (or does it?), a connection to Internet resources makes no impact on your organization if users don't use it.

Training topics should cover the use of browser software, including Web browsing and e-mail operations. Cover the use of search engines as well, to help users perform research and download the information they need. And don't forget to discuss security issues such as avoiding confidential information in Internet e-mail, and the possibility of computer viruses hiding in any downloaded file. Of course, the best way to teach is by example – so be sure you practice whatever you preach to your users.

Implementing the Internet Code of Ethics

When you install a computer network, it's important to train your users not only on the technical aspects of using the network, but also on the rules of etiquette and ethics associated with sharing and consuming network resources. In addition to knowing what they can do, users need to know what they shouldn't do. In an internal LAN environment, you can design, communicate, and enforce your own set of rules that match the needs of your organization. But when your users connect to the Internet, they're playing an away game in a field with a set of already established rules. Ignoring the rules can potentially affect many individuals and businesses throughout the world. The freedom of connecting globally comes with certain responsibilities.

As far back as 1989, before the Internet popularity boom, the Internet Activities Board (IAB) published a paper called *Ethics and the Internet*. It's basically a set of "thou shalt not" commandments, to help the uninitiated understand the boundaries of acceptable behavior. In a nutshell, users shouldn't try to gain unauthorized access to resources, disrupt the intended use of the Internet, waste resources (human, network, or computer bandwidth), destroy information integrity, or compromise the privacy of other users. Of course, these rules apply equally well to your internal LAN environment. (If you have access to the Internet, you can find the IAB paper online at `http://ei.cs.vt.edu/~cs3604/lib/WorldCodes/IAB.html`.)

The real world of the Internet is full of people who spend their time breaking these rules. For example, the act of spamming, which I mentioned in Chapter 3, wastes network bandwidth, hard disk space, and the time of hundreds or even thousands of people. Some folks have nothing better to do than find new ways to disrupt the Internet, steal or modify information, or accumulate personal information about users. As a result, an increasing number of safeguards have been developed to prevent certain types of attacks and abuses. Unfortunately, new ways to abuse the Internet are constantly being developed, requiring development of new defensive weapons all the time.

This is an area where training your users is critically important. Ignorance of the rules can reflect badly on the individual user and on your organization – and you certainly don't want a bad reputation of global proportions. Be sure to include the rules of the road (that is, the information highway) while you train your users in the mechanics of network navigation. As a network administrator, do your part to ensure that your users don't contribute to the problem. Teach them to act as responsible network citizens.

Worrying About Internet Security

Securing the data and other resources on your network from unauthorized access and tampering is an important concern. As a network administrator, you should be worried about it. Attaching one or more computers to the Internet poses a far greater security risk than does a cloistered LAN environment. On the Internet, you have literally millions of people potentially gaining access to your network. Many of those people have nothing better to do than find ways to access your network. It's sad, but true. So before you jump into connecting your organization to the Internet, be sure you understand the security implications first, and take steps to avoid breaches. Read Chapter 12, which is devoted to network security.

Summary

In this chapter, you've read an overview of the Internet and the issues associated with connecting your organization's network to it. You've learned what's involved in establishing low- and high-speed connections, and how to shop for an ISP. You've also discovered the steps required to implement and test a Web site. You now have the background you need to dig deeper into the details of establishing your own network. In Part II, I delve into the nuts and bolts of designing and implementing your network based on Windows 98. Part II begins with Chapter 5, where I fill you in on the details of establishing your network infrastructure.

Part II

Creating a Computer Network

Chapter 5

Designing Your Network Infrastructure

IN THIS CHAPTER

- Understanding network topologies and technologies, and how they differ
- Exploring and comparing LAN and WAN connection options
- Connecting your network: hubs, bridges, switches, routers, and gateways

IN THIS CHAPTER, you'll learn the concepts associated with designing the logical layout of your network, as well as issues involved with creating the physical network infrastructure. By the end of this chapter, you'll understand the differences between various network topologies, cabling options, and the roles played by specialized devices including gateways, bridges, routers, and switches. You'll also have the information you need to decide whether or not you want to tackle installing the infrastructure yourself. There's a lot to consider when making these decisions, so let's get started.

Understanding Network Topologies

As you learned in earlier chapters, networks require both network adapter hardware in each device to be connected, and some physical (or wireless) connection to hook them all together. If you consider a two-node network, you can think of the network adapters as the tin cans, and the connection as the string between them. But most real-world networks include more than two nodes, and this leads to many different ways to string them together.

The arrangement of network nodes and connections between them is called the network's *topology*. It's simply a map of the layout of nodes and connections in the network. Three network topologies predominate today – namely, *bus*, *star*, and *ring*. I discuss each of them in the following sections.

Understanding Bus Topology

In the *bus* network topology, you connect each node to the network along a single piece of network cable, called a bus. (If you're familiar with the term *bus* in the context of motherboards, the idea is similar. The bus provides the path for the data, and devices tap into the bus along its length to communicate with other devices.) As shown in Figure 5-1, network nodes essentially tap into the bus at convenient locations along the way. Data travels from a node out onto the bus until it reaches the ends of the cable. At each end of the bus, a device called a *terminator* is installed to prevent data signals from reflecting back onto the bus and causing errors. (Unlike Hollywood's *Terminator*, the network bus terminator prevents data from saying "I'll be back!") A terminator is a special resistor device that's attached to an electrical ground. When the transmitted data hits the terminator, it doesn't go any farther.

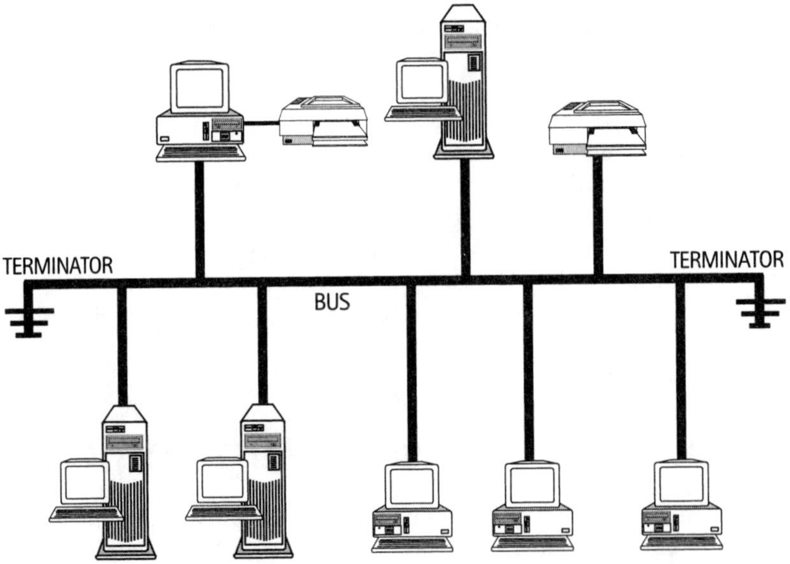

Figure 5-1: The bus network topology connects each node to a single length of cable, terminated at each end.

Reliability of the bus topology can be a problem in all but the smallest networks. If the single cable acting as the bus is severed at any point, the entire network can go down. Even if many of the nodes are still connected to each other on the bus, a severed cable is no longer terminated correctly. Although it's the lowest cost topology to implement, I don't recommend selecting the bus topology unless you're dealing with a total of three or four computers in the same room, and all the network cabling is easily accessible.

Understanding Star Topology

In the *star* network topology, you connect each network node to a central device called a *hub*. Small LANs with less than eight nodes usually need only one hub. Larger networks can require many hubs, and hubs can be connected to each other to tie all the nodes together into a single network. Figure 5-2 shows an example of a network using the star topology. The network in this example actually consists of two stars, each centered on its own hub. The hubs are tied together to provide a single cohesive network.

Hubs are usually connected together to expand the number of nodes in the network. Hubs typically allow four, eight, or sixteen nodes before another hub is required. In Figure 5-2, for example, the upper hub uses seven of its eight connections for attaching nodes, and its eighth to connect to the other hub. This approach of connecting stars together is also sometimes used when setting up a WAN. If two branch offices each have their own star topology LANs, you can connect the two LANs together by connecting the two hubs together via a WAN connection.

The concept of connecting hubs isn't restricted to networks. Airlines typically select a handful of major airports as hubs, and create their routes based on traveling through these hubs. You can still get from any city to any other city, but you may have to travel through a hub or two along the way. So it is with the data on a star topology network. Every network node is connected, but data must travel through one or more hubs between its source and destination.

NOTE

One difference between airline hubs and network hubs is the role of the hub itself. Airline hubs, such as the Dallas-Fort Worth International Airport, for example, can be the beginning or end of a trip. In contrast, a network hub is always *between* the source and destination of the data. The data source and destination are always network nodes connected to the hub — never the hub itself.

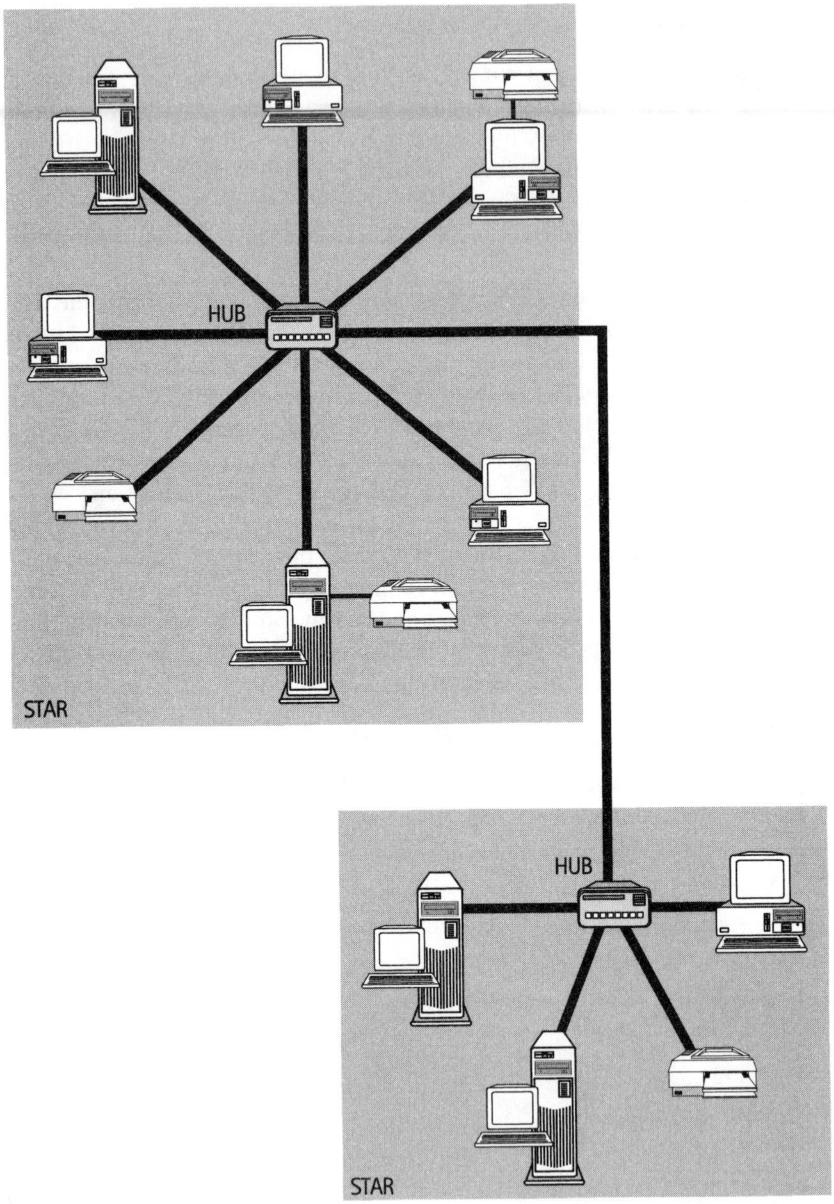

Figure 5-2: The star network topology connects each node to a centralized network hub.

You get what you pay for when selecting a network topology. Star topologies are more expensive to implement than bus topologies. You must invest in at least one hub, even if you want to connect only two computers together. Each addition of four, eight, or sixteen nodes to the network may require an additional hub. In contrast, bus topologies require no additional external hardware, beyond the inexpensive terminators at each end of the bus.

Understanding Ring Topology

The ring network topology is shaped just like its name implies – it's made up of an unbroken circle of network nodes. Essentially, each node is directly connected to its two immediate neighbors. Data on the network flows in one direction around the ring, traveling from one node to the next along the way. Figure 5-3 illustrates the ring topology.

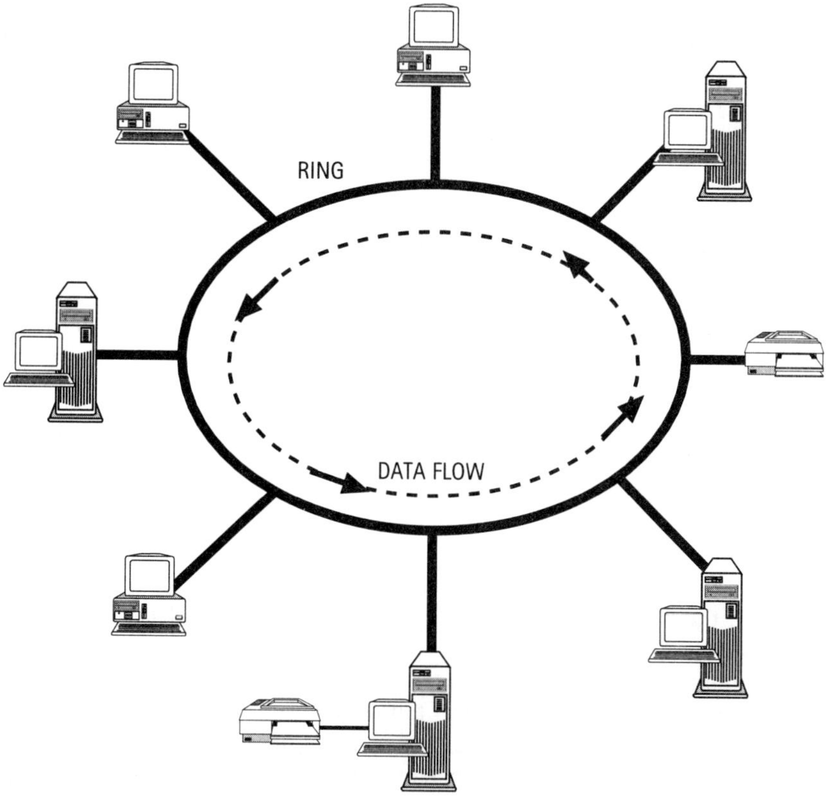

Figure 5-3: The ring network topology connects each node to its neighboring nodes, forming an unbroken ring.

Conceptually, a ring is like a bus that has had its two ends brought together. In other words, a ring is like a circular bus, to which all nodes are directly attached. The ring topology can be plagued with reliability problems because it depends on an unbroken link between each adjacent node on the network. If the ring is broken at any point along the way, the entire network stops functioning.

Sniffing for Trouble

No, Lassie. Timmy hasn't fallen down a well again. As you've seen, each topology discussed so far allows each node to see all the network data as it travels by. This isn't always a bad thing. Network diagnostic tools, called network analyzers or sniffers, enable network administrators to legitimately eavesdrop on network traffic to discover and diagnose problems.

In the past, these products were very expensive – in the $25,000 ballpark. Now the software is available at little or no cost – Microsoft gives away its sniffer software, called Network Monitor, free with Windows NT Server and Systems Management Server. What it doesn't give away is the detailed knowledge and experience a person needs to interpret the raw data as it comes across the network. (Incidentally, Microsoft's internal code name for the Network Analyzer product was *Bloodhound*, because it's such a great sniffer.)

Physical and Logical Topologies

In the topology discussion so far, I've focused on the physical layout of the network in terms of cabling and hubs. This is known as the *physical topology* of the network. But the physical topology doesn't really tell the whole story. Each network also has a *logical topology*, which describes how data actually travels on the network. The physical and logical topology of the network can be the same, but often they aren't.

Think of the physical topology as the network layout you'd see if you looked at the physical network from outside. To understand the physical topology, you completely ignore how the data travels, and focus instead on the appearance of cables, hubs, and nodes that make up the network. To understand the logical topology, you need to become one with the data traveling on the network. Pretend you are the data, and follow the path it takes. The path you follow defines the network's logical topology.

Why is this important? Well, it turns out that most networks today use a physical star topology, but may have the logical topology of a bus, a star, or a ring. The internal wiring of the cables and hubs determines the network's logical topology. So there are different types of hubs, connectors, and wiring, depending on the logical topology of the network you're implementing.

For example, a physical star topology may be wired with a logical bus topology. Unless the hub itself fails, a break in a single cable won't bring down the entire network – just the node attached to the broken cable. A physical star topology can also be used to implement a logical ring topology, as shown in Figure 5-4. Notice that the data travels in one direction only, creating a logical ring.

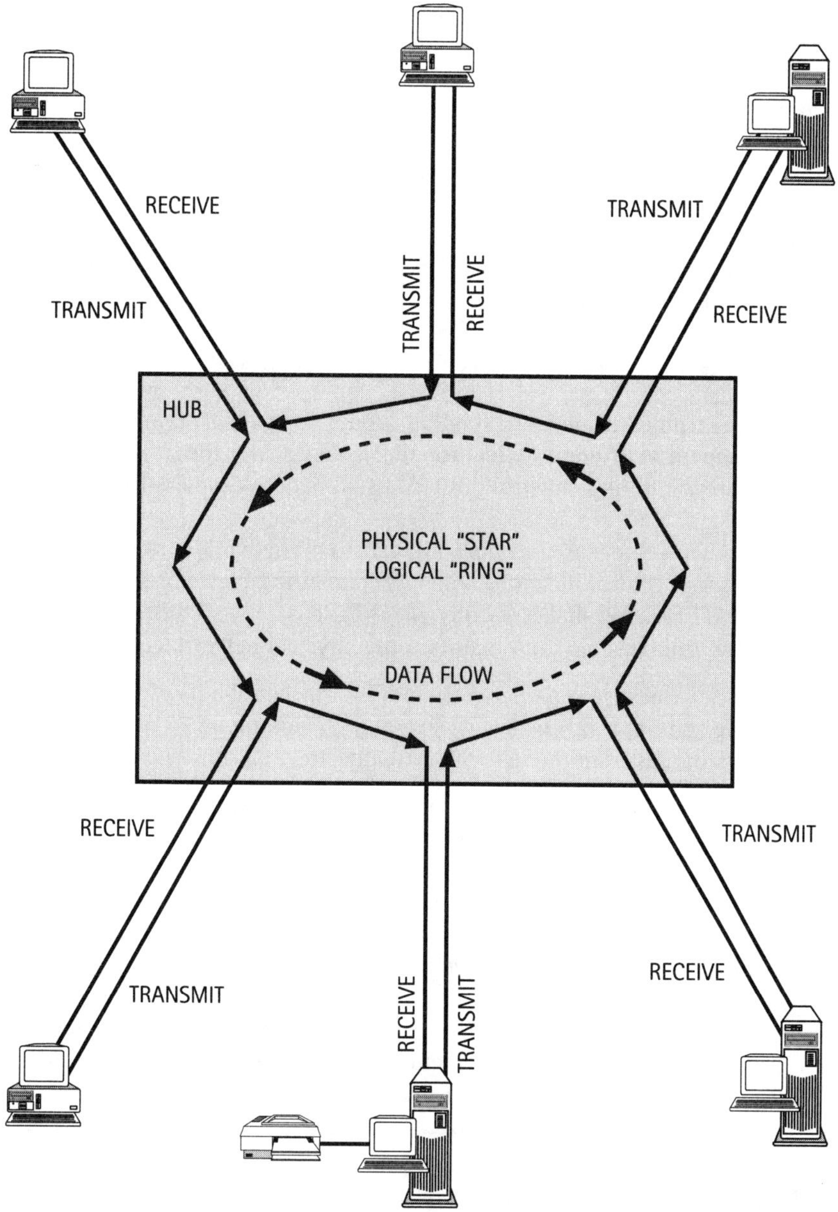

Figure 5-4: A physical star topology can be used to implement a logical ring topology, using an appropriate hub.

Hubs come in many different flavors, because they can be wired to implement any of the three basic logical network topologies. For example, a hub that implements a ring topology, such as the one shown in Figure 5-4, is called a *multistation access unit* (or *MAU* or *MSAU*). Moreover, a hub can be either passive or active. A *passive hub* simply acts as a central wiring point, and does nothing to the signals that pass through it. In contrast, an *active hub* can provide a wide range of features. In its most basic form, an active hub amplifies transmitted signals, to prevent distortion and lost data. High-end active hubs can offer features that include sophisticated network management, diagnostics, and reporting capabilities. I discuss hubs in more detail later in this chapter.

Choosing Between Network Topologies

The most prevalent physical network topology today is the star topology, even if it's used to implement a different logical topology. Here's why the star has become the standard approach to implementing other logical network topologies:

- **Convenience** – The star configuration causes all network wiring to converge in a central location, typically in a wiring closet or server room. This central location makes it convenient for the network administrator to configure, troubleshoot, and maintain the physical network connections.
- **Flexibility** – Because each network node is attached via its own dedicated cable, the star approach makes it very easy to add, move, or remove individual nodes from the network without affecting other nodes.
- **Intelligence** – As manufacturers create increasingly smarter hub devices, star topologies can take advantage of the intelligence built into these devices, including centralized network management and advanced troubleshooting capabilities. Even if a network doesn't use intelligent hubs today, having the physical star topology in place makes it possible to insert intelligent hubs in the future.

Table 5-1 presents a summarized comparison of the network topologies I've discussed in the previous sections. I've included external hardware requirements, relative costs, reliability, and security considerations.

TIP

If you're creating a LAN from scratch, your best bet is to plan a network based on the physical star topology. It will provide the most convenience and flexibility as your network and your requirements change and grow in the future.

Table 5-1 COMPARISON OF NETWORK TOPOLOGIES

Characteristics	Bus Topology	Star Topology	Ring Topology
External hardware required	Terminators at each end of bus	Hub (active or passive)	MAU hub
Relative hardware cost	Low	Moderate	High
Reliability	Dependent on single cable bus	Dependent on central hub(s)	Dependent on MAU and cable paths to each node

Understanding Network Technologies

Didn't we just discuss this? Even networking veterans often confuse the concepts of network topologies (describing the physical or logical layout of a network) with *network technologies*, which are standard ways of signaling and communicating over the network. These standards specify exactly how nodes address each other, negotiate for use of the network, and transmit information. You can think of network technologies as the building codes, and network topologies as the house plans. Both are important in establishing your network infrastructure.

Two network technologies predominate today: Ethernet and Token Ring. Other network technologies are still in use – one of the more popular ones is called ARCnet – but because it's a relatively slow network technology, I won't discuss it here. In the following sections, I focus on the two technologies you're most likely to encounter in existing networks, or in designing your own new network from scratch.

CAUTION

For some strange reason, the two competing network technologies have created zealots in the networking community. People who strongly believe in either Ethernet or Token Ring will often defend their chosen technology with an almost religious fervor. As a network administrator, you should be aware of this schism, and be sensitive to the high level of emotions present when this debate surfaces in your organization. Try to remain objective about your choice of network technology, stay cool during the debates, and who knows — you may win some converts to your side.

Understanding Ethernet Technology

Ethernet, originally developed in 1973 at Xerox, is by far the most popular network technology in use today. (Don't repeat this fact to a Token Ring fanatic, or he might spin around until his head explodes.) The logical topology of an Ethernet network is always a bus. The predominant physical topology used to be a bus as well, but has been eclipsed in recent years by the star topology. Ethernet can use any of several network cabling approaches, which I discuss later in this chapter.

ACCESSING THE BUS

Because Ethernet is logically a bus, data is transmitted to every node on the network. Each node sees every transmission, and receives transmissions destined for it based on the address of its network adapter. This approach to sharing a single cable for all transmissions is known as the *multiple access* method. Only one node can successfully transmit at any given time, so the nodes must agree on a way to share the cable without interfering with each other. The Ethernet standard specifies how the nodes share the bus.

Before a node starts transmitting, it briefly listens to the bus for other traffic. This activity is known as *carrier sensing.* If another node is already transmitting, the node desiring to transmit tries again later. If there's no other traffic on the bus, the node begins transmission. This approach avoids transmissions stepping on each other – in most cases.

AVOIDING COLLISIONS

If the network becomes busy, it's more and more likely that two nodes will want to transmit exactly at the same time. When this happens, they both listen to the bus for other traffic, find none, and start their respective transmissions simultaneously. The two transmissions collide, leaving a pile of incomprehensible data on the bus. Who's going to clean up this mess? Both nodes detect the collision, back off for a while, and then try again later. This behavior is called, as you might guess, *collision detection.*

When a collision occurs, both transmitting nodes need to wait for a short, random period of time. If the waiting time were always the same, the two nodes would attempt to transmit again simultaneously and collide again. By delaying randomly, one of the nodes will win the race on the next attempt to transmit on the bus.

If this behavior isn't completely clear, consider a telephone party line. If you pick up the phone and someone else is already using the line, you politely and quietly hang up the phone and try again later. This activity is analogous to Ethernet's carrier sense behavior. On the other hand, if you and another party pick up the phone to use it at exactly the same moment, neither of you will hear a conversation. So you both start dialing, and completely mess up the phone line. When you both realize what has happened, you hang up, and you both try again later, hopefully at different times. This activity is analogous to Ethernet's collision detection behavior.

NOTE: In learning about Ethernet, you may encounter the acronym *CSMA/CD*, which stands for *carrier sense multiple access with collision detection*. The scary thing is that you now know exactly what behavior this acronym describes. Welcome to the inner sanctum of Ethernet network knowledge.

Understanding Token Ring Technology

Token Ring network technology was originally developed at IBM in 1984. Many people still consider Token Ring to be an IBM proprietary approach, even though it's an industry standard network technology. This belief has been fueled by the fact that Token Ring is most often found in "blue" organizations that use IBM mainframes and other products. It just hasn't caught on in volume the way Ethernet has. Nevertheless, as you'll see in this section, Token Ring does have some technical advantages over Ethernet. (Don't repeat this statement to an Ethernet zealot, or you might find yourself improperly terminated.)

One reason for its lower popularity is its higher relative cost to implement. Adding a single node to a Token Ring network can cost two to four times what adding a node to an Ethernet network costs. Logically, a Token Ring network has a ring topology – there's a surprise. As I mentioned earlier in this chapter, though, it isn't implemented as a physical ring. Instead, it uses a special hub that's wired especially for Token Ring. When you plug a node into the hub, you're essentially adding that node into the logical ring. Figure 5-4 illustrates this concept.

ACCESSING THE RING

Token Ring technology uses a very different access method from the Ethernet approach. A special message, called a *token*, is continuously circulated in one direction around the logical ring. If the token passes by a node that wants to transmit on the network, the node grabs the token, tacks on the data it wants to send, and puts the message back on the ring. The message continues its journey around the ring until it's delivered to its destination. Until the message arrives, no other nodes can send any data. A node can't transmit anything until it sees the token come by again. If a node sees the token but has nothing to say, it simply passes the token on to the next node in the ring. This access method is called *token passing*.

What if the circulating token stops circulating? This happens occasionally, although no one knows where the lost token really goes. (Perhaps it ends up in the sock drawer with all the matchless socks.) To solve this problem, one node on the ring is given the responsibility of detecting and regenerating lost tokens. This special node is called the *active monitor*.

CHOOSING TOKEN RING

The token passing access method avoids the collisions and random waiting periods inherent in the Ethernet world. Therefore, message delivery time is more predictable in a Token Ring environment. This behavior makes Token Ring ideal for installations that require a guaranteed periodic opportunity for each node to transmit on the network.

An excellent example of this requirement can be found in an automated factory. Each computer or robot needs to be able to report problems and status immediately, without being locked out by other nodes. If many failures occur at about the same time, as they often do in factories, several nodes need to report status and ask for help simultaneously. The potential collisions and waiting periods in the Ethernet technology could spell disaster in this environment.

Token Ring is also well-suited for networks that require access to IBM mainframe computers and minicomputers. The hardware, software, and support required to connect these systems to this network technology are readily available.

Understanding LAN Cabling Options

Over the years, manufacturers have developed networks that run on just about any type of wiring. However, they haven't all proved to be good approaches. As a result, only a handful of standard connection approaches has survived. In the following sections, I discuss each of the standard approaches used for physically connecting devices to a LAN.

The signals that are transmitted on network cables have two natural enemies: interference and attenuation. *Interference* is caused by nearby electrical devices or other wiring that causes stray signals to mix with the real data. Even the wires within the cable itself can interfere with each other unless steps are taken to prevent it. If interference is bad enough, it can lead to slow network performance and lost data.

Attenuation is the loss of strength in a signal due to electrical resistance within the cable itself. In general, the longer the cable, the worse the attenuation. This phenomenon leads to limits on cable lengths. If you exceed these limits, you're likely to encounter poor performance and lost data as attenuation weakens the transmitted signals. You're about to learn that different cabling technologies have different levels of susceptibility to interference and attenuation.

Figure 5-5 illustrates the major types of network cabling you'll learn about in the following sections. Each has a slightly different wiring and insulation configuration, affecting its bandwidth as well as its immunity to interference and attenuation. In the following sections, I discuss each type and tell you how it's wired and how it behaves.

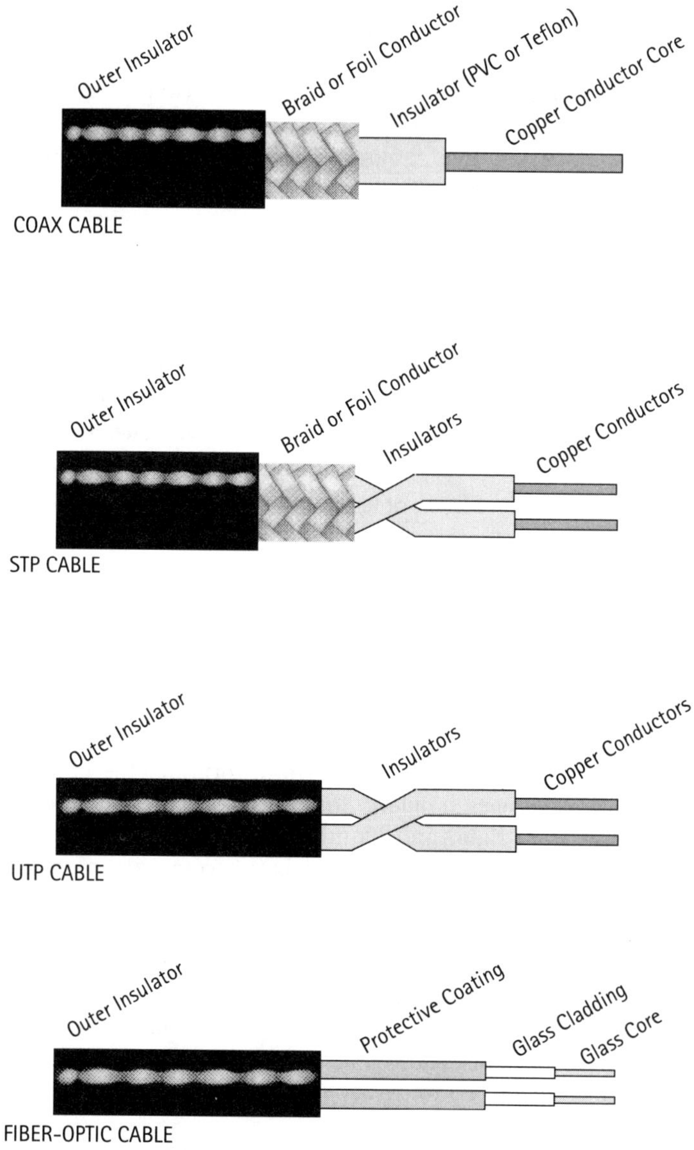

Figure 5-5: Four standard types of network cabling offer a range of performance characteristics.

Understanding Coaxial Cable

If you have cable television, you know what *coaxial cable*, or *coax*, looks like. Coax networking cable isn't exactly the same stuff, but it's very similar. Before 1990, most computer networks used coax; today, however, coax is nearing obsolescence in all but the very smallest networks.

A typical coax cable consists of two conductors centered on a common central axis – hence the name *coaxial.* As you see in Figure 5-5, the two conductors are insulated from each other and from the outside world. The inner copper conductor carries the signal and is either solid, as shown in Figure 5-5, or stranded. The outer conductor acts as a shield, and is made of copper braid, mesh, or foil. The outer insulator is typically made of rubber, Teflon, or plastic.

NOTE

Shielding cuts down on data transmission errors by absorbing external stray signals (called *electromagnetic interference, EMI,* or simply *noise*), to keep them from entering the cable. It also prevents EMI from getting out of the cable and affecting data transmission on nearby cables. In electrically noisy environments such as factories, additional shielding may be required. Coax with one layer of foil and one layer of braided metal is known as *dual-shielded* cable. Coax with two layers of foil and two layers of braid is called *quad-shielded.*

Although several flavors of coax exist, you're likely to encounter one of two common forms – namely, *thinnet* or *thicknet.* Thinnet, often called *thin Ethernet* or *RG-58,* is about a quarter of an inch thick, is flexible, and is relatively inexpensive. It's definitely the most common type of coax in use today, so it's the one you're most likely to encounter in existing networks. The earliest form of Ethernet coax cabling is called thicknet, or sometimes *standard Ethernet.* Thicknet is about twice as thick as thinnet, is much more rigid, and its outer jacket is typically yellow. (Based on these three characteristics, thicknet cable has become affectionately known in the industry as "frozen yellow garden hose.")

Whenever you install cable in an office environment, you need to be concerned about meeting fire codes. Depending on where you're installing your network cabling, you'll need to decide on the appropriate cable grade to install. Coaxial cable is available in two grades: *PVC* (polyvinyl chloride) and *plenum.* PVC material is used in most coax cable for both the internal and external insulation layers. Plenum refers to the area in many buildings between the false ceiling and the floor above.

If you're running coax in the exposed areas of an office (for example, behind desks, along walls, and so forth), you can use PVC grade cable. Unfortunately, when PVC burns, it gives off poisonous gases. Because the air in the plenum areas eventually becomes the part of the air breathed by everyone in the building, fire codes prohibit running PVC cable in the ceiling, in walls, and under floors. That's where plenum cabling comes in. Its insulators use special fire resistant materials that are designed to produce a minimum amount of smoke when burned. Plenum cabling is a bit less flexible than PVC cable, and it's more expensive.

CAUTION

If you don't pay attention to local fire codes, electrical codes, and engineering permit requirements before installing your network, you're just asking for trouble. Most localities require permits before you can install cables in walls, ceilings, and so forth. If you end up installing the wrong cable grades, you can get in trouble with the law, lose time and money when you have to redo the job, and potentially take lives if a fire breaks out. This tragedy is completely avoidable. Either educate yourself and do the job right the first time, or hire a reputable contractor to do it for you.

An Ethernet network implemented using coax thinnet is often referred to as *10Base2*. This means it transmits data at 10Mbps over a cable that can carry a signal roughly two times 100 meters (185 meters). The *Base* in 10Base2 is short for *baseband* transmission, which uses the entire communication capacity of the cable to transmit a single digital data signal. *10Base5* refers to thicknet that runs at 10Mbps and has up to 500-meter segments (five times 100 meters). You don't have to remember exactly how these terms are derived, but I guarantee you'll see them used in many coax-compatible product specifications. Table 5-2 summarizes the differences between 10Base2 and 10Base5.

TABLE 5-2 COAX CABLE COMPARISONS

Characteristics	Thinnet (10Base2)	Thicknet (10Base5)
Connector to network adapter	BNC, connected to the segment	AUI connected to transceiver, connected to the segment
Maximum length of a segment	185 meters	500 meters
Maximum nodes per segment	30	100
Maximum number of segments	5	5

Continued

TABLE 5-2 COAX CABLE COMPARISONS *(Continued)*

Characteristics	Thinnet (10Base2)	Thicknet (10Base5)
Maximum total network length	925 meters	2,500 meters
Relative cost (equipment and installation)	Low	High
Relative installation difficulty	Low	High

TIP

If you're installing or adding nodes on a coax network, be sure to select network adapters that can handle both coaxial cable and UTP (which I discuss later in this chapter). Called combo cards, these network adapters enable you to migrate easily to UTP without changing network adapters. The small additional cost for these combo cards is insignificant compared to the cost of opening up your computers a second time to replace the network adapters.

Understanding Shielded Twisted-Pair Cable

Twisted-pair cables contain at least one pair of insulated copper wires twisted around each other. The twists cut down on EMI from external sources; the more twists per unit of cable length, the better its resistance to EMI. Cables can contain any number of twisted pairs, depending on how the cable is to be used. There are two types of twisted-pair cables – shielded and unshielded.

As shown in Figure 5-5, *shielded twisted-pair* (*STP*) cable consists of a pair (actually, one or more pairs) of twisted pairs surrounded by a conducting shield similar to that found in coax. (Contrary to popular belief, STP cable contains no motor oil of any kind. It had to be said.) The combination of twists and shielding cuts down significantly on EMI.

IBM Type 1 Token Ring cable is the only type of STP cable still commonly used today. STP's costs and capabilities are about on par with those of coax. For Token Ring networks installed in electrically noisy environments such as warehouses and manufacturing facilities, STP remains an excellent choice. STP has been losing popularity steadily, in favor of the cheaper and more versatile *unshielded twisted-pair* cable, discussed in the next section.

Through Thick and Thin

So, which type of coax is right for your network? Once you decide that coax is the way to go (and don't decide that until you've reviewed the other cabling options in this chapter), you need to trade off cost for distance. As shown in Table 5-2, thinnet can transmit data up to about 600 feet before the signal starts to degrade. In contrast, thicknet is capable of transmitting up to about 1,640 feet — but this longer distance comes at a price.

Thinnet is much less expensive than thicknet, both in terms of equipment and installation hassles. In fact, it has become known in the industry as *cheapernet.* (Remember my explanation of the term *SneakerNet* in Chapter 1? It's okay to laugh now.) Thinnet attaches directly to network adapters using small inexpensive *BNC* connectors. (BNC stands for *British Naval Connector.*)

In the thicknet world, on the other hand, each network adapter requires a device called a *transceiver* (which is short for *transmitter-receiver*) and a special cable between the transceiver and the adapter. The special cable is called a *drop cable,* which connects to the *AUI* (*attachment unit interface*) on the network adapter. The AUI connector is known as a *DIX* connector, in deference to its three developers: Digital, Intel, and Xerox.

The transceiver attaches to the thicknet cable via a connector known as a *vampire tap* — making its connection by literally piercing through the cable to contact the inner conducting core. (Doesn't this seem like a macabre way of accessing your data?) Moreover, thicknet's inflexibility makes it much more difficult and time-consuming to install, especially in tight spaces and around corners. (I said corners, not coroners. Thicknet isn't all a chamber of horrors.)

Based on this tradeoff between transmission length and cost, you'll sometimes see thicknet used as a longer-distance interconnection between smaller networks that use thinnet. Refer to Table 5-2 for a summary comparison of the two types of coax cabling.

Understanding Unshielded Twisted-Pair Cable

Unshielded twisted-pair, or *UTP,* is fast becoming the most common approach to network cabling. As shown in Figure 5-5, UTP consists of two insulated copper wires twisted around each other. Unlike STP, UTP has no extra shielding, so it's more susceptible to EMI. The maximum length of a UTP cable is about 328 feet. UTP has been used for everything from traditional telephone cable to high-speed data networks. Different standards are used for each UTP application. The standards break down UTP cabling into five categories (sometimes called levels), which are summarized in Table 5-3. The higher the category number, the better the grade of cable.

TABLE 5-3 UTP CABLE CATEGORIES

Category (Level)	Twisted Pairs	Data Rate	Characteristics
1	1 or 2	Voice only. Do not use for data.	Traditional telephone voice cable, not used for data transmission.
2	4	Up to 4Mbps	Data transmission typically in the range of 1Mbps to 4Mbps. Used for voice and PBX, but not typically used for LANs.
3	4	Up to 10Mbps	Bare minimum used for Ethernet (up to 10Mbps) and Token Ring (up to 4Mbps).
4	4	Up to 16Mbps	Usable for Ethernet (10Mbps) or Token Ring (up to 16Mbps).
5	4	Up to 100Mbps	Usable for Ethernet, Token Ring, or Fast Ethernet (100Mbps).

Many modern buildings are prewired with extra twisted pairs to accommodate future cabling needs. If the right category of UTP is used for the extra wiring, you can take advantage of it when setting up your computer network. But don't even try to use UTP wiring that isn't designed for the speed of your network. For example, don't use standard telephone wiring to connect an Ethernet network. It won't work, because the cable doesn't have the appropriate twisting and other electrical characteristics required for data transmission at LAN speeds.

TIP

Regardless of the initial speed of your LAN, if you're going to wire with UTP cable, don't install anything less than Category 5 cabling everywhere. It's somewhat more expensive than the other categories, but it's well worth the investment. Not only will it yield the highest reliability, it will also give you the flexibility of moving to Fast Ethernet (100Mbps) and other technologies without rewiring your whole world. Installing anything less than Category 5 is a waste of time and money. If you already have UTP below Category 5 installed, consider replacing it with Category 5 down the road.

An Ethernet network implemented using UTP (or STP) is often referred to as *10BaseT*. This means it transmits data at 10Mbps over a baseband cable that uses twisted-pair cabling. Likewise, *100BaseT* and *100BaseTX* are used to describe a 100Mbps network. Again, you don't have to remember where the terms came from. You'll encounter them in your network literature travels.

If you're installing or adding nodes on a 10BaseT UTP Ethernet network, it's a good idea to select network adapters that can operate at either 10Mbps or 100Mbps. That way, you won't have to open your computers and replace network adapters if you decide to switch to 100Mbps Ethernet in the future. All you'll need to replace are the external wiring hubs. Although the cost for 100Mbps-capable network adapters is higher (usually 10 to 50 percent higher than 10Mbps adapters, depending on features), you should weigh it against the future cost of opening your computers and replacing adapters.

UTP Installation Do's and Don'ts

Category 5 UTP cable is manufactured to exacting specifications. To ensure top performance and reliability of your network, you need to handle and install it properly. Too much stretching or bending can alter the characteristics of both the conductors and the insulation—and that potentially affects the transmission properties of the cable. If the cable becomes kinked, for example, just straightening it out may not return it to its original performance. There's an art and skill to proper cable installation that comes with training and experience.

When pulling cable during installation, don't exert more than 25 pounds of force. Anything more will permanently stretch the cable and alter its performance. Don't let the cable kink or knot either. This alters the twists within the cable, again permanently affecting performance. Avoid bending the cable at right angles (or any acute angles) when turning corners or connecting to network equipment. Instead, arrange enough slack in the cable to have sweeping bends.

If you use staples or tie-wraps to secure cable, be sure the fasteners don't crush, squash, or puncture the cable. When running cables in the plenum area, use appropriate hooks or channels to support them. Don't simply drape the cables or rest them on ceiling tiles or light fixtures—cables can stretch under their own weight. Never run cables in traffic areas where people might walk on them, even if they're protected by mats and cushions. (I encountered a client who installed a network this way, and they couldn't figure out why they had so many network problems.)

Understanding Fiber-Optic Cable

Fiber-optic cable is made of glass or plastic fiber instead of copper. It transmits data by using pulses of laser light, rather than by traditional electrical means. This approach makes it virtually immune to both EMI, attenuation, and corrosion. As a result, it's great for high-speed data transmission across relatively long distances. You can use fiber-optic cable to transmit data at 100Mbps or faster across many miles without signal degradation. In fact, fiber-optic networks that transmit as fast as 1Gbps have been demonstrated, and they can theoretically operate at more than one terabit (one trillion bits) per second. What's more, there's never a possibility of a short circuit in fiber-optic cable.

> NOTE
>
> Fiber-optic cable is more secure than any of its copper cousins, because it can't easily be tapped. It's relatively easy to tap and eavesdrop on data from copper-based cable that transmits using electrical signals. With the right equipment, you can detect and interpret data from the pulses radiated externally from the copper cable — but because fiber-optic cable uses light for data transmission, it's nearly impossible to access the data from outside the cable. (I say *nearly impossible*, because there are exceptions. Very expensive devices exist for tapping fiber-optic transmissions. They bend the cable slightly, and can detect the minute amount of light that escapes from the bend.) Relative to other cabling approaches, though, fiber-optic is much more resistant to tapping.

So if fiber-optic cable holds all the keys to reliable, high-speed, secure data transmission, why doesn't everyone just "go into the light?" Well, it's becoming increasingly difficult to answer that question. In the past, the cost of installing a fiber-optic network infrastructure was many times that of an equivalent UTP installation. These days, however, fiber installations cost 10 to 20 percent more than Category 5 UTP. Still, that cost difference can be significant, depending on the size of your network. But fiber-optic network adapters are still much more expensive than UTP adapters – costing five to ten times more than UTP. This price gap will narrow over time, as more manufacturers offer fiber-optic network adapters. You'll want to assess whether the extra cost is justified in your situation.

As shown in Figure 5-5, fiber-optic cable consists of two glass fibers, each surrounded by a layer of glass called *cladding*. (Some fiber-optic cable uses plastic for the fiber, but it can't span the distances that glass can. Plastic fiber-optic cable is limited to about 900 feet.) Although data can travel in either direction along a single fiber, network adapters and other equipment have been designed to transmit data in only one direction per fiber. That's why a fiber-optic cable consists of two fibers – one for transmitting and one for receiving.

CAUTION: The laser used to transmit data across fiber-optic cable is powerful and dangerous. Be sure that you and anyone who works with the cable heeds all the warnings provided with the cable and network equipment. If you look down the end of a transmitting cable, the laser can severely burn your retinal tissue.

Because of its traditionally high cost, you typically find fiber-optic cable used in portions of large networks. For example, Microsoft uses fiber-optic cable as a high-speed link between the many buildings on its corporate campus. Within each building, it uses Category 5 UTP cabling. Fiber-optic cable is a perfect choice to connect buildings, because it isn't metal and therefore doesn't attract lightning. Its speed and reliability minimize or eliminate performance bottlenecks between the networks it connects together.

In general, fiber-optic cabling is a good choice for any segments of the network where you expect to see high traffic, long physical distance, or the need for highly secure and EMI-resistant transmission. As the cost difference diminishes, you'll see fiber-optic cable placed into service in a broader range of environments. Dare I say that more networks will be given high-fiber diets?

TIP: While fiber remains more expensive than UTP, the bulk of the difference now boils down to a set of special tools, proper installation training, and the labor required to properly attach connectors to the cable. The advent of simpler connectors has gone a long way in reducing the overall cost of fiber. If you're planning to get someone else to install your network infrastructure, it's worth getting estimates on both UTP and fiber-optic installations. The added benefits of a fiber-optic infrastructure might be worth the extra cost.

Rules of do's and don'ts, similar to the UTP rules discussed in the previous section, apply to fiber-optic cable installation. Each manufacturer provides detailed specifications on how hard you can pull the cable, how acutely you can bend it, and how to properly splice and connect it. (In the fiber-optic world, the act of attaching connectors to the ends of the cable has become known as *connectorizing*. Isn't it amazing how new words emerge in our complex world? First we had motives, then motivations; pretty soon we'll be "motivationing" each other to engage in proper "connectorization!")

An Ethernet network implemented using fiber-optic cable is sometimes referred to as *10BaseFL* for 10Mbps networks, and *100BaseFX* for Fast Ethernet 100Mbps networks. 10BaseFL means that it transmits data at 10Mbps over a baseband cable that uses fiber-optic cabling, with a segment length of up to 2000 meters.

NOTE: Work is progressing toward a standard for Gigabit Ethernet, which reaches data rates up to 1Gbps using fiber-optic cable. At the time of writing, the standard is about to be ratified. Meanwhile, standards committees are also working on a 1Gbps Ethernet standard that uses copper-based UTP cable.

Understanding Wireless Networks

Wireless technology uses either optical or radio techniques to transmit data. (In a sense, wireless technology puts the "ether" back in "Ethernet." No connectorization here.) As costs have come down and transmission speeds have increased, wireless networking technology has become an increasingly viable alternative to traditional cabled networks. It's especially ideal for providing temporary or portable connections to existing networks, extending the reach of traditional networks beyond the limits of cabling infrastructure.

NOTE: The term *wireless* is a bit misleading. Wireless networks almost always require some amount of cabling between certain components. And you rarely find wireless technology used independently of a traditional cabled network. Most networks that use wireless connections are actually hybrid networks — combinations of both cabled and wireless approaches.

CHOOSING WIRELESS NETWORKING

So, why not select wireless as the perfect overall networking solution? After all, it's convenient, doesn't require (much) wiring, and is certainly more flexible than traditional cabled networks. Well, there are currently two cons associated with wireless networking – namely, its relatively high cost and its relatively low transmission speeds. If you measure your network investment in terms of dollars per unit of bandwidth, wireless networking offers one of the lowest networking values. Because of its high cost and low transmission speed, wireless is a good alternative only if you have a concrete need for it.

In the simplest case, you may have a subset of network users whose jobs require that they be mobile during the work day. Wireless networking may be an ideal solution for them to periodically check and send e-mail, update warehouse inventory, or perform other specific tasks from any location within your facility. Many hospitals have adopted wireless technology for doctors and nurses, enabling them to update patient records electronically without having to plug into a network outlet. Some automobile rental agencies have equipped some of their employees with wireless devices that enable quick car check-in, billing, and printing out of receipts on the car lot.

You may have a facility that can't be wired for some reason. For example, if your organization occupies a structure that has historical significance, you may be prohibited from installing traditional network cabling. Or, the structure may be constructed in a way what would make cabling too expensive. In these situations, wireless technology may be the only networking alternative available to you.

UNDERSTANDING WIRELESS TECHNOLOGY

Most wireless implementations involve connecting wireless nodes to a traditional cabled network. To create a wireless connection to an existing LAN, you need to install a wireless *transceiver* (essentially a network adapter without a cable) in the node you want to connect. Back on the cabled network, you need another transceiver to handle communication with one or more of these wireless nodes. The transceiver that's physically attached to the cabled network is typically called an *access point.* An access point sends and receives data to and from nearby nodes that have their own transceivers. It's physically attached to a node on the cabled network via a cable. Depending on the wireless technology used and the physical distance covered by the network, you may need more than one access point to handle subsets of the wireless nodes.

Wireless networks can be implemented using one of several technologies, including infrared, radio, cellular, and satellite. In the following sections, I discuss the important issues and terminology associated with these wireless networking technologies.

INFRARED NETWORKING Infrared networks transmit and receive data using a high-intensity infrared light beam similar to, but more powerful than, the beam used by a television remote control. Data transmission speeds can reach up to 10Mbps in ideal circumstances. A wireless network that approaches standard Ethernet speeds sounds great, until you consider its limitations. Infrared devices have a hard time transmitting any farther than about 100 feet. And because they're susceptible to interference from strong light sources (such as windows), they can become unreliable in some business environments. If walls or other objects lie between the cabled network and the wireless nodes, infrared devices won't work at all.

Several infrared approaches exist, each with its own set of limitations. *Line-of-sight* networks require a completely clear line of sight between the sending node and the receiving node. If someone walks between the two, the wireless connection is broken until there's a clear path again. In some environments, this can translate to many attempts to send the same data, greatly reducing the effective data transmission rate.

Scatter networks attempt to get around this limitation by shooting the signals at walls and ceilings. The signals bounce around until they eventually reach the receiving node. Unfortunately, this approach is limited to a small physical area, and the signal bouncing can significantly slow down transmission speed. *Reflective* networks place a small line-of-sight transceiver closer to the wireless nodes. These intervening transceivers forward transmissions to and from a common access point transceiver. This approach cuts down on the problems encountered with the line-of-sight and scatter techniques, but doesn't eliminate them completely.

Laser networking technology is similar in concept to infrared. It requires an unbroken direct line of sight between sender and receiver. People or objects that get in the way will block transmission. Laser technology is more expensive than infrared, and doesn't overcome infrared's line-of-sight limitations.

NARROW-BAND RADIO *Narrow-band radio* (sometimes called *single-frequency radio*) uses an approach similar to a radio station. The sender and receiver agree on and tune to a specific radio frequency. Because the signal is broadcast in what amounts to a 15,000 square foot area, line of sight isn't required. However, these high frequency broadcast signals can't usually penetrate load-bearing walls or steel. Barring this limitation, narrow-band radio can effectively transmit between 4Mbps and 5Mbps – under half the speed of standard Ethernet. This approach offers a tradeoff between transmission speed and network flexibility.

SPREAD-SPECTRUM RADIO To overcome the limitations of narrow-band radio, *spread-spectrum radio* broadcasts its transmissions over a range of radio frequencies instead of just one. It divides the available frequencies into channels, which are sometimes called *hops*. (These aren't the same kind of hops a brewery has, unless of course the brewery uses this type of wireless network.) All the wireless nodes in the network agree on and synchronize to a specific *hop timing* – the length of time they tune in to a specific hop or channel. Although this approach typically yields transmission speeds around 256Kbps, some products can offer up to 4Mbps.

Spread-spectrum products exist that let you implement a truly wireless network. Netwave offers a good example of this technology. By installing Netwave adapters into several laptop computers, you can create a peer-to-peer network without running cabling anywhere. You can then connect this wireless network to a traditional cabled network by adding a Netwave access point to one of the cabled nodes.

Extending the Wireless Reach

If you need to connect existing LANs and don't have the luxury of running cables between them, you might consider connecting them using wireless technology. For example, if your organization occupies two buildings across the street from each other, you could install a *wireless LAN bridge* between them. (I discuss network bridges in detail later in this chapter. For now, think of the wireless bridge as a virtual cable for data transmission between the LANs in the two buildings.)

This technology typically uses spread-spectrum radio to link LANs that can't be connected by traditional cabling for either cost or pragmatic reasons. It can save the potentially high recurring cost of leased lines between buildings. It can also provide a connection in environments were no other physical connection is possible. For example, local laws might prohibit running cable either under or over the street between your sites. Depending on weather conditions and obstructions, sort-range wireless bridges enable connections over a distance of up to three miles, whereas long-range systems can reach up to 25 miles.

MOBILE NETWORKING If you have many users who travel with laptops or handheld PDAs (personal digital assistants), and they need to stay in touch with your network for e-mail and file transfer, mobile wireless technology may be worth considering. Mobile networking typically uses wireless network adapters that communicate with your cabled network using cellular telephone technology. Portable nodes communicate with either radio towers or low-orbit satellites to send and receive data.

Although mobile networking offers the ultimate level of convenience, its transmission speed is quite slow. Depending on conditions and error correction features, speeds range anywhere from 8Kbps to 19.2Kbps. Compare this range with mainstream modem speeds, which are between 28.8Kbps and 56Kbps, and you'll get a feeling for how painfully slow this technology is. Small amounts of data, such as text-only e-mail messages, work well – but transfers of large blocks of data may cause your users to toss their PDAs into the nearest river.

Mobile network devices typically use either packet-radio technology or cellular technology. *Packet-radio* transmits data in small chunks called packets. In addition to the data, the packets include information about the source and destination nodes. Packets travel up to a satellite, which broadcasts them back to the earth. Only devices that have an address that matches the destination address can receive the packets. *Cellular Digital Packet Data* (*CDPD*) transmits data packets between voice calls using existing cellular telephone equipment. Data is transmitted whenever the cellular network isn't busy. Even in a society where cellular phones are everywhere, there's lots of available bandwidth for these data transmissions.

Understanding WAN Connection Options

Recall from Chapter 1 that a WAN (wide area network) covers longer physical distances than a LAN. WANs are often used to connect multiple sites together into a unified network. It's sometimes impractical or impossible to string your own network cable between physical sites, especially if the intervening property isn't owned by your organization, or the distance is more than a couple of miles. Therefore, WAN connections require solutions that are often more complex and sometimes more costly than LAN connections. In the following sections, I discuss the WAN connection options available to you.

The costs of implementing and leasing analog and digital lines presented in this section are approximate and will vary over time from region to region. Moreover, not all services are available in all areas. Be sure to check with your telecommunications carrier for a list of specific services and prices before you get your WAN budget completed and approved.

Data in the Sky

Communication satellites orbit the earth in such a way that they remain in the same place in the sky relative to the satellite stations on earth. Once pointed at a particular satellite, a station on earth doesn't have to keep adjusting its aim. The satellites are in what's called *geosynchronous* orbit (synchronized with the earth's rotation).

Because satellites are so far away from the earth, they introduce a communication delay of about 0.27 seconds on each leg of the trip. Data traveling from its original source to its final destination can be delayed up to 0.54 seconds. As a result, satellite links may not be suited for some applications that require immediate, real-time data transmission.

Understanding Analog Connections

From a financial perspective, the least expensive way to connect LANs at different sites together is via the existing *public switched telephone network* (*PSTN*). You can think of this worldwide voice network as one large WAN link, if you're willing to live with its slow speed and variable reliability. In the following sections, I discuss the key issues associated with using PSTN as the network infrastructure for your WAN connections.

DIAL-UP AND DEDICATED ANALOG LINES

The simplest and least expensive analog connections are dial-up connections. Each session requires that your modem dial a phone number to establish a new session. As a result, the quality (speed and reliability) of a session is only as good as the telephone network circuits connected for that particular session. If you've had experience dialing into an ISP to access the Internet, you've probably seen the transmission speed vary from one session to the next. In general, the longer the distance covered by the connection, the less consistency you'll see in the quality from one dial-up session to the next. For example, local calls tend to provide more consistency than long-distance or international calls.

If you need a persistent connection with consistent speed and reliability, consider a dedicated leased analog line. For a monthly fee, a leased line provides a connection that's constantly active and ready to transmit data. Leased lines are also typically faster and more reliable than dial-up connections, and their consistent quality is often guaranteed by the service provider. The fee is much higher than that of a standard dial-up line, because the service provider must dedicate resources to the line whether you're using the connection or not.

So, how do you decide which approach is better? If you need infrequent access and you're not concerned with inconsistent connection speed and reliability, dial-up lines are fine. If you need a consistent connection continuously, then consider investing in a dedicated leased line. If you plan on large amounts of network traffic over your WAN connections, however, you should consider one of the digital alternatives discussed in the following sections.

REMOTE ACCESS SERVICE

Recall from Chapter 1 that *RAS* (pronounced *rass*, for *Remote Access Service*) provides the capability of dialing into your network from a remote location, and acting as a remote node on the network. Windows 98 includes both a RAS client (remote component) and a RAS server to provide access to the network. The Windows 98 RAS server can accept only one connection from a remote client. (Windows 95 included only the RAS client. The Windows 95 RAS server was available as an add-on component in the Microsoft Plus! package.)

NOTE: If you need a RAS server that accepts more than one simultaneous remote client connection, you'll need to use Windows NT Server. Its included RAS server can handle up to 256 remote clients at a time.

RAS is the primary mechanism for remote connections. You'll find in the Windows 98 interface and in the documentation that RAS is often referred to as *Dial-Up Networking*, or *DUN*. DUN software communicates with and controls the devices used to connect your networks to your telecommunications system.

When connecting to the analog phone system, you'll need a modem at each end of the connection. A *modem* (which stands for *modulator-demodulator*) converts digital signals from your PC to analog signals for transmission over the telephone lines. (These analog signals are audible sounds – actually, downright unpleasant screeching sounds, if you ever listen to two modems conversing.) This action is called *modulation*. At the other end of the connection, a modem converts the analog signals from the phone line and turns them back into digital signals. This is known as *demodulation*. Both a RAS client and a RAS server require their own modems. The RAS server modem answers a call from a RAS client modem to establish the remote network connection.

As I discussed in Chapter 4, you shouldn't consider using modems any slower than 28.8Kbps. Modems claiming 33.6Kbps and 56Kbps employ some form of compression, and the modems at each end of the connection need to be capable of compatibly handling the higher speed transmissions. Actual speeds vary depending on the quality of your wiring and the amount of interference present along the entire connection.

TIP: There are two ways to cut down on headaches during your RAS implementation. First, when you select modems for use with Windows 98 or Windows NT RAS, make sure they're on the operating system's hardware compatibility list (HCL). The listed modems have been successfully tested in the RAS environment. Other modems may work, but choosing products from the list will remove one unknown from the mix. Second, it's best to use the same make and model of modem on both ends of your RAS connections. Subtle differences in the behavior of modems from different manufacturers (or modems with different feature sets) can lead to problems that are often very difficult to diagnose.

VIRTUAL PRIVATE NETWORKING

RAS is great if you're close enough to the office to make a local phone call to dial into the server. But it can get pretty darned expensive if you're on a business trip and need to dial a long-distance number for access. RAS still works, but the extra expense can add up, especially if you need to access the network for lengthy periods. Some businesses get toll-free phone numbers to shift the cost from the caller to the business, but somebody ends up paying in the end.

If you already have an account on the Internet with a national ISP that provides unlimited access via a local phone call, wouldn't it be great to simply use the Internet itself to connect to your office network? If your ISP provides local access numbers nationwide, you can connect to the Internet from almost anywhere without making a long-distance call. If there were a way to securely transmit data over the Internet, and make it all seem as if you've dialed directly into your network, you'd never have to pay long-distance charges. In Windows 98, Microsoft has provided the tools you need to make this happen.

Virtual private networking, or VPN, is a new feature of Windows 98 that enables you to securely access your networks across the Internet. It uses a special network protocol that encases your data in a secure "tunnel" and transmits it over the Internet to its destination site. The protocol used by VPN is called PPTP, which stands for *Point-to-Point Tunneling Protocol.* I discuss protocols in more detail in Chapter 6. For now, just remember that a protocol is a language that both sender and receiver agree upon.

Like RAS, VPN uses Dial-Up Networking (DUN) to establish the network connection. For example, let's say you take your laptop to a faraway city. To connect to your network back at the office, you would first use DUN to dial a local number to connect to your ISP, and then set up a second connection (or "tunnel") into your office network via the Internet. You can also use VPN over dedicated analog lines, to maintain a permanent network connection to the Internet – and between your organization's sites.

Your ISP may provide special requirements and instructions for setting up a tunnel connection to your network. For example, it may need to give you a special logon name for this type of connection. Be sure to contact your ISP before attempting to set up a VPN.

Understanding ISDN Lines

Integrated Services Digital Network, better know as *ISDN*, was designed to be the digital successor to the existing public switched telephone network (PSTN). It's a completely digital dial-up service, and doesn't provide for a dedicated line. Like many dial-up services, ISDN typically requires a basic monthly fee and incremental fees based on your connect time or the volume of data you transmit. ISDN comes in two flavors, which I discuss in the following sections.

Although ISDN has been around in one form or another for nearly 20 years, it isn't yet available everywhere. If you need information about the level of ISDN service in your area, or need to know which of the Regional Bell Operating Companies (RBOCs) handles your area, contact the National ISDN Hotline. Their telephone number is 1-800-992-ISDN, and their e-mail address is `isdn@cc.bellcore.com`. Appendix B provides pointers to additional ISDN information resources.

BASIC RATE ISDN

Basic Rate ISDN, or *BRI,* is the most common form of ISDN, intended eventually to replace standard analog telephone lines. Designed to provide the maximum data rate that could use existing wiring, BRI includes three distinct transmission channels. The first two channels, called *B channels,* each transmit data at 64Kbps.

The third channel, called the *D channel* (no, not the Disney Channel), runs at a much slower 16Kbps. The B channels are dedicated to transmitting data, while the D channel handles all the handshaking, management, and housekeeping tasks. To reflect this relationship of the B and D channels, you'll sometimes see BRI referred to as *2B+D.*

In some regions, telecommunications carriers provide ISDN B channels that transmit at 56Kbps, rather than 64Kbps. This approach provides backward compatibility with older phone systems that use 8Kbps of the 64Kbps for control signaling. Be sure to ask about the B channel transmission rate of your carrier's ISDN service, so you know how much bandwidth you're really buying.

Placing all the control signaling on the D channel enables the B channels to use their full bandwidth for data transmission. Combining both B channels together, you can achieve a data rate of up to 128Kbps. Rates can go even higher if both ends of the connection support data compression.

Don't be fooled by people or brochures that try to convince you that BRI provides a full 144Kbps data rate. They're not doing the math correctly. Remember that the D channel is dedicated to control signaling — not to data transmission. So the BRI data rate isn't 64+64+16=144Kbps. It's really only 64+64=128Kbps. If your carrier quotes the 144 number, you'll have some idea of how much (or how little) they know about ISDN.

PRIMARY RATE ISDN

Primary Rate ISDN, or *PRI*, is also made up of B channels and a D channel – but it offers a lot more bandwidth than BRI. Instead of just two B channels, PRI provides 23 of them. Also, it expands the D channel from 16Kbps to 64Kbps. As with BRI, the PRI D channel is used exclusively for control signaling, giving the B channels the freedom to transmit only data.

By combining all the B channels together, you can achieve a data transmission rate close to that of a T1 line, which I discuss later in this chapter. In fact, just as BRI was designed to provide the maximum data rate over existing phone wiring, PRI was designed to handle the maximum data rate provided by a T1 line. A T1 line provides just the right amount of bandwidth to support the PRI's 23 B channels and one D channel. By aggregating all the B channels together, you can achieve a data rate of nearly 1.5Mbps.

NOTE: You may encounter mention of *Broadband ISDN*, or *B-ISDN*. This is basically a refinement of the ISDN standard that commonly supports data rates of 51Mbps, 155Mbps, and 622Mbps. B-ISDN uses ATM and SONET technologies, which I discuss later in this chapter.

As I mentioned before, ISDN costs will vary from one region to the next. Likewise, depending on the state of local telephone switching equipment, you may find that the lead time for ISDN installation varies widely as well. You'll find a list of pointers to additional information on regional availability and costs of ISDN in Appendix B.

Understanding DSL Technology

Digital Subscriber Line, or *DSL*, is a relatively new digital technology that uses existing copper telephone wiring as a high-speed digital pipeline. Only the equipment at each end of the connection needs to change. The existing copper telephone wiring doesn't need to be replaced. DSL uses software and hardware to clean up the transmission problems associated with copper wire, allowing for higher transmission speeds and increased reliability.

If you elect to subscribe to a DSL service, you need special hardware and software at your end of the connection. But this isn't the real stumbling block. The telecommunications carrier has to install special equipment at its end, as well. This factor has slowed the progress of DSL adoption considerably – at the time of writing, it's only available in selected test markets. However, because the carrier's DSL equipment is significantly less expensive than ISDN equipment, DSL technology should be adopted more aggressively than ISDN has been. If all goes well in the test markets, many experts predict that DSL will begin broad deployment sometime in 1999 or 2000, and will overtake ISDN in popularity within two years after that.

TIP Check with your telecommunications carrier to see if it offers any DSL services. If it doesn't, you'll have to wait for the DSL circus to come to your town; if it does, it's definitely worth considering for your WAN and Internet connections.

When you read about DSL, you usually see some other letter attached to the beginning of term – and the letters always seem to be different. Table 5-4 presents a rundown of the many flavors of DSL service, and what the acronyms really mean. The term xDSL refers generically to the collection of DSL technologies listed in Table 5-4. Appendix B contains some pointers to additional information on DSL technologies.7

TABLE 5-4 SUMMARY OF DIGITAL SUBSCRIBER LINE (DSL) TECHNOLOGIES

DSL Type	Definition	Maximum Distance (feet)	Downstream Rate	Upstream Rate
ADSL	Asymmetric DSL	18,000	1.544Mbps to 8.448Mbps	16Kbps to 640Kbps
VDSL (or VADSL)	Very-high-data-rate DSL (or Very-high-speed DSL) is a very fast version of ADSL.	4,500	12.96Mbps to 51.84Mbps	1.5Mbps to 2.3Mbps
HDSL	High-bit-data-rate DSL is aimed at efficiently transmitting T1 over copper lines. It uses two wires to achieve duplex communication.	18,000	1.544Mbps to 2.048Mbps	1.544Mbps to 2.048Mbps
SDSL	Single-line DSL (or Symmetric DSL) is a single-wire version of HDSL.	9,000	160Kbps to 2.048Mbps	160Kbps to 2.048Mbps

The data transmission rates in each flavor of DSL depend primarily on the distance covered, although the size of the copper wire and the amount of interference present along the way are also factors.

Understanding T1 Lines

T1 is the most popular high-speed digital line in use today. Using two pairs of wires (one pair for transmitting, the other for receiving), it can transmit voice, data, and video at up to 1.544Mbps. T1 lines are expensive to lease, costing between $1,500 and $2,500 per month depending on your region. If the price tag and bandwidth don't match your budget or communication requirements, you can order as little or as much T1 as you want.

T1 lines are made up of 24 distinct 64Kbps channels. If you don't need the full bandwidth or can't afford a full T1 line, you can lease a subset of the available channels. This less-expensive service is called *Fractional T1* or *FT-1*. On the flip side, if you can afford T1 and need even more bandwidth than a single T1 line provides, you can combine more than one line together by leasing a service called *Multiple T1*. (In case you encounter these terms on your T1 shopping trip, *DS-0* refers to a single 64Kbps T1 channel, *DS-1* refers to a full 1.544Mbps T1 line, *DS-1C* refers to two T1 lines, and *DS-2* refers to four T1 lines. This numbering scheme seems almost logical – but not quite.)

NOTE: T1 service isn't available in all countries, but fear not — in Europe, a similar service called *E1* is available. E1 is faster than T1, transmitting at up to 2.048Mbps. *Euro-ISDN* makes use of the additional bandwidth by including 30 B channels in their Primary Rate ISDN (PRI), rather than the 23 channels that are standard in North America. For a discussion of B channels, see the section titled "Understanding ISDN Lines," earlier in this chapter.

If your bandwidth needs go much beyond three T1 lines, you may want to consider leasing a T3 or Fractional T3 line, which I discuss in the next section.

Understanding T3 Lines

T3 is a digital leased line similar to T1, but it operates at much higher data rates. T3 is the highest capacity leased line service available today, achieving data rates up to 45Mbps. While T1 can be implemented with copper wire, T3 requires a high-frequency connection such as fiber-optic cable.

T3 isn't cheap. A single T3 line can cost between $65,000 and $85,000 per month. But like T1, T3 can be leased on a fractional basis (called Fractional T3 or FT-3). You can lease an FT-3 line with as little bandwidth as 6.3Mbps – the equivalent of four T1 lines.

Understanding ATM Connections

Asynchronous Transfer Mode (ATM) is a high-speed network technology that can be used to implement LANs or WANs. It can accommodate voice, data, fax, real-time video, CD-quality audio, imaging, and very large data (multi-megabit) transmissions. ATM was originally defined in 1988, as part of the B-ISDN definition. ATM typically transmits data at a rate between 155Mbps and 622Mbps.

Theoretically, ATM can transmit at 1.2Gbps and beyond. In fact, it can reach that speed over SONET optical lines. You'll find, however, that most commercial ATM adapters will only go as high as 155Mbps — not too shabby as network data rates go, but certainly not up to the full potential of ATM. But more adapters capable of 622Mbps are fast emerging to take over as the most common ATM speed.

ATM isn't restricted to any particular type of cabling. ATM networks have been implemented using coax, twisted-pair, and fiber-optic cabling. To take advantage of all of ATM's capabilities, however, you need to use a very high bandwidth connection method such as FDDI (at 100Mbps), SONET (from 155Mbps to 1.2Gbps and above), or T3 (at 45Mbps). I discuss some of these in the next section.

There's a lot of excitement and hype surrounding the ATM technology, but the fact remains that it's very immature. It requires special hardware and very high bandwidth connections to reach its full potential. Moreover, implementing and supporting ATM currently requires knowledge and experience that isn't widely available. It's okay to get excited about ATM, but keep these factors in mind as you evaluate it.

Understanding Your Other Options

Beyond the services discussed so far in this chapter, many telecommunications carriers offer additional services at various prices and speeds. Here is a brief overview of some of these services, which may or may not be available in your area:

- **Digital Data Service (DDS)** provides a relatively low-speed dedicated digital service that can transmit at rates ranging from 2.4Kbps to 56Kbps.
- **Switched 56** provides a dial-up 56Kbps LAN-to-LAN digital connection. Most local and long-distance telecommunications carriers now offer this service. It's typically less costly than a dedicated digital line. Switched 56 is a specialized form of DDS.

- **Frame Relay** was designed to support B-ISDN, discussed earlier in this chapter. It's built around fast fiber-optic networks, so it assumes high reliability. Data transmission ranges from 56Kbps to 1.544Mbps.
- **Fiber Distributed Data Interface** (FDDI) is a specification that describes a 100Mbps token-passing ring designed to use fiber-optic cabling. Its maximum ring length is 62 miles, so its application to WANs is limited. FDDI uses two rings, providing redundancy if one of the rings fails.
- **Synchronous Optical Network** (SONET) is an emerging technology that takes advantage of fiber-optic technology to transmit voice, data, and video at more than 1Gbps. It uses a basic transmission rate of 51.84Mbps, and offers higher data rates by applying a multiplier to this basic rate.
- **Switched Multi-megabit Data Service** (SMDS) provides transmission speeds between 56Kbps and 34Mbps. It's only offered in selected regions. SMDS uses technology similar to ATM. Just as FDDI forms a dual-ring topology, SMDS forms a dual-bus topology.

NOTE: As I mentioned earlier in this chapter, you can use wireless technology to link buildings together and avoid stringing or leasing cable altogether. One approach is microwave technology. It's used by satellites and is currently the most widely used method for long-distance telephone transmission in the United States. You can use it to provide line-of-sight network links between satellites and ground stations, between adjacent buildings, or between sites that lie on either side of a large flat area such as a lake.

Selecting a WAN Strategy

The array of WAN connection choices available to you will be trimmed down based on your region and what services your telecommunications carrier provides. Once you know what's available, the selection boils down to your specific application and what it will cost you. If the amount of bandwidth you plan to use is fairly constant, you're better off with a service that charges a flat rate (such as T1, for example). On the other hand, if your requirements for bandwidth vary widely, you may want to consider a "pay for what you use" plan that charges based on the time you're connected and the amount of bandwidth you actually use. Services such as ISDN fall into this category.

As you can see by now, planning is critically important in selecting the right type of WAN connection for your environment. Mistakes in this area can be expensive, both in terms of dollars and lost productivity. To make the correct choices, you'll need to know ahead of time what bandwidth you require and what sort of data traffic patterns you expect to have. To achieve this, you'll either need to educate yourself on the details of what each of your applications and operating systems requires, or you'll need to bring in an experienced network designer to help.

Connecting Your Network Together

You can create very small, simple networks using only cables and network adapters attached to your computers and other devices. (You can even get away with using no cable in a very small wireless network.) But as your network grows in size and complexity, you'll need other networking devices to tie everything together correctly. For example, even a network of two computers may need special equipment installed between them, if the distance between the computers exceeds the maximum specified cable length.

It's important to understand the roles of various network components as you design your initial network and plan for its future growth. In the following sections, I discuss many of the key networking components you're likely to consider in your network design process.

Connecting to Hubs

I introduced the concept of hubs earlier in this chapter. Hubs are the most common piece of networking equipment you're likely to require as you build and expand your network. They're used to implement both Ethernet and Token Ring networks, and can create just about any logical network topology using the physical star topology. Hubs can be cascaded to let you expand your network by adding additional hubs, cables, and nodes. (See Figure 5-2 for an example of cascading hubs.) As you've already seen, hubs come with various capacities and features.

TIP

Hubs are a critical component in most networks, so you need to safeguard them to avoid network downtime. In networks containing more than a couple of nodes, it's best to install your hub devices out of the way, preferably in a wiring cabinet or closet. This protects them from accidental or malicious tampering. I visited one installation where the hubs were velcroed under the network administrator's desk, and every time he sat down his knees knocked one or more cables out of the hub. He kept wondering why his network kept going down. Be smart — install your hubs out of harm's way.

USING DUMB HUBS

Dumb hubs are the simplest and least expensive form of hubs. A dumb hub simply acts as a central wiring box, accepting transmitted signals and passing them on to other nodes attached to the hub. (Which nodes get the signals next depends on how the hub is internally wired.) It contains no additional electronics to boost transmission signals or provide any network management features. Dumb hubs are becoming less popular these days, except in very small networks. To reflect this, some people refer to these devices as *workgroup hubs*.

USING SMART AND INTELLIGENT HUBS

Smart hubs represent the second generation of network hub hardware. They typically perform signal amplification to improve signal quality and cut down on lost data due to interference and attenuation. (I discussed these problems earlier in this chapter.) Some smart hubs give you limited network management capability by enabling you to program how the hub operates. Many smart hub products enable you to plug in diverse types of network cabling and tie them together into a single cohesive network. For example, you'll commonly find smart hubs that contain 16 UTP connections and one BNC coax connection.

CAUTION

A few smart hub products come in the form of an internal adapter that plugs into a computer's motherboard. Sometimes called *card hubs,* these devices are usually quite limited compared with their external hub counterparts. They also have the disadvantage of potentially soaking up a lot of the computer's CPU bandwidth and slowing it down significantly. I recommend that you leave card hubs out of your network design.

Intelligent hubs take a leap forward in features. They provide all the features commonly found in a smart hub, usually handle a more diverse array of cabling and network topologies, and offer more sophisticated management features. Some of these products enable you to easily and automatically switch connections to diagnose and fix problems with cables or ports. Others are able to sense trouble and quickly resolve certain types of problems by placing redundant hardware into service. Intelligent hub products can also play host to other types of network devices, including routers and bridges. (I discuss these devices later in this chapter.)

TIP

If you're developing a network containing more than 30 nodes, or you plan to grow it to that size soon, or you plan to evolve your LAN into a WAN, consider making the extra investment in an intelligent hub. The larger or more complex your network, the more you can take advantage of intelligent hub features.

Repeating Yourself

No, this isn't a section about rapid-fire rifles. Repeaters are among the simplest network devices – they're only slightly more complicated than cable. A *repeater* does exactly what its name implies. It takes an incoming signal into one end and repeats it verbatim out the other end. Sounds a lot like what a cable does, so why bother with a repeater? The answer is simple – repeaters amplify the incoming signal before repeating it.

Recall from earlier in this chapter that electrical resistance in cabling caused the transmitted signal to deteriorate over long distances. This attenuation phenomenon places strict limits on the cable length. What's more, as the transmitted signal gets very weak, it's more vulnerable to interference. Combining attenuation with interference yields a signal that's unrecognizable by its destination node. If you add a repeater along the way, while the signal is still recognizable, you can clean it up and boost its energy before sending it on its way.

The need for repeaters is generally dictated by the length of cables you run in your network. If you need to exceed the length specifications for a specific cable type, or if your environment contains a lot of external interference, you probably need to install repeaters. Your choice of hubs may also be a factor. If they already act as repeaters, you need only consider the length of cables between the hubs and the network nodes attached to them.

Don't rely heavily on using multiple repeaters on extremely long cable installations throughout your network. Although most repeaters will let you use more than one in a given run of cable, they typically impose limits on the maximum number of repeaters you can use on one stretch of cable. Be sure to check with the repeater manufacturer for these limitations before you design a network around them. Also, keep in mind that repeaters add delays to your network that can cause nodes to retransmit data, causing horribly slow network performance. A good rule of thumb is to keep the total number of repeaters in your network to four or less.

Some repeaters can transmit data from one type of cable to another, if they accept the right physical connections. This feature is especially useful if two different departments independently created two different types of networks, and it's your job to make them talk to each other. For example, a repeater with the right connectors can move data from a thinnet coax cable to a fiber-optic cable. If you need to join pieces of networks in more complex ways, consider using bridges instead of repeaters. For example, getting an Ethernet network to connect to a Token Ring network requires a bridge. I discuss bridges in the next section.

Building Bridges

Network *bridges* go a step beyond repeaters to link networks together in more meaningful ways. You can think of a bridge as a smart repeater. Like repeaters, bridges amplify signals and can convert signals from one cabling type to another. But if a portion of your network is overloaded with traffic and is dragging down the performance of the entire network, you can use a bridge to isolate the high-traffic segment. Moreover, you can use bridges to increase network reliability and security. Bridges can break your network into isolated segments so that a problem on one segment has no effect on the rest of the network. Also, if you have sensitive data traveling over the wire, you can isolate it to a specific segment to minimize the chance of eavesdropping.

A bridge is much smarter than a repeater because it analyzes a portion of the data transmitted across it. For example, a bridge typically builds and maintains its own list of network addresses on each network segment attached to it. (The network adapter in each node has its own unique network address.) As a result, the bridge allows only those transmissions destined for a different segment to pass through it. Some transmissions, called broadcasts, are destined for all nodes on the network. In this case, the bridge can forward the transmission to all attached segments.

Because they interpret the destination information in the data being transmitted, bridges can be programmed to filter transmissions – effectively isolating a network segment on one side of the bridge from the rest of the network. You may want to do this for one or more of the following reasons:

- **Performance** – If one part of your network is extremely busy, you may not be able to control the generation of traffic, but you can prevent it from affecting the entire network. Let's say that your marketing department is doing a lot of video conferencing over the network. This generates a large amount of data transmission. If you install a bridge between the marketing department and the rest of the network, you can isolate the other departments from marketing's video traffic. The marketing network segment won't see improved performance, but other departments will.
- **Reliability** – If one of your departments is trying out a new NOS, new network hardware, or something else that may cause problems on the network, you can keep them from bringing down the entire network. For example, if your MIS department is trying out a beta (pre-release) version of a new NOS before deploying it company-wide, you can install a bridge between MIS and the rest of the network. Then, even if a bug in the NOS brings the network to its knees, only the nodes on the MIS network segment will be affected.
- **Security** – If you want to keep honest people honest and make life more difficult for dishonest people, you may want to limit certain types of sensitive data to specific parts of the network. Doing this cuts down on the chance of eavesdropping. For example, your human resources

department may regularly share files over the network that contain salary levels, performance reviews, disciplinary records, and so forth. If you install a bridge between human resources and the rest of the network, the sensitive data won't travel across the bridge from the human resources network segment. Of course, if someone in that department explicitly sends the data across the bridge to a node on the other side, the bridge doesn't stop it. The bridge will only isolate data that's transmitted between nodes within the human resources segment.

NOTE

Because bridges require some level of intelligence, PCs can make great bridges. Standalone bridge devices are available, but PCs are frequently used to play this role. With at least two network adapters and appropriate software installed, a PC can perform all the functions of a standalone bridge device. Because the traffic passing through or being filtered by a bridge can be high, server-class computers are typically used to perform this function. In fact, you'll often see powerful PCs doing double duty as both file servers and bridges.

Tomorrow's Weather — Isolated Broadcast Storms

Broadcast storms occur when so many messages are broadcast on the network that the available network bandwidth is nearly saturated. This condition is sometimes caused by a failing network adapter or a bug in the network software. Either way, a broadcast storm can take down your entire network within minutes.

You can use bridges to isolate your network into multiple segments. Then, when a broadcast storm rolls in, the bridge can prevent the storm from spreading beyond the segment of the network where it started. Using a bridge this way is sort of like having a weather control machine that's able to confine the storm to an isolated area. The bridge won't help you predict the storm, but your network will do a better job of weathering it.

In the simplest case of bridge use, two LANs or network segments are connected by a single bridge. The first part of Figure 5-6 illustrates this basic configuration. In the real world, all but the very small networks require more than one bridge. When you need multiple bridges, a couple of network design choices are available – namely, cascading and backbone configurations. I discuss them in the following sections.

CASCADING BRIDGE CONFIGURATION

In the *cascading* bridge configuration, shown in the second part of Figure 5-6, network segments are linked together by bridges in a linear fashion. The overall network consists of a segment, a bridge, another segment, another bridge, and so forth. For data to get from segment A to segment D, it must travel across all the bridges and segments in between.

Of the two configurations, the cascading approach is the least efficient and least reliable approach. Why? There are three main reasons. First, bridges introduce some delay to the transmission. If a series of them introduces enough delay, the data will be resent and will generate a lot of unnecessary network traffic. Second, the more devices the data must pass through to reach its final destination, the more chance it has of encountering interference. Third, if a single bridge fails, all the segments (including bridges and nodes) become completely inaccessible to the rest of the network.

BACKBONE BRIDGE CONFIGURATION

Because of the efficiency and reliability problems inherent in the cascading approach, the *backbone* bridge configuration has become the more popular way to go. In this configuration, each bridge for each segment is directly linked to the others via a common cable called a backbone.

As you can see in the third part of Figure 5-6, the backbone configuration requires one additional bridge to support the same number of segments. As a result, this approach costs more than the cascading approach discussed in the previous section – but the efficiency and reliability limitations of the cascading approach are eliminated. Data travels through two bridges at most, regardless of the source and destination segments. This means shorter delays and less chance of interference. Also, the single failure of a bridge affects only the segment attached to that bridge; the remainder of the bridges and segments continue to function.

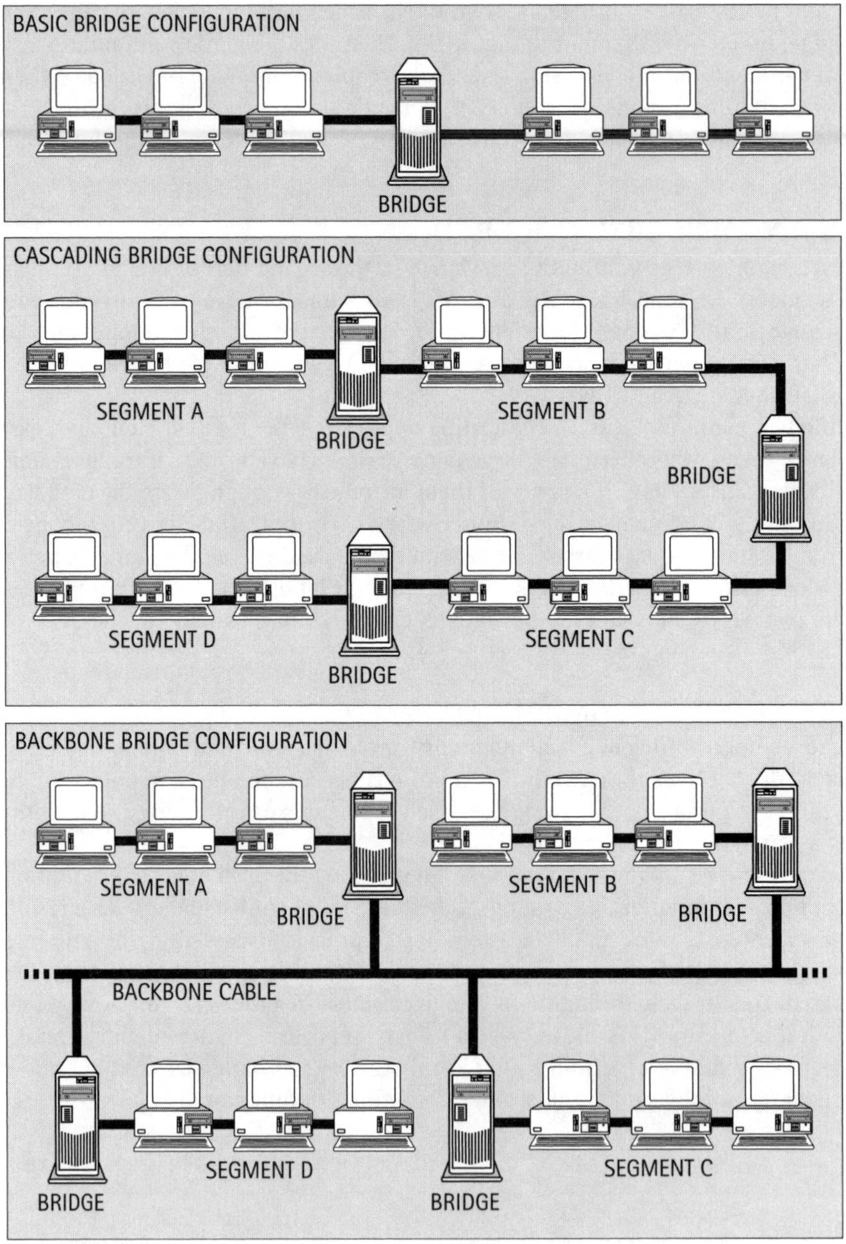

Figure 5-6: Bridges on the network can be configured in either cascading or backbone configuration

Although Figure 5-6 illustrates a bus topology for simplicity, network segments joined by bridges can have any network topology. If, for example, the segments used the star topology, you would attach the bridge to the hubs of the two segments being bridged. Keep in mind that you can also use bridges to connect network segments with differing topologies (bus, star, and ring) and differing technologies (Ethernet and Token Ring).

Turning on Switches

A network *switch* is similar in concept to both an intelligent hub and a bridge. Like an intelligent hub, a network switch is a software-manageable central wiring point for network cabling. Like a bridge, a switch also performs filtering functions to improve network performance. The main goal of a switch is to reduce network contention by creating temporary virtual connections between the source and destination nodes. A switch filters out traffic that isn't destined for a node attached to a specific port, so each node sees much less network traffic. It accomplishes this feat by switching ports on and off as needed.

On the surface, a switch looks much like a hub. Instead of simply passing incoming data back out to every port, however, a switch contains enough intelligence to learn (or be programmed with) the network node addresses associated with each port, and it stores them in an internal table. When data is transmitted, the switch creates a temporary path between the source and destination nodes, and the data is transmitted only through that path. No other nodes can see the data – only the source and destination nodes see it. The entire bandwidth of the network (say, 10Mbps) is provided for the data transmission on this dedicated – but temporary – path between the source and destination nodes. Also, as you might guess, collisions are reduced dramatically.

The physical topology of a switched network is a star — the switch plays the same physical role as a hub. However, the logical topology of a switched network doesn't really match a bus, ring, or star. The logical topology of a network that's based on switches is sometimes referred to as a *switched topology*. I discussed physical and logical topologies earlier in this chapter.

Some sophisticated switches provide features that support disaster recovery. They can accept alternate configurations that can go into effect if disaster strikes, or automatically detect and isolate network problems to prevent the entire network from going down. The unaffected portion of the switch and network can continue to operate normally, once the offending ports have been switched off. (Do you see yet where the term switch came from?)

There has been a tendency in the industry, over the past few years, to replace hubs with switches to improve network performance. As hubs become increasingly intelligent, though, it's getting more difficult to distinguish between switches and hubs. Switches still have the advantage over hubs of reducing extraneous network traffic and collisions.

Planning Trips with Routers

As your network grows in size and complexity, bridges may not be adequate to achieve efficient communication between all of your network segments. If you have several segments with differing network technologies and you're running different network protocols on them, you may need a device that can find the best path for moving and filtering data between segments. The good news is that this type of device is available – it's called a *router.* (With all due respect to Bob Vila, this isn't the same kind of router you'd use to make a countertop.)

Routers can do everything bridges can do, including filtering traffic, isolating traffic, and connecting network segments together. But they're more intelligent than bridges. A bridge can reach into the network addressing information of each transmission, and figure out how to improve the performance of delivering data.

Some routers talk to each other, sharing status, address, and routing information. (Routers use special network protocols behind the scenes to accomplish this. I discuss these protocols in Chapter 6.) The router can then use this information to avoid slow or failed network connections. Routers internally store and use information about known network addresses, how to connect to other networks, the possible paths between routers, and the costs of sending data over those paths. This information is kept in an internal table called a *routing table.* (It's sounding more and more like an episode of *This Old House*, isn't it?)

Bridges also keep track of information in routing tables; however, a bridge's information is limited to a list of the network addresses of nodes on either side of the bridge. Routing tables in routers, on the other hand, contain significantly more information about the entire network and the status of specific paths through it. It's unfortunate that manufacturers of these devices chose to use the term *routing table* to refer to these very different entities. Keep the context in mind when you see the term *routing table* used.

Actually, two major types of routers are available to you: static and dynamic. A *static router* requires that you manually enter into the routing table all the addresses, network configuration information, and routes to take for data delivery. Static routers always send data on exactly the same path, regardless of network conditions and regardless of whether the specified route is the shortest or most efficient path. Any changes in routes or network configurations must be entered manually into the routing table. All these inconveniences are balanced by the advantage of better security. The network administrator maintains complete control of how data is routed through the network.

Dynamic routers automatically discover all the routes through the network, so much less manual configuration is involved. Depending on a number of factors, dynamic routers make real-time decisions on how best to route each data transmission. As a router senses heavy traffic, slow response, or errors in one part of the network, sending a packet through that segment is given a higher cost relative to other paths. The next transmission will take a different, lower-cost path to its destination, if one is available. Some network administrators consider dynamic routers less secure, because they never know how a given transmission might be routed to its final destination.

TIP

Routers can take the form of dedicated, standalone devices, or you can implement them using a computer, network adapters, and appropriate routing software. Because a router's task can be both CPU-intensive and I/O-intensive, it's a good idea to use a server-class computer in the router role. Assigning a computer to be both a file server and a router simultaneously may not be efficient or practical. If the server is out of expansion slots for network adapters, if it's already fully burdened by its server tasks, if it's not conveniently located for interconnection with other segments, or if you use a high-speed backbone, you should consider installing a dedicated router.

Entering Gateways

No, I'm not going to talk about the famous computer manufacturer with the distinctive cow-like shipping cartons. The term *gateway* is often used generically to describe a wide range of network devices. A gateway is really just a translator that takes data transmitted in one form and converts it to another form. If I spoke only French and you spoke only Japanese, for example, we would need an interpreter that understands both languages and both cultures. The interpreter not only provides a translation of the words in both directions, but must also add any necessary inflections and additional words to ensure that the entire meaning is conveyed and understood. Also, the interpreter needs to follow appropriate protocol to avoid any international incidents. In the network world, a gateway functions as the interpreter.

A gateway can be implemented as hardware, software, or a combination of both. In each case, the gateway performs a translation and makes changes to the control information or data that's actually transmitted to its ultimate destination. Routers that translate between different network technologies are often referred to as gateways. In this case, the gateway (router) translates between two incompatible technologies (such as Ethernet and Token Ring). Gateways are also used to translate between incompatible network protocols. (I discuss protocols in Chapter 6 – but for now you can think of the language translation analogy.) Gateway Service for NetWare is a classic example of a protocol gateway that translates between a Windows NT Server-based network and Novell's NetWare.

NOTE

One common use of gateways is for translation between PC-based networks and mainframes or minicomputers. Many large systems don't recognize computers attached to LANs. But if you need access to your minicomputer or mainframe from nodes on the PC network, you can designate one computer as the gateway. Using appropriate software, nodes on the network can access many of the resources provided by the large systems. Microsoft SNA Server is an example of this type of gateway — it translates between a Windows NT Server network and IBM's SNA (systems network architecture).

The term *gateway* is used to refer to a piece of software that translates data between incompatible application formats. For example, you'll frequently see gateways used to tie two or more incompatible e-mail systems together. If you send an e-mail message from your AOL account to an Internet address, that message must go through an AOL-to-Internet gateway. An Internet-to-AOL gateway is required to translate incoming e-mail. Likewise, if your organization uses Lotus cc:Mail, you need both a cc:Mail-to-Internet gateway and an Internet-to-cc:Mail gateway if you want to send and receive e-mail to and from Internet addresses.

Summary

Your understanding of the available network topologies, technologies, connection options, and specialized network equipment is important as you design, plan, implement, and grow your network. In this chapter, you've learned about the bus, star, and ring network topologies. You've also seen how physical and logical topologies can differ. I then introduced you to the two predominant network technologies – Ethernet and Token Ring. Next, you attended a crash course in network cabling and wireless technologies for LANs and WANs. Finally, you learned about several key network components that perform critical roles as your network grows in size and complexity.

In Chapter 6, you'll study a model of network design that illustrates how network hardware and software components function and interact. You'll learn about Windows 98 network protocols, their strengths and weaknesses, and how to chose the right protocols for your network. You'll also see how the devices I've discussed in this chapter interact with network protocols. Finally, you'll understand how the NOS uses network protocols to achieve meaningful communication across a network.

Chapter 6

Passing Data Across a Network

IN THIS CHAPTER

- Examining the layers of modular networking architecture
- Understanding and using network device drivers and protocols
- Exploring the differences between interconnectivity and interoperability

IN THIS CHAPTER, you'll learn about an industry standard model of network design that illustrates how networking components – both hardware and software – work together. You'll also learn about the network protocols in Windows 98 and how to choose between them. Finally, you'll see how network interconnectivity and interoperability are achieved. By the end of this chapter, you'll have a solid conceptual foundation for Windows 98 networking components.

Examining the Layers of Networking

Windows 98 and other network operating systems have implemented a layered, modular networking architecture. The architecture is based on an industry standard called the Open Systems Interconnect (OSI) Reference Model. First released in 1984, it has become an international standard and guide to network design.

The OSI model defines an approach to networking in which each layer is responsible for a very specific portion of the networking function. The OSI reference model is, as its name implies, a model – most real-world protocols don't adhere to it exactly, but use it as a basis for their designs. The model provides a solid framework for understanding the software and hardware components of networking and how they interact with each other. It also provides a starting point for network troubleshooting by describing where network components fit and how they're supposed to function.

> **NOTE** One of the main goals in developing the OSI model was to provide a blueprint to hardware and software vendors, enabling them to develop individual networking components that would work together compatibly. Although the OSI model doesn't match most existing networks, it's gone a long way in establishing enough standardization to enable components from different manufacturers to work well together.

Understanding the OSI Reference Model

The OSI reference model describes the flow of data in a network from the lowest layer, representing the physical network connection, to the highest layer, representing the services used directly by applications. As shown in Figure 6-1, data passes from one layer to the next in its journey from its source to its destination. Each layer communicates directly with the layer immediately above it and immediately below it. This approach yields a simple, modular design in which each layer plays a specific, well-defined role.

The goal of each layer is to perform its assigned responsibility as a service to the layers above it. Its secondary goal is to hide all the gory details of the lower layers from the layers above it. Ideally, a layer should be able to treat the layer below it as a magic black box that does whatever needs to be done to complete its task. In a sense, each successive layer, as you travel up the OSI model, represents a higher level of abstraction.

When two network nodes communicate with each other, the network software at each layer assumes it's communicating directly with the same layer on the other node. A sort of virtual communication path exists between corresponding layers on the two nodes. You can see these virtual communication paths in Figure 6-1. No virtual path is needed between corresponding physical layers, because they're physically connected to each other by the network hardware itself.

Consider how data is sent from an application on Node A to an application on Node B, illustrated in Figure 6-1. The data begins its journey at the highest networking layer on Node A and travels down each successive layer on Node A until it reaches the physical network. On its way, additional control information is added to the data to ensure that it gets to its intended recipient (Node B) in good shape. The information travels over the physical network, and arrives at the lowest layer on Node B. It then travels up each successive layer on Node B until it reaches the application there. On its way up through the Node B layers, the control information that was added on Node A is stripped off, layer by layer, until the application receives the original data that was sent by the application on Node A.

In the following sections, I discuss in detail the roles and responsibilities of each layer in the OSI reference model. You'll see how these layers relate to the components of Windows 98 networking and to the network hardware components you learned about in Chapter 5. By the end of this discussion, you'll view the seven-layer networking model as a seven-layer piece of cake.

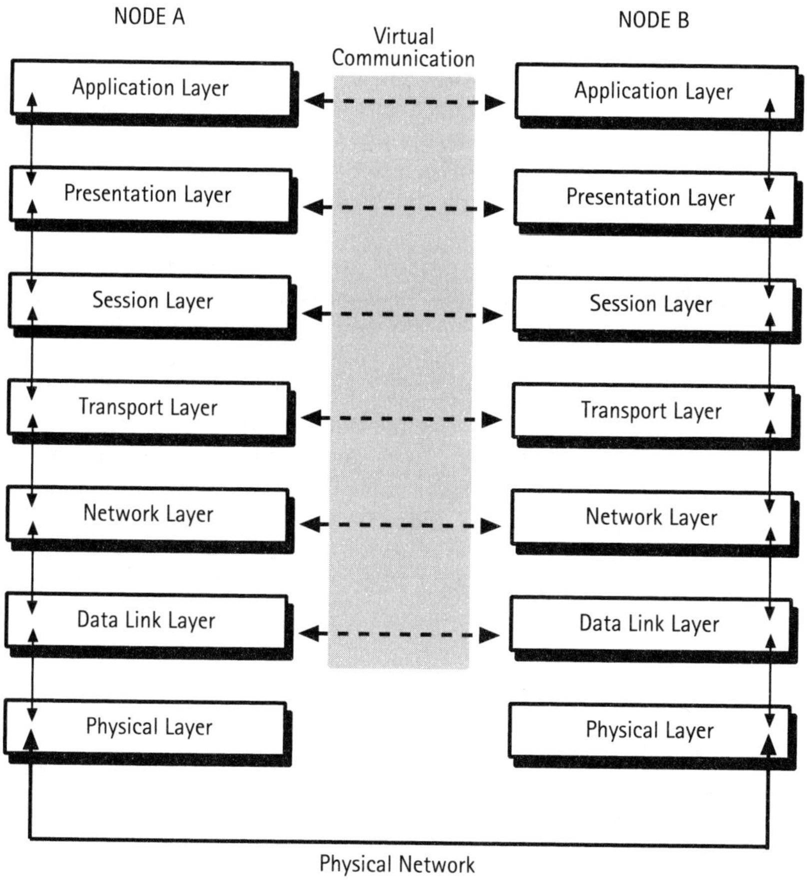

Figure 6-1: The OSI reference model divides network communication into seven layers.

Exploring the Physical Layer

The *physical layer*, or *layer 1*, is responsible for transmitting raw binary data on the network cable (or over a wireless connection). As the lowest layer of the OSI reference model, it's the closest to the actual network hardware. In fact, it includes the hardware associated with the network cable itself. The physical layer deals with both the physical specifications of how network nodes are connected and the electrical details of how raw data bits are actually transmitted and received over the connection medium.

On the hardware front, the physical layer spells out the specific requirements for the network cable itself. It defines all aspects of cabling, connectors, and cable placement rules – even down to the number of pins on cable connectors and which signals each pin carries. Of course, in a wireless network there's no cable to specify. In this environment, the physical layer treats the wireless medium as a virtual cable, specifying all the requirements and characteristics of the physical (or should

I say metaphysical?) network connection. The physical layer also specifies the network adapter that attaches a node to the connection medium.

Beyond the hardware itself, the physical layer defines exactly how data bits are represented when they're transmitted on the cable. It includes such details as what voltage represents a binary 1, what voltage represents a binary 0, the timing of these binary signals, and so forth. In a wireless environment, the physical layer specifies similar details that fully describe how raw binary data is transmitted through the air.

A repeater operates exclusively at the physical layer of the OSI model. The data packets handled by the repeater are exactly the same coming in as they are going out, so you can't use a repeater to link two different network technologies. In that sense, the repeater is no more functional than a length of network cable. However, a repeater can convert from one physical medium to another (that is, from one type of cable to another). And, of course, it boosts the signals along the way.

All other network devices that transmit or receive any type of information on the network also operate at the physical layer of the OSI model. They must abide by the physical specifications of the cable and transmit according to the physical layer's electrical and timing rules. As you'll see later in this chapter, however, the smarter network devices also operate at higher levels of the OSI model as they perform their tasks.

Exploring the Data Link Layer

The *data link layer*, or *layer 2*, takes the raw stream of data bits transmitted on the physical layer and begins to apply some structure to it. The data link layer packages the raw stream of data into manageable, logical chunks of information called *frames*. (The official OSI term for a frame is a *physical-layer-service-data-unit*. Be grateful that I stick with the term *frame* throughout this book.)

A frame includes the data to be transmitted as well as information about the source and destination of the transmission. A frame also includes information that helps the recipient of the transmission detect whether the data arrived intact. This additional information essentially surrounds the original data – you might even say the additional information *frames* the data. The actual format of the additional frame information differs depending on the network technology. Ethernet frames, for example, don't have the same format as Token Ring frames. The data link layer contains the knowledge of how to form correct data frames to match the network technology in use.

The data link is responsible for preparing data frames for transmission, receiving data frames, managing the network access method, and assuring error-free node-to-node communication. The process of detecting and recovering from transmission errors is the most complex activity undertaken by the data link layer. Beyond the data actually transmitted, the sending and receiving nodes must somehow communicate the status of transmitted data and arrange for retransmission whenever something goes wrong. In a nutshell, the sender must wait for the receiver to acknowledge that the data arrived intact. Let's look at a simple case of a sender transmitting one data frame to a receiver:

1. The data link layer on the sending node calculates an *error-detecting code* and embeds it into the data frame. The sender then transmits the frame through the physical layer to the receiving node, and waits for the receiver to send an acknowledgment frame.
2. The data link layer on the receiving node receives the data frame from the physical layer, and uses the error-detecting information embedded in the frame to determine whether the data arrived intact. Depending on the results, one of the following takes place:
   a. If the receiver finds that the data arrived safely, it immediately sends an acknowledgment frame to the sender, and then passes the received data frame up to the next layer. The transmission was successful.
   b. If the receiver finds that the data was corrupted in transit, it completely discards the data frame. No acknowledgment frame is sent.
3. Back at the sender, if an acknowledgment frame arrives, all is well and life goes on. The whole process can start again at Step 1.
4. If the sender doesn't receive an acknowledgment frame within a certain timeout period, it retransmits the original data frame to the receiver. The process starts over at Step 1 again. In this situation, the sender assumes that one of three things happened:
   a. The data frame never arrived at its destination, so no acknowledgment frame was sent. This can happen if the destination address is corrupted during transmission, for example.
   b. The data frame was found by the receiver to be corrupt and was discarded, so no acknowledgment frame was sent.
   c. The data arrived intact, and the receiver sent back an acknowledgment frame, but the acknowledgment frame itself was lost.

In the last scenario, the data actually arrived at its destination unharmed, but the sender has no way of knowing this because the acknowledgment didn't come back. So it has no other choice than to blindly retransmit the original data frame and hope for an acknowledgment frame to return. Life just became more complex for the data link layer — the receiver must now recognize and throw away duplicate data frames when they arrive.

Much Ado About Errors

What's all this about error checking? If the network cables and other network devices are all installed and working properly, don't we have a reliable network? These are reasonable questions, considering the investment of time and money that goes into planning and implementing a reliable network.

But the fact of life is that errors can and do occur on all networks. Errors can be caused by external interference from the environment, internal interference between wires in a cable, failing or marginal network devices, signal attenuation on excessively long cables, and even bugs in network software. Because errors are inevitable, it's important to have an easy way of detecting them and recovering from them. You wouldn't want corrupted data to travel across a network and be stored in a file on a server – especially if that file contains your payroll information.

Therefore, the data link layer bends over backwards to make sure that data is delivered reliably to its destination. That way, none of the other layers above it has to worry about whether the data transmitted arrived at its intended destination.

NOTE

This sequence of events is a bit oversimplified. In a real network, you wouldn't want the data link layer on the sending node to sit idle, pining for an acknowledgment from the receiver. If the layers above it have more data frames to send over the network, the data link layer should continue sending them as quickly as possible. Meanwhile, data frames from other nodes are arriving from the network and need to be error-checked and passed up to the upper layers. Thus, the data link layer must keep track of all the outstanding data frames it has transmitted, and process acknowledgment frames as they arrive. These activities add yet another dimension of complexity to the data link layer.

CHECKING FOR ERRORS

The whole mechanism of providing reliable data transmission hinges on the error-detecting code I mentioned earlier. What is this error-detecting code, and how is it used to detect transmission errors? Before transmitting a data frame, the sender calculates what is known as a CRC, which stands for either cyclic redundancy code or cyclic redundancy check (depending on the prevailing wind direction). A CRC can be very simple – as simple as the arithmetic sum of all the data bytes being transmitted. If the sum overflows the width of the CRC, the extra bits are simply lopped off the end. CRCs can also be quite complex, involving all sorts of mathematical formulas that most sane folks don't want or need to understand. (There's a branch of computer science that deals with finding more efficient and complex ways to generate CRCs. Believe me, life's too short for you to worry about the internal details of CRC generation.)

Today, CRCs are commonly generated in hardware on the network adapter itself. On the receiving side, the network adapter recalculates the CRC based on the data in the frame. It then compares this CRC with the one embedded in the received data frame. If they match exactly, the data arrived safely and the sender transmits an acknowledgment frame. If the two CRCs don't match, the data frame is known to be corrupt and is discarded.

NOTE

It's important to keep in mind that the CRC is just an error-detecting code. Its purpose is purely to signal whether or not the data arrived intact. If it signals data corruption, the entire data frame must be retransmitted. Later in this book, and in other literature, you'll encounter discussions of *error-correcting* codes. These codes contain enough information to reconstruct corrupted data when certain types of transmission errors occur. An error-correcting code can restore data to its original form without the need for retransmission.

Are We There Yet?

Now that I've defined the physical and data link layers, are we ready to transmit data from node to node on the network? The answer is a qualified "yes." With the combination of these two layers, you can transmit and receive small chunks of data and ensure that the data arrives at its destination intact. For truly meaningful communication to take place between nodes, however, we need to employ some of the higher layers. I discuss them later in this chapter.

In the real world, the combined physical and data link layers of the OSI reference model are typically dealt with in the network adapter hardware, the physical network connection, and the network adapter device driver. So, all of this frame communication is made possible by a combination of hardware and software.

CREATING SUBLAYERS

You've seen that the data link layer has quite a few responsibilities to fulfill. As a result, this layer can become fairly complicated, in terms of both hardware and software. One way to simplify and modularize a design involves dividing up the problem into smaller, more specialized chunks. The data link layer can be split into two distinct *sublayers*, each taking on a specific subset of responsibilities. (It's ironic that adding more layers, terminology, and acronyms to the OSI model is designed to simplify your life.)

The lower of the two sublayers is called the *media access control sublayer*, or *MAC sublayer*. As its name implies, the MAC sublayer handles all the details of managing the network technology's access method. In an Ethernet environment, the MAC sublayer deals with implementing the CSMA/CD access method, which I described in Chapter 5. In a Token Ring environment, the MAC sublayer manages the token passing access method (also described in Chapter 5). The idea behind the MAC sublayer is to hide or encapsulate the access method management functions from the rest of the data link layer's responsibilities. The MAC layer is also responsible for ensuring an error-free communication path between nodes by retransmitting data frames and throwing away duplicate frames when necessary.

The higher of the two sublayers is known as the *logical link control sublayer*, or *LLC sublayer*. (I know it sounds like one of those new limited liability companies, but it's not.) The LLC is primarily responsible for managing connections between network nodes, and for controlling the flow of data frames using the acknowledgment scheme I discussed earlier in this chapter. By being split out as a separate sublayer, the LLC can do its job without worrying about the lower-level transmission details handled in the MAC sublayer. Figure 6-2 illustrates the relationship between the data link sublayers and the seven-layer OSI model.

Addressing Addresses

Just as each home or business has a unique postal address assigned to it, each network adapter also has a unique address assigned to it. Your home address was probably assigned by a builder or local government entity. A network adapter is typically assigned its address by the adapter manufacturer. (This address is sometimes referred to as a *node address*, but this isn't entirely accurate. A network node – a computer, printer, or other device – may contain more than one network adapter. If this is the case, a network node might have more than one address on the network.)

Because so many entities on a computer and on a network have addresses, it's sometimes important to be more explicit when talking about them. Strictly speaking, a network adapter address is known as a *MAC sublayer address*, or simply *MAC address*. When you see or hear this term (and you will), you'll know that the address in question is the unique address assigned to a network adapter.

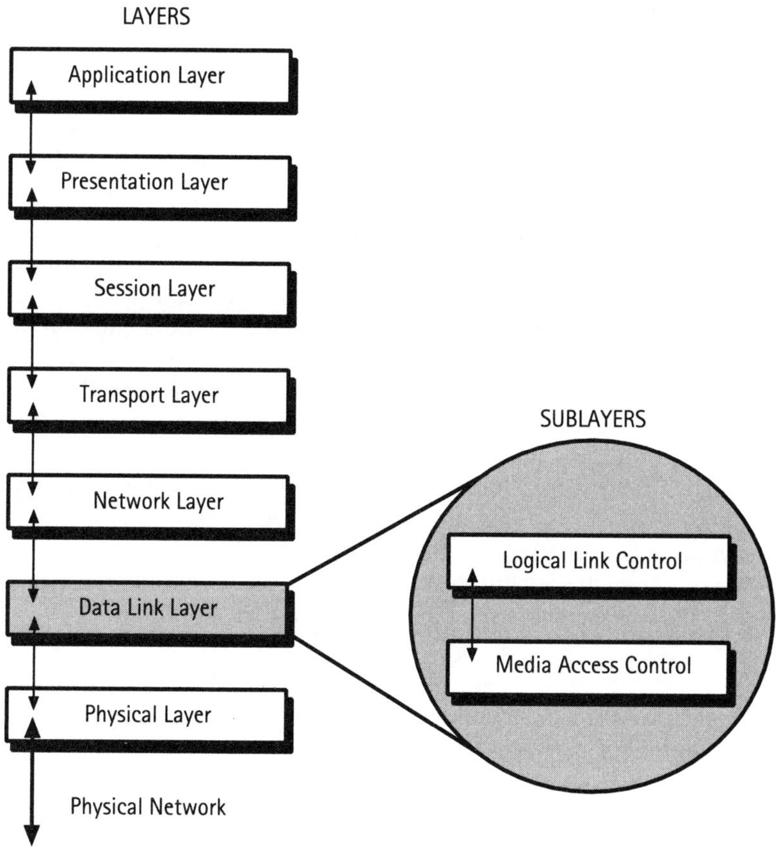

Figure 6-2: The data link layer is divided into two sublayers — logical link control (LLC) and media access control (MAC).

NOTE A network bridge, which I discussed in Chapter 5, operates at the data link layer. More specifically, bridges work at the MAC sublayer level. In fact, bridges are sometimes referred to as MAC layer bridges. (Mac Layer Bridges is the one Bridges son that chose a non-show-business career. But he shows up on the networks.)

NOTE Windows 98 network adapter drivers and driver support functions operate at the data link layer of the OSI reference model. The drivers provide low-level services to Windows 98 network protocols, which are implemented at higher layers of the model. I discuss network adapter drivers and network protocols later in this chapter.

Exploring the Network Layer

The *network layer,* or *layer 3,* relies on the layers below it for rudimentary node-to-node communication. It's responsible for addressing data transmissions and translating logical addresses (or names) into physical addresses. In addition, the network layer determines the route the data will take from the sender to the receiver, based on network conditions and other factors. The network layer operates on data *packets,* just as the data link layer operates on data frames. Data packets contain the original data, of course, along with some additional addressing and control information. A large packet may need to be translated into a sequence of smaller frames before the network layer sends it to the data link layer and out onto the network.

The network layer adds important network addressing information that's used to select a route for the packet, to send it efficiently on its way to its final destination, even if that destination is on another network. You may wonder why it's necessary to select a route at all. When you plan a trip, there are usually many possible routes between you and your destination. Some are long, some are short, some slow, some temporarily congested. After weighing all these factors, you select a route and go with it. The network layer does the same thing. If it didn't, it would have to flood all possible paths on the network with the same packet. For performance reasons, it's much better to select a route and send that packet on that specific route.

Different networks select routes in different ways. One may use a static, manually updated routing table — always selecting the exact same route between two given nodes. Another may dynamically determine the best possible route by monitoring the network for traffic conditions and slow or failing network segments. Regardless of how a route is chosen, the network layer provides the addressing information that makes routing possible.

A key responsibility of the network layer involves breaking up large data packets into smaller pieces and then reassembling them at the other end. Why is this important? The lower layers of the OSI reference model are restricted to sending and receiving data frames of certain sizes. If you want to transmit a file or some other chunk of data that exceeds the maximum data frame size, you're out of luck – unless you have a way of breaking up and reassembling the data. That's where the network layer comes in. On the sending side, it detects when a packet is too long, and breaks it into several separate data frames. It also embeds enough information in the frame to enable the receiving end to package the data together into its original form.

Routers operate at the network layer. They can route packets across multiple networks. A router can reach into a data packet, reading and interpreting the embedded addressing information stored inside the packet. It can then use this information to update its routing tables and make more intelligent decisions when other packets come along.

Exploring the Transport Layer

The *transport layer,* or *layer 4,* is responsible for ensuring that all packets are delivered efficiently, delivered without error, and processed in the same sequence they were sent, with no missing or duplicate packets. Using acknowledgments and error recovery, the transport layer provides a reliable source-to-destination (or end-to-end) packet delivery service. In this regard, the transport layer is similar to the data link layer, which provides reliable node-to-node delivery. The difference is one of scope – the transport layer guarantees delivery from beginning to end, on a path that may visit many nodes along the way.

> NOTE: Because of transmission errors, packets may not be delivered in the same order in which they were originally sent. For example, packets that never arrive at their destination are retransmitted, creating the potential for packets to arrive out of their original sequence. The transport layer is responsible for ensuring that packets are processed on the receiving end in the same order in which they were originally sent — even if they were received in a different order. Therefore, sequencing information is part of what the transport layer adds to the transmission.

Once you have the transport layer in place (along with all the layers below it), the OSI reference model begins to look like a real live network. With it, a process running on one node can communicate with a process on another node. The two processes can send data to each other in the form of *messages*. The transport layer works with messages passed from the layers above it (or sometimes directly from a process). It converts the messages into packets before passing them down to the network layer. At the receiving end, the transport layer converts packets into messages before delivering them to higher layers.

The transport layer is interested in packaging data for efficient transmission. It may take a very long message and break it into multiple sequential packets. In this regard, the transport layer acts like the network layer, which breaks long packets into smaller data frames. The transport layer also does the opposite. It may combine several short messages into one long packet before passing it down to the network layer. On the receiving end, the transport layer may need to assemble multiple packets into one long message, or break a packet into several short messages. Control information embedded in the packet by the transport layer lets the receiving end know how the packet should be converted back to the original message (or messages).

Exploring the Session Layer

The *session layer*, or *layer 5*, is an application-oriented layer. It enables application processes on two different nodes to establish, communicate over, and terminate an end-to-end connection called a *session*. Instead of focusing on delivery of individual messages, which is already handled quite nicely by the transport layer, the session layer focuses on managing the entire dialog between the two processes. It controls who transmits when, and for how long. And just as the transport layer ensures in-sequence delivery of packets, the session layer ensures in-sequence delivery of messages.

The session layer introduces the concept of data *checkpoints*. Periodically, during the session, one process can inform the other that it has received and processed the data sent up to a certain point in the conversation. This notification is the checkpoint. If the network fails or the connection is lost for some other reason, only messages transmitted after the last checkpoint need to be retransmitted.

Transaction-based processing is also handled by the session layer. It provides a mechanism to ensure that a sequence of individual commands is carried out completely or not carried out at all. For example, if you're updating a database over the network, you may need to execute a sequence of three database commands to complete the transaction. If you don't execute all of the commands, the database could be left in an inconsistent state. By treating the three commands as an "all or nothing" transaction, you can avoid this problem.

The session layer also deals with security issues during the establishment of a session, to ensure that both ends have the appropriate rights to create and use the connection. These activities may include looking up security information based on the users running the applications, or even triggering a dialog box that asks a user for a password.

NOTE

Windows 98 network protocols, which I discuss later in this chapter, are typically implemented in the session, transport, and network layers of the OSI reference model. In other words, network protocols perform the functions and offer the services that these three layers are defined to provide. There are exceptions to this rule, but most protocols live within the confines of these layers.

Exploring the Presentation Layer

It make more sense to think of the *presentation layer*, or *layer 6*, as a transformation layer or translation layer. But we're stuck with its given name. The presentation layer controls the formats used to exchange data between network nodes. At the sending node, the presentation layer translates application data into a commonly recognized form. On the receiving node, it translates the data from the common form to an application-specific form.

Layer 6 is called the presentation layer because it controls how the network presents itself to your applications. What specific translations does the presentation layer perform? The possible responsibilities include character set conversion, data encryption and decryption, data compression and expansion, file format translation, and graphics command expansion.

This is the one layer in which the original application data can change before it goes out on the network and after it arrives from the network. In all other layers, you can assume that the original data portion of the message, packet, or frame is left unaltered.

Direct Your Attention to the Redirector

Windows 98 includes a key component called the network *redirector.* It intercepts all I/O requests from applications and determines whether they can be handled locally or must be handled over the network. If a request can't be handled locally, the redirector *redirects* the request to the network. In addition to basic file services such as open, read, and write, the redirector provides mechanisms for sending messages directly between applications. It intercepts all requests to transmit or receive data to or from a remote network resource, and shields the application from the fact that the resources are networked.

Microsoft uses the term *redirector* to refer to this NOS component in all of their operating systems, including MS-DOS, Windows 3.1, Windows for Workgroups, Windows 95, Windows 98, and Windows NT. (If you're familiar with NetWare, Novell uses the term *requester* to refer to this component of their NOS.) Windows 98 includes two redirectors. Client for Microsoft Networks provides support for Microsoft networking. Microsoft Client for NetWare Networks supports Novell NetWare networking, if your Windows 98 nodes need to talk to NetWare servers.

The redirector operates at the application and presentation layers of the OSI reference model. All of the services provided by the redirector fall into one of these two layers. A network software component called the *server* (not to be confused with network nodes that act as servers) also operates at this level, and services remote requests from the redirector. The redirector and server components communicate with each other using a protocol called *SMB,* which stands for *Server Message Block.*

All the lower layers of the OSI reference model support these high-level application functions. Freed from the details of data translation, session management, reliable message delivery, routing, and low-level communication, the application layer focuses on access to network resources, control of the flow of messages, and helping applications recover gracefully from error conditions.

Gluing the Model Together

As you've seen in the discussion of each of the seven OSI model layers, each layer adds some additional information to the data for its own purposes as the data makes its way down the layers to the physical network. A conglomeration of the original data and all the additional control information is sent over the network to its final destination. As the data makes its way up through the layers on the destination node, the control information is removed by each successive layer until the original application data is presented to the application. The layers of control information are added to the message (or packet or frame) either as *headers* (attached to the beginning of the message) or as *trailers* (attached to the end of the message). Figure 6-3 illustrates this concept.

NOTE

The illustration of layered control information shown in Figure 6-3 isn't completely accurate, because some layers either break messages into several smaller chunks, or collect small messages and create larger chunks. But the concept of adding and removing headers and/or trailers at each layer is accurate, no matter how messages are broken up or put back together.

Another way to think of this layering technique is to consider an onion or one of those nesting toy dolls you find at airport gift shops. As application data (the core of the onion or the smallest nested doll) travels down the layers of the OSI model, new layers are added. On the receiving end, the same layers are removed in succession until you're left with the original core data.

Now consider the illustration of the data packet in Figure 6-3. If you take the lowest packet and turn it on its end, it appears to have different layers of information stacked on top of one another. Protocols running at each layer of the model added their information to the top of this stack. Can you see why the vertical list of protocols is often called the *protocol stack*? (Now where did I put that pancake mix?)

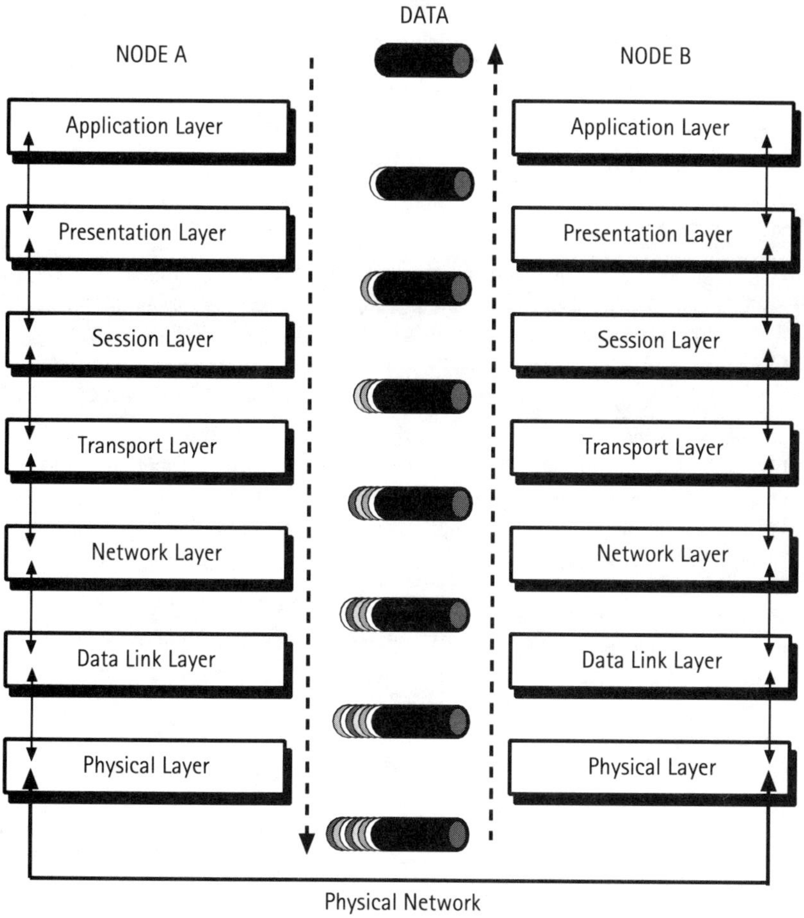

Figure 6-3: Each layer adds control information to the data before transmission and removes it after transmission.

Understanding Network Device Drivers

Now that you've been exposed to the OSI reference model and how it relates to the major NOS and hardware components, it's important to understand how the major software components fit together. Just as I did with the OSI model, I start with the lowest-level software component – the network adapter device driver. Then, later in this chapter, I discuss the network protocols that make use of these drivers.

Gaining a Driver's Perspective

If you've been around computers for very long, you may be aware that the creation of device drivers — the software that directly manipulates hardware devices — is considered something of a mysterious black art. Device drivers are traditionally very difficult to develop and test, and few engineers dare to tread in this nether region of software development.

In the network device driver arena, a significant revolution has been taking place over the past ten years. In the late 1980s, no standards existed for network drivers. Network adapter manufacturers had to write their own drivers, and each of those drivers had to include the network protocol as well. The combined device driver and network protocol occupied a single block of code. (This type of driver is sometimes called a *monolithic driver* — similar in design to the huge slab in *2001: A Space Odyssey*.) To support a new protocol, the manufacturer had to write a whole new monolithic driver. To support a brand new operating system platform, the manufacturer had to write a complete set of new drivers to cover all the supported network protocols. The situation was a living nightmare.

As the need to run more than one network protocol increased, another flaw in the monolithic driver approach surfaced. Because each network adapter could have only one device driver, it could also run only one protocol. If you required two protocols, you had to have two network adapters each running different drivers. Unfortunately, many of these monolithic drivers were designed to assume the node contained only one network adapter. When a second adapter was introduced, many of these drivers fell on their faces.

A solution was needed that would decouple the network protocol from the device-dependent part of the driver. A standard interface was needed between these two layers, enabling virtually any protocol to work on top of any device-specific driver. Moreover, it would be great if the solution allowed the drivers to work on more than one operating system platform.

Introducing NDIS

The *Network Driver Interface Specification* (*NDIS*) describes the software interface between a network adapter driver and the underlying network hardware, the network protocol above the driver, and the operating system on which the driver runs. Microsoft and 3Com jointly developed the NDIS standard, which has gone through several revisions to reach the current version of NDIS 5.0. Here are the advantages to the NDIS approach to network adapter drivers:

- **Single driver per adapter model** – NDIS eliminates the need to create a new driver for each combination of adapters and protocols. The manufacturers can create a single NDIS driver for a new network adapter, and not worry about network protocols at all. Protocols are completely decoupled from NDIS device drivers.
- **Multiple protocol support** – A properly written NDIS driver can support multiple network protocols running above it. As protocols are added, removed, or replaced, the underlying NDIS driver doesn't change at all.
- **Multiple adapter support** – NDIS drivers can run on multiple network adapters within the same computer. This makes it easy to expand network capacity or create bridges and routers using multiple adapters and appropriate software.
- **Multiple operating system support** – Properly written NDIS drivers can run without change on Windows 95, Windows 98, and Windows NT. Digital Equipment Corporation (DEC) uses the NDIS approach under VMS and Ultrix. Network adapter manufacturers need only develop one NDIS driver to support multiple operating systems.

Of course, network adapter drivers aren't the only components that need to abide by NDIS rules. Network protocols that run on top of NDIS drivers must be written to communicate with the drivers through the well-defined NDIS interface. Once a network protocol is written to the NDIS standard, it can run on top of any NDIS driver without requiring modification. Everybody wins.

TIP

NDIS has become an industry standard approach to network adapter device drivers on the Windows operating system platforms. Windows 98 and other Microsoft networking products include NDIS drivers for the most popular network adapters. Adapter manufacturers also supply their own NDIS drivers. Before investing in network adapter hardware, be sure to check whether NDIS drivers are available for the network adapters you plan to use.

Examining NDIS Interfaces

One important goal of NDIS is to isolate the driver from the operating system details, enabling it to run unchanged on multiple operating systems. This is accomplished by supplying a library of common OS functions on each platform. The library is the *NDIS wrapper*, since it isolates the driver from its surrounding environment. So, NDIS defines three standard interfaces:

- **Driver/hardware interface** – The NDIS driver communicates directly with the underlying network hardware in a standard way. Conceptually, this interface exists below the NDIS driver and above the network adapter hardware.
- **Driver/protocol interface** – The NDIS driver and the network protocol communicate with each other through a standard interface. Conceptually, this interface exists above the NDIS driver and below the network protocol.
- **Driver/operating system interface** – The NDIS driver communicates with the operating system, in a standard way. Conceptually, this NDIS wrapper interface surrounds the NDIS driver.

NDIS drivers and the NDIS interfaces operate within the MAC sublayer of the OSI model's data link layer. Figure 6-4 illustrates the relationship of the NDIS interfaces to the OSI reference model. The shaded areas in Figure 6-4 represent interfaces between layers or interfaces to the operating system. They don't constitute actual layers themselves.

TIP

At about the same time NDIS first appeared, Novell and Apple developed a similar network device driver model called Open Datalink Interface, or ODI. It provides essentially the same capabilities as NDIS. Microsoft operating systems support ODI drivers as well as NDIS drivers, but they provide better technical support for NDIS. If your network adapter hardware has both NDIS and ODI drivers available, opt to run the NDIS driver.

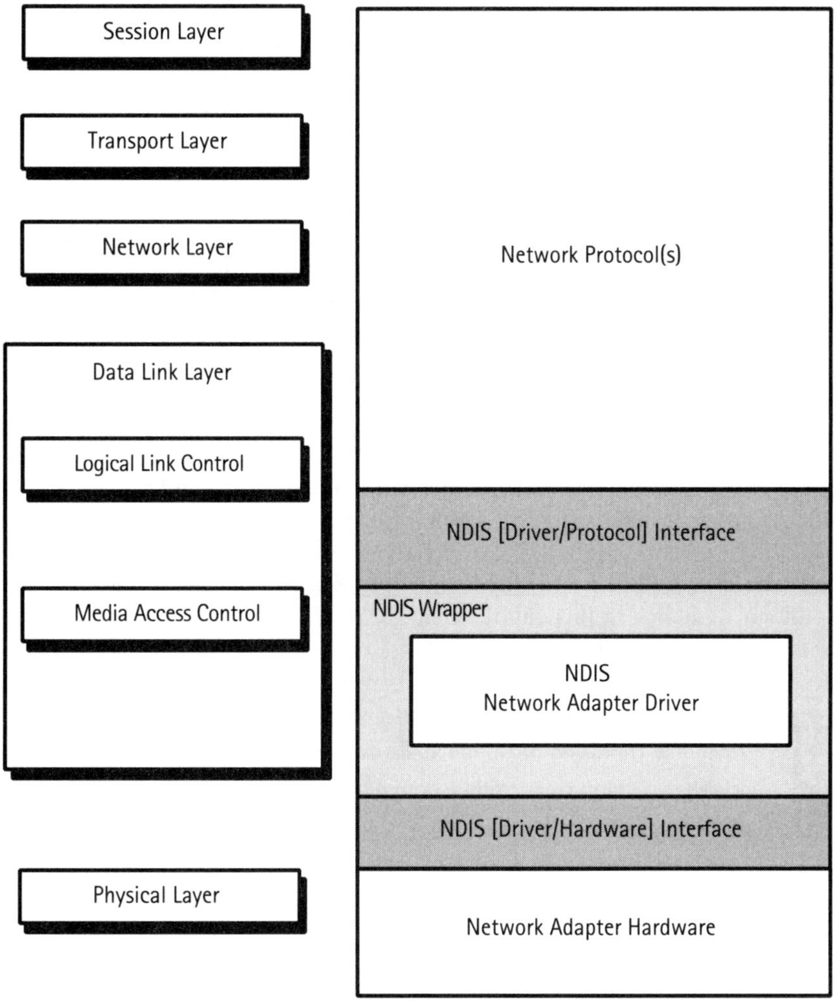

Figure 6-4: NDIS drivers and interfaces exist in the MAC sublayer.

Understanding Network Protocols

Now that you understand the Windows 98 approach to low-level network adapter device drivers, it's time to climb up to the network protocol above the driver. Recall that a network protocol is a language and set of rules that nodes agree to use to communicate over the network. Protocols exist in one form or another at every layer of the OSI reference model. In this section, however, I zoom in on the protocols that live in the session, transport, and network layers of the model. Network protocols at this level are sometimes called *transport protocols*, to distinguish them from protocols that operate in other layers.

Many different network protocols exist, at all layers of the OSI model. Windows 98 includes support for several industry standard network protocols, and it lets you install other protocols supplied by third parties. If you need to, you can run more than one protocol on a node at the same time – even on a single network adapter. In the following sections, I cover the most popular and useful protocols you're likely to encounter or at least consider in your Windows 98 network.

Understanding NetBEUI

NetBEUI (pronounced *net-boo-ee*) is a network protocol that was originally developed in 1985 by IBM. Although it has some shortcomings, it's used in all Microsoft networking products (including MS-DOS and all versions of Windows and Windows NT) as well as IBM's OS/2 and LanServer products. In a small, purely Microsoft network, NetBEUI is a good network protocol choice. In fact, it's the fastest protocol available in this environment.

NOTE: The NetBEUI acronym stands for *NetBIOS Extended User Interface.* (This is a particularly confusing definition, because it includes yet another acronym and it has nothing to do with user interfaces.) *NetBIOS* stands for *Network Basic I/O System*. So NetBEUI really stands for *Network Basic I/O System Extended User Interface*. But all you really need to remember is how to correctly pronounce NetBEUI.

The original idea behind the NetBIOS protocol was to provide a way for applications to communicate with network hardware without requiring any additional network software. This approach is similar in concept to a PC's built-in BIOS, which enables the operating system to communicate with standard PC devices. Many applications have been written over the years to use NetBIOS services. However, network hardware has become diverse and complex, and there's a need to run other network protocols to interact with different operating systems and environments. Rather than abandon or rewrite all the NetBIOS applications out there, NetBIOS has become an *application programming interface* (*API*) that sits on top of other network protocols.

The Windows 98 implementation of the NetBEUI protocol operates mostly within the network layer of the OSI reference model. Portions of its functionality are also part of the transport layer and data link layer. The NetBIOS interface sits in the session layer, above the NetBEUI protocol.

NETBEUI ADVANTAGES

The NetBEUI protocol is small, fast, and efficient. It takes up very little memory relative to other protocols, so it works well on older, lower-end computers running MS-DOS. (NetBEUI may be the only practical protocol choice for some computers running MS-DOS.) It introduces minimal overhead, so transmission on the network is fast. Microsoft includes NetBEUI with all of its networking products, making it a sure bet for compatibility – at least on Microsoft networks. Windows 98 includes both protected mode and real mode support for NetBEUI, enabling you to run both Windows and MS-DOS applications that make use of its network services.

NetBEUI uses text names to identify and address individual network nodes. You can assign each computer or device a unique name such as KEN486, TOWERA, FINANCE1, or BIGSERVER. In addition, there's almost no other configuration required by this protocol. Once you assign names to computers and install the protocol, you're ready to communicate. These attributes make NetBEUI relatively easy to configure and maintain – some other protocols require a great deal of up-front configuration before you can put them to work.

NETBEUI DISADVANTAGES

Unfortunately, NetBEUI is not a routable protocol. It doesn't contain enough information to send packets from one network to another. Therefore, if your network needs or will need a router, keep in mind that NetBEUI packets won't be able to travel across it. This Achilles' heel limits the use of NetBEUI to small, simple networks. See Chapter 5 for a discussion of routers.

NetBEUI runs into trouble on large networks for another reason. When a node wants to communicate with another node by name, it sends out a broadcast on the network. These broadcast messages go everywhere, even across bridges. If the network is busy (which is often the case for large networks), the broadcast may need to be resent, creating even more traffic and slowing things down. The bigger and busier your network becomes, the worse this problem gets.

> Don't even attempt to use NetBEUI if you plan on having more than 200 nodes on your network. Not only will you encounter performance problems, but you'll run into another NetBEUI limitation: it doesn't let you establish more than 254 sessions over the network. Some applications take up more than one session, and the operating systems themselves occasionally use sessions in the background. Therefore, if everyone is using the network, and some applications are soaking up more than one precious session, some of your users will end up waiting for sessions to become available. As a network conservative, I recommend staying under 50 nodes in a NetBEUI network.

Although it works with some IBM products, NetBEUI is now considered strictly a Microsoft protocol. It's an industry standard only because Microsoft operating systems are industry standards. If you plan on running only Microsoft operating systems on your network nodes, NetBEUI is in the game as a protocol choice. However, if you're going to connect to operating systems from other vendors (for example, NetWare or UNIX), NetBEUI won't get you there.

TIP

If you have to use NetBEUI to communicate with existing low-end clients running MS-DOS or older versions of Windows, by all means use it. If your network is under 50 nodes, you don't plan to grow it, and you don't have or plan to have routers in your network, NetBEUI is still a good choice. If you're designing a new network that doesn't have to communicate with existing NetBEUI nodes, however, you may want to consider using one of the more flexible protocols discussed later in this chapter. For maximum flexibility, consider using TCP/IP, which I discuss later in this chapter.

Understanding IPX/SPX

IPX/SPX is the network protocol traditionally used on Novell NetWare networks. (I say "traditionally" because, in some of their key products, Novell has been moving toward using TCP/IP, which I discuss later in this chapter.) IPX/SPX stands for internetwork packet exchange/sequenced packet exchange. Its primary function in the Windows networking world is the capability to connect to NetWare servers in a mixed network environment. It can also be used as the main protocol in a pure Microsoft network.

Microsoft provides support for applications that use the NetBIOS interface by allowing the NetBIOS component to operate on top of the IPX/SPX protocol. This approach lets you continue to use older applications even if you change to the new protocol. Microsoft also includes the Client for NetWare Networks, which is essentially the NetWare requester (or redirector) that I mentioned earlier in this chapter. It operates at the application and session layers of the OSI model and implements the NCP (NetWare Core Protocol).

IPX/SPX Advantages

IPX/SPX is nearly as small and fast as NetBEUI. Unlike NetBEUI, IPX/SPX is routable, so for larger or more complex networks that use routers (or will use routers in the future), it's a more appropriate choice. Of course, if you're putting together a mixed network that includes NetWare servers, you'll need to use IPX/SPX on any Windows nodes that communicate directly with these servers.

Windows 98 includes both protected mode and real-mode support for IPX/SPX, enabling you to run both Windows and MS-DOS applications that make use of its network services. Applications that are written to use the NetBIOS interface can run with Microsoft's implementation of the IPX/SPX network protocol, which is called *NWLink*.

IPX/SPX DISADVANTAGES

Relative to NetBEUI, IPX/SPX takes up more resources and is a bit less efficient. So if you don't need a routable protocol, or you don't need to connect to NetWare servers, consider NetBEUI as an alternative.

IPX/SPX was a Novell-proprietary protocol for a long time. It's an industry standard now for two reasons. First, NetWare had (and still has) a majority of the networking market share. Second, Microsoft developed its own version of IPX/SPX when it became clear that many customers needed to support mixed Microsoft/Novell networks. The long-term future of IPX/SPX is uncertain, though, since both Novell and Microsoft have quickly moved toward adopting TCP/IP as the default standard protocol for their networking products. (I discuss TCP/IP in the next section.)

> NOTE: Windows 98 includes both the Microsoft IPX/SPX-compatible Protocol and the Novell IPX ODI Protocol. When configuring IPX/SPX for use with Windows 98, I recommend that you select the Microsoft protocol.

Understanding TCP/IP

TCP/IP, which stands for transmission control protocol/internet protocol, is the most flexible and most complex protocol option available on Windows 98. It enables you to connect and communicate across networks that use different hardware architectures and run different operating systems. You can use TCP/IP to communicate on pure Microsoft networks, or on mixed networks with products such as IntranetWare and UNIX. Connecting to the Internet is straightforward, because TCP/IP is the protocol used there.

TCP/IP is more than just a network protocol – it's typically referred to as a protocol suite. Beyond the basic network protocol, the suite includes a large number of utilities designed for managing and diagnosing connections. In addition, it includes several high-level protocols that perform specific functions including file transfer, network management, and so forth.

> **NOTE** Software developers use two basic approaches to developing TCP/IP applications. Some use the old NetBIOS interface, which Microsoft supports by supplying a thin translation layer between NetBIOS and TCP/IP. More modern applications use the Windows Sockets or Winsock interface. It gives developers familiar with Windows a relatively easy way to create TCP/IP-enabled applications.

TCP/IP ADVANTAGES

The main advantage of TCP/IP is its flexibility. Virtually every operating system platform now supports it, so running it on your network opens up the possibility of connecting to just about any other computer, network device, or network. By definition, TCP/IP is routable, so migrating to large or complex networks doesn't pose a problem. The fact that TCP/IP is the language of the Internet should tell you something about its capability to deal with large networks and multiple networks.

The two networking leaders, Microsoft and Novell, are both converging on a TCP/IP-centered universe. Microsoft has systematically increased its support for the TCP/IP protocol by improving its implementation with each new Windows operating system release. Microsoft now uses TCP/IP as the primary network protocol on its huge corporate network. What's more, Microsoft has now made TCP/IP the default protocol during installation of both Windows 98 and Windows NT. Novell has taken a bit longer to diverge from its proprietary IPX/SPX-centered universe, but it's now producing TCP/IP products as well.

TCP/IP has been around since the 1970s, and the number of tools and techniques for managing and troubleshooting it has proliferated. While this can add to its complexity and create a bit of a learning curve for the new network administrator, it also provides a tremendous resource that other protocols lack.

> **NOTE** One interesting protocol that's part of the TCP/IP suite is called *SNMP*, which stands for *Simple Network Management Protocol*. It operates at the application layer to collect and report statistics, device status information, configuration information, and performance data behind the scenes. The protocol is composed of two pieces: an agent and a manager. *SNMP agents* run on hubs, routers, and individual nodes to collect and store information. *SNMP managers* request and report the information, or use it to make automated decisions (much like I did when I was a manager). SNMP also enables some of the remote administration functions I discuss in Part III.

TCP/IP DISADVANTAGES

The biggest drawback of TCP/IP is its relative complexity. It presents a steep learning curve – people have spent entire careers learning about the nitty-gritty details of TCP/IP. If your goal in life is to learn everything there is to know about the TCP/IP suite, you should probably abandon your plans for early retirement. Alternatively, you could get yourself cloned, and assign each clone several years' worth of reading and training.

One important drawback of TCP/IP is the requirement that each network node must be assigned a unique numeric address, called an IP address. In fact, each network adapter must have its own IP address, so a node containing more than one network adapter has more than one IP address. If your network doesn't connect directly to the Internet and never will, you can assign private IP addresses. If your network is connected to the Internet, however, those IP addresses must be different from all other addresses used anywhere in the world. TCP/IP imposes administrative overhead, because you have to obtain a block of unique IP addresses from a central authority and assign them to individual nodes on your network. I cover IP addresses and Windows 98 TCP/IP installation and configuration in more detail in Chapter 9.

A number of techniques have been devised to simplify the assignment, use, and management of IP addresses. For example, *DNS* (*Domain Name System*) provides a global database that translates friendly computer names such as `www.rentcontrolled.com` into cryptic IP addresses such as 162.20.23.255. A protocol called *DHCP* (*Dynamic Host Configuration Protocol*) is another example. It was developed to automatically dole out addresses to network nodes as they show up on the network. To take advantage of this, a computer on the network must be assigned the role of DHCP server, responsible for managing and assigning IP addresses to nodes.

TIP

If your network consists entirely of Windows 98, you won't be able to use DHCP for assigning IP addresses. Microsoft offers DHCP only on Windows NT Server, so you need at least one Windows NT Server computer on your network to use the DHCP approach. If your network is small, assigning and reassigning IP addresses manually isn't a huge hassle. But if your network grows to 10 or more nodes, you're better off adding a Windows NT Server node running DHCP.

Understanding DLC

Windows 98 includes the *DLC (Data Link Control)* network protocol to enable your network to communicate with certain network printers. For example, the HP JetDirect series of printers requires the use of the DLC protocol. You can also use DLC to connect your network to IBM mainframes and minis, including the AS/400. DLC is the underlying protocol used by Microsoft SNA Server, which runs on Windows NT Server. Windows 98 includes DLC support for 32-bit, 16-bit, and MS-DOS applications.

When using DLC to communicate with a network printer, you need to install the DLC protocol on the computer that's acting as the print server for the network printer. Other nodes that send jobs to the print server can use any standard protocol, and don't need to have DLC installed.

The DLC protocol operates in the data link layer (as if its name didn't give away that fact). It corresponds almost exactly to the logical link control (LLC) sublayer within the data link layer.

Selecting Your Network Protocols

Now that you've gone through an explanation of the key Windows 98 network protocols, it's time to work on deciding what protocol (or protocols) you need on your network. Table 6-1 presents a useful summary comparing the characteristics of NetBEUI, IPX/SPX, and TCP/IP. You can use this table to help decide on the protocols you'll use on your network.

Talking to the Apples

If you have Apple Macintosh computers, can you hook them up to your Windows 98 network? Well, yes and no. Apple's network protocol, called AppleTalk, supports LocalTalk (a proprietary connection), Ethernet (called EtherTalk), and Token Ring (called TokenTalk). Therefore, hooking the wires together may not be a problem, but getting the dissimilar nodes to understand each other is a different story.

Like TCP/IP, AppleTalk is a suite of protocols that operate at several levels of the OSI reference model. These protocols aren't compatible with those that run on the Windows 98 platform. However, there is hope. Windows NT Server includes a feature called Services for Macintosh, or SFM. It enables a Windows NT Server computer to act as a file and print server to Macintosh computers running AppleTalk. Once you get the files on the NT Server machine, your Windows 98 (and other) computers can access the files over standard network protocols.

TABLE 6-1 CRITERIA FOR SELECTING NETWORK PROTOCOLS

Characteristics	NetBEUI	IPX/SPX	TCP/IP
Capability to transmit across routers	No	Yes	Yes
Best for corporate intranet	No	No	Yes
Best for large networks	No	No	Yes
Best for pure Microsoft networks (no routing)	Yes	No	No
Best for pure Microsoft networks (with routing)	No	No	Yes
Best for small LANs	Yes	Yes	No
Best for WANs	No	No	Yes
Ease of client configuration	High	High	Low
Ease of network administration	High	High	Low
Interoperability with NetWare	No	Yes	No
Interoperability with the Internet	No	No	Yes
Interoperability with UNIX	No	No	Yes
Level of industry standardization/interoperability	Low (Microsoft and IBM)	Low (Novell and Microsoft)	High
Performance for application servers (client/server)	Low	Medium	High
Performance for file and printer sharing	Medium	High	Medium
Performance on small networks	High	Medium	Medium

Interconnectivity and Interoperability

The two networking terms I hear bandied about most frequently are *interconnectivity* and *interoperability*. These terms represent critically important network concepts. In my experience, though, the majority of people who use these terms in conversation either don't know what they mean or incorrectly use them interchangeably. I don't want you to fall into either category, so I've devoted this section to briefly explaining these terms and the differences between them.

Understanding Interconnectivity

The term interconnectivity implies that a physical connection exists between one or more entities – but that's all it implies. To achieve interconnectivity, you can simply hook together several computers using Ethernet network adapters, a hub, and UTP cables. The cards may even send occasional data frames to each other. However, the connection isn't useful until you add compatible protocols to each node on the network. Until then, the interconnectivity you've achieved doesn't serve a useful purpose.

Understanding Interoperability

Interoperability, on the other hand, implies that entities are working together to get something useful accomplished. It's a step up from interconnectivity. To achieve interoperability, you need to provide your network nodes with all the right software and hardware components to enable them to communicate with and understand one another. You can find interoperability at many levels, but true interoperability is achieved only when you're running compatible protocols in the first five layers of the seven-layer OSI model. This enables nodes to send and receive useful information. If you add interoperability at the highest two levels, you can get applications to work cooperatively together over the network.

Windows 98 and other operating systems enable you to run more than one protocol stack on the network at the same time. Doing this can make a node interoperable with other nodes that may be running dissimilar protocols. For example, assume that Node A runs NetBEUI, Node B runs TCP/IP, and Node C runs both NetBEUI and TCP/IP. Node C is interoperable with both Nodes A and B, even though A and B aren't interoperable with each other.

Homogenous vs. Heterogeneous Networks

Why is it important to achieve interoperability with nodes running dissimilar protocols? Why not simply select compatible hardware, operating systems, and network protocols from day one, and run the same thing on every network node? Well, that's exactly how networks start out – as *homogenous* networks. Nodes achieve full interoperability with each other because they're all running a single standard protocol stack.

In practice, this condition doesn't last very long, and may never exist to begin with. If you're inheriting an existing network or computers, you may find it impractical to convert them all to compatible operating systems and protocols. (The added costs of hardware upgrades and user training can make this prospect even more unpleasant.) Perhaps you need to run an application that only exists on a certain operating system that's different from the one your other computers are running. Or perhaps you're tying together two smaller incompatible networks, and the cost of ripping out and replacing wiring is prohibitive. Or, you may begin to adopt a new network technology, but can't afford to roll it out to the entire network all at once. There are many reasons why you may need to run dissimilar nodes on your network.

The bottom line is that most real-world networks, even if they start out as homogenous, evolve into *heterogeneous* networks eventually. Cabling, network technologies, operating systems, and protocol stacks can end up differing from node to node. This is where the concept of interoperability becomes important, both in the planning and implementation stages of creating your network.

Summary

In this chapter, you've covered a lot of ground – or maybe climbed a lot of stacks. You've learned about the OSI reference model, which describes a layered approach to designing networks. You've discovered how this model relates to and helps explain several hardware and software components of networks. I discussed the key network protocols offered by Windows 98, and provided some insights to help you select the protocols that meet your needs. Finally, you learned the difference between interconnectivity and interoperability, and why interoperability is important.

In Chapter 7, I help you understand the key differences between network operating systems – from Microsoft and from other vendors. You'll learn all you need to know to make intelligent decisions about which network operating systems are right for your particular environment.

Chapter 7

Selecting a Network Operating System

IN THIS CHAPTER

- Understanding and selecting modern network operating systems
- Examining Microsoft network operating systems, new and old
- Exploring a variety of network operating system alternatives

IN THIS CHAPTER, I show you what to look for in a network operating system. Then, you'll learn about the similarities and differences between each of the Microsoft operating system products. You'll be able to look at most of them side by side in a table to help in your evaluation process. Finally, I discuss several important non-Microsoft network operating systems you may encounter as you design and implement your network. By the end of this chapter, you'll have a solid foundation for selecting your NOSs.

Understanding Network Operating Systems

I briefly introduced the concept and content of a network operating system, or NOS, in Chapter 1. Now that you have a more in-depth understanding of the hardware and software components that make up a network, let's discuss NOS features in the context of what you've learned so far. Here, I focus primarily on modern NOSs, which integrate networking functions directly into the operating system. Microsoft Windows 98 is one of these products.

Reviewing NOS Features

A typical modern NOS consists of the following set of components:

- **Network adapter drivers** – One or more network adapter drivers, and the capability to install third-party drivers.
- **Transport protocols** – One or more transport protocols that may or may not run simultaneously on a node.
- **Application layer components** – One or more network redirector/server components that may or may not run simultaneously on a node.
- **Network administration tools** – A set of graphical or text-based utilities that enable you to install, configure, monitor, and maintain network-related features.
- **Traditional operating system** – At the core, an operating system that offers non-networking services including memory management, file I/O, and so forth.

This certainly isn't an exhaustive list, nor can you assume that every NOS contains all of these components. To be fully functional, however, a NOS requires some form of each of these elements. Some items, such as administration tools, may be offered in an add-on package at extra cost.

A NOS usually includes an entire protocol stack, covering all the OSI reference model layers – from the software portion of the physical layer all the way up to the application layer. Not all NOSs have something at every layer, but the point is that they're fully functional because they provide all the services required to create a usable network.

Some NOSs are available in packages that include the entire physical layer — network adapters, cables, hubs, and so forth. Such bundles are often called network starter kits, and they sometimes represent a good value. However, you should make sure that all the hardware components fit into your overall network plan.

Many NOS products include a set of network adapter drivers that support the most popular adapter hardware. If NOS doesn't include the driver for a specific adapter, it provides a mechanism to install a driver supplied by the network adapter manufacturer. Some NOSs, such as Windows 98, include more than one transport protocol – giving you the choice of running one or more of them on your network.

At the application layer, a NOS may also include more than one redirector, to support different brands of networks. For example, Windows 98 includes both the Client for Microsoft Networks, which uses the SMB protocol, and the Client for NetWare Networks, which uses the NCP protocol. See Chapter 6 for a discussion of drivers, protocols, and redirectors.

TIP

Microsoft offers both 16-bit and 32-bit versions of some of its Windows 98 networking software components. The 16-bit versions provide compatibility with some older applications that require them. Whenever possible, though, opt to use the 32-bit components. This way, you can avoid maintaining a series of manual configuration files (such as AUTOEXEC.BAT, PROTCOL.INI, and NET.CFG) by storing all settings in the Registry. The 32-bit components are also faster and more reliable than their 16-bit counterparts.

Network administration tools can range from networking features built directly into general utilities (such as the capability to connect to a shared directory using Windows Explorer) to standalone utilities designed specifically for network administration (such as Net Watcher). Additional tools are usually available from the NOS manufacturer or from third parties. For example, Microsoft offers a useful set of tools in the Windows 98 package, and provides even more in the Windows 98 Resource Kit.

The portion of the NOS that's considered to be a traditional operating system may be built directly into the NOS, or it may run underneath the NOS. For example, Windows for Workgroups, which I discuss later in this chapter, runs on top of a preexisting copy of MS-DOS, and requires its presence for file access and other local OS functions. Windows 98, on the other hand, has its own well-hidden version of MS-DOS built in. And Windows NT is a complete standalone operating system that requires no other underlying operating system to run. It includes all the OS functions required for file access and other activities.

Achieving NOS Reliability

Whether or not the operating system is included in the NOS, its overall design has a dramatic effect on the reliability of the NOS. If you've been around PCs for a while, you're probably used to an occasional hang (or lock-up, or freeze, or crash, depending on where you were raised). In MS-DOS and early versions of Windows, hanging and rebooting were just a fact of life. When this happens on your desktop system, I'll bet you express a little frustration, reboot the computer, and move on. But you accept it, because the problem and its solution only affect you and your own work.

Once you start connecting computers together and sharing resources, however, the impact of your computer freezing up reaches beyond your desktop and affects other network users. Let's say you have a peer-to-peer network, and you're sharing a printer and a set of database files with other users. If your computer hangs, for whatever reason, the printer and files are no longer accessible to the other users. If they try to access your shared resources, they'll get error messages. Worse yet, if they were in the middle of using the resources, they may even end up with corrupted files on your computer. At the same time, if other nodes are trying to send data to your node, they'll end up retrying several times. This extra traffic can slow down your network's performance, affecting everyone involved.

In the following sections, I discuss some key operating system features that contribute to performance and reliability of your nodes and your network.

MULTITASKING

Perhaps the most important operating system feature required by today's demanding networks is *multitasking*. This refers to the capability of the operating system to enable progress on more than one task at a time. In a computer with a single CPU, the operating system enables each task to progress for a short period of time (called a *time slice*), and then lets another task have a chance to run. If a computer contains more than one CPU, and the operating system supports multiple CPUs, the OS can assign one task to each CPU and run the tasks in parallel. If the number of tasks exceeds the number of available CPUs, the operating system must revert to time slicing between the tasks that need to be performed.

> **NOTE:** There are cases in which a multitasking operating system isn't required for networking. For example, if you have a computer running the single-tasking MS-DOS operating system and you have an application that runs only under MS-DOS, you can use this computer as a network client. But I highly recommend a multitasking NOS for clients, and consider multitasking a necessity for servers.

COOPERATIVE MULTITASKING There are two approaches to multitasking: cooperative and preemptive. In *cooperative multitasking* (sometimes called *non-preemptive multitasking*), the individual tasks decide when to give up the CPU to another task. In this environment, a task runs as long as it wants, to the exclusion of all other tasks. Nothing can preempt its hold on the CPU. When the task is ready to yield the CPU to another task, it must explicitly give up control. Microsoft Windows for Workgroups and Novell NetWare are examples of cooperative multitasking network operating systems.

In *preemptive multitasking*, the operating system has complete control over deciding when a given task runs. At any time during a task's execution, the operating system can preempt it, and assign another task to the CPU. This approach prevents any one task from monopolizing the CPU's time, and lets the operating system quickly shuffle priorities based on external events that may require immediate attention. (Although preemptive multitasking is the opposite of cooperative multitasking, it's never called uncooperative multitasking. It just had to be said.) Windows 98, Windows 95, and Windows NT are examples of preemptive multitasking operating systems.

PREEMPTIVE MULTITASKING Preemptive multitasking is critically important in a network environment. Why? There are two main reasons, involving performance and reliability. On the performance front, consider the fact that, in a networked computer, a lot is going on behind the scenes that you never see. Besides running your applications, the NOS must constantly monitor the network for incoming data, manage transmission of data that needs to go out on the network, and handle any network error conditions that may occur. Some of these events require immediate attention. For example, if data is coming in from the network, the NOS may need to pass it on to an application and start listening for another message immediately. If this doesn't happen quickly enough, the computer might miss the next message, causing the other end to retransmit the data. This can slow down the entire network. A NOS has to be able to drop whatever it's doing right away, handle the network-related event, and then pick up where it left off.

Perhaps more important is the reliability benefit of preemptive multitasking. Recall that cooperative multitasking lets the applications control CPU usage, whereas preemptive multitasking lets the operating system have all the power. Now consider an uncooperative software application running in a cooperative multitasking environment. The application may contain bugs, or it may just want all the CPU time it can get. Either way, if the application fails to yield control of the CPU for long periods of time (or even forever), the computer can't do anything else. If it needs to pay attention to the network or some other activity, it can't until the application gives up on its filibuster. The only way to resolve the problem is to restart the system. This is unacceptable behavior in a networked environment. Preemptive multitasking keeps applications from holding up the entire system.

NOTE: The problem I've described isn't really the fault of the operating system. It's the fault of the application. The operating system approaches just have different degrees of vulnerability to application bugs. Cooperative multitasking OSs are completely vulnerable, whereas preemptive multitasking OSs are virtually immune. No matter how much you test a software product, it will have bugs in it. The key to success is finding and fixing the right set of bugs, so that those remaining are either trivial or will never be encountered in normal use of the product. This philosophy becomes even more critical in a cooperative multitasking environment.

When you select a NOS for your network, I strongly recommend one that's designed to perform preemptive multitasking. It will result in a more reliable and efficient network that will cause fewer headaches.

MEMORY PROTECTION

Memory's cheap these days, so why protect it? Can't you just buy more? Well, I'm not talking about that sort of memory protection. I'm referring to a key reliability feature present in many (but not all) operating systems.

Most modern CPUs (that is, ever since the Intel 386) enable you to keep applications from stepping on each other's memory, or from stepping on the operating system's memory. Each application (or the OS itself) runs in a separate virtual memory space. Any attempts to access memory outside this space won't work. Without this protection, a buggy (or malicious) application can scribble into memory that belongs to other tasks and crash other applications, or in the worst case, crash the operating system itself. Some operating systems protect the OS from errant applications, but don't keep applications from hurting each other.

Even if the CPU provides this protection feature, the operating system must be designed to take advantage of it. Why don't they all do this? The most basic reason is simplicity. Software developers can create a much simpler, smaller operating system if they don't have to worry about managing memory protection. The second reason is efficiency. As the CPU makes the transition from one virtual memory address space to another (that is, from one application to another), a small cost is incurred. Some operating system developers argue that the lost time in making these transitions far outweighs the risks inherent in an unprotected memory design.

If application and operating system software were bug-free, there would be no need for memory protection. But the sad truth is that no software is bug-free. The even sadder truth is that the most common software bug involves accessing an invalid memory address. In an OS with memory protection, this class of bug results in an error in the application, with no effect on other applications or on the OS itself. In an OS without memory protection, it's anybody's guess what will happen, but a system crash is a likely outcome.

TIP

When it's time to select a NOS, opt for one that has memory protection. You can't count on applications being bug-free, and the small price of reduced performance is well worth it when compared with the cost of recovering a crashed system and waiting for it to come back up. I'm not saying that memory-protected operating systems don't crash — but they're much less vulnerable to application bugs that are outside of their control.

Exploring Microsoft Operating Systems

In the following sections, I cover each of the Microsoft operating systems. In discussing them, I focus on the networking capabilities and features that are relevant to networking, rather than on a comparison of every operating system feature.

Keep in mind that you don't need to pick just one NOS and run with it on every node in your network. Yes, doing so could make life simpler for you and your users. But if you're tying together existing computers, you can certainly have a mixture of operating systems running throughout your network – as long as they're interoperable with each other. And as you learn about other operating systems, you may find that a certain mixture better meets the needs of your organization. See Chapter 6 for a discussion of interoperability.

Exploring Windows 98

I introduced you to Windows 98 in Chapter 1, and you've been learning about its capabilities throughout this book. In this section, I fill in a few more details and compare Windows 98 with other Microsoft operating system offerings, described in the sections to come.

Windows 98 is a standalone, preemptive multitasking operating system with built-in networking capabilities. It offers full memory protection between individual 32-bit applications, and between applications and the operating system. (To maintain compatibility with Windows 3.*x*, it doesn't protect 16-bit Windows applications from each other.)

You can run most 32-bit Windows applications (sometimes called *Win32* applications) on Windows 98, whether they're written for Windows 98, Windows 95, or Windows NT. It doesn't run all Win32 applications because some of them use features that are specific to Windows NT (for example, security features). In addition, Windows 98 runs nearly all 16-bit MS-DOS and Windows 3.*x* applications.

The Windows 98 operating system can play the role of a node in a peer-to-peer network, or the role of a client in a Windows NT Server-based network. It can also be a client to NetWare and UNIX servers, which I discuss later in this chapter. The basic NOS architecture remains the same as Windows 95.

XREF

In Chapter 9, I show you how to install and configure Windows 98 network software.

NEW FEATURES

Among the many added features in Windows 98, here are some that relate directly or indirectly to networking:

- **Tighter Internet/intranet integration** – With the introduction of the Active Desktop, you can place active links to Internet sites directly on your desktop, making them only a mouse click away. The desktop can be a combination of icons for local applications and files, and for remote resources. Windows 98 also includes a light version of FrontPage and Personal Web Server, enabling you to author and publish Web content. (See Chapter 4 for more information.) You can even set Windows 98 utilities to act more like Web pages, enabling you to single-click on links rather than double-click on icons.
- **Broader hardware support** – Windows 98 adds support for ATM (Asynchronous Transfer Mode), DVD (Digital Video Disc), USB (Universal Serial Bus), FireWire, power management, and others. (I discuss devices further in Chapter 8.) Windows 98 also includes support for NDIS 5 network adapter drivers, which better support a wider range of high-speed network technologies.
- **Enhanced networking features** – Windows 98 includes Winsock 2, an upgrade to the popular Windows-based Internet programming interface. Microsoft also completely rewrote the TCP/IP protocol to improve its performance. It added new ISDN drivers, improved dial-up networking, included a single-line RAS server, and added VPN (virtual private networking) capabilities.
- Performance improvements and bug fixes – Microsoft tightened up performance in many areas, including program loading and networking. It improved disk space usage with the new FAT32 file system. Microsoft also fixed many bugs that plagued Windows 95 – including networking issues.

TIP

Windows 98 is more reliable than Windows 95. Aside from its new features, it contains more than 5,000 bug fixes — resolving problems that were present in the retail Windows 95 product. (This may sound like a large number of bugs in Windows 95, but it's actually small for a product that's been widely used for more than three years.) Even the beta releases of Windows 98 were more stable than Windows 95. If you're already running Windows 95 and you experience problems with it, I highly recommend upgrading to Windows — even if you don't use the new features. If you can't afford to upgrade every node, at least upgrade the ones that will act as peer servers.

This isn't an exhaustive list, but it does cover the items that relate to your use of Windows 98 as a NOS. Clearly, Windows 98 doesn't represent a quantum leap in features and usability, like Windows 95 did. It's more of an evolutionary release – evolving to support new hardware, evolving to integrate better with the Internet, and evolving to become faster and more reliable.

Windows 98 is really a bridge product between Windows 95 and Windows NT, both of which I discuss later in this chapter. As I mentioned in Chapter 1, Microsoft will merge the Windows 98 and Windows NT 5.0 product lines into one over the next couple of years. There will likely be several flavors of this product, tuned for different network roles and organization sizes – but all of the products will be based on the same NT operating system core.

TIP

If you're building a small peer-to-peer network, Windows 98 is the way to go. If you're building a small dedicated server network in which security isn't a critical issue, Windows 98 can be the client NOS of choice. If security is an issue, however, or if your network is more than a few nodes, I highly recommend Windows NT Workstation for your client nodes. I discuss Windows NT later in this chapter.

NETWORK CLIENT SUPPORT

Windows 98 has built-in support for being a client to either Microsoft or Novell servers. The Microsoft client is called Client for Microsoft Networks, and the Novell client is called (as you might guess) Client for NetWare Networks. Also, if you're running servers with NetWare 4.*x* or higher, you can take advantage of the built-in Service for NetWare Directory Services (NDS). This component enables you to easily log on to an NDS tree, just as if you were logging on to a Microsoft network. (I discuss NetWare and NDS later in this chapter.)

DCOM SUPPORT

A new operating system component, the *Distributed Component Object Model* (*DCOM*), is included in Windows 98. It provides a way for a distributed application, whose individual pieces might run anywhere on the network, to communicate over the network in a seamless and secure way. A DCOM-enabled application may be distributed over a mixture of nodes running Windows 98 or Windows NT. (This operating system component was originally called *Network OLE*, for *Network Object Linking and Embedding*.)

FAT32 FILE SYSTEM

Windows 98 includes a more efficient version of the traditional FAT file system. Called FAT32, it changes the on-disk structure to allow more efficient use of space on the hard disk. In contrast to the old MS-DOS FAT file system, which has become known as FAT16, the new file system uses a smaller cluster size. (A *cluster* is the smallest unit of disk storage that the file system can obtain as it creates or grows a file.) This approach minimizes wasted hard disk space, especially on large disks.

> NOTE: FAT32 is also available in Windows 95 *OEM Service Release 2* (*OSR2*), which shipped preinstalled on new computers for several months prior to the Windows 98 release. The Windows 95 version provides the same features as the Windows 98 version, and the on-disk structures are identical.

FAT32 breaks the 2GB partition size barrier that plagued earlier versions of Windows and MS-DOS. With FAT32, you can create and access hard disk partitions all the way up to 127GB. (At the time of writing, it's tough to find a hard disk larger than 30GB, so this limit should last a while. But 127GB is only a partition size limitation. If huge hard disks show up, you can always create multiple 127GB partitions!) FAT32 hard disks can be up to 2TB (terabytes) in size. (A *terabyte* is a trillion bytes, a ten-digit number.) What's the catch? The hard drive can't be any smaller than 512MB.

FAT32 is also more reliable than FAT16. For example, it automatically detects when Windows 98 wasn't shut down properly, and performs a disk scan the next time the system is rebooted. If necessary, it can relocate the drive's root directory and use the backup copy of the file allocation table. Also, FAT32 backs up additional critical file system data in the boot sector. All of these features make it less susceptible to partial hard disk failures.

> NOTE: FAT16 refers to both the MS-DOS *FAT* file system and the default Windows 95 *VFAT* file system. Both of these flavors of FAT16 have identical on-disk structures, so they're fully compatible with each other. The difference lies in performance — FAT for MS-DOS uses a real-mode 16-bit driver, while VFAT uses a protected-mode 32-bit driver. But the type of driver used has no effect on the on-disk structure, which is considered FAT16 in both cases. VFAT was first introduced as an option in Windows for Workgroups 3.11, and became the only file system supplied in Windows 95. VFAT is the default option in Windows 98, unless you explicitly convert to the new FAT32 file system.

Although it sounds too good to be true, FAT32 also speeds up application loading time, by up to 50 percent. Its small cluster size enables a new Windows 98 version of the Disk Defragmenter to move portions of the application around on disk, to create the most efficient approach to loading it into memory.

You can choose to convert your existing FAT16 file system to FAT32 during Windows 98 installation, or use the Drive Converter Wizard to convert it later. When you perform the conversion, Windows 98 defragments the new file system and optimizes it for FAT32.

CAUTION: Unlike FAT16, FAT32 isn't supported by most Microsoft or non-Microsoft operating systems. The only other OSs that support it are Windows NT 5.0 and Windows 95 OSR2. (The retail version of Windows 95 doesn't support FAT32.) Keep all this in mind as you make the decision to convert to FAT32. All of these operating systems can access data on your FAT32 hard disk over the network, but if you want any of them to be able to read your physical hard disk directly, you should stick with FAT16.

Why focus so much attention on FAT32? In a networked environment, improved file I/O performance translates directly to improved network performance and efficiency. This is especially true on server nodes that must get information on and off the hard disk as quickly as possible – on behalf of multiple users. Improved reliability is also critically important; you want to minimize the possibility of a corrupted or unusable volume, especially if you're sharing it with others. Finally, it's important to support large hard disks and partitions. Network servers (whether they're dedicated or peer-to-peer) fill up quickly as more information is shared and more applications are used to manage it. Servers especially need to be able to access large hard disks efficiently.

Exploring Windows NT

Windows NT is Microsoft's most reliable and powerful network operating system, targeted primarily at computer networks in businesses and other organizations. It is a fully 32-bit preemptive multitasking operating system with complete protection between applications and the operating system. Its design was influenced by other operating systems including Mach, UNIX, OS/2, and VMS.

Although this book focuses primarily on Windows 98 networking, I also dig into some details about the Windows NT operating system. I have two reasons for doing this. First, Windows NT is the next step up from Windows 98 in terms of reliability, capacity, and networking features. As you complete your network plan, you may find that you need Windows NT right out of the — so having enough information to know whether you need it is important. Second, because Windows 98 and Windows NT 5.0 will merge into a single NT-based product line over the next couple of years, anything you can learn about Windows NT now will serve you (and your network) well.

Here's a brief outline of Windows NT's key attributes:

- **Reliable** – Windows NT fully protects the operating system from errant applications, keeps applications from harming each other, and provides advanced features that prevent loss of data – minimizing the impact of hardware failures. Windows NT is much more bullet-proof than other Windows operating systems, including Windows 98.
- **High-performance** – Windows NT provides a pure 32-bit architecture, highly efficient I/O operations, and advanced performance analysis tools. Both Windows 95 and Windows 98 still include 16-bit operating system components.
- **Usable** – Windows NT offers simple installation, Plug and Play (in version 5.0), easy-to-use graphical utilities, and the same user interface as Windows 95. (The Windows NT 5.0 user interface is the same as Windows 98). It includes powerful tools to make administration of computers and networks easier. Windows NT also enables users to log on just once to the network to gain access to all appropriate shared resources.
- **Compatible** – Windows NT provides a high level of compatibility with computer systems, hardware devices, software applications, and many types of networks. In addition to running 32-bit Windows applications, it can run the following application types: 16-bit MS-DOS, 16-bit Windows 3.*x*, 16-bit OS/2 1.*x*, and 32-bit POSIX.
- **Secure** – Windows NT offers high levels of security to control access to individual resources and files on a per-user basis. It provides both network and local security. Windows NT meets security standards required by many U.S. government contracts.

- **Scalable** – Windows NT can take full advantage of computers containing multiple CPUs (up to 32), large amounts of memory, and very large hard disks. It also supports server *clustering,* to spread the computing workload between multiple server computers.
- **Portable** – Windows NT runs on both the Intel x86 architecture and the DEC Alpha architecture. It's designed to be easily portable to other popular CPU architectures in the future.

I won't cover all the features that support these attributes. I'll just focus in on some key elements that are relevant to your NOS decision process.

APPLICATION COMPATIBILITY

Windows NT runs most 32-bit Windows applications, whether they're written for Windows NT, Windows 98, or Windows 95. In addition, Windows NT runs most 16-bit MS-DOS and Windows 3.*x* applications without a hitch. However, Windows NT isn't quite as compatible as Windows 98 or Windows 95. Why? Some 16-bit MS-DOS or Windows 3.*x* applications attempt to perform operations that NT considers unsafe or breaches of security. To keep OS/2 customers happy, Windows NT includes an OS/2 Subsystem that enables customers to run their legacy 16-bit OS/2 1.*x* text-based applications.

In an effort to make Windows NT a player in the U.S. government computing marketplace, Microsoft decided to include the capability to run 32-bit POSIX applications. What is *POSIX*? It stands loosely for *Portable Operating System Interface based on UNIX.*

ALPHA PROCESSOR SUPPORT

In addition to supporting the Intel x86 CPU architecture, Windows NT also runs on the DEC Alpha architecture. This platform has become increasingly popular in the graphics workstation market, especially in 3-D CAD, rendering, and animation. The Alpha processor is even finding its way into servers that require lots of CPU power, especially in client-server application environments. DEC and other companies develop and market an increasingly fast and powerful array of Alpha CPUs, chipsets, motherboards, and complete single-processor and multiprocessor systems.

> **NOTE:** Although Alpha-based systems run most 16-bit MS-DOS and Windows 3.*x* applications, they do so through software emulation in Windows NT. The emulation software is becoming more efficient with each Windows NT product release, and increasing CPU clock speeds improve the situation, but it's still emulation software. An x86-based system executes these applications much more efficiently.

Not all NT software developers offer both an x86 and an Alpha version. Based on relative CPU market share, some have chosen to support only the x86. In that sense, the x86 platform has more software available for it than the Alpha platform has. To alleviate the potential software dearth, DEC and Microsoft have developed a software technology called FX!32. DEC offers it free to Alpha end-users, and many Alpha-based system manufacturers distribute it with their new computers. In addition, some NT x86 application vendors supply FX!32 with their software, to enable customers with Alpha-based computers to run their x86 NT applications.

FX!32 is neither an emulator nor a binary translator – it's actually a hybrid combination of both. (It's a floor wax and a dessert topping!) This technology includes an x86 instruction emulator, a complete 32-bit x86 environment, and a background translator that converts sequences of x86 instructions into streams of Alpha instructions. Each time you run an x86 application, FX!32 accumulates more and more translated chunks of Alpha code, so execution gets faster each time you run the application. (This speed improvement diminishes once FX!32 has translated most of the commonly executed code into native Alpha instructions.) As with 16-bit x86 emulation, when the x86 application calls a 32-bit Windows API, FX!32 transfers control to the native Alpha APIs.

NTFS FILE SYSTEM

Although Windows NT is compatible with the FAT16 file system (and NT 5.0 is compatible with the FAT32 file system), NT provides its own unique file system to support underlying operating system features. *NTFS* (which, not surprisingly, stands for *NT File System*) has the following attributes that set it apart from other PC file systems:

- **Recoverability** – To avoid losing data, NTFS goes out of its way to maintain a consistent state of on-disk structures. It uses a transaction approach to updates, and typically takes only a few seconds to recover from improper shutdowns. It keeps redundant copies of its critical data, and can mark and skip bad sectors on the fly.

> NOTE: NTFS recoverability doesn't take any steps to recover lost data. For example, data not yet written to disk when an improper shutdown occurs is lost forever. What NTFS recovery does guarantee is the validity of on-disk file system structures, so that other files and the partition itself aren't affected.

- **File security** – NTFS stores permission information at the file level, so you can assign permissions to users and groups on a file-by-file or directory-by-directory basis.
- **Data compression** – With NTFS, you can compress the data in a single file, all the files in a directory, or all the directories on a partition. The compression ratio can be as high as 2:1, but depends on the nature of the data being compressed.
- **Data encryption** – Windows NT 5.0 adds data encryption to the list of NTFS features. The data within individual files can be stored in encrypted form, and can be decrypted using public and private keys.
- **Large disk support** – NTFS supports hard disks up to 16EB (*exabytes*) in size. (In case you're wondering, 16EB is 16 quintillion bytes, a 20-digit number.) Like FAT32, NTFS uses smaller cluster sizes than FAT16, making more efficient use of large hard disks. It's even more efficient than FAT32 on disks larger than 8GB.
- **Volume set support** – You can expand an existing NTFS partition by logically appending an empty partition from another hard disk. This feature enables you to expand an NTFS volume without repartitioning.
- **POSIX and Macintosh support** – NTFS provides the unique file system support required by POSIX applications and by Macintosh clients.

Windows NT supports both the FAT16 and NTFS file systems. (Windows NT 5.0 also supports FAT32.) However, NTFS is only supported under Windows NT – no other commercial operating system products will read from or write to it. Other operating systems can access data on your NTFS partition over the network, but if you want any of them to be able to read your physical hard disk directly, you need to use FAT16 (or FAT32 on NT 5.0).

FAULT TOLERANCE

Windows NT provides a set of features collectively known as *fault tolerance*. These features enable you to automatically store redundant copies of data, and quickly restore them if a hard disk failure occurs. NT fault tolerance implements a software approach to a technology called *RAID*, which stands for *Redundant Arrays of Inexpensive Disks.*

By using multiple hard disks and writing to them simultaneously in one of several ways, you can easily recover from a single hard disk failure. As a side benefit, you can achieve performance improvements by spreading the data across multiple disks and writing to each one simultaneously. In Chapter 13, I discuss RAID in more detail. Here's an overview of the RAID approaches supported in software by Windows NT:

- **RAID 0 (stripes without parity)** – This approach provides no redundancy; it's done purely for improved performance. An array of 2 to 32 hard disks creates a single large partition. Data is written to or read from the partition in a *striped* fashion across all the hard disks, enabling many I/O operations to occur in parallel.
- **RAID 1 (mirroring and duplexing)** – This approach uses two hard disks, and one completely *mirrors* the contents of the other. When data is written to one disk, the other disk gets a copy of the same data. (If separate disk controllers are used, this technique is called *duplexing*.) If either disk fails, the surviving hard disk takes over automatically until the failed disk can be replaced. This feature isn't available in Windows NT Workstation.
- **RAID 5 (stripes with parity)** – This approach uses an array of 3 to 32 hard disks, striping data across them just as in RAID 0. However, one of the disks is dedicated to storing *parity* information, which allows recovery of the data if one of the disks in the array fails. (Actually, the parity information is also spread across all the disks, so that no single disk contains all the parity information.) When a hard disk fails, NT automatically reconstructs the missing data using the parity information until the failed disk can be replaced. This feature isn't available in Windows NT Workstation.

NOTE

You can achieve RAID fault tolerance using other operating systems such as Windows 98 and Windows 95. To do this, you need a RAID device that performs all the redundancy and recovery in hardware. This approach obviates the need for fault tolerance features within the operating system, and it will likely run faster than with the software approach. Windows NT can use hardware RAID as well. In this case, the NT software doesn't need to do anything special — the RAID array just looks like one large disk to NT. However, hardware RAID devices are more expensive when compared with off-the-shelf hard disks and controllers.

WINDOWS NT WORKSTATION

Windows NT Workstation is tuned to operate at peak performance in an interactive desktop environment. Because of its reliability and high performance, it's ideal for high-end graphics applications including computer aided design (CAD), digital video, and 3-D animation. It also makes an ideal platform for software development.

Windows NT Workstation supports up to two multiprocessor CPUs. (If you need to run it on a computer containing more than two CPUs, you must obtain a special version of the product from the multiprocessor computer vendor. The operating system is limited to a maximum of 32 CPUs.) Windows NT Workstation includes peer-to-peer networking, but the built-in server imposes a limit of up to ten clients.

WINDOWS NT SERVER

Windows NT Server has been optimized to provide an efficient, easy-to-administer dedicated server designed for sharing files, devices, and applications. It offers additional features to improve reliability, centralize and ease network administration tasks, and allow remote access to the network. There is no limit on the number of network clients.

Windows NT Server supports up to four multiprocessor CPUs. If you need to run it on a computer containing more than four CPUs, you have to get a special version of the product from the computer vendor. The operating system is limited to a maximum of 32 CPUs.

NOTE: The latest version, Windows NT Server 5.0, includes NT's answer to Novell's NDS global directory. It's called Microsoft *Active Directory*, or *AD*. This feature helps you organize and administer all the shared resources on the network. To take full advantage of Active Directory in a Windows NT Server-based network, your client computers need to be running Windows NT Workstation 5.0 or greater. Windows 98 and other versions of Windows can access resources on the network, but won't have full access to the capabilities of AD. (I discuss NDS later in this chapter.)

In addition to its optimization for use as a network server, Windows NT Server includes the following enhancements to Windows NT Workstation.

- **Fault tolerance** – Windows NT Server adds options for maintaining redundant copies of data, automatic recovery from crashes, live backups of security databases, and replication of data to other servers.
- **Services for Macintosh** – Windows NT Server can act as a Macintosh file server, a Macintosh print server, and an AppleTalk router.
- **Remote Access Server** – Windows NT Server includes a version of RAS that allows up to 255 simultaneous dial-in connections to a single server.

- **Domain administration** – NT Server 4.0 organizes nodes into groups called domains. Each domain has a separate security database that enables a user to log on once to gain access to all appropriate resources. Domains can be told to trust each other, to avoid duplicate security information in multiple places on a large network. NT Server 5.0 has replaced this approach with Active Directory.
- **Active Directory** – NT Server 5.0 introduces the new Active Directory (AD) scheme, which enables you to organize your network, nodes, users, and other information into a completely hierarchical structure. It uses *organizational units* (*OUs*) to produce a hierarchy of any depth. It overcomes the administrative inconveniences of the domain approach, and lets you include more detailed information in its global database.
- **DHCP Server** – To avoid the time and effort required to manage IP addresses on a network running the TCP/IP protocol, NT Server can act as a DHCP server. It automatically doles out IP addresses as needed, and takes them back when they're not needed. See Chapter 6 for discussions of TCP/IP and DHCP.

WINDOWS NT SERVER ENTERPRISE EDITION

About a year after releasing Windows NT Server 4.0, Microsoft released a third flavor of the NT product – Windows NT Server Enterprise Edition. This is the youngest addition to the Windows NT product family. It includes all the features of Windows NT Server listed in the previous section, with the following additions:

- **Support for up to eight CPUs** – The number of multiprocessor CPUs supported jumps from four in Windows NT Server to eight in this edition. You don't need to obtain a special version of the software from your computer vendor, unless the number of CPUs exceeds eight.
- **Support for up to 3GB of application RAM** – NT Workstation and Server split 4GB of memory equally between applications and the operating system (applications are limited to 2GB of RAM). Enterprise Edition includes a feature called *4GB Memory Tuning* (*4GT*), which increases the application limit to 3GB and decreases the OS limit to 1GB. In systems with large amounts of RAM, this feature can improve performance by 20 percent or more when running memory-intensive applications.
- **Microsoft Cluster Server (MSCS)** – MSCS lets you cluster two servers together, enabling one to take over automatically if the other fails. This feature provides a higher level of availability for critical data. The server cluster appears as a single server to client nodes, and the automatic transition from one to the other (called *failover*) is invisible to users.

- **Microsoft Transaction Server (MTS)** – MTS provides transaction protection for large-scale distributed applications that may tie together thousands of computers. It is designed to preserve data integrity by tying together multiple operations and treating them as "all or nothing" transactions. MTS also includes tools for deploying these applications. It's tightly integrated with Microsoft Message Queue Server, enabling it to roll back both message sends and receives that may be part of an aborted transaction.
- **Microsoft Message Queue Server (MSMQ)** – MSMQ provides guaranteed delivery of messages between components of large-scale distributed applications, even over unreliable (but low-cost) connections. It's tightly integrated with MTS. (MSMQ is also available free for NT Server in the Windows NT Server Option Pack.)

Exploring Windows 95

Microsoft Windows 95, released in 1995, was the first version of Windows that didn't require a preexisting copy of MS-DOS underneath. Windows 95 includes its own version of MS-DOS built into the operating system package. Because it's a preemptive multitasking operating system, Windows 95 is more suitable for use as a peer-to-peer network node than Windows 3.1 or Windows for Workgroups. It offers full memory protection between individual 32-bit applications, and between applications and the operating system. (To maintain compatibility with Windows 3.*x*, Windows 95 doesn't keep 16-bit Windows applications from harming each other.)

You can run most 32-bit Windows (Win32) applications on Windows 95, whether they're written for Windows 95, Windows 98, or Windows NT. Windows 95 doesn't run all Win32 applications because some of them use features that are specific to either Windows NT or Windows 98. In addition, Windows 95 runs nearly all 16-bit MS-DOS and Windows 3.*x* applications.

Windows 95 can play the role of a node in a peer-to-peer network, or the role of a client in a Windows NT Server-based network. It can also be a client to NetWare and UNIX servers, which I discuss later in this chapter. Windows 95 includes essentially the same underlying peer-to-peer networking capabilities as Windows for Workgroups.

With Windows 95, however, networking became easier – primarily because of the introduction of Plug and Play technology. When used with the latest hardware, this feature enabled the operating system to configure devices (including network adapters) automatically. It saved the time, effort, and training required to install and configure network hardware. Coupled with the new, easier-to-use graphical interface, Windows 95 made peer-to-peer networking easier than ever. For information on installing Windows 95 networking, see Appendix A.

Exploring Windows for Workgroups

Windows for Workgroups 3.11 (often called WfW) was the first Microsoft operating system to include networking capabilities. It basically consists of Windows 3.1 with built-in drivers, protocols, redirector, server, and administration utilities – everything required for peer-to-peer networking.

Windows for Workgroups enhanced the performance of file I/O by introducing the VFAT file system. Its on-disk structure is completely compatible with the FAT file system used on MS-DOS, but it uses a 32-bit protected-mode driver to speed up file access. This feature made it relatively attractive for use as a peer-to-peer file server.

Microsoft's support of Windows for Workgroups is dwindling. If you can afford the upgrade from WfW, I recommend switching to Windows 98.

Exploring Windows 3.1

Windows 3.1 is a 16-bit operating system that introduced higher reliability and more functionality than its Windows 3.0 predecessor. It doesn't have network capabilities built in, but it can be upgraded to support the same set of networking features that Windows for Workgroups provides. Windows 3.1 requires a copy of MS-DOS running underneath, to supply access to local devices and files.

Windows 3.1 uses cooperative multitasking and doesn't provide memory protection between applications. This makes it especially vulnerable to hangs and crashes caused by applications. On the plus side, it runs all 16-bit Windows (Win16) applications – mainly because it *is* 16-bit Windows! Actually, only a few applications out there use features specific to Windows for Workgroups – and Windows 3.1 can't run them. But it can run some Win32 applications, with special help from a little something called Win32s.

Microsoft's support of 16-bit versions of Windows has all but vanished. If you can afford the upgrade from Windows 3.1, I recommend moving your Windows 3.1 network nodes to Windows 98, even it is means upgrading your hardware.

> NOTE: You can upgrade a Windows 3.1 system to add networking capabilities by installing an add-on product supplied by Microsoft. It brings your Windows 3.1 installation up to the level of Windows for Workgroups. Windows 3.1 peer-to-peer network software is also included on the Windows NT Server CD-ROM. See Appendix A for instructions on installing network software on Windows 3.1.

Exploring MS-DOS

Microsoft introduced MS-DOS in 1981 as a standalone, single-tasking operating system for the IBM PC. (It has become generically known in the industry as DOS, and as PC-DOS in the IBM world.) The user interface is completely based on text commands. MS-DOS was required to act as the underpinnings of Windows 3.*x* and Windows for Workgroups. A version of MS-DOS is also built into Windows 95 and Windows 98. MS-DOS isn't required at all to run Windows NT, however. For compatibility with existing software, Windows NT includes a version of the MS-DOS command language and the capability to emulate MS-DOS behavior for existing applications.

> At the time of writing, MS-DOS 6.22 is the latest version of this operating system. Microsoft has no plans to release future versions, because virtually every new computer comes with Windows 98, Windows 95, or Windows NT preloaded. Windows 98 and Windows 95 include some MS-DOS code, which is sometimes called MS-DOS 7. Other manufacturers, such as IBM, have released versions numbered greater than 6.22 for the systems they supply.

I discussed the evolution of networking on MS-DOS in Chapter 1. The product still doesn't include built-in network functionality – you have to get the client software from Microsoft. Because MS-DOS is a single-tasking operating system, it's definitely not a good choice for a server. (This is one key reason for the amazing success of Novell's NetWare server in the early 1980s. I discuss NetWare later in this chapter.) It's not a great client either, but it may be the only choice for nodes that don't have the hardware horsepower to run Windows. Moreover, if you have an MS-DOS application that won't run under Windows, you may be forced into running MS-DOS.

> Windows NT Server includes the MS-DOS network client on its CD-ROM. You can also obtain the client software from Microsoft. See Appendix A for instructions on how to install MS-DOS client networking software.

Exploring Non-Microsoft NOSs

As I mentioned in Chapter 6, real-world networks typically include (or evolve to include) NOSs with differing capabilities from a variety of manufacturers. If your job involves pulling existing networks together, you may run into them immediately. Because heterogeneous networks are so common, I've covered several important non-Microsoft network operating systems in the following sections.

Exploring Novell NetWare

In the early 1980s, Novell developed and sold a product called NetWare, a dedicated server network operating system for Intel x86 computers. The NetWare server NOS is a cooperative multitasking operating system that's specifically designed to be used as a dedicated server – it's not suitable for doing double-duty as a workstation. It provides security features including user and group authentication, as well as restrictions at both the disk and individual file levels.

The Novell networking architecture is proprietary. Novell doesn't publish internal specifications covering the protocols it uses. This approach has had the effect of preventing competitors from developing fully functional NetWare components. It has also limited NetWare's growth in a world where interoperability is becoming increasingly important. Over the last few years, Novell has recognized this and added support for interoperability with UNIX, Macintosh, and Windows NT platforms.

The NOS is designed with a monolithic architecture, consisting only of the kernel and a set of application and service modules. These modules are called *NetWare Loadable Modules*, or *NLMs*. While this approach yields high levels of raw performance, its reliability depends on proper execution of every module. NetWare provides no protection between applications or between an application and the kernel. In other words, a single errant application module can take down the entire server. Moreover, since NetWare uses cooperative multitasking, an application that refuses to release control of the CPU (either because of a bug or because it's just plain greedy) can also prevent the server from running.

Early versions of NetWare were written entirely in Intel x86 assembly language, which maximized performance but eliminated portability. It also created a nightmare whenever a new, higher-performance Intel processor came out. Although the existing version of the software ran on the new CPU, Novell had to rewrite chunks of the NOS to take advantage of many of the hardware performance improvements. Consequently, after Intel released the 80386, Novell decided to rewrite the NOS in the C programming language.

The Privilege of Reliability

I don't mean to paint a completely bleak picture of a NOS that's constantly crashing due to application problems. In fact, NetWare is quite reliable in real-world installations. If it weren't, it wouldn't have the market share it still enjoys.

But NetWare's design leaves it vulnerable to application bugs, making it very expensive and difficult to develop an NLM and test it well enough to ensure overall server integrity. You have to rely on either Novell or the NLM developer to take the extra care necessary in their development and testing activities. This requirement has cut down on the number of software developers willing to create new NLMs.

Before NetWare 4.*x*, the kernel and all NLMs had to run side by side in the CPU's most privileged mode (called Ring 0 in the Intel world). Everyone could step on and crash everyone else, but the NOS didn't suffer the performance penalty of jumping in and out of privileged mode. In NetWare 4.*x*, Novell provides the capability to force an NLM to run at a lower privilege level (Ring 1), thus protecting the kernel and other components from getting stepped on. Reliability problem solved? Not really.

This approach imposes a performance penalty when the CPU must switch back and forth between the different privilege modes. Rather than live with this slowdown, most folks use this feature for testing purposes only. As soon as an NLM seems to be reliable, it gets thrown back into the Ring 0 mix with the kernel.

NetWare product releases have loosely followed the same schedule as Intel processor releases. The first version, NetWare 86, ran on 8086 and 8088 CPUs. NetWare 2.*x* was designed for the 286, and version 3.*x* was tuned for the 386. At that point, correlation between NetWare versions and CPU products became fuzzy. NetWare 4.*x*, NetWare Lite, Personal NetWare, and intraNetWare are all Intel-based products, but aren't geared for any specific CPU model. Of these, NetWare 4.*x* and intraNetWare survive. intraNetWare, a strategic response to Windows NT, bridges the gap between NetWare LANs and Internet and intranet environments.

NetWare 4.*x* was a totally revamped design with heftier hardware requirements. In it, Novell introduced *NetWare Directory Services* (*NDS*) to compete directly with Banyan VINES' directory service. Before NDS, each NetWare server maintained its own security database, known as the *bindery*. It contained user and group accounts and their rights to access resources on that server. If users needed access to resources on other servers, they needed separate accounts on each one. The bindery approach led to users having to remember different passwords on different servers, or users setting a single password on all their accounts. Either way, this was an inconvenient and insecure way of life.

NDS treats everything on the network as an object – servers, shared resources, and even users and groups. It organizes these objects into a hierarchical tree structure. Objects within the hierarchy can be either resource objects or container objects. *Resource objects* are the leaf nodes of the tree – representing actual network resources. *Container objects* let you organize resources in various ways, regardless of their physical locations or connections. For example, you may want to collect all the shared printers together into one logical container. Or, you may want to assign all the resources in a department to a single logical container. The NDS tree is stored as a database that's constantly replicated to all servers within the tree. Rather than logging on to an individual server, a user logs into the entire NDS tree to access available network resources.

Although NDS provides great flexibility and convenience in terms of organizing and managing users and resources, it can still become unwieldy in large networks. If you have many users logging on, and many changes taking place in the NDS database, the replication traffic between servers can begin to bog down the entire network.

The NetWare client software is simply a set of add-on products for existing operating systems. Novell offers client software that accesses both bindery and NDS information for all of Microsoft's desktop operating systems – including MS-DOS, Windows 3.1, Windows 95, Windows 98, and Windows NT. Microsoft has developed and included its own version of NetWare client software, giving it away for free with the operating system. However, because Novell's networking architecture remains closed, Microsoft's versions can't always do everything that Novell's can. The Microsoft developers just don't have all the information on NetWare internals that the Novell developers have.

To take advantage of NDS features, client software must be upgraded. NetWare 4.*x* still works with older clients, however, because it can emulate the older (bindery) versions of the server. Unfortunately, a NetWare 4.*x* server that has to do this emulation takes a serious hit to its performance. Updating the clients, although painful and expensive, is a much better solution when moving to NetWare 4.*x*.

Novell created a formidable combined sales, training, and reseller force for the NetWare product line. It was able to capture the lion's share of the PC-based dedicated server networking market early on. NetWare is still considered strong at sharing files and printers, but isn't considered as strong in the role of an application server. Compared with other available server NOS products, NetWare is typically more difficult to install and maintain. Nevertheless, Novell still holds its server market share lead today – though its share is eroding rapidly as Microsoft Windows NT skyrockets in the marketplace.

Exploring Banyan VINES

In 1983, Banyan Systems chose the dedicated server NOS approach as well. It introduced *VINES*, which is loosely an acronym for *Virtual Networking System*. Banyan VINES server software is a preemptive multitasking operating system based on a UNIX core. VINES clients are add-ons that run on top of MS-DOS, Windows, OS/2, or UNIX. VINES includes a component called *StreetTalk*, which offers organization and management features similar to Novell's NDS. In fact, many of the NDS features were driven by having to compete with the VINES directory.

Like Novell, Banyan defined its own set of proprietary network protocols, following the OSI reference model closely. So, although VINES isn't interoperable with systems using standard protocols, the protocol functions are relatively easy to understand. Parts of these protocols are very similar (but not identical) to TCP/IP.

VINES is a bit less complex than NetWare, and it takes certain steps to make it easier to distinguish between shared resources. VINES is good for sharing files and printers, but is not generally considered a good application server.

Exploring Artisoft LANtastic

In contrast to both Novell and Banyan, Artisoft focuses primarily on the peer-to-peer networking model. Its LANtastic product line was successful for many years because of its ease of installation, ease of use, and low overhead on computers that had little memory to spare. Like Banyan and Novell clients, LANtastic peer-to-peer software consists of network software that runs on top of MS-DOS, Windows, OS/2, Windows NT, and other operating systems.

NOTE: Artisoft also ventured into the world of dedicated servers by offering a product line called CorStream. It was essentially NetWare with an easier-to-use LANtastic interface, but it wasn't as popular as Artisoft's peer-to-peer products.

LANtastic uses a proprietary protocol that's similar, at the application layer, to the SMB protocol. (To be as confusing as possible, I'll mention that the LANtastic protocol is called SNB. It sure made it tough to sit around a conference table discussing how to get SNB to talk to SMB.)

LANtastic enjoys most of its success in small businesses that don't want to climb the NetWare learning curve or hire consultants to manage their networks. However, that success has waned in recent years. Once Microsoft started including full peer-to-peer networking capabilities in its Windows operating systems (especially Windows 95), Artisoft had a difficult time competing. It still has a solid customer base, though, because of its large number of loyal resellers and consultants, the products' relative ease of use, and the products' capability to run on older computers and operating systems.

Exploring Everybody's UNIX

Originally developed at AT&T Bell Labs in the early 1970s, UNIX has been a true network operating system from day one. It uses preemptive multitasking, and most versions support multiprocessor computers. For legal reasons, AT&T licensed the source code for UNIX to universities, creating a generation of UNIX operating system gurus, and feeding the UNIX marketplace with more software utilities than you could possibly count in a lifetime.

Written mostly in the C programming language, UNIX has proven to be easily portable to a wide range of CPU architectures. As a result, you'll find a flavor of UNIX available for many non-PC-based workstations, in addition to the PC platform.

CAUTION

Easy portability is both a blessing and a curse to the UNIX operating system. On the blessing side, it means that UNIX can be ported quickly to just about any CPU architecture that can execute instructions. On the curse side, it leads to tremendous fragmentation in the UNIX market. Because it's so easy to port, just about everyone who can fog a mirror has come out with a different version of UNIX. There's no central authority that controls what is and isn't a UNIX operating system product.

A large number of different UNIX flavors exist. There are free versions of UNIX, such as NetBSD and Linux. Sun Microsystems offers Solaris for the Sun platform, Hewlett-Packard offers HP-UX, and DEC sells Digital UNIX and Ultrix. Silicon Graphics, the company that makes some of the computer hardware used for Hollywood special effects, has its own version of UNIX called IRIX. Santa Cruz Operations (SCO) sells OpenServer, which is today's leading UNIX NOS for the Intel-based PC market.

Most UNIX versions (other than the free ones) are tuned specifically to a vendor's hardware for optimum performance. On many systems, this approach has given UNIX a distinct performance advantage over other NOSs. Because the versions have been developed or modified independently, however, it's anybody's guess as to whether a particular version includes a particular feature or utility. (Nervous about the Windows NT juggernaut, UNIX vendors have banded together several times in an effort to standardize their wares – without success.)

The complexity of UNIX in the operating system arena is similar to the complexity of TCP/IP in the network protocol arena. You could spend a career trying to learn everything there is to know about UNIX and all of its thousands of utilities and switches.

Exploring IBM OS/2

OS/2, which stands for Operating System/2, was jointly developed by IBM and Microsoft. The initial goal was to take advantage of the new Intel 286 processor (yes, OS/2 is that old) by creating a true 16-bit multitasking graphical operating system. By 1989, the companies had jointly released two versions – a text-based version and a graphical version. Both were 16-bit, preemptive multitasking, memory-protected operating systems.

When IBM inherited the OS/2 project from Microsoft, it continued and completed development of a 32-bit version, which evolved into today's OS/2 Warp Server. OS/2 is based on LAN Manager, so it's compatible with Microsoft networking. At the redirector level, OS/2 uses the SMB protocol.

NOTE: OS/2 has been dying a slow death for several years. It's still used by IBM loyalists or in certain situations where an application is available only on the OS/2 platform. Few software developers are making any investment in creating new applications for OS/2, because its market is so small and doesn't appear to be growing. However, you may encounter it in existing installations.

Summary

In this chapter, you've seen how network operating systems differ, and how certain products fill specific needs in your networked environment. You've been exposed to the key features of Microsoft's operating system products, as well as those from other manufacturers. At this point, you probably know which NOS (or NOSs) you need, or at least which ones you need to learn more about.

In Chapter 8, I fill you in on how to select the right hardware to design powerful and efficient clients and servers for your network. Then, in Chapter 9, I show you how to install, configure, and test network hardware and Windows 98 network software in your computers.

Chapter 8

Choosing Client and Server Hardware

IN THIS CHAPTER

- Establishing and prioritizing your network design objectives
- Designing your Windows 98 hardware system: starting fresh or upgrading
- Selecting the right CPU, motherboard, and devices
- Selecting the right network adapter

IN THIS CHAPTER, I discuss the key hardware topics to consider in designing and preparing your computers for Windows 98 and your network. Understanding the implications of computer hardware is important, whether you're installing and running Windows 98 on existing hardware, you're upgrading existing hardware, or you have the luxury of specifying and purchasing new computers.

Because networked computers potentially provide services to many clients at once, a single component in one computer can affect the productivity of many users. Therefore, component reliability and performance take on greater importance when computers are networked together. By the end of this chapter, you'll have the knowledge and tools you need to select the right hardware for all your Windows 98 computers.

Designing Your Windows 98 Hardware

Whether you're upgrading an existing computer or specifying a new one, you'll find valuable information in this section. Here, I cover the key Windows 98-compatible hardware components that relate directly or indirectly to networking.

Throughout this chapter, I emphasize achieving high performance and reliability on individual networked computers and on the overall network. Both are important in achieving the greatest user productivity benefits from your network.

Picking a CPU for Windows 98

In this section, I walk you through the process of selecting a central processor to use with Windows 98. Even if you're going to run the operating system on existing hardware, you'll find useful information about CPU upgrade options that might be available to you. Keep in mind that your choice of CPU will have a downstream effect on several other hardware decisions you'll make later in this chapter.

> NOTE: If you're considering Windows NT as part of your network design, additional options are available to you that I won't discuss here. As I mentioned in Chapter 7, Windows NT supports computers based on the DEC Alpha CPU in addition to the Intel x86 CPU. NT also supports multiprocessor systems — computers containing more than one processor. Selecting Windows NT hardware is beyond the scope of this book, but many of the performance concepts I discuss in this chapter apply to Windows NT equally well.

PICKING THE RIGHT INTEL CPU

As I'm sure you're aware, Intel offers several flavors of x86 architecture CPUs. (The term *x86* refers generically to the family of Intel products, including the 8086, 80286, 80386, 80486, and Pentium technologies.) New models at new speeds arrive in a continuous stream. At a minimum, Windows 98 requires at least a 486 CPU running at 66MHz. Keep in mind that Microsoft's minimum CPU requirements are indeed bare minimums. Later on, I discuss what I recommend you put into practice in the real world.

Table 8-1 provides a comprehensive picture of the current Intel CPU arena, at the time of writing. In the table, I've focused only on processors that are compatible with Windows 98.

TABLE 8-1 INTEL PROCESSORS COMPATIBLE WITH WINDOWS 98

Intel Processor Model	Processor Clock Rate (MHz)	System Bus Clock Rate (MHz)	Level 1 (Primary) Cache Size (Bytes)	Level 2 (Secondary) Cache on the Processor (Bytes)
i486DX2	66	33	8K	0
i486DX4	75	25	16K	0
i486DX4	100	33	16K	0

Intel Processor Model	Processor Clock Rate (MHz)	System Bus Clock Rate (MHz)	Level 1 (Primary) Cache Size (Bytes)	Level 2 (Secondary) Cache on the Processor (Bytes)
Pentium	60	60	16K	0
Pentium	66	66	16K	0
Pentium	75	50	16K	0
Pentium	90	60	16K	0
Pentium	100	66 or 50	16K	0
Pentium	120	60	16K	0
Pentium	133	66	16K	0
Pentium	150	60	16K	0
Pentium	166	66	16K	0
Pentium	200	66	16K	0
Pentium MMX	166	66	32K	0
Pentium MMX	200	66	32K	0
Pentium MMX	233	66	32K	0
Pentium Pro	150	66	16K	256K
Pentium Pro	166	66	16K	512K
Pentium Pro	180	60	16K	256K
Pentium Pro	200	66	16K	256K
Pentium Pro	200	66	16K	512K
Pentium Pro	200	66	16K	1M
Celeron (Pentium II)	266	66	32K	0
Pentium II	266	66	32K	512K
Pentium II	300	66	32K	512K
Pentium II	333	66	32K	512K
Pentium II	350	100	32K	512K
Pentium II	400	100	32K	512K

Table 8-1 includes both the internal CPU clock rate and the external bus clock rate – the speed at which the CPU interacts with surrounding devices. The combination of these rates significantly influences the overall performance of the computer, so both rates are vitally important. If the clock rate of the CPU is higher than the bus clock rate, the CPU contains a multiplier circuit that causes the processor to run proportionally faster than the other system components. Clock multiplying offers huge performance boosts if you're running primarily CPU-bound software. You'll see very little difference when running I/O-intensive applications, though, because the system bus speed limits overall I/O performance. (*I/O* refers to *input/output*, the transfer of data between a CPU and a peripheral device.)

NOTE: The internal data bus width represents another important performance factor. All the processors listed in Table 8-1 are considered 32-bit CPUs. However, the Pentium processors (Pentium, Pentium MMX, Pentium Pro, and Pentium II) are capable of moving data around internally 64 bits at a time. This design further improves the speed of handling data within the CPU — processing more data in the same amount of time.

A *cache* (pronounced "cash") is a high-speed memory area that keeps recently used data and software instructions readily available to the CPU, in case they're needed. Caches are used to increase performance by minimizing the number of times the CPU has to access slower main memory. Each of the listed Intel processors includes an internal *Level 1 cache*, sometimes called a *primary cache*. The 486 CPU uses the entire cache for a mixture of instructions and data. The other Intel processors divide the cache into two equal parts, using half for caching instructions and the other half for caching data.

The Pentium Pro and Pentium II designs move the *Level 2 cache*, or *secondary cache*, from its traditional home on the motherboard to the CPU device itself. This approach both reduces system cost and improves performance. I discuss more details of caches and motherboards later in this chapter.

INTEL'S 486 The absolute minimum Intel CPU for Windows 98 is a 486DX2 running at 66MHz. If you must run Windows 98 on this class of computer, you'll need to stock up on plenty of that virtue they call patience. If you're specifying a new system, I strongly recommend opting for a Pentium-based computer. 486-based computers, because of their small cache and slow system bus speeds, make running

Windows 98 a pretty darned unpleasant experience. If you must install it on a 486 computer, however, I recommend upgrading the CPU to a 486DX4, which runs at about 100MHz. Not all motherboards are compatible with this upgrade, so check with your motherboard manufacturer.

INTEL'S PENTIUM Appearing first in 1993, the Intel Pentium processor introduced a 64-bit data bus to Intel's line of CPUs. (Intel had planned to call this product the 586, and that's what everyone else expected – but when the courts told Intel that it couldn't copyright numeric names, it christened the new chip *Pentium.*) The Pentium CPU contains two instruction pipelines, enabling the execution of up to two instructions in each clock cycle. Up until this time, this architectural feature had appeared only in *RISC* (*Reduced Instruction Set Computer*) processors, so the Pentium began to blur the line between traditional RISC and *CISC* (*Complex Instruction Set Computer*) architectures. Table 8-1 includes a list of the Pentium processors.

Avoid the 60MHz and 66MHz Pentium CPUs like the plague. Even if someone tries to pay you to take one of these systems, walk away quickly. These processors run at very high temperatures, and have had some nasty heat dissipation problems. A few vendors were able to design around the problems with strategically placed heat sinks and multiple cooling fans. But many vendors were unsuccessful, creating systems that sometimes behave erratically, usually at the worst possible times. Life is short, so if your goal is a reliable computer — and it should be — avoid these CPU speeds.

The Pentium includes an on-chip 16K Level 1 cache, which it functionally separates into two parts – an 8K instruction cache and an 8K data cache. Most Pentium motherboards include a slot for external Level 2 cache, ranging in size from 256K to 2MB. When you specify your Pentium-based computer, always opt for the largest possible external cache.

Overall, the Pentium offers a significant performance improvement over 486-based computers. Because the cost difference is so small, and because more and more software now requires a Pentium CPU, I recommend that you don't consider anything less than a Pentium to run Windows 98.

TIP

Bus speed is vitally important to overall system performance. Because many computer specifications don't explicitly list the speed of the system bus, you can still avoid slow bus speeds by avoiding certain CPU speeds. Table 8-1 shows that Pentium CPUs running at 60, 75, 90, 120, and 150MHz operate with a system bus speed below 66MHz. Finding out the speed of the bus in a 100MHz Pentium-based computer requires a little more digging, because it can use either a 50MHz or 66MHz bus. In this case, you'll have to find out the actual bus speed from the manufacturer. The overall speed of systems with a bus speed below 66MHz is often lower than that of computers based on slower processors with a faster bus speed. So, avoid these processor speeds and be sure your system bus speed is at least 66MHz.

INTEL'S PENTIUM MMX *MMX*, which stands for *Multi-Media Extensions*, introduces three architectural enhancements to the basic Pentium design described earlier. First, Intel has added 57 new instructions to the standard Pentium instruction set. Specifically designed to provide a performance boost to multimedia applications, the new instructions help manipulate video, audio, and graphical data efficiently. Software developers who want their applications to take advantage of these new instructions must write (or rewrite) their software to use those instructions explicitly. (Intel's *Designed for Intel MMX* logo is your signal that a software product uses one or more of the new MMX instructions.)

The second MMX enhancement involves a process called *Single Instruction Multiple Data* (*SIMD*), which enables one instruction to operate on many pieces of data. Think of this feature as the difference between using a single e-mail address to communicate with a large number of people versus sending messages to many individuals manually. You can automatically send one e-mail message to a large group of people by sending it to a single mailing list address. Otherwise, you must manually send the same e-mail message many times to many different individual addresses. Again, software developers must design their applications to use this feature if they want to take advantage of it.

The third MMX enhancement, and perhaps most important in the short term, is a 32K on-chip Level 1 cache – that's double the size of the non-MMX Pentium processors. The MMX CPU uses 16K for instructions and 16K for data. The increased cache size is the one MMX feature you can automatically benefit from right away – no new software is required.

Do you really need to pay a premium for MMX? At the time of writing, a relatively small percentage of applications actually take advantage of the MMX instructions. Until software comes along that uses these MMX instructions, you won't see any benefit from them. That said, however, MMX is definitely worth considering for several reasons. First, the doubling of the cache alone has resulted in a

10 to 20 percent performance boost over non-MMX Pentium CPUs running at the same clock speed. Second, when the MMX-enabled software does arrive *en masse*, you'll be equipped to take immediate advantage of it. Third, Intel has promised to include MMX technology in future processor lines, so this isn't just some technological sidetrack. Of course, if the software you plan to run on Windows 98 already uses the new instructions, that's one more strong argument in favor of investing in MMX. Finally, non-MMX CPUs are getting harder to find in the marketplace. Intel is definitely phasing out its older Pentiums in favor of MMX-equipped CPUs.

INTEL'S PENTIUM PRO Intel started designing the Pentium Pro way back in 1991. At that time, Intel designers predicted that by 1995, the industry would have certainly abandoned all 16-bit software, and we would be living in a purely 32-bit world. Based on this assumption, the Pentium Pro is highly optimized for pure /32-bit applications and operating systems. But when you toss 16-bit software at it (including DOS, Windows 3.*x*, 16-bit applications, and parts of Windows 98 and Windows 95), the Pentium Pro is slower than a standard Pentium processor running at the same clock rate.

As a result, if you run Windows NT and 32-bit applications exclusively, the Pentium Pro makes a great CPU choice. If you plan to run Windows 98 or Windows 95, however, I recommend either sticking with a standard Pentium (or Pentium MMX), or springing for a Pentium II, which I discuss later in this chapter. Because Windows 98 and Windows 95 still contain 16-bit code, they perform relatively poorly on a Pentium Pro.

TIP

If you do end up choosing a Pentium Pro, avoid crippling the computer with a slow bus speed by staying away from the 180MHz Pentium Pro CPU. Table 8-1 shows that the 180MHz Pentium Pro operates with a system bus speed of only 60MHz. Combining this factor with a smaller cache, overall speed on these systems can be lower than that of computers based on the 166MHz Pentium Pro. Make sure your motherboard's bus speed is at least 66MHz.

In my view, the Pentium Pro has several strikes against it. First, the Level 1 cache size in the Pentium Pro remains at 16K. You can get twice as much Level 1 cache by selecting either the less expensive Pentium MMX or the more expensive Pentium II. Second, the Pentium Pro doesn't include the MMX instructions, and Intel has not announced plans to add them in future versions of this CPU. This isn't a big issue today, but it may be in the future, as more software takes advantage of MMX instructions. Third, the Pentium Pro imposes a performance penalty on all 16-bit software. This is more of a short-term issue as 16-bit software fades into the distance, but it's still important if you plan to run either Windows 98, Windows 95, or any 16-bit applications.

INTEL'S PENTIUM II The Pentium II processor is Intel's top-of-the-line CPU. Functionally, this 7.5 million transistor device combines the best of the Pentium Pro and Pentium MMX technologies. You can think of the Pentium II as a Pentium Pro with a larger Level 1 cache, MMX instructions, and improved performance for both 32-bit and 16-bit software. In addition, like the Pentium Pro, the Pentium II is designed to make developing multiprocessor computers relatively easy.

The Pentium II departs from the conventional flat CPU package with pins sticking out the bottom, and instead uses a proprietary *Single Edge Contact*, or *SEC*, cartridge. (No, this isn't the same SEC that investigates corporate executives for insider trading.) The cartridge contains the CPU itself along with both the Level 1 and Level 2 caches mounted within the package. This design enables all the components within the package to operate at higher frequencies, effectively doubling the Level 2 cache speed over a standard Pentium or Pentium MMX Level 2 cache. The SEC package is oriented vertically, and slips into a motherboard edge connector called *Slot 1*. Unlike the Pentium and Pentium Pro CPU sockets, the SEC Slot 1 looks more like a motherboard expansion slot. Intel has promised that future versions of the Pentium II will be compatible with the Slot 1 connector.

Because Intel uses the new Slot 1 CPU connector, you can't upgrade from any previous Pentium technology without replacing the motherboard. (When Pentium II CPUs were hard to come by, a few manufacturers designed motherboards with sockets for both the Pentium Pro and Pentium II. But now that Pentium II processors are readily available and prices are falling, the market for these hybrid motherboards has all but vanished.)

Is the Pentium II the way to go? Sure, if you're willing to pay the price premium. With a large Level 1 cache, higher clock rates, MMX instructions, a large and fast integrated Level 2 cache, and other performance improvements, it does a great job of running Windows 98 and applications today and into the future. However, I can't make the decision for you. The Pentium, Pentium MMX, and Pentium Pro (and the 486, in desperate times) are all capable of running Windows 98. You'll need to examine the relative costs and benefits for your particular situation, based on your applications and your system design objectives.

INTEL'S CELERON To compete in the sub-$1000 PC market, and still make customers feel good about their purchases, Intel introduced the Celeron. It's essentially a Pentium II processor, with one critical difference: as shown in Table 8-1, the Celeron has no integrated Level 2 cache. In every other respect, it's exactly the same as a Pentium II.

The lack of an integrated Level 2 cache is a critical performance problem. Future Celeron products will contain small integrated Level 2 caches, but they still won't perform as well as Pentium II processors. Some benchmarks show that the Celeron running at 266MHz performs more slowly than a Pentium MMX at 233MHz. With the introduction of Celeron (and other products that I discuss later in this chapter), it's no longer possible to judge relative CPU performance by comparing clock speeds alone. My advice is to steer clear of any system based on the Celeron processor — performance-wise, you're much better off with a cheaper Pentium MMX.

INTEL CPU UPGRADES If your plans include upgrading an existing CPU to a faster one, either today or in the future, you may be able to simply swap out the processor, depending on your current processor speed and your motherboard design. Equipped with the appropriate CPU socket or slot, you can select an Intel OverDrive Processor as a replacement. In most cases, the replacement requires only a few minutes to install. Table 8-2 presents a number of available Intel upgrade options. In the table, I've focused only on CPUs that are compatible with Windows 98.

TABLE 8-2 INTEL PROCESSOR UPGRADE OPTIONS

Current Intel Processor Model	Current Processor Clock Rate (MHz)	System Bus Clock Rate (MHz)	Socket or Slot Required on Motherboard	New Intel Processor Model	New CPU Clock Rate (MHz)
i486DX	33	33	Socket 1, 2, or 3	i486DX2	66
i486DX	25	25	Socket 1, 2, or 3	i486DX4	75
i486DX	33	33	Socket 1, 2, or 3	i486DX4	100
i486DX	66	33	Socket 1, 2, or 3	i486DX4	100
i486DX or SX	20 or 25	20 or 25	Socket 2 or 3	Pentium	63

Continued

TABLE 8-2 INTEL PROCESSOR UPGRADE OPTIONS *(Continued)*

Current Intel Processor Model	Current Processor Clock Rate (MHz)	System Bus Clock Rate (MHz)	Socket or Slot Required on Motherboard	New Intel Processor Model	New CPU Clock Rate (MHz)
i486DX2 or SX2	50	25	Socket 2 or 3	Pentium	63
i486DX or SX	33	33	Socket 2 or 3	Pentium	83
i486DX2 or SX2	66	33	Socket 2 or 3	Pentium	83
Pentium	60	60	Socket 4	Pentium	120
Pentium	66	66	Socket 4	Pentium	133
Pentium	75	50	Socket 5 or 7	Pentium	125
Pentium	75	50	Socket 5 or 7	Pentium MMX	150
Pentium	90	60	Socket 5 or 7	Pentium	150
Pentium	90	60	Socket 5 or 7	Pentium MMX	180
Pentium	100	66	Socket 5 or 7	Pentium	166
Pentium	100	66	Socket 5 or 7	Pentium MMX	166
Pentium	120	60	Socket 7 (296 pins)	Pentium	180
Pentium	120	60	Socket 7	Pentium MMX	180
Pentium	150	60	Socket 7	Pentium	180
Pentium	150	60	Socket 7	Pentium MMX	180
Pentium	133	66	Socket 7	Pentium	200
Pentium	133	66	Socket 7	Pentium MMX	200
Pentium	166	66	Socket 7	Pentium	200
Pentium	166	66	Socket 7	Pentium MMX	200
Pentium	200	66	Socket 7	Pentium	233

Current Intel Processor Model	Current Processor Clock Rate (MHz)	System Bus Clock Rate (MHz)	Socket or Slot Required on Motherboard	New Intel Processor Model	New CPU Clock Rate (MHz)
Pentium	233	66	Socket 7	Pentium	266
Pentium Pro	150	66	Socket 8 (387 pins)	Pentium Pro	166
Pentium Pro	150	66	Socket 8	Pentium Pro	200
Pentium Pro	166	66	Socket 8	Pentium Pro	200
Pentium Pro	180	66	Socket 8	Pentium Pro	200
Pentium II	266	66	Slot 1 SEC (242 pins)	Pentium II	300
Pentium II	300	66	Slot 1 SEC	Pentium II	333
Pentium II	350	100	Slot 1 SEC	Pentium II	400

Intel's upgrade requirements are very strict regarding the CPU socket on your motherboard. To complicate matters further, different motherboards operate the CPU at different voltages, and you can adjust some motherboards for multiple voltage settings. With all these variables at play, you need to check the detailed specifications of your motherboard, your computer's documentation, and the Intel OverDrive compatibility list to make sure the upgrade CPU you purchase is truly compatible with your computer. You can find additional details about Intel's OverDrive upgrades at `www.intel.com/overdrive/personal/odpfaq.htm`.

CAUTION: Never use a standard Pentium MMX processor to upgrade an existing non-MMX Pentium, unless you're absolutely sure your motherboard is configured to provide the correct voltages. Intel designed the OverDrive MMX CPUs to work as upgrades to non-MMX processors, but standard Pentium MMX CPUs assume that your motherboard hardware can accept standard MMX processors. If you put a standard MMX CPU into a motherboard that wasn't designed for it, the computer may appear to work properly for a while. However, you could end up permanently damaging your CPU, your motherboard, or both, due to voltage differences.

In some computers, older BIOS code may not be able to operate correctly with higher-speed, upgraded CPUs. Before upgrading, check with your computer, motherboard, or BIOS manufacturer to determine whether you need to upgrade your BIOS at the same time you upgrade your CPU. It's especially important to upgrade your BIOS before installing an MMX processor upgrade. If you don't, your computer may lock up every time you try to boot it. More information on BIOS upgrade requirements is available at `www.intel.com/overdrive/bios/`.

CAUTION

Intel explicitly states that its OverDrive processors won't work properly when installed in multiprocessor computers. The truth is that some do and some don't. Check with Intel on the specific CPU upgrade you're considering before attempting to use it in a multiprocessor computer. This is important only if you're planning to upgrade the operating system to Windows NT later on.

Because of the significant changes in the CPU package interfaces to the motherboard, there's no upgrade path from the Pentium to either the Pentium Pro or Pentium II. To make these leaps, you'll need a new motherboard designed for the new processor. Likewise, you can't upgrade today from a Pentium Pro to a Pentium II; however, Intel has announced future plans to release Pentium II OverDrive processors that will upgrade existing Pentium Pro-based systems.

Screen Savers Can Cost You

Consider the innocuous screen saver — useful, whimsical, even downright entertaining at times. The screen saver concept is great, because it lets you protect your long-term investment in your computer's video monitor. But just as television can numb our minds and credit cards can bleed us financially dry, screen savers can suck the very life out of your CPU. In a network environment, you need to select the right screen saver, or you'll run into trouble.

Some screen savers (for example, some of the 3-D OpenGL screen savers) are very CPU-intensive. If you run one on a server (or peer) computer, the computer can end up spending more CPU cycles on the screen saver than on processing network clients' data. What's more, screen savers can be buggy pieces of software — especially the more complex ones that fly kitchen appliances or bathroom fixtures across the screen. Under the right conditions, a screen saver can crash a computer.

My bottom-line advice here is to use a low-impact, simple screen saver. I'm a big fan of the blank-screen choice. Sure, it isn't exciting, but it won't eat up your computer's precious CPU cycles, and probably won't crash the system either.

UNDERSTANDING NON-INTEL CPU OPTIONS

Cyrix, AMD, and other CPU manufacturers offer several lower-cost, x86-compatible alternatives to Intel processors. They position some of these products as upgrades, and others as core components of low-cost, name-brand computers. In addition to lower prices, these products sometimes offer faster CPU performance and additional features. In the following sections, I present some details on the Cyrix and AMD processor products.

One significant advantage of these products is their use of the standard Socket 7 found on most existing Pentium motherboards. You can often take advantage of the increased speed and features of these processors without having to invest in a brand new motherboard. Recall that, in the Intel arena, if you want to move from a Pentium to either a Pentium Pro or Pentium II, you need a new motherboard to accommodate the new CPU design.

Based on my experience at Microsoft and with many users in the field, I have mixed feelings about these products. On one hand, many customers use them and achieve excellent results. In these cases, the alternative CPUs represent a great price-performance value. On the other hand, some folks who use these processors have trouble installing Windows on them, or end up with system behavior that's sometimes difficult to diagnose. Most of these problems have been chalked up to subtle incompatibilities with Intel x86 architecture. In some cases, users have solved the problem simply by replacing the CPU with an Intel brand processor. Thus, you face some amount of risk in choosing these products, and some network administrators don't want to deal with the potential drain on time and money in an experiment that may save only a few dollars on each computer.

> NOTE: To be fair to these Intel competitors, the reason for this type of strange behavior isn't always the processor's fault. Sometimes, it's caused by a mismatch between the CPU and motherboard voltages. If you decide to use these products, make sure you check the CPU voltage specifications in your motherboard or computer documentation, and verify that they exactly match those of the CPU itself. If there's a mismatch, you could end up with anything from unexplained random behavior to a permanently damaged CPU, motherboard, or both.

All of these CPU products claim Intel x86 compatibility. For legal reasons, the manufacturers must design the CPUs virtually from scratch, and duplicate the functionality of the Intel x86 architecture without duplicating the internal logic that makes an Intel x86 what it is. The manufacturers have done a great job, but with literally millions of transistors on the chip, it's difficult to achieve 100 percent compatibility. Even if all the instructions operate exactly the same as on an Intel processor, a non-Intel CPU may have slight timing differences that you may never see manifested – or they might wreak havoc with some other hardware or software component in your system.

Picking a Motherboard for Windows 98

Even if you're purchasing an off-the-shelf computer, you need to be aware of what to look for in a motherboard. If you're thinking of upgrading an existing computer by replacing its motherboard, then you should definitely read this section. Your choice of motherboard will influence downstream decisions about your computer's hardware, and if you make the right choices at this stage, later decisions will be easier for you.

RIDING THE BANDWIDTH BUS

Ever since IBM introduced the first PC in 1983, a number of bus architectures – good, bad, and even ugly – have graced the PC landscape. Interestingly, today's typical motherboards are sort of like a May–December romance, combining the oldest bus architecture with the youngest. In this section, I present the pros and cons of the major bus architectures available to you, and provide some recommendations for your Windows 98 computers.

UNDERSTANDING THE ISA BUS The motherboards in the original IBM PC and PC/XT included 8-bit expansion slots. Because IBM decided to open the PC architecture to anyone who wanted to design adapters, many hardware manufacturers jumped on the bandwagon. When the PC/AT arrived, IBM widened the standard expansion bus to 16 bits. The new bus was backward compatible with the existing 8-bit expansion adapters. Today, there are literally thousands of adapters designed to use this bus architecture. Due to its wide industry acceptance and support, both the 8-bit and 16-bit buses have earned the name *ISA* (*Industry Standard Architecture*).

Compared with other available bus architectures, ISA is relatively sluggish. Theoretically, its maximum data transfer rate is 8MB per second, but in practice, data travels between 1.5MB and 5MB per second. Existing motherboards with only ISA slots are 486-based. Pentium-based motherboards typically have a combination of ISA and PCI slots, to offer both the high speed of PCI and compatibility with existing ISA adapters. (I discuss the PCI bus later in this chapter.)

I don't recommend motherboards with only ISA slots — not only because they're 486-based, but because disk, video, and network performance is painfully slow. To exacerbate the performance problem, ISA adapters that perform *DMA* (*Direct Memory Access*) can only do so to the first 16MB of RAM. Normally, more RAM is a good thing for performance, but if an ISA adapter attempts to do DMA above the 16MB threshold, Windows 98 has to copy the data to and from a buffer in the lower 16MB of RAM, where the DMA can actually take place. This slows down I/O to a pathetic crawl. So, if you do use ISA slots, don't use them for anything that needs to be fast, such as network adapters, disk controllers, or video adapters. And if the ISA adapter performs any DMA operations, don't use it in a computer with more than 16MB of RAM. (I discuss DMA in Chapter 9.)

The average number of ISA slots provided on new motherboards is shrinking with each passing month. Eventually, ISA slots will go away completely, as more and more adapters move to PCI. The PC98 specification, which computer manufacturers will need to follow to earn the Microsoft *Designed for Windows* logo, requires that most ISA slots and adapters disappear by the end of 1999.

The entire PC industry is quickly moving away from ISA altogether. The only two reasons for having ISA slots today are modems and sound cards. Sound cards are now appearing for the faster PCI bus, which I discuss later in this chapter. Non-ISA modems are appearing as well. And of course, you always have the external modem alternative. If you're designing a new PC, whether it's a server or a client, I suggest you avoid designing it around any ISA devices.

UNDERSTANDING THE MCA BUS Four years after it introduced the first PC, IBM tried to regain control of the PC architecture by releasing the PS/2 computer. This revolutionary design included a brand new, proprietary expansion bus called the *Micro Channel Architecture*, or *MCA*. It accommodates both 16-bit and 32-bit data paths, and pushes the data at a rate of up to 40MB per second. IBM wanted this superior design to eclipse the ISA bus completely, but the licensing fees it levied on hardware manufacturers discouraged all but a handful from designing MCA adapters.

As a network administrator looking toward the future, you should be aware that MCA is a dead end. You'll be able to maintain and upgrade your MCA-based computers for some time, but virtually all hardware manufacturers have put all their resources into developing for the PCI architecture, which I discuss in a later section. If you're acquiring new computers, I don't recommend the MCA bus.

UNDERSTANDING THE EISA BUS The *EISA* bus architecture is the product of a PC industry revolt against IBM. In 1988, computer manufacturers who had built their businesses on the open PC architecture needed an answer to IBM's 32-bit MCA bus design. Few wanted to pay IBM licensing fees, so several manufacturers united, under the leadership of Compaq, to create the *Extended Industry Standard Architecture* (*EISA*).

Unlike MCA, EISA is fully compatible with ISA adapters, and represents a completely open architecture. The consortium of hardware manufactures (the rebel forces) didn't want to cut off their ISA revenue stream, so instead of creating a whole new bus architecture from scratch, they decided to maintain full compatibility with the existing 8-bit and 16-bit ISA standards. Each EISA slot can accept either an EISA adapter or an ISA adapter, enabling you to mix and match them as needed. From a performance viewpoint, the price of maintaining ISA compatibility limits the data transfer rate to about 33MB per second, somewhat slower than the MCA bus. Most industry pundits considered this a worthwhile tradeoff, considering the number of ISA adapters already on the market.

UNDERSTANDING THE PCI BUS The *Peripheral Computer Interface* (*PCI*), developed by Intel, represents the current standard high-speed expansion bus in the world of Intel (and even some Macintosh) computers. Originally designed around the Pentium CPU, the 33MHz PCI bus offers a 64-bit data path – twice the width of either the MCA or EISA buses. It's also the first bus architecture to fully support Plug and Play. At the time of writing, the latest PCI bus designs can operate at up to 66MHz – the speed of the system bus – providing a data transfer speed of up to 264MB per second. Even faster PCI buses are on the horizon.

Several versions of PCI have found their way to market, causing some confusion and compatibility issues to surface, and slowing the widespread adoption of this standard. Today's PCI versions 2.0 and 2.1 transfer data at 132MB per second. PCI 3.0 promises to achieve the full potential of PCI at 264MB per second – at the cost of replacing your motherboards and adapters with components compliant with the PCI 3.0 standard. You'll be able to run older PCI adapters in new PCI 3.0 motherboards, but the old adapters will run at the old PCI 2.*x* rate. Confusion over versions and speeds notwithstanding, PCI is now solidly in place as the industry standard for expansion of computers based on the Pentium, Pentium Pro, and Pentium II.

PCI-equipped motherboards typically provide between three and six PCI slots, supplemented by one or more ISA or EISA slots. (The ratio of PCI slots to non-PCI slots is steadily increasing, to the point where you'll soon see motherboards with only PCI slots and no ISA slots.) The PCI/ISA combination is the most common one today. In this configuration, the PCI bus I/O controller talks directly to the CPU on a 32-bit path at a speed of 33MHz. The PCI controller communicates with the PCI adapters and the ISA I/O controller at the same high bandwidth. The ISA I/O controller then slows the data down to 8MHz and jams it through a 16-bit data path to and from ISA adapters.

TIP

Debugging PCI compatibility problems can be extremely frustrating. Although many of these issues have now been shaken out, go the extra mile and check with your motherboard and adapter manufacturers to be sure that all your PCI components will work together. And, of course, use the Microsoft Hardware Compatibility List (HCL) as a road map to Windows 98 compatibility.

From a performance perspective, the more empty PCI slots on your motherboard, the better. Why? First, regardless of whether you're targeting a server or a client, PCI provides the I/O speed to make the Windows 98 operating system and applications perform well. Second, PCI adapters fully support Plug and Play, so they're automatically configurable by Windows 98. Third, because of the availability of standardized PCI chipsets, PCI motherboards and adapters are very cost-effective components. Finally, more and more hardware manufacturers are migrating to PCI. As a result, you have an ever-widening choice of PCI adapters available to you.

NOTE

In a computer with both PCI and ISA slots, the PCI slot that is adjacent to the ISA slot is usually shared. You can install an adapter in either the PCI slot or the ISA slot, but you can't have an adapter in both. The two slots share the same metal bracket at the rear of the PC case, so they would occupy the same space. Keep this in mind when counting the number of available slots on a PCI/ISA motherboard.

In a client computer running Windows 98, you'll probably want to install at least your video and network adapters in the PCI slots. In a server computer, network and storage adapters should be your first PCI priority. If you plan to implement network bridging (requiring two or more network adapters), you'll need all the empty PCI slots you can find.

CAUTION

In your motherboard investigation, you'll encounter two types of Pentium and Pentium II motherboards — AT and ATX. They differ in their physical shape, their I/O connections to the system unit, and their power requirements. Be sure that your chosen motherboard is compatible with the system unit you select to house it. ATX motherboards require an ATX system unit with an ATX power supply. Most Pentium II motherboards are ATX components, but some still use the AT design.

UNDERSTANDING THE AGP BUS In 1997, Intel introduced the *Accelerated Graphics Port*, better known as *AGP*. (You may occasionally see AGP defined as *Advanced Graphics Port*. Don't you just love acronyms with multiple meanings?) This technology provides graphics adapters with direct, high-speed access to system RAM. Intel designed AGP to bring realistic 3-D graphics to PCs at a lower cost than traditional PCI-based 3-D video adapters. If your application involves 3-D graphics, you know that the market is fragmented, and truly high-performance adapters can run from several hundred dollars to several thousand. Intel wants to bring many of these 3-D capabilities into the PC mainstream via AGP.

AGP takes two physical forms: a single expansion slot or an AGP video interface built directly onto the motherboard. For the most flexibility, choose the expansion slot approach. That way, you'll be able to take advantage of new AGP video adapters as they become available.

Intel didn't design the AGP bus as a replacement for the PCI bus. The two will continue to coexist peacefully on the same motherboard. AGP specifically targets high-performance graphics, and is not intended for general-purpose I/O. That's why you'll see only one AGP slot on the motherboard. In the future, the PCI bus will independently migrate to faster and wider versions, as I mentioned in the previous section.

SELECTING THE RIGHT BUS SPEED

Most existing Pentium-based motherboards operate with either a 66MHz or 100MHz bus speed. You should consider 66MHz as the minimum – motherboards with slower bus speeds have noticeable performance problems. Moreover, a 66MHz buys you the most flexible set of CPU upgrade options.

If you want to maximize the useful life and upgradability of your computer, however, consider a Pentium II motherboard with a 100MHz bus. Although this translates to a CPU with a minimum of 350MHz, choosing a 100MHz system bus now will enable you to upgrade the CPU up to 800MHz in most cases.

UNDERSTANDING MOTHERBOARD I/O OPTIONS

In addition to the adapter slots on your motherboard, most modern motherboards include several built-in I/O ports to which you can directly attach peripheral devices. Back in the early days of the 486 and prior processors, motherboards had no built-in I/O ports – you had to install one or more adapters to handle ubiquitous needs such as floppy drives, hard disks, serial ports, parallel ports, and so forth. Not so, anymore.

Today's typical motherboard includes at least one parallel port, two RS-232 serial ports, and one hard disk interface (usually an IDE interface, which I discuss later in this chapter). Some products include a second hard disk interface to double your disk expansion capabilities.

The latest AT and ATX motherboards include *Universal Serial Bus* (*USB*) ports. USB is a peripheral bus standard developed by a group of seven companies including Microsoft, Compaq, DEC, IBM, Intel, NEC, and Northern Telecom. It's designed to bring Plug and Play capabilities to external peripheral devices by automatically configuring them when you physically attach them to the computer. You can connect up to 127 USB devices, including mice, printers, monitors, keyboards, digital joysticks, telephony devices, scanners, speakers, and digital cameras.

Too Much of a Good Thing

As computer manufacturers try to squeeze more and more functionality into lower-priced computers, they're taking many cost-cutting measures. One approach has been to reduce the number of expansion slots, and build more features directly into the motherboard. As a result, some of today's motherboards include built-in network adapters, video adapters, SCSI bus adapters, or some combination thereof. (I discuss these devices later.) Although folding these components into the motherboard can lower the initial system cost (compared with purchasing all the components separately), I'm not a big fan of them. Here's why.

These three technology areas are changing rapidly — more rapidly than other areas of the PC industry. As a result, it's likely you'll want to replace these components before you replace your entire computer. When you do, two things will happen. First, you won't be able to remove the old component and let someone else in the organization inherit it. This sort of hardware trickle-down phenomena is very common in both large and small organizations, and is important for saving costs and boosting employee morale. (Even hand-me-down hardware is like manna from heaven, if it noticeably improves your sluggish computer's performance.) From a cost viewpoint, the moment you replace a built-in device with a new adapter, you've paid for two devices and can only use the new one. All of this assumes, of course, that you can easily disable the built-in device.

Second, you'll use up a motherboard expansion slot to accommodate the new adapter. Next to cost savings, freeing up expansion slots is the biggest advantage of a motherboard with built-in adapters. The moment you replace the adapter, that advantage disappears. On motherboards with many built-in adapters, this can be even more of a problem — some manufacturers reduce the cost of their motherboards by cutting down on the number of expansion slots they provide. The thinking is, "Hey, it's got a SCSI built in, so the customer doesn't need that extra PCI slot for a SCSI adapter. Let's remove the slot."

So, think twice about choosing a motherboard with these built-in devices. Assume that you'll need to replace them all with new adapters within a year or two. Then, do the math on the number of expansion slots you'll need and the total cost you'll have to bear.

USB can transmit data at only 12 megabits per second (or about 1.5MB per second), so it's designed primarily for low-speed devices. You wouldn't want to attach hard disks or high-speed CD-ROM drives to a USB port. It's unclear, at the time of writing, how universally accepted USB will become. Most motherboard manufacturers are already on board (so to speak), but USB devices aren't exactly jumping off the shelves yet. Some analysts believe that the higher-speed FireWire technology, which I discuss later in this chapter, may replace USB.

UNDERSTANDING POWER-SAVING OPTIONS

More and more motherboards are emerging that support advanced power-saving features. Windows 98 supports the latest power management techniques, including *OnNow*, a comprehensive system design that addresses system and device power control. It describes a PC that's always turned on but appears to be turned off, and responds immediately to external events such as user input. OnNow involves changes to the operating system (in this case, both Windows 98 and Windows NT 5.0), device drivers, hardware, and even some applications. So even though Windows 98 supports OnNow, you may not reap all the benefits until all of your hardware and software supports it.

OnNow relies on *ACPI*, which stands for *Advanced Configuration and Power Interface*. ACPI is an industry specification developed by Microsoft, Intel, and Toshiba. Its goal is to establish operating system control of system power, device power, CPU power, Plug and Play configuration, system events (including addition or removal of devices), battery management, and thermal management. The area of thermal management is becoming hotter and hotter these days. (Okay, arrest me for excessive pun usage.) With CPUs and motherboards running at higher frequencies, disks spinning at increasingly dizzying rates, and more adapters installed than ever, effective control of excessive heat is important. Some Pentium and Pentium II motherboards already include heat sensors and exhaust fan motor controls to support these features.

COUNTING YOUR MOTHERBOARD CACHE

To paraphrase the highly successful Martha Stewart, "A lot of cache – it's a good thing." The bigger your Level 1 and Level 2 caches are, the better your computer's performance will be. Selecting a Level 1 cache size is simple, because it's embedded on the CPU chip. Always opt for the CPU with the largest Level 1 cache. Level 1 cache has the greatest impact on performance, because it operates at speeds closest to the actual CPU speed. So don't pinch your pennies here. Level 1 cache is expensive for a reason – it's extremely fast.

The Level 2 cache situation is a little less straightforward. Some CPUs supply the Level 2 cache in the CPU package, whereas others rely on external cache installed on the motherboard. If the CPU you choose provides its own Level 2 cache (for example, the Pentium Pro and Pentium II), pay the premium for the maximum cache available. Otherwise, choose a motherboard that has ample room for external Level 2 cache.

On-chip Level 2 cache makes for a much faster system than Level 2 cache that lives out on the motherboard. An integrated Level 2 cache can run at nearly CPU speed, but external Level 2 cache is constricted by the speed of the system bus. In fact, on a 100MHz bus, RAM can respond just as quickly as an external cache, so adding an external Level 2 cache to these systems doesn't really improve performance. If you have a choice, opt for a CPU that has an integrated Level 2 cache.

Most mainstream Pentium motherboards offer either 256K or 512K of Level 2 cache. If you have a choice between 256K and 512K, opt for the latter. A few manufacturers offer Pentium motherboards designed to handle up to 2MB of Level 2 cache. For example, motherboards based on the VIA VT82C580VP Apollo-VP chipset provide this feature.

PLANNING FOR RAM EXPANSION

When selecting your motherboard, you'll need to consider its RAM expandability. Nearly all motherboards provide sockets for RAM expansion. (I discuss the details of RAM types later in this chapter.) The total amount of RAM in your computer depends on the motherboard design and the capacity of the memory modules you use. As you'll see later in this chapter, more RAM is almost always better for Windows 98 performance – so opt for a motherboard that will accept as much RAM as possible. Even if you don't invest in all the RAM up front, don't buy a motherboard that limits you to anything less than 128MB. Motherboard limits of 512MB up to 4GB are available.

When you're evaluating your motherboard, pay attention to any special rules for RAM expansion before you make your purchase. I know one network administrator who was burned when he purchased a motherboard with twice as many RAM sockets as competing products. He incorrectly assumed that he could upgrade the RAM size to twice the capacity of the other motherboards. But in the fine print, the motherboard manufacturer required that memory modules above a certain size occupy every other slot, with the remaining slots left empty. The motherboard was no more expandable than its competitors — it just had more memory expansion slots. Don't make the same mistake. Read the fine print before you buy.

In the next section, I discuss how much RAM you'll need in your Windows 98 computer, and what types of RAM are available to you.

Picking RAM for Windows 98

The easiest and least expensive way to improve performance of your Windows 98 computer is to add system RAM, especially since the price of memory has dropped so dramatically. The easiest way to cripple your Windows 98 computer is to run with too little RAM. In the following sections, I provide the information you need to analyze the amount and type of RAM you need in your Windows 98 computer.

PICKING THE RIGHT AMOUNT OF RAM

Windows 98 requires a minimum of 16MB of RAM, but Microsoft recommends 24MB or more. The 16MB size is really a bare minimum, if you just want to run the operating system and one application. If you're going to run network software and several applications, however, I recommend moving to 32MB. RAM is inexpensive compared with the performance boost it yields. And if you're planning to run many applications simultaneously, or your computer is acting as a dedicated server or peer server, 64MB of RAM is even better. You can get away with the 16MB minimum on your Windows 98 computers, but it's worth a little extra money to avoid wasted productivity as your users wait for their computers or the server to respond to requests.

These recommendations are rules of thumb, but there's no substitute for analyzing your application requirements to determine the optimal amount of RAM you need. If you know which applications your users will be running, look at their recommended RAM sizes. (Ignore their minimum requirements, and focus on their recommendations.) As best you can, determine which applications will be run simultaneously, add the Windows 98 Microsoft recommendation of 24MB, and arrive at a RAM size that should comfortably run your set of applications. Just remember that adding even more RAM will almost always increase performance. Other factors to consider include the number of clients a server is serving, the sizes of open data files, and the sizes of running applications.

PICKING THE RIGHT TYPE OF RAM

The computer RAM landscape can be pretty confusing these days. Falling prices have brought more network administrators to the check-out counter, but they're faced with an unprecedented array of memory choices, along with new acronyms to describe them. In the following sections, I provide the details you need to know in deciding which type of RAM to use.

UNDERSTANDING PHYSICAL RAM CONFIGURATIONS Two types of physical RAM configurations reign – SIMMs and DIMMs. A *SIMM*, which stands for *Single In-line Memory Module*, is a small circuit board containing enough chips to add anywhere from 256K to 64MB of RAM to your computer. A SIMM connects to the motherboard via an edge connector with either 30 or 72 pins. The 30-pin SIMMs represent older, slower technology, and are getting harder to find. Contemporary motherboards accept the 72-pin variety.

Several manufacturers offer products that let you convert one or more older 30-pin SIMMs to 72-pin SIMMs, enabling you to recycle your RAM for use in newer motherboards. While this is a great idea in theory, quality and reliability of these devices vary widely. Moreover, even with the best quality converters, you'll likely encounter flaky behavior if you mix RAM speeds and brands together. I don't recommend these devices. RAM prices have fallen, so spend your money on memory, and not on unreliable converter devices. You may spend a few more dollars, but you'll save yourself lots of time and trouble down the road.

Regardless of the number of pins, SIMMs attach to a 32-bit data bus on the motherboard. To achieve the full 64-bit data path of the Pentium architecture, you typically need to install SIMMs in pairs. Installation requirements vary with each motherboard, so check your motherboard manufacturer's documentation before adding SIMMs.

A *DIMM*, which stands for *Dual In-line Memory Module*, is similar in concept to a SIMM. It contains enough chips to add between 16MB and 128MB, and attaches to the motherboard with a 168-pin edge connector. Because each DIMM has access to the entire 64-bit data bus, you can add DIMMs one at a time – so DIMMs are more flexible in terms of upgrading your computer's memory. As you'll see later in this chapter, DIMMs are also used as the vehicle for some of the fastest RAM available.

For RAM expansion flexibility, some motherboards provide slots for both SIMMs and DIMMs. They're great if you have spare SIMMs and you haven't yet invested in faster DIMMs. In theory, you can populate both sets of slots with RAM, but be careful not to cripple your computer's performance! Most of these motherboards access all the memory at the speed of the slowest RAM you've installed, so even one installed 72-pin SIMM can drag your DIMMs down to SIMM-like performance. If you want top memory performance, don't mix the two flavors together.

UNDERSTANDING RAM TECHNOLOGIES If you've shopped for RAM upgrades recently, two things should be clear – prices have fallen to an all-time low, and the number of RAM acronyms have climbed to an all-time high. So just when you can afford any type of RAM, you're faced with more confusing choices than ever. In the following sections, I help you understand the variety of RAM options, and which ones will suit your needs.

STANDARD DRAM – Standard DRAM (Dynamic RAM) is the most widely used and certainly the cheapest of all types of memory in PCs today. It's been around for many years, and has steadily (although not dramatically) increased in speed. You'll find it packaged as 30- and 72-pin SIMMs, living in everything from 386-based computers to current systems. Older computers use DRAMs with speeds in the 70 to 80 nanosecond range. Current motherboards accept 60 nanosecond DRAM components. There's lots of old DRAM floating around the marketplace, so check to make sure the DRAM in your computer is the appropriate speed for your motherboard.

Never mix RAMs with different speeds in your computer. Even if all your RAM is faster than the speed required by your motherboard, mixing speeds can cause erratic system behavior that's difficult to diagnose. Make sure all of your RAM uses identical speeds. If possible, don't mix RAM brands, either. Minor differences between manufacturing processes can lead to subtle differences in timing, again leading to erratic and enigmatic behavior.

SRAM – *SRAM* (*Static RAM*) is significantly faster than DRAM, but it costs a lot more per byte. This relatively high cost has consigned SRAM to serve as external Level 2 cache in today's computers. Unless you're adding external cache to your motherboard, the SRAM choice probably won't surface in your shopping trip.

SDRAM – Sometimes confused with SRAM, *SDRAM* (*Synchronous DRAM*) currently represents the state of the art in affordable high-performance PC memory. This high-speed RAM technology synchronizes itself with the system clock, giving it the capability to operate at the CPU's external data bus speed (typically 66MHz or 100MHz). SDRAM comes in 168-pin DIMM modules. Compared to a standard DRAM speed of 60 nanoseconds, SDRAM offers a blazing 10 nanosecond speed.

I highly recommend using SDRAM in new systems. You do pay a premium for SDRAM's higher speed, but the improved system performance justifies the extra cost. Of course, your choice of this memory technology narrows your selection of motherboards to those with SDRAM capability.

TIP

Manufacturers are now offering SDRAM modules that can operate at bus speeds of 100MHz and higher. Even if you're using a 66MHz motherboard today, consider the future of your SDRAM. If you plan to use the memory modules in other computers down the road, it makes sense to purchase the higher-speed versions now.

EDO RAM – *EDO* (*Extended Data Output*) RAM is a flavor of DRAM that offers faster memory access speeds. As a rule, EDO RAM isn't compatible with 486 and early Pentium computers, because the motherboard manufacturer must design the board to handle this type of memory. The original idea behind the introduction of EDO was the elimination of the need for Level 2 cache. Why? At the time, Level 2 cache SRAM was very expensive, and computer vendors were looking for ways to reduce system costs without sacrificing performance. Since the introduction of EDO, however, Level 2 cache prices have fallen, and some CPUs (like the Pentium Pro and Pentium II) provide their own built-in Level 2 caches.

CAUTION

If you plan to use the EDO RAM you buy today in future systems, bear two things in mind. First, some Pentium Pro motherboards aren't compatible with EDO RAM, because Intel didn't design early versions of the Pentium Pro CPI chipset to handle EDO RAM. Second, the PC world is quickly moving toward SDRAM. Just as PCI slots will one day completely replace ISA slots, the day will come when SDRAM DIMM slots will replace today's 72-pin SIMM slots.

ECC RAM – *Error Checking and Correcting* (*ECC*) *RAM* is yet another form of DRAM – one that's smart enough to correct its own errors! By storing additional parity-like bits, ECC memory is able to detect the occurrence of a single-bit error and change it back to the correct value using the redundant stored bits. It can also detect double-bit errors. The ECC capability adds another layer of reliability to your computer – a layer that can cost you a hefty price premium. At the time of writing, you should expect to see ECC RAM priced 20 to 40 percent more than standard DRAM. When ECC RAM becomes more popular and plentiful, that price difference will diminish.

The Pentium II processor contains built-in support for ECC RAM (more specifically, ECC SDRAM), so many Pentium II-based motherboards support it. A number of Pentium Pro motherboards also let you use ECC. Check with the manufacturer of your computer or motherboard to determine whether ECC RAM is an option.

If extremely high reliability is on your list of design goals, strongly consider using ECC RAM. A memory parity error can crash Windows 98, so many network administrators select ECC RAM for use in their server computers. In doing this, they can spread the extra cost over many users. ECC RAM introduces a small performance penalty, but for the increased reliability, it's well worth it.

Picking Windows 98 Storage Devices

In this section, I fill you in on what you need to consider when selecting storage devices such as floppy drives, hard disks, and CD-ROM drives. I also cover the available technologies and their strengths and weaknesses in a Windows 98 environment.

PICKING A HARD DISK

In this section, I show you which hard disk options are available to you, what the tradeoffs are between them, and how much disk space you're likely to need on your Windows 98 computer. If you haven't looked at the market for hard disks recently, you'll find a widening array of choices accompanying constantly plummeting prices.

The amount of free hard disk space you'll need for Windows 98 itself varies depending on whether you're upgrading from a previous version of Windows, and which optional Windows 98 components you install. The total amount of required free disk space also depends on whether you're going to use the FAT16 or FAT32 file system, discussed in Chapter 7. Here are the basic disk space guidelines:

- **Upgrade installations** – These require 150MB to 250MB of additional free space, depending on existing Windows components and any additional components you install. An extra 50MB is required if you elect to back up your Windows 95 system files during the upgrade process.
- **Clean installations** – These require 150MB to 360MB of free space, depending on the Windows 98 components you choose to install.

NOTE

The Windows 98 Setup program, which installs the operating system, requires 150MB of free disk space to upgrade from Windows 95. If you're performing a clean install, or you're upgrading from Windows 3.1 or Windows for Workgroups, Setup requires 180MB of free space. Some of this space is regained after Setup removes temporary files created during the upgrade process.

Of course, this disk space accounts only for Windows 98 itself. You'll need to add in the free disk space requirements of any applications you plan to install, as well as sufficient storage for your data files. Hard disk space is also required by the Windows 98 swap file, which grows and shrinks depending on RAM size, application activity, and available disk space. Assume the file will require space equal to the amount of RAM in the computer, and then add 16MB to that figure.

UNDERSTANDING IDE The *Integrated Drive Electronics* (*IDE*) technology remains the most popular and least expensive hard disk interface for mainstream PCs. You can connect up to two IDE devices to a single controller. When you have multiple IDE devices, one acts as master and the other as slave. This seemingly innocuous approach leads to the most significant performance flaw in the IDE world – you can access only one drive at a time. The master–slave approach also leads to a reliability concern. If the master drive fails, the slave drive doesn't function either.

You can get around both issues by placing the two drives on two separate IDE controllers. If you're lucky, your motherboard has two of them. If you're unlucky, you'll need to burn another expansion slot to add a second controller. However, down the road when you add two more drives to your computer (for a total of two on each IDE controller), you'll run into the same performance and reliability issues again. Each controller can address only one drive at a time.

Even if you're willing to live with this design, your computer is limited to a grand total of four IDE drives – a long-term limitation that may be unacceptable, especially for computers that act as servers. Moreover, due to BIOS limitations in older motherboards, IDE drives are often limited to a maximum size of about 504MB each in ISA bus computers. Finally, IDE is limited to hard disk devices only, and doesn't directly support connecting CD-ROM drives. Newer technologies, which I discuss in the following sections, address some of these limitations.

CAUTION

While it's true that IDE is designed specifically for hard disks, you can attach ATA CD-ROM drives and tape drives to it in most cases, but not all. The industry has agreed on a standard called *ATAPI*, or *Advanced Technology Attachment Packet Interface*, to support these non-hard-disk devices. ATAPI-compatible hardware is inexpensive, and you can plug ATAPI devices into a standard IDE cable. However, if your IDE controller is a caching controller or performs some other intelligent function, it must be aware of ATAPI for your ATAPI devices to function properly. Older intelligent IDE controllers assume that all attached devices are hard disks, and this assumption can cause serious problems for ATAPI CD-ROM drives and other devices.

UNDERSTANDING EIDE The *Enhanced Integrated Drive Electronics* (*EIDE*) standard builds on its IDE predecessor. Although individual drive performance is better, performance suffers when you try to access multiple drives simultaneously. You can put two drives on two separate EIDE controllers to get around this serialization, but the minute you add a third or fourth drive, you run into the problem again. In theory, the EIDE standard defines the use of up to four controllers, allowing a total of up to eight devices (two devices on each channel). In practice, however, most of the EIDE hardware and BIOS software available supports only two controllers. So in the real world, EIDE maintains the limit of a total of four devices attached to a total of two controllers.

UNDERSTANDING ULTRA DMA/33 *Ultra DMA/33* (also called *Ultra ATA* and *Ultra DMA*) is a new EIDE-based communication standard that boosts the data transfer rate up to 33MB per second. If you have both a controller and a drive that are capable of Ultra DMA/33, you'll see a big difference in performance relative to the IDE and EIDE interfaces. Motherboards that use the Intel 430TX, 440LX, 440BX, or later chipsets incorporate this feature. PCI motherboards that don't have this capability can use a separate PCI Ultra DMA/33 adapter.

The good news about Ultra DMA/33 is that it uses the same cable as IDE, and Ultra-capable drives can coexist with older EIDE and IDE drives on the same cable. Ultra DMA/33 achieves its higher data rate by virtually widening the bus, transferring twice as much data in each clock cycle. Non-Ultra drives attached to an Ultra DMA/33 controller operate at the slower 16.6MB per second data transfer rate. Likewise, if you attach an Ultra drive to a non-Ultra (IDE or EIDE) controller, the drive still works, but at the slower 16.6MB rate.

If you plan to attach both an older IDE drive and a newer Ultra DMA/33 drive to a controller that's capable of Ultra DMA/33, do your homework. Check with the controller or motherboard manufacturer to verify that your controller is capable of using independent timing for both master and slave devices. Some controllers slow everything down to the speed of the slowest attached drive, wiping out any Ultra DMA/33 performance benefits.

Now for the bad news. For all its added speed, Ultra DMA/33 is still IDE. It has the same master-slave limitations I mentioned earlier. SCSI technology, which I discuss in the next section, overcomes these limitations.

UNDERSTANDING SCSI Even with the increasing speed and falling prices of IDE technologies, the most flexible and highest performance storage solution is *SCSI*, which stands for *Small Computer Systems Interface*. (SCSI is pronounced *scuzzy*, but that's certainly no reflection on the quality of this technology. After you get over your initial snickering about its name, you'll discover that SCSI really means business.) SCSI has been around for many years, and has had a chance to mature and stabilize while still moving forward in terms of performance improvements.

SCSI, defined by the X3T10 committee of *ANSI* (*American National Standards Institute*), originally emerged as a non-device-specific communication bus for connecting devices to small computers. Its roots lie in technology developed as early as 1979 by Shugart. Adopted by the Macintosh and later by the PC, SCSI lets you attach up to seven physical devices to a single adapter, and each of those devices can include up to eight logical devices. More recent SCSI adapters let you connect up to 15 physical devices, and dual-channel versions that support up to 30 devices at once are also available.

SCSI technology is superior to IDE in several key areas. SCSI lets you connect many more devices, and offers a broader range of device types – including scanners, printers, tape drives, and other devices. It also takes advantage of the latest high-speed devices, such as hard disks that spin at up to 10,000RPM. But one of SCSI's most significant advantages is its capability to communicate with multiple devices simultaneously. This capability improves performance on any computer that attempts to access multiple drives simultaneously. For example, a network server may share multiple drives over the network, and several client requests may be pending at any given time. A SCSI device can receive an I/O request, disconnect until the I/O operation has completed, and allow other devices to perform I/O operations in the meantime.

The SCSI world used to be a simple one, but continuing advances in the technology have led to an increasingly daunting array of choices. Today, several SCSI flavors exist, each with slightly different characteristics. Table 8-3 summarizes the characteristics of the available SCSI technologies at the time of writing.

TABLE 8-3 CHARACTERISTICS OF AVAILABLE SCSI TECHNOLOGIES

SCSI Interface Type	Data Bus Width (Bits)	Maximum Data Transfer Rate (MB per second)	Implementation Notes	Maximum Cable Length (Feet)
SCSI-1 or SCSI-1 Narrow	8	5	Original SCSI bus	20
Fast SCSI, Fast SCSI-2, or SCSI-2 Narrow	8	10	Doubles the bus frequency of SCSI-1from 5MHz to 10MHz	20

Continued

TABLE 8-3 CHARACTERISTICS OF AVAILABLE SCSI TECHNOLOGIES *(Continued)*

SCSI Interface Type	Data Bus Width (Bits)	Maximum Data Transfer Rate (MB per second)	Implementation Notes	Maximum Cable Length (Feet)
Wide SCSI, Wide SCSI-2, orSCSI-2 Wide	16	10	Widens the data path of SCSI-1 from 8 bits to 16 bits	20
Fast-Wide SCSI, Fast-Wide SCSI-2, or SCSI-2 Fast-Wide	16	20	Wide (16-bit) bus running at 10MHz	10
UltraSCSI Narrow, Fast 20, or UltraSCSI Fast 20	8	20	Doubles the bus frequency of Fast SCSI-2 from 10MHz to 20MHz	5
UltraSCSI Wide, Fast 40, UltraSCSI Fast 40, or Ultra-Wide SCSI	16	40	Widens the data path of UltraSCSI Narrow from 8 bits to 16 bits	5
Ultra2 SCSI LVD	16	80	Emerging technology, increases frequency, allows longer cables	36

Fast SCSI – The original SCSI specification (sometimes called SCSI-1) allows the SCSI bus to operate at up to 5MHz, resulting in a maximum data transfer rate of 5MB per second. *Fast SCSI* effectively doubles the rate at which data is transmitted. The Fast SCSI specification raises the bus frequency to 10MHz, letting the bytes fly. Fast SCSI is one of several technologies under the general umbrella called *SCSI-2*. SCSI-2 devices can talk to the SCSI host adapter on their own initiative, and this can sometimes confuse older SCSI-1 adapters. At a minimum, I recommend that you make sure any SCSI adapter you choose is capable of understanding SCSI-2.

Hurry Up and Wait

If you've spent much time around hard disks, you've probably noticed that they occasionally stop transferring data for a few seconds. The heads make that familiar grinding noise as they move back and forth over the disk's surface. Your application appears to hang briefly, waiting patiently for the drive to continue working. Suddenly, everything's back to normal again.

This behavior is especially noticeable when you're attempting to copy large files or capturing digital video. When this happens to your hard disk, it's likely that the drive is going through a *t-cal* (*thermal recalibration*) cycle. As the drive heats up, it occasionally checks and adjusts its mechanics to ensure that it can still read and write data correctly.

At best, t-cal behavior is annoying when your applications become unresponsive. At worst, it's completely devastating to time-critical applications such as digital video and audio capture. Moreover, when a t-cal cycle takes place on a network server, it can affect many of your users at once. Several manufacturers offer drives that defer or completely eliminate the need to perform t-cal operations. If you don't want to be a t-cal victim, consider spending the extra money for drives tuned for *AV* (*audiovisual*) applications.

Fast SCSI is one of several technologies under the general umbrella called *SCSI-2*. SCSI-2 devices can talk to the SCSI host adapter on their own initiative, and this can sometimes confuse older SCSI-1 adapters. At a minimum, I recommend that you make sure any SCSI adapter you choose is capable of understanding SCSI-2.

Unless you really enjoy a good headache, pay particular attention to the total cable length of your UltraSCSI bus. As shown in Table 8-3, the maximum cable length drops down to only five feet. It's amazing how many cable vendors sell 9-foot-long UltraSCSI cables, calling them UltraSCSI only because the connectors happen to be compatible with UltraSCSI devices. Don't exceed the five-foot maximum, or you're just asking for trouble. And while you're at it, do what you can to educate your SCSI cable vendor on UltraSCSI length requirements.

UNDERSTANDING SCSI CABLING REQUIREMENTS SCSI devices work just fine, as long as you properly configure the devices and the SCSI bus itself. Unfortunately, proper SCSI configuration isn't as straightforward as for other types of PC devices. As a network administrator, be aware that SCSI bus configuration problems are the second most common class of reported hardware problems, according to technical support professionals. If part of your charter involves configuring or maintaining computers containing SCSI hardware, you'll need to become a resident expert on proper SCSI bus configuration. In this section, I discuss these important topics.

Single-ended and differential SCSI – Most widely available SCSI devices today are called *single-ended SCSI.* A single-ended SCSI bus uses a single wire for one bit of information. A high voltage level on the wire represents a logical zero bit, and a low voltage level represents a logical one bit.

Differential SCSI devices are less common. A differential SCSI bus uses two wires, instead of just one, to represent a single bit. One of the wires carries the same type of signal as a single-ended SCSI wire. The second wire carries its logical inversion. A single bit of information is defined by the difference between the signals on the two wires, rather than the level of voltage on a single wire. Because the receiving end uses the difference (or *differential*) between two signals, information can travel longer physical distances with less degradation from external noise than single-ended SCSI. This characteristic enables you to use longer cable lengths on differential SCSI buses. If you need to exceed the cable length limits shown in Table 8-3, or if your computer will operate in an electrically noisy environment, consider implementing a differential SCSI bus. It can extend your cable reach to up to 75 feet.

Although both single-ended and differential SCSI devices use the same connectors, they're electrically different and are therefore incompatible with each other. You need a differential SCSI adapter to drive differential SCSI devices. Don't try to mix the two types on the same SCSI bus – they won't work together.

SCSI termination – The most common source of trouble in any SCSI bus configuration is improper termination. To achieve both reliability and high performance, you must terminate the SCSI bus correctly. If you don't, you're in for many frustrating problems including unbootable systems, flaky behavior, invisible or disappearing devices, and poor I/O performance. In some cases, your system may behave normally for a while, and then suddenly fail in one of several frustrating ways. Even if an improperly terminated SCSI bus appears to work just fine, you may not notice the frequent data errors and retries that will drag your system performance to its knees.

SCSI uses special electrical resistors to terminate the bus. A SCSI bus requires proper termination of the devices at both ends, so commands and data don't end up reflecting back onto the bus. (You've probably seen an example of this type of signal reflection if you've ever seen "ghosting" on your TV screen. It's caused by a mismatch between your cable system or antenna and your TV. The ghost image is generated by the original signal being reflected back to your TV receiver. Unless you're really into the paranormal, this sort of interference is usually considered a bad thing.) However, terminating the devices at each end of the bus is only half the battle. You also need to be absolutely sure you don't terminate any of the devices in between, otherwise some devices won't be able to communicate.

Some contemporary SCSI adapters, which offer both narrow and wide SCSI connectors, can be a bit confusing to configure. For example, the Adaptec AHA-2940W SCSI adapter provides three connectors – an external wide connector, an internal wide connector, and an internal narrow connector. Adaptec lets you use any two of the three connectors, but you can't use all three of them. Why? The SCSI bus must have exactly two ends, and the devices at those ends must act as terminators. If you could attach devices to all three connectors, you'd have a three-ended SCSI bus – a creature you might find in a Lewis Carroll novel, but definitely not in a computer system.

SCSI adapters handle termination in different ways. Traditionally, SCSI adapters have controlled termination with manually configured resistor packs or switches. More recent offerings enable you to control termination through software. Most SCSI adapters in laptops or built into the computer's motherboard provide their own termination and generally don't let you change it. Many of the latest adapters are able to sense whether connectors have SCSI devices attached, and change their termination status automatically.

TIP

If your SCSI adapter claims to provide automatic termination by sensing whether devices are attached to each connector, be sure to read the fine print in your manufacturer's manual. If you attach devices to more than one connector on the adapter, some adapters have trouble figuring out whether or not to terminate the bus. You may need to tell the adapter what to do.

SCSI disk drives, tape drives, CD-ROM drives, scanners, and other SCSI devices likewise take different approaches to termination. They include removable termination resistor packs, jumpers, and switches. Whether or not a particular device is terminated is anybody's guess. Read the device documentation to find out how to set termination on your SCSI devices.

Choosing active or passive termination – Two types of termination exist in the SCSI world: passive and active. Regardless of the approach you select, you should configure all your devices to use the same type of termination. Of the two approaches, active termination is the better choice for both reliability and performance. What is active termination? One or more devices provide what's called *termination power* to the SCSI bus. Most modern SCSI devices offer the option of providing termination power, but some older or less expensive devices don't. If none of your devices offer to supply termination power, you can supply it externally using an active terminator device, which I discuss later in this section.

TIP

If you're using active termination on your SCSI bus, and you have more than three devices attached, it's a good idea to let multiple devices supply termination power to the bus. If possible, configure one device to provide termination power for every three devices on the bus. Don't worry about providing too much termination power — all SCSI devices include components to protect themselves from this situation.

Unfortunately, because different manufacturers use termination resistors of varying quality and resistance, some SCSI devices do a good job of terminating the bus and some don't. Even if your bus appears to have proper termination, you may still have problems with it. You can sometimes solve this simply by moving other devices to the end of the bus and using them as terminators.

TIP

Some SCSI devices don't work well if they're used as the terminating device and are also supplying termination power to the bus. I've seen a few Iomega ZIP drives that display this behavior. If termination looks correct and you're still having problems, try letting a non-terminating device supply the termination power. If that doesn't work, try using a different device for termination.

Although you can typically reach a working configuration, trial-and-error approaches such as this can be a real time drain – so much for the "science" in computer science. What's a network administrator to do? You can take a more expensive and more effective approach to solving the SCSI termination problem by using separate *active terminator* devices. These devices plug into the end of your SCSI bus, independent of the SCSI devices themselves. They supply the correct termination power and resistance, virtually eliminating all of the SCSI termination headaches I've discussed. Some of these devices include diagnostic LEDs that help you detect bus activity and evaluate the quality of the SCSI signals. At the time of writing, prices for these devices range from $60 to $120 each.

In the real world, I've found that you can often get away with either passive or active termination on a non-Ultra narrow SCSI bus (that is, SCSI-1 or Fast SCSI), although active termination does improve both reliability and performance. With the higher transfer rates associated with wide SCSI and Ultra SCSI, active termination becomes a necessity. If you can possibly afford it, I recommend that you opt for active termination. In the long run, the time you save will be well worth the extra cost.

Planning Ahead for Windows NT Fault Tolerance

If you're planning to upgrade the computer to Windows NT and take advantage of fault tolerance features, you may need to alter your hardware decision-making up front – especially in the hard disk subsystem arena. Whether you're considering RAID 0, RAID 1, RAID 5, server clustering, or some combination thereof, you'll need to consider fault tolerance hardware requirements. That way, you'll avoid spending extra money on the right devices later.

All drives that participate in a RAID array, regardless of the RAID level, should be SCSI devices. Moreover, they should all have the same performance characteristics to avoid bottlenecks caused by slow individual drives. Because Windows NT fault tolerance features send I/O requests to multiple drives simultaneously, IDE and EIDE drives become horrible performance bottlenecks in a RAID environment. SCSI is the only way to go. At a minimum, both RAID 0 and RAID 1 require two hard disks with equal-sized partitions on each drive. RAID 5 requires a minimum of three hard disks with equal-sized partitions on each drive.

You may decide instead to use a hardware-based RAID solution. This approach removes the small software overhead imposed by Windows NT RAID, and even removes the need for Windows NT, in some cases. However, the hardware can be more costly. Typically, a hardware RAID drive array comes in a self-contained cabinet, and looks to the operating system like a single drive.

Cabling for SCSI – Once you understand and have chosen a solution to the termination problem, you need to consider the quality of your SCSI cables. After bad termination, the next leading cause of data errors and flaky SCSI behavior is poor-quality cables. This is no place for saving your pennies. Although it's great that SCSI adapter manufacturers throw in a free internal SCSI ribbon cable, my advice to you is to throw it out with the packing material. For best performance and reliability, you're going to need well-shielded, tight-fitting cables, preferably with gold connectors. For internal connections, try to get Teflon cables and avoid letting any part of the cable lie flat against the computer's metal case or power supply.

Never exceed the cable length limits of the SCSI technology you're using. If you do, you're likely to encounter the same types of problems that improper bus termination causes. Use Table 8-3 as your guide. If you use external SCSI drive enclosures, don't forget to include the extra length of cabling used inside them when calculating your total SCSI cable length. A single drive enclosure typically adds nearly a foot of length to the bus.

TIP If you find that you must exceed the specified cable length limits, you can sometimes get around these limitations by using a SCSI repeater. (I discussed the concept of repeaters briefly in Chapter 5.) Inserting a SCSI repeater on the bus regenerates the signals and can double the bus length. Repeaters have the additional advantage of improving reliability, especially in electrically noisy environments. These devices can run anywhere from $150 to $450, depending on features.

PICKING A CD-ROM DRIVE

These days, a CD-ROM drive is a must for most applications and operating systems. Having a CD-ROM drive attached locally to a computer makes life easier for the user, and once you have a network, you can share CD-ROM drives across it. In a computer that acts as a server, though, I recommend installing a local CD-ROM drive. It makes software installation and maintenance much easier. It also enables you to access a CD-ROM while you troubleshoot network problems – without having to rely on a working network.

Client computers can benefit from CD-ROM drives as well, but the argument is less compelling. If much of a user's local software is CD-ROM-based, and the user will constantly be changing CD-ROMs in a shared drive, opt for a local drive on the client computer. If you have several users who need to access a common database on a CD-ROM, for example, consider sharing a drive over the network.

Windows 98 supports both EIDE and SCSI CD-ROM drives. If you're designing a new computer, I recommend opting for a SCSI drive. Even though the cost is a bit higher, the flexibility of SCSI is superior. In addition, many SCSI CD-ROM drives have larger built-in caches, which enhance their performance. Finally, IDE CD-ROM drives soak up more CPU time during data transfers than do SCSI CD-ROM drives. Shy away from CD-ROM drives that attach to proprietary interfaces on an audio adapter – they tend to require special drivers that sometimes don't work well. And don't even bother considering parallel port CD-ROM drives – all are painfully slower than their SCSI or IDE counterparts.

Microsoft specifies a minimum CD-ROM drive speed of 1X for Windows 98 (are there slower CD-ROM drives?), but they recommend at least an 8X drive. If your computer is a server and you're sharing the CD-ROM, or if you're doing full-screen multimedia playback on a workstation, go for the fastest SCSI CD-ROM drive you can find. Some manufacturers are producing Ultra DMA/33 CD-ROM drives and adapters, which promise effective speeds of up to 50X. By the time these components are plentiful, you'll see SCSI CD-ROMs achieve the same or better performance. So even if you're tempted to go with an IDE CD-ROM drive, I still recommend sticking with SCSI.

CD-ROM changers (sometimes called CD jukeboxes) can be a good solution in a single-user environment, where the user needs convenient, sequential access to the contents of several CD-ROMs. If you need to share multiple CD-ROMs over the network from a single workstation or server, however, don't use a CD-ROM changer. The time and mechanical wear and tear required to perform the internal CD-ROM changes can drive you and your network users batty. If you need to provide access to multiple CD-ROMs over the network, install separate CD-ROM drives instead. If you want to install several drives in a single cabinet without giving up precious expansion bays in your server's system unit, you can opt for a SCSI-based external CD-ROM cabinet.

PICKING A BACKUP TAPE DRIVE

As a network administrator, you're probably responsible for defining or implementing your organization's backup program. If you're attaching several Windows 98 computers to a network, you'll probably need at least one tape drive. One drive is enough, if you're willing to perform backups over the network. (I discuss performing network backups in Chapter 13.)

I strongly recommend staying far away from drives that attach to the computer's floppy controller. They're painfully slow, often unreliable, very limited in capacity, and they typically use tape media that isn't portable to other drives. In my experience, they're downright unpleasant to use. A few IDE tape devices are available, but they suffer from one or more of the same problems as tape drives that attach to the floppy controller. (In my consulting practice, I've never had a client who was satisfied with one of these drives.)

When choosing a tape drive, go with SCSI, and if you can possibly afford it, select a 4mm DAT tape drive. They're fast, reliable, and can store between 2GB and 12GB on a single tape at up to about 2MB per second. The DAT format standards continue to roll forward, with discussions underway for a future 48GB tape capacity at 6MB per second.

Most DAT tape drives include a media recognition system that forces you to use tapes that meet the *DDS* (*Digital Data Storage*) specification. Qualified tapes include special stripes on the tape's leader. Some drives let you configure them to use standard DAT audio tapes, which haven't been certified for computer data. Don't be tempted to save money by disabling this feature and using standard audio DAT tapes. Although non-DDS tapes may appear to work, they can threaten the integrity of your data. Backups are important, so don't put them at risk.

If you have more money to spend and less time to waste, Digital Linear Tape (DLT) may be the answer. DLT lets you put up to 35GB on a single tape at 5MB per second. You'll pay a premium for DLT, but you can nearly triple the speed and capacity of your backups. Of course, standards in this arena are marching forward as well, with promises for higher capacities and faster speeds in the future. Because of their higher price, I generally don't recommend them for small Windows 98-based peer-to-peer networks. If you're using Windows NT Server on a larger network, however, the extra capacity and speed can better justify the extra cost.

Data compression is important for achieving advertised tape capacities. Look for a tape drive that performs its own data compression in hardware. Some drives on the market rely on software data compression, expecting the computer to deliver data in compressed form. On average, if you choose a tape drive that relies on software compression, you'll achieve about half the advertised tape capacity. Many backup applications support software compression, but it's more efficient to use a drive that performs compression in hardware.

Picking a System Unit

As a network administrator, you'll find that your system unit needs will vary from one computer to another, depending on the system's requirements and plans for future expansion. Except for laptop systems, most Windows 98 computers will eventually end up equipped with multiple drives and adapters, so you should plan for maximum expandability and heat dissipation whenever possible. Consider the number of internal and external drive bays, their sizes, the number of cooling fans, and the power supply capacity. Client computer power supplies should support at least 250W. Server computer power supplies should be 300W or higher, since they'll probably have to accommodate more installed devices.

In some situations, even the tallest tower system units don't provide the expansion room or cabling access you need. If you need to install many computers and associated peripherals in a fairly small space, and you need quick and easy expandability, you may want to consider a rack mount approach. Individual components can be mounted to a vertical rack, allowing expansion from the floor to the top of the rack. You can even install multiple servers in a single rack and control them all from a single keyboard, mouse, and monitor using an electronic switch unit.

TIP

In a network with ten or more nodes, it's a good idea to keep an extra PC power supply handy in case one fails. This is especially true for computers acting as servers, because a downed server can affect all users. Some system units and racks include redundant power supplies, which take over if the primary supply fails. You can also get system units with hot-swappable power supplies that can be replaced without having to open the case or shut down the computer.

Picking a Network Adapter

In Chapter 5, I discussed the network technologies and cabling options available to you, but I didn't delve into selecting a network adapter. That decision depends on the network technology and cabling decisions you've already made, as well as the computer hardware decisions covered earlier in this chapter. Now that you've decided on a network technology (for example, Ethernet), an approach to your cabling infrastructure (for example, UTP), and the hardware you plan to use for clients and servers, it's time to decide which network adapters you need. In the sections that follow, you'll see which factors you need to consider as you select your network adapters.

ADDRESSING NETWORK COMPATIBILITY

The adapters you choose must be fully compatible with both the network technology and the cabling you've decided to install. Ethernet and Token Ring adapters are two different animals – you won't find a single adapter that handles both technologies. Therefore, the network technology you've chosen narrows the field of adapter choices right off the bat.

Once you enter the Ethernet realm, your selection of network adapter cabling connections isn't quite as straightforward. Some adapters have a single connector for a specific type of cabling (such as UTP, coax, and so forth). Other network adapters, called *combo adapters* or *combo cards*, offer more than one type of cabling connection. You can configure a combo adapter through software or jumpers to use one of the two connectors for network communication.

For example, a typical combo adapter a few years ago boasted both a thick Ethernet connector and a coax (BNC) connector. As network installations migrated from expensive, inflexible thicknet to cheaper and more flexible thinnet, they could change their cabling infrastructures without requiring the purchase of new network adapters. More recently, typical combo cards include a coax connector and a UTP (RJ45) connector, to facilitate easy migration from coax to the UTP cabling. Other connector combinations are available, as well.

If you're installing a UTP infrastructure (Category 5, if you took my advice in Chapter 5), a combo adapter doesn't really buy you much. All your network adapters need is a UTP connector. If you're starting off with a small coax network and you plan to grow into a UTP network, however, a coax/UTP combo adapter is the ideal choice. If you're gluing together existing network segments with different types of cabling, and you think this mixed environment will be around for a while, choose combo adapters for your new computers. Doing this enables you to move the computers around between different network segments without having to replace adapters.

NOTE

Ease of configuration is another important consideration when selecting a network adapter — especially in large networks. If some or all of the settings require that you open the computer's cover and change jumpers or switches, you'll be in big trouble if you have to reconfigure more than a handful of systems. Software configurable adapters are much easier to deal with, even if you have to load manufacturer-supplied utilities to make configuration changes.

The final consideration for Ethernet network compatibility is network speed. The two most common speeds today are 10Mbps and 100Mbps. Some adapters will run only at 10Mbps, but virtually all 100Mbps adapters will operate at either speed. If you're putting together a 100Mbps Ethernet network, be sure that all your adapters are capable of this higher speed. Even if you install a 10Mbps network today, consider spending a little extra on dual 10/100Mbps adapters. Then, when it's time to switch to 100Mbps, all you need to do is change your hubs. You won't have to change your network adapters.

The adapter landscape in the Token Ring world isn't as complex. Once you've selected the cabling for your Token Ring network, the only remaining issue is ensuring compatibility with the speed of your ring. Token Ring networks run at one of two speeds – 4Mbps and 16Mbps. If you choose an adapter that isn't compatible with your chosen speed, it won't work. Most adapters today operate at either speed. So, for maximum flexibility, it's best to select adapters that are capable of running at both.

TIP

Over the last few years, network adapters have dropped dramatically in price, making networking more affordable. Now that network adapters are commodities, the dizzying array of brands has driven many network administrators to select adapters based purely on price. Don't fall into this trap. Network adapter reliability is critical to the success of your organization. Flaky hardware, buggy drivers, and adapters that fail frequently are unacceptable. I strongly recommend that you choose well-known, reliable brands such as Intel, 3Com, Digital, or SMC for Ethernet, and IBM, Proteon, or Madge for Token Ring. Much of Microsoft's internal network uses the Intel EtherExpress adapter series.

ADDRESSING OS COMPATIBILITY

It's important for your chosen network adapters to be compatible with Windows 98, or with whatever operating system you plan to run. Nearly every network adapter on the market today has an NDIS driver written for it – whether it's included with the operating system or supplied by the adapter manufacturer. (See Chapter 6 for a discussion of NDIS.) With an NDIS driver, you can probably operate the network adapter under Windows 98, Windows 95, or Windows NT.

Windows 98 provides a number of tested network adapter drivers on its CD-ROM. They're part of the *Windows 98 Driver Library* (*WDL 98*). On the CD-ROM, go to the \DRIVERS\NETLAN directory, and then to the directory that matches your network adapter name or manufacturer. If the directory contains installation instructions, follow them. If not, simply copy all the files to a floppy disk, and follow the instructions in \DRIVERS\README.TXT. I cover installation of network adapter drivers in Chapter 9.

If you're considering installation of more than one network adapter in a single computer, either now or in the future, check with the manufacturer to be sure that both the hardware and driver support this configuration. Some drivers are written and tested assuming there's only one network adapter in the system, and they crash miserably if you try installing two or more adapters. It's best to plan for this eventuality up front, so you don't have to mix and match brands and drivers later just to get around a poorly written driver.

TIP If you plan to migrate to Windows NT in the future, it's a good idea to check the Windows NT Hardware Compatibility List to make sure the network adapter has been tested with that operating system. Select an adapter that's compatible with both Windows 98 and Windows NT, so you don't have to buy a new network adapter when you upgrade the operating system. Keep in mind that Windows NT's compatibility restrictions are narrower than those of Windows 98.

COMPUTER COMPATIBILITY

Of course, the network adapter you select must be compatible with the computer in which you install it. It needs to be compatible with the bus slot on the motherboard, and can't conflict with other devices already installed in the system.

Whether your computer is going to act as a client, server, or both, I highly recommend that you use a PCI network adapter in a PCI motherboard slot. ISA network adapters are cheaper, but they don't perform nearly as well – they create a bottleneck for data flowing to and from your system. (I discussed some of the problems with the ISA bus earlier in this chapter.) If you don't have PCI slots, and you have a choice between EISA and ISA, choose EISA for better performance. Of course, MCA-based computers don't have much choice – an MCA adapter is the only way to go.

If the network adapter you select isn't Plug and Play, you need to do your homework on which resources your computer uses (including IRQs, I/O addresses, memory mapped addresses, and DMA channels) before installation. These internal resources are scarce, so adapters that limit your configuration choices may not work at all, depending on what else is installed in your computer. The more configuration choices the adapter provides, the more likely you'll be able to get it to work in a given computer. Stay away from 8-bit ISA network adapters. They're still around today, but they're extremely slow and they offer a very limited number of IRQ settings.

TIP

Network adapters occasionally fail — they either cease to communicate or start talking gibberish on the network. It's a good idea to have at least one spare network adapter on hand, in case one fails — unless, of course, your network adapter supplier is right next door and is open seven days a week.

Summary

In this chapter, I've presented a lot of information and advice about how to design the hardware for your Windows 98 computers. In Chapter 9, you'll find out how to install your networking hardware and software and configure your computers for network communication.

Chapter 9

Installing Windows 98 Networking

IN THIS CHAPTER

- Installing and testing a network adapter
- Installing and configuring Windows 98 network software
- Testing your network's hardware and software setup

IN THIS CHAPTER, you'll learn what's required to properly configure and install network adapters in your Windows 98 computers. Whether or not the adapter is Plug and Play, you'll understand how to get Windows 98 to recognize and work with it. Then, I show you how to install and configure Windows 98 network software, including network device drivers and protocols. You'll also find out how to set up the Windows 98 client (redirector) and server components, and how to make sure you've done it right.

Installing Network Adapter Hardware

If your computer came with the network adapter already installed, you can skip this section for now and proceed to the section titled "Installing Windows 98 Network Software." When you need to install or replace a network adapter in the future, you can come back to this section for the information you need.

Because each network adapter has slightly different installation requirements, you'll need to refer to the manual that came with your adapter for detailed installation and configuration information. In this section, I present steps and information required for many network adapter installations, to help increase your chances of getting it installed right the first time.

If you're not comfortable opening the computer's case and installing an adapter, assign this task to a qualified technician or consultant. If you don't follow proper electrical grounding procedures, you could damage both your network adapter and your computer's motherboard.

Preparing to Install Your Network Adapter

Whenever you change the hardware configuration of a computer, there are always a few preparatory steps you should take. Before you open the computer to install your network adapter, I recommend that you complete the following steps:

1. Gather the necessary tools for adapter installation: a screwdriver and a grounding wrist strap. Also, prepare a static-free surface on which to work.
2. Gather the materials that came with your network adapter, including installation instructions, floppy disks, or CD-ROMs.
3. Have at least a portion of your network infrastructure installed or available, so you can use it to test your network adapter. For example, in a UTP network, you would need at least one hub and two UTP cables. (See Chapter 5 for a discussion of network infrastructure topics.)
4. If this is your first network adapter installation, allow time for installing adapters on two computers, so you can use them together to test your adapter installations. I discuss testing your network adapter installation later in this chapter.
5. Have all other devices installed in the computer, and verify that they're working properly, with no hardware conflicts. Ideally, all decisions about hardware components discussed in Chapter 8 should have been made already. (You can certainly change your hardware configuration later, but it's best to start with a known working configuration before adding your network adapter.)
6. Have Windows 98 installed and running properly before installing the network adapter. This is not absolutely necessary, but it helps with hardware detection and installation, which is covered later in this chapter.
7. Prepare a list of all resources used by existing devices in the computer. You may need this information even if both your computer and network adapter are equipped for Plug and Play. If Windows 98 is already installed, this step is easier than it first appears. I discuss approaches to gathering this information later in this chapter.

TIP

This last step is critically important. It requires some extra effort and detective work to uncover all the configuration details of your devices, but it will help you immensely should you encounter problems with your network adapter installation. Having all this information available will also come in handy the next time you need to add a device to your computer. Whatever you do, don't discard this hard-earned information after you've successfully installed your network adapter. Even if you store this information electronically, I recommend keeping a printed copy on file or near the computer.

UNDERSTANDING SYSTEM RESOURCES AND CONFLICTS

If you've worked with PCs for a while, you know that resource conflicts (more than one device trying to use the same internal system resource) can sometimes render a computer or device completely useless. Each device needs to use its own unique set of resources for the device or system to function properly. If the resource assignments to devices overlap, they are said to *conflict.* Four basic types of system resources can be assigned to a device: IRQs, I/O addresses, memory-mapped addresses, and DMA channels. Not all devices use each of these resource types.

The *IRQ*, or *interrupt request*, is a hardware signal line that a device uses to get the immediate attention of the CPU. The device uses this line to communicate the completion of an event (for example, a read or write operation). The CPU immediately stops (or *interrupts*) what it's doing and lets the device driver process the event. As soon as the event is handled, the CPU can go back to whatever it was doing before it was so rudely interrupted. The advantage to this approach is that the CPU doesn't have to constantly ask the device whether it has completed an I/O operation. The interrupt signal automatically notifies the CPU, so the CPU doesn't have to worry about polling the device. An *interrupt controller* handles the flow of interrupts through one or more IRQs to the CPU.

An *I/O address* (sometimes called an *I/O port* or *I/O port address*) is a special storage location through which a device and the CPU can directly communicate. (*I/O* stands for *input/output.*) I/O addresses can be used to send and receive data or perform control and status functions. Using a set of I/O instructions, the CPU can write directly to or read directly from the device hardware. A device may use one I/O address for all operations, or it may use a range of I/O addresses.

A *memory-mapped address* is another approach to accessing I/O ports. Instead of using special instructions to perform I/O operations, the CPU can simply read or write specific locations in RAM. The addresses of those locations are *mapped* directly to I/O ports on the device – so storing and retrieving data to and from memory addresses effectively writes to or reads from the device hardware. A device may be designed to use I/O addresses, memory-mapped addresses, or both to perform I/O.

A *DMA channel* is a hardware circuit external to the CPU that enables a device to access RAM directly without going through the CPU. (*DMA* stands for *direct memory access*.) This approach to I/O improves performance by freeing up the CPU from data transfers between the device and RAM. A *DMA controller* consists of hardware that controls the flow of data through one or more DMA channels.

Most network adapters, for example, require one IRQ, 1 to 16 I/O addresses, and 4KB to 64KB of memory address space. All of these resources must be unique – they can't overlap with resources assigned to other devices in the system. Although the Plug and Play features of the adapter, the motherboard, and Windows 98 may all work together to handle resource assignments and conflict avoidance, in many cases you'll need to intervene.

The first step in avoiding conflicts involves gathering your current configuration information. There are several approaches to this task, including the following:

- **MSInfo utility** – This Windows 98 tool lets you easily see which hardware resources are currently used, and which ones are free for new devices to use. (I show you how to do this later in this chapter.)
- **CMOS configuration utility** – The CMOS utility built into your motherboard's BIOS may provide useful information about the built-in devices and which resources they consume. You can typically find out about built-in serial ports, parallel ports, disk controllers, and so forth.
- **Network adapter utilities** – Some network adapter manufacturers supply their own utility software with the adapters, enabling you to detect unused resources and configure your network adapter to use them safely.
- **EISA configuration utility** – On an EISA-based computer, you can use the configuration utility that came with the computer to collect resource information on your installed EISA adapters. (See Chapter 8 for a discussion of the EISA bus.)
- **MCA reference disk** – On an MCA-based computer (such as an IBM PS/2), the reference disk that came with the computer can collect the resource information for installed MCA adapters. MCA computers will also automatically detect resource conflicts after you install a new adapter. (See Chapter 8 for a discussion of the MCA bus.)
- **Other configuration utilities** – Other utilities are available to gather and report device configuration information and resource assignments. If you haven't installed Windows 98 yet, and you can boot the computer to MS-DOS 6.22 (or higher) or Windows for Workgroups 3.11, then you can run the MSD utility that came with the operating system. Alternatively, you can use one of many third-party utilities, including CheckIt, Norton Utilities, QA Plus, and Probe.

None of these approaches is guaranteed to give you a complete picture of the resources that every device is using. If you have legacy ISA adapters, for example, you may still need to open up the computer and look at the jumper settings, even after using one or more of these techniques. In some cases, a device may be installed, but the operating system can't see which resources it's using unless a device driver is installed and running.

LIVING WITH PLUG AND PLAY

As I mentioned in Chapter 8, Plug and Play can be either a dream or a nightmare. It all depends on how the network adapter manufacturer interpreted the Plug and Play specification, how the motherboard BIOS manufacturer implemented it, and which other devices are installed in your computer. In this section, I cover a few key issues associated with installing a network adapter in a Plug and Play environment.

If you have non-Plug and Play devices installed, you'll need to account for them in your motherboard's CMOS settings. Set aside resources that are used by non-Plug and Play devices, so the Plug and Play mechanism doesn't assume they're free to use. Each BIOS and motherboard manufacturer has a different approach to changing these settings, so consult your computer or motherboard manuals for details.

If you're out of available resources, such as *IRQs* (*interrupt requests*), you may be able to free some up by disabling unused devices on your motherboard. For example, if you're using SCSI devices and you're not using any IDE (or EIDE, or UltraDMA/33) devices, you can disable one or both of the built-in IDE controllers. Likewise, a second unused serial port is fair game for freeing up resources, if the CMOS setup program lets you do this.

Incorrect CMOS settings can have dramatic effects on your computer's reliability and speed. Make sure you change only the settings that must be changed, and be sure to change them correctly. The descriptions of some settings can be cryptic, so consult the documentation. If you aren't comfortable making these changes, consult an experienced technician or consultant.

In a Plug and Play environment, it's a good idea to add one device at a time. If you add multiple devices at the same time, Plug and Play logic (and I use that term loosely) can become confused and may not configure every device correctly. As I mentioned earlier in this chapter, I recommend getting all other devices installed, configured, and running before installing your network adapter. Doing this will cut down on the variables if you have to troubleshoot your installation.

If your motherboard and other installed components comply with the PCI 2.1 standard (or greater), the PCI hardware itself can sometimes resolve interrupt conflicts for you. But if you have any non-Plug and Play devices, you still have to gather their resource information to make sure you don't create conflicts.

In an ideal world, where all devices and motherboards cooperate, installation of a Plug and Play network adapter would consist of physically installing it, watching Windows 98 detect it, and letting Windows 98 automatically install the right driver for it. Believe it or not, this occasionally happens. If it does, great. But even if you're installing the same make and model of network adapter in many computers, you're likely to run into at least one system configuration that requires some additional work.

In the worst-case scenario, you may have to completely disable the adapter's Plug and Play logic to configure the adapter properly. Most ISA Plug and Play network adapters have an option to let you do this, although it could mean having to boot the system under MS-DOS to make it happen. In the following sections, I present the information you need to configure your adapters manually, in order to avoid hardware resource conflicts.

If you're comfortable with experimentation, and all your components (network adapter, motherboard, and installed devices) are capable of Plug and Play, you may just want to install the adapter without doing all the homework discussed here. Keep in mind that if it doesn't work, you'll need to physically remove the adapter and research the usage of existing hardware resources.

USING THE MICROSOFT SYSTEM INFORMATION UTILITY

If Windows 98 is already installed on your computer, you can quickly and easily determine the list of resources used by existing components in your computer. The Microsoft System Information (MSInfo) utility is included with Windows 98, and provides a detailed view of hardware resources and other information.

To gather system resource information using MSInfo, perform the following steps:

1. Click Start → Programs → Accessories → System Tools → System Information.
2. In the left side of the window, click the plus (+) next to Hardware Resources.

3. Under Hardware Resources, click IRQs. A list of each IRQ and its use is displayed. As shown in Figure 9-1, unused IRQs are labeled as free.

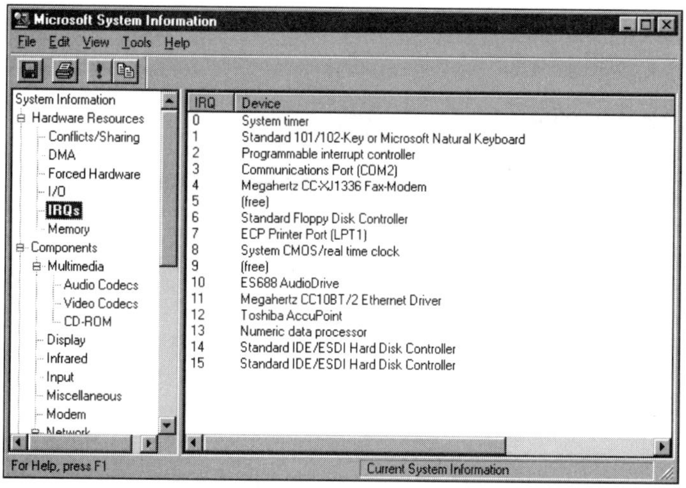

Figure 9-1: The MSInfo utility enables you to gather information on IRQs, I/O addresses, memory-mapped addresses, and other resources..

4. For a similar list of DMA channels, I/O address ranges, and memory-mapped address ranges, click DMA, I/O, or Memory, respectively.

5. To print the configuration information for future reference, click File → Print.

CAUTION

Unfortunately, there's no way to print just a portion of the information gathered by MSInfo. If you decide to print a report, be sure to have plenty of paper handy. A typical report can range between 40 and 90 pages, depending on the hardware and software installed on the computer. Alternatively, you can use the Edit menu in MSInfo to select and copy individual pages of information to the Clipboard for use in other applications.

Two other sections under Hardware Resources may be useful to you in avoiding or resolving resource conflicts. Forced Hardware lists the devices that have user-specified resources assigned – as opposed to resources automatically assigned by the system. Older devices and devices that Windows 98 can't automatically detect are also shown here. Conflicts/Sharing displays any resource conflicts or resources that are shared between devices.

TIP

MSInfo should be your first stop in Windows 98 when troubleshooting a system. Not only can you examine information about installed hardware and software, but you can also launch several diagnostic utilities. I discuss these further in Chapter 14.

MAKING IRQ ASSIGNMENTS

IRQs are the scarcest hardware resource commodity in the computer. Of the 16 IRQs in a PC, only two aren't already assigned to standard PC devices. Each device that needs an IRQ must use a unique one – Windows 98 doesn't allow two devices to share a single IRQ. Table 9-1 lists each IRQ, its typical device assignment, whether or not it's available for other devices, and some additional information.

Not all PCs are configured with all the devices listed, and unused built-in devices can usually be disabled by reconfiguring the computer's CMOS settings. So, depending on what's installed and enabled in your computer, you may have more IRQs or fewer IRQs available for your network adapter to use.

Table 9-1 TYPICAL IRQ RESOURCE ASSIGNMENTS

IRQ Level	Resource Assignment	Available	Comments
0	System timer (15ms clock tick)	No	This IRQ is tied permanently to the PC's internal system timer, and can't be used by other devices.
1	Keyboard controller	No	This IRQ is tied permanently to the PC's keyboard, and can't be used by other devices.
2	Interrupt controller (cascaded from IRQ 9)	Not recommended	This IRQ isn't really an IRQ at all. It's used to tie together the PC's two interrupt controllers. IRQ 2 is triggered whenever IRQs 8 through 15 are active. Although some adapters let you use it, you should avoid using it.

IRQ Level	Resource Assignment	Available	Comments
3	Secondary serial port (COM2 or COM4)	Maybe	This IRQ is typically used by the second RS-232 serial port or modem, if any. If no such device exists, this IRQ may be available for other devices.
4	Primary serial port (COM1 or COM3)	Maybe	This IRQ is typically used by the first RS-232 serial port or modem, if any. If no such device exists, this IRQ may be available for other devices.
5	Secondary parallel port (LPT2)	Maybe	This IRQ is sometimes used by a second parallel port, or by some audio adapters. If no such device exists, this IRQ may be available for other devices.
6	Floppy drive controller	No	This IRQ is tied permanently to the PC's floppy disk controller, and can't be used by other devices.
7	Primary parallel port (LPT1)	Maybe	This IRQ is used by the first parallel port, if any. If no such device exists, this IRQ may be available for other devices.
8	System CMOS real-time clock	No	This IRQ is tied permanently to the PC's CMOS real-time clock, and can't be used by other devices.
9	Interrupt controller (cascaded to IRQ 2)	Not recommended	This IRQ isn't really an IRQ at all. It's used to tie together the PC's two interrupt controllers. IRQ 9 is triggered whenever IRQs 8 through 15 are active. Although some adapters let you use it, you should avoid using it.

(Continued)

Table 9-1 TYPICAL IRQ RESOURCE ASSIGNMENTS *(Continued)*

IRQ Level	Resource Assignment	Available	Comments
10	Not used by standard PC device	Yes	This IRQ may be used by add-in devices.
11	Not used by standard PC device	Yes	This IRQ may be used by add-in devices.
12	Mouse port (PS/2 or bus mouse)	Maybe	This IRQ is used by a PS/2 or bus mouse, if any. If no such device exists (that is, if you have a serial mouse), this IRQ may be available for other devices. (A serial mouse uses IRQ 3 or IRQ 4.)
13	Numeric data processor (NDP)	Never	This IRQ is tied permanently to the PC's math coprocessor, and can't be used by other devices.
14	Primary hard disk controller (IDE, EIDE, UltraDMA/33)	Maybe	This IRQ is used by the primary IDE (or EIDE, or UltraDMA/33) hard disk controller, if any. If no such device exists (that is, if you have a SCSI adapter and hard disk), this IRQ may be available for other devices.
15	Secondary hard disk controller (IDE, EIDE, UltraDMA/33)	Maybe	This IRQ is typically used by a secondary IDE (or EIDE, or UltraDMA/33) hard disk controller, if any. If no such device exists, this IRQ may be available for other devices.

MAKING I/O ADDRESS ASSIGNMENTS

In addition to needing an IRQ, it's likely your network adapter will also require one or more I/O addresses. There are a lot more I/O addresses than there are IRQs, but once again you need to make sure they don't conflict with any existing devices. The network adapter manufacturer may also limit you to a small number of I/O address choices, making the conflict avoidance game more challenging.

Get Your Priorities Straight

IRQs are sometimes referred to as *interrupt levels*, because they represent a prioritized list of interrupts. The lower the IRQ number, the higher its priority. Therefore, if two events simultaneously trigger both IRQ 3 and IRQ 5, the device connected to IRQ 3 will be serviced first.

Because of the way interrupt controllers are arranged in the PC, however, IRQs 8 through 15 actually have higher priority than IRQs 3 through 7. So the IRQ priorities, from highest priority to lowest, are: 0, 1, 2, 8, 9, 10, 11, 12, 13, 14, 15, 3, 4, 5, 6, 7.

You can take advantage of this knowledge by placing higher-speed devices in the IRQ 8 to 15 range, and lower-speed devices in the IRQ 3 to 7 range. It's best to put network adapters and disk controllers (or SCSI adapters) in the high priority IRQ 8 to 15 range, if possible. Lower-speed devices such as modems and printers are best left in the low priority range of IRQs.

NOTE: The manufacturer doesn't always tell you the full range of I/O addresses the network adapter uses, so it's not always easy to figure out whether the range will conflict with another device. As a rule of thumb, assume that if you're given only the starting I/O address, the adapter uses a range of 16 addresses. For example, if you're given a starting I/O address of 300 and no range is specified, assume that the adapter uses 300 through 30F.

MAKING MEMORY-MAPPED ADDRESS ASSIGNMENTS

Some network adapters also require a range of memory-mapped addresses to make I/O more convenient for the CPU. Once again, this range must be unique to the device, and can't overlap with memory-mapped address ranges used by other devices.

MAKING DMA CHANNEL ASSIGNMENTS

Many network adapters and other devices use DMA (direct memory access) channels provided by the PC to transfer data directly to and from system RAM, completely bypassing the CPU. DMA channels are a scarce resource within the PC, and they can't be shared among multiple devices.

Most PCs reserve DMA channel 0 and DMA channel 2 to use for refreshing DRAM and supporting floppy drive DMA, respectively. (See Chapter 8 for a discussion of DRAM.) Some PCs use DMA channel 4 instead of DMA channel 0. The rest of the eight DMA channels are available for built-in or add-in devices. Once again, make sure you use one of the techniques discussed earlier in this chapter to determine the DMA channels used by other installed devices.

CONFIGURING YOUR NETWORK ADAPTER

Some network adapters are configured via on-board jumpers or switches, whereas others can be configured completely through software. Older adapters typically require some manual configuration; newer ones rely on software settings. If your network adapter settings are handled completely in software, you can proceed to the next section, "Installing Your Network Adapter." If you need to set the adapter manually, you're in the right place.

> Leave the network adapter in its anti-static bag until you're ready to work on it. While handling your network adapter during manual configuration, be sure to wear a grounding anti-static wrist strap.

Here are some typical manual settings required by network adapters. (On software-configurable adapters, similar settings are available, either through utilities provided by the manufacturer or through Windows 98 features.)

- **Computer hardware resources** – Switches or jumpers may need to be set to select the network adapter's IRQ, I/O addresses, memory-mapped addresses, and DMA channel. Adjust these settings accordingly to use the available resources you discovered earlier in this chapter. Be sure to write them down for future reference.
- **Combo connector selection** – If you're installing a combo network adapter (one that has two different types of physical network connections), you may need to select which connector you're going to use when you connect to your network. Selecting the wrong connector is one of the most common configuration errors made during Ethernet adapter installation.
- **Network speed selection** – Token Ring network adapters can run at either 4Mbps or 16Mbps. Likewise, most Ethernet adapters operate at either 10Mbps or 100Mbps. You may need to set a switch or jumper to cause the adapter to operate at the correct network speed. In the Token Ring arena, setting the adapter to the wrong speed is the most common configuration error.

If your network adapter uses switches for configuration, don't use the end of a pencil to change the switch settings. Not only does it leave a mess, but the pencil lead can flake off and fall into the switch — and that may cause a short circuit. Instead, use a paper clip or pen to set switches.

Installing Your Network Adapter

Once you've performed any required manual configuration, install the network adapter in your computer according to the instructions provided by the adapter's manufacturer. At this point, don't physically connect the adapter to your network. If the manufacturer includes only driver software, you'll use Windows 98 to install and configure the drivers. (I cover Windows 98 driver installation later in this chapter.)

If your manufacturer includes a software configuration program, it's probably an MS-DOS-based utility. Boot the computer into MS-DOS mode and run the utility according to the manufacturer's instructions.

Some configuration utilities refuse to run under the version of MS-DOS that's part of Windows 98. If you run into problems, try booting the computer to MS-DOS using a boot floppy, and run the utility from there. You may have to copy the contents of the manufacturer's floppy onto the MS-DOS boot floppy before you can run it.

When you've finished running the configuration software, it's best to shut down the computer completely (that is, power it down), leave it off for a few moments, and power it back up again. Although manufacturers don't always include this step, I've encountered several adapters that won't work correctly until you do this.

Even small static discharges can destroy your network adapter, your motherboard, and other internal components. While installing your network adapter, wear a grounding anti-static wrist strap. Attach the strap to the case of your computer or to a properly grounded work surface. Be sure to turn off your PC before attempting installation. If you use the computer case as a ground, leave the PC power cord plugged in for proper grounding. But whatever you do, make sure you turn off the PC first.

Testing Your Network Adapter

Before continuing with Windows 98 network software installation, it's a good idea to test the network adapter, if possible. This can catch configuration problems or defecting adapters before you spend time installing drivers and protocols. Occasionally, network adapters don't work, and it's better to catch this early before you spend too much time scratching your head over what's going wrong.

If the network adapter manufacturer supplies a diagnostic utility, use it to test the adapter. Better diagnostic utilities include both a local test, which checks the adapter configuration itself, and a network test, which actually communicates with another network node. The latter test typically requires two computers running the same diagnostic software.

TIP

Don't test newly installed adapters over your production LAN, unless the LAN isn't being used for actual work. Defective or incorrectly configured adapters can wreak havoc on your network, interrupting service to your users. Also, the amount of data sent by diagnostic tests can be so huge that it can bring your network to its knees (if networks had knees). Your best bet is to isolate these tests on a small, separate network — as small as two nodes and a hub. If you must run the tests over your production network, try not to do it during business hours.

Installing Windows 98 Network Software

In this section, I show you how to install and configure the network software included with Windows 98 to get your network adapter up and running. You'll learn what you need to know before proceeding with the installation, and you'll get a step-by-step view of what it takes to get the hardware and software working together.

Preparing for Network Software Installation

In this section, I discuss some key preparatory steps you need to take before proceeding with network software installation. You'll need to determine where the network adapter driver is, what you're going to name your computer, and which protocols you plan to install.

FINDING YOUR NETWORK DRIVER

Before installing your network adapter, you need to find out where the driver will come from. Most network adapters arrive with a floppy disk or CD-ROM that contains drivers for Windows 98 and other operating systems. Some adapters don't provide any software, but the documentation tells you which built-in Windows 98 driver to install.

Alternatively, the manufacturer may point you to the Windows 98 CD-ROM. Windows 98 provides a number of tested network adapter drivers on its CD-ROM in the *Windows 98 Driver Library* (*WDL 98*). Go to the \DRIVERS\NETLAN directory, and then to the directory that matches your network adapter name or manufacturer. Copy all the files to a floppy disk for use during installation.

Regardless of where the driver comes from, you should arm yourself with either a diskette or the name of the built-in Windows 98 driver before you begin installation.

SELECTING COMPUTER NAMES

Each computer on the network needs a unique name. This name is used to distinguish the computer for all other network nodes. During the Windows 98 network configuration process, you need to select a name for the computer in which you've installed a network adapter. The computer name can be up to 15 characters long, and can't include any spaces. The name can include alphabetic, numeric, and the following special characters: `! @ # $ % ^ & ( ) - _ ' { } .` ~. I show you how to assign this name to the computer later in this chapter.

> CAUTION
>
> Consider your choice of computer names carefully. Once you establish the computer name of a dedicated server or peer-to-peer node that may act as a server, other computers will refer to it by name when accessing its shared network resources. If you decide to change the computer's name later on, all clients (or peers) that access its shared resources will have to change the name to which they connect. In a very small network with few users, this may not be a big deal. In a large network with many users, however, changing the name of a server can be a major productivity hit.

To avoid having to change computer names, pick a convention that's based on a fairly stable entity and stick with it. For example, using names associated with departmental or functional units tend to endure (for example, FINANCE01, SALES10, DISTRIBUTION, or ENGINEERINGB). Names that have nothing to do with anything real also work well (for example, FRODO16, BILBO88, or GANDALF100). Another approach is to name the computer according to the information it provides (for example, SOURCECODE1 or REPORTS).

Avoid computer names that map directly to names of people, unless the computer will always act as a client and never as a server. (Remember that, in a peer-to-peer network, any computer can act as both a client and a server at the same time.) Try also to avoid using computer names to refer to the location of the equipment. Names like KIMSERVER or ROOM18 are poor choices if Kim leaves or changes departments, or if the server moves from Room 18 to some other room, building, city, or state. Names like WAREHOUSE might be all right, if it refers to the warehouse function and not necessarily the location of the server.

> NOTE: In small networks, it's OK to name peer-to-peer computers on people's desks based on the employees' names, as long as the resource sharing they do is incidental. For example, if they just use the server functionality to occasionally transfer files between computers, then changing the name of the computer later isn't a problem. But if a computer offers a continuous service, such as a shared printer or a repository for departmental files, you should use another convention for naming the computer.

SELECTING A WORKGROUP NAME

Every Windows 98 computer must be assigned to a workgroup. The workgroup is used to logically associate groups of computers together. Workgroup names have the same rules as computer names, which were discussed in the previous section. However, workgroups aren't unique – you can assign all of your computers to the same workgroup.

The default workgroup name is WORKGROUP. (Now that took a lot of imagination to concoct.) I recommend that you select your own workgroup names for each logical grouping of computers. For example, if your network covers two departments, each with its own network resources, you could create one workgroup for each department (for example, FINANCE_GROUP and SALES_GROUP). Later in this chapter, you'll find out how to assign a Windows 98 computer to a WORKGROUP.

PREPARING FOR NETWORK PROTOCOLS

Choose the network protocols that you're going to run on your network. I discussed individual network protocols in Chapter 6, so if you haven't yet selected the protocol (or protocols) you want to run on your network, you need to do that now. Table 6-1 presents a summary of criteria for selecting network protocols. I show you how to install and configure Windows 98 network protocols later in this chapter.

If you plan on installing the TCP/IP protocol, you'll need several additional pieces of addressing information, which I discuss in the following sections.

ARRIVING AT AN IP ADDRESS As I mentioned in Chapter 6, each network adapter that uses the TCP/IP protocol needs a unique IP address. Each adapter is called a *host* in the TCP/IP world. There are two approaches to selecting IP addresses for hosts. If the hosts will ever be attached to the Internet, you need to use *globally unique IP addresses*. As its name implies, a globally unique IP address is different from the IP address of any other host in the world. Your ISP can provide a range of valid unique addresses to use in your network. If, however, your hosts will never connect to the Internet, you can opt to use *private IP addresses*. These addresses aren't globally unique, but as long as they're uniquely assigned within your own network, you can use them.

Whether you use globally unique or private IP addresses, you have two choices for how to assign addresses to individual hosts. The first is called *static IP addressing*. It's the most straightforward approach, but the least convenient. In static addressing, you manually configure the IP address of each host. This can be time-consuming if your network contains more than a handful of nodes.

NOTE: If you install more than one network adapter in a computer or other network device, and more than one of the adapters uses TCP/IP, the computer or device is said to be *multihomed*. Remember that each network adapter requires its own IP address, so you need to assign more than one IP address to a multihomed computer.

The more desirable approach is called *dynamic IP addressing*. IP addresses can be assigned and reassigned to individual hosts automatically. There are three types of dynamic IP addressing available in Windows 98:

- **ISP assigned IP addressing** – For dial-up Internet connections, you can configure your host to be automatically assigned an IP address when it connects to your ISP.
- **DHCP assigned IP addressing** – If you have a Windows NT Server (version 3.5 or later) host on your network, you can configure it as a DHCP server, which doles out IP addresses automatically to your other hosts. (See Chapter 6 for a discussion of DHCP.) Windows 98 cannot be set up as a DHCP server, so if you don't have a Windows NT Server host on your network, you can't use this addressing option.
- **Automatic private IP addressing** – Windows 98 will automatically assign a private IP address, if it can't find a DHCP server on the network. The assigned address will only work on the internal network – it's not valid for Internet access.

Before you install the TCP/IP protocol, you need to determine whether you want to use globally unique or private IP addresses. If you decide on globally unique addresses, you need to contact your ISP to obtain a valid Class C or Class B address. Then, you need to decide whether you want to use static or dynamic addressing to assign IP addresses to your individual hosts.

Anatomy of an IP Address

Just what does an IP address look like? An IP address is really just a number – actually, a series of four numbers – that uniquely defines a network adapter within a network. IP addresses are expressed in what's called *dotted-decimal notation*, in which the four numbers in a series are separated by periods. For example, 127.248.15.6 could be an IP address. The individual numbers range from 0 to 255, so they can be represented in eight bits. But instead of being called bytes, these numbers are referred to as *octets* – an archaic reference from the time before the term *byte* even existed.

The Internet community has sliced and diced these numbers in various ways, to accommodate networks of different sizes. Three classes of IP addresses have emerged as standard. Class A uses the first byte (or octet) as a network address, and the remaining bytes as a host address. With a Class A address, you can deal with 126 networks and 16,777,214 hosts within each network. Class B uses the first two bytes for the network address, and the other two for the host address. It can accommodate 16,384 networks, with 65,534 hosts per network. Finally, a Class C IP address uses the first three bytes for the network address and only the final byte as the host address. It can handle a whopping 2,097,151 networks, but each network can contain only 254 hosts.

ISPs typically assign organizations either Class C or Class B addresses, depending on the size of the organization's network. The values 0, 1, and 255 have special meaning and should not be used in a standard IP address. IP addresses that begin with either 10 or 169.254 are reserved for private IP addressing, and are not valid on the Internet.

RESOLVING TCP/IP NAMES Most folks prefer to deal with computers using names, rather than cryptic IP addresses. To do this, you need some way of automatically translating between meaningful computer names and their associated numeric host addresses. Windows 98 provides several mechanisms for handling this job, which is known as *name resolution*. I discuss those approaches in this section.

Domain Name System – *DNS* (*Domain Name System*) is a global distributed database that maps a hierarchy of names to their IP addresses. You've probably seen DNS names on the Internet – for example, `fred.flagrant.com`. A DNS name has two parts: a domain name and a host name. The host name (fred) maps to a specific IP address of a host on your network. The domain name (flagrant.com) is actually a hierarchy that might consist of several levels of detail.

For example, fred.sales.western.flagrant.com contains four levels in the domain name hierarchy. It represents a commercial organization (.com), a specific organization name (flagrant), a geographic region within the organization (western), and a department or function within that region (sales). The default host name of your Windows 98 computer is the computer name I discussed earlier in this chapter. I show you how to change that name later in this chapter.

If you're attaching your network to the Internet, your ISP will supply you with a couple of IP addresses that point to DNS servers. (Alternate DNS servers are contacted if the primary ones are unavailable.) Those servers perform the translation from names to IP addresses for you. If you're not attaching to the Internet, you'll need to set up one or more DNS servers within your network. If you stick with a Windows environment, you'll need Windows NT Server to implement a DNS server, or you'll need third-party DNS server software that doesn't require Windows NT Server to run.

NOTE: DNS provides a static mapping between names and IP addresses. It's not a good choice if you're using DHCP or some other dynamic approach to IP address assignment.

Microsoft WINS – No, I'm not talking about the outcome of a government lawsuit. *WINS* (*Windows Internet Naming Service*) offers a more dynamic approach. It uses Windows NT Server (version 3.5 or later) as a WINS server to provide the same type of service as DNS. The advantage of WINS is that it works hand-in-hand with DHCP to automatically update the distributed database of name-to-address mappings.

To implement a WINS server, you need a Windows NT Server computer running the included WINS server software. You also need a WINS component on your Windows 98 computers – it's installed automatically when you install the Microsoft TCP/IP protocol. Because WINS servers and DHCP servers both require a fixed IP address (that isn't assigned dynamically), it's a good idea to have one Windows NT Server computer act as both a DHCP server and a WINS server. You can establish additional WINS servers as backups, in case the main WINS server goes down. Windows 98 supports up to 12 WINS servers.

NOTE: Using Windows NT Server 4.0 or later, you can set up both DNS and WINS to work together. If you take this approach, you can take advantage of dynamic IP addressing on your network (handled by WINS), and the global hierarchy of the Internet (handled by DNS).

Other name resolution approaches – Windows 98 supports additional name resolution approaches, but they're not as popular or as desirable as the mechanisms discussed so far. One is called *broadcast name resolution*. In this environment, each computer broadcasts its name and IP address on the network, and other nodes need to keep track of these announcements. They also need to challenge attempts to register duplicate names or addresses. This approach works only for small networks, and its network traffic overhead can be high.

The most ancient of all methods uses static text files, called *host tables*, that simply contain a list of IP addresses and their associated host names. Host tables are maintained manually using text editors such as Notepad. Windows 98 can use this approach if none of the other methods is available. A file called HOSTS is used to map DNS style names to IP addresses, while a file called LMHOSTS maps computer names to IP addresses. When DNS isn't available, Windows 98 can use its local HOSTS file; the LMHOSTS file takes over if WINS isn't available.

Installing and Configuring Network Software

Once your network adapter is physically installed in the computer, you need to get Windows 98 to recognize and use it properly. The first step in this process, after physical adapter installation, is booting Windows 98 with the new hardware.

The remainder of this chapter assumes that you have physically installed the network adapter in your computer, and that the Windows 98 operating system is already installed on the computer. If you haven't installed the adapter yet, go back to the beginning of this chapter.

If the adapter you've installed is a Plug and Play device, Windows 98 will attempt to detect it automatically, and may install the appropriate device driver as well. You'll be able to determine this by watching the onscreen messages during the boot process. (These messages appear after the Windows 98 background appears, but before your desktop icons appear.) If it looks as though Windows 98 recognized the hardware and installed the appropriate driver, you can proceed to the section titled "Verifying device driver installation."

Windows 98 may recognize the hardware correctly and call it by the right name, but the operating system may not have a built-in driver available for it. It's also possible that Windows 98 realizes there's a new device installed, but doesn't know what type of device it is. In either case, you'll be prompted during the boot process to optionally provide a device driver from the adapter manufacturer. At this point, insert the driver disk provided by the manufacturer (or the one you created from the Windows 98 CD-ROM earlier in this chapter) and follow the prompts.

If Windows 98 doesn't seem to detect the driver at all – which is likely if it's not a Plug and Play device – you'll need to resort to other means of installing the driver. If this happens, proceed to the section titled "Manually installing the device driver" later in this chapter.

VERIFYING DEVICE DRIVER INSTALLATION

After Windows 98 has detected the network adapter and installed the driver for it, it's a good idea to verify that the driver is indeed installed and running properly. This is a fairly simple task, but an important one to help avoid needless troubleshooting later on. To verify network adapter driver installation, perform the following steps:

1. Click Start → Settings → Control Panel. In Control Panel, double-click the System icon.
2. In the System Properties dialog box, click the Device Manager tab. Click View devices by type. Under Computer, all device types are listed alphabetically.
3. Look for a type called Network adapters. If you find it, proceed to Step 4. If that type isn't listed, the device driver isn't installed. Proceed to the section titled "Manually installing the device driver."
4. Click the plus sign (+) to the left of Network adapters to expand its contents. Under Network adapters, look for an entry that matches the make and model of your network adapter hardware.
5. If you find your adapter listed, as shown in Figure 9-2, double-click the entry and proceed to Step 6. If you don't find your adapter, proceed to the section titled "Manually installing the device driver."

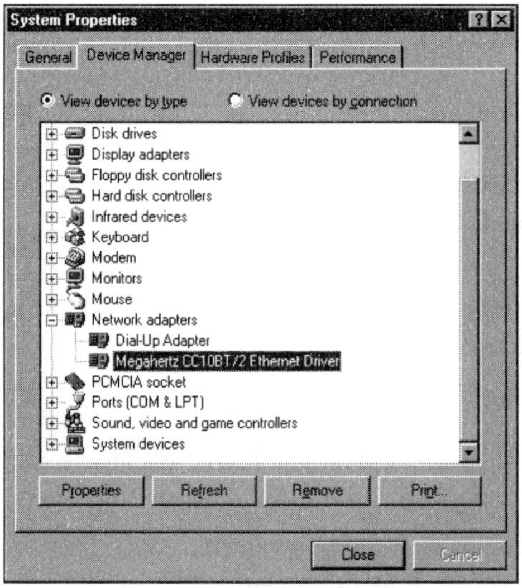

Figure 9-2: The Device Manager tab lists all currently installed devices, and enables you to view and modify configuration details.

6. In the Driver Properties dialog box, click the General tab. In the Driver status area, read the status of the device driver. If all is well, the status should read "This device is working properly." If that's the case, you have verified that the driver is installed and running. Click OK.

Whether or not the driver is running, proceed to the section titled "Configuring the device driver." You'll need to verify and possibly change the driver settings, now that the driver is installed.

MANUALLY INSTALLING THE DEVICE DRIVER

If Windows 98 doesn't detect the network adapter during the boot process, you need to install the device driver manually. To do this, perform the following steps:

1. Click Start → Settings → Control Panel. In Control Panel, double-click the Add New Hardware icon.
2. In the Add New Hardware Wizard dialog box, click Next, and click Next again. Windows 98 searches for newly installed Plug and Play hardware.
3. If Windows 98 presents a list of the Plug and Play devices it finds, you'll be asked if the device you're trying to install is on the list. If it is, click Yes, select the network adapter from the list, click Next, and follow the prompts to install the driver. If it isn't listed, click No and then click Next.
4. When asked if you want Windows to search for new non-Plug and Play hardware, click Yes, click Next, and click Next again. Windows 98 attempts to detect non-Plug and Play hardware. A gas gauge indicates its progress.

> NOTE: Depending on your hardware configuration, this hardware detection process may cause your computer to hang. If you see no progress in the gas gauge indicator and no disk activity for several minutes, shut down the computer and restart Windows 98. Go through the steps again to reach Step 4, and click No instead of Yes. Then proceed to Step 5. You want Windows 98 to skip automatic hardware detection this time around.

5. If no hardware is detected, click Next and proceed to Step 7. Otherwise, proceed to Step 6.
6. Click Details to see the list of detected devices. If the network adapter is included in the list, click Finish. You may be prompted to insert the Windows 98 CD-ROM to complete installation of the driver. Follow the prompts to complete driver installation. Then proceed to Step 11.

NOTE: If other new devices were detected besides your network adapter, you may be prompted to install their drivers as well. Follow the prompts and insert the appropriate floppy disks or CD-ROMs as requested.

7. As shown in Figure 9-3, under Hardware types, click Network adapters and click Next. Under Manufacturers, click the name of the network adapter manufacturer and proceed to Step 8. If you don't see your network adapter manufacturer, proceed to Step 10.

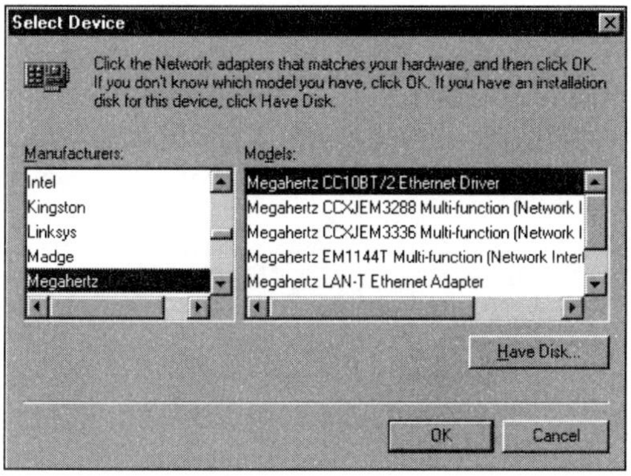

Figure 9-3: The Add New Hardware Wizard enables you to specify the make and model of the network adapter you're installing.

8. As shown in Figure 9-3, under Models, click the specific model of your network adapter and proceed to Step 9. If you don't see your network adapter model, proceed to Step 10.

9. Click OK. You may be prompted for the Windows 98 CD-ROM or a floppy disk to complete installation of the driver. Follow the prompts to complete driver installation. Then proceed to Step 11.

10. Click Have Disk. Insert the floppy disk or CD-ROM containing the network adapter device driver and follow the prompts to complete driver installation.

11. Driver installation is complete. If the Add New Hardware Wizard dialog box is still visible, click Cancel. You may be prompted to restart the computer for the changes to take effect. Do so.

Now that you've manually installed the network adapter's device driver, you'll want to verify and possibly modify the driver configuration. I show you how to do this in the next section.

CONFIGURING THE DEVICE DRIVER

Once the device driver is installed, either automatically by Windows 98 or manually by you, it's time to verify that the driver is configured properly. If it isn't, you need to modify the configuration to get the adapter to work correctly. In the following sections, I show you how to verify and correct resource assignments, resolve resource conflicts, and modify other device driver settings.

ASSIGNING RESOURCES Whether or not your network adapter is a Plug and Play device, you need to determine whether resources were detected and assigned properly to the device. Follow these steps:

1. Click Start → Settings → Control Panel, and double-click the System icon. In the System Properties dialog box, click the Device Manager tab. Click View devices by type.
2. Click the plus sign (+) to the left of Network adapters. Under Network adapters, click the name of the network adapter you just installed, and then click Properties.
3. In the Driver Properties dialog box, click the Resources tab, as shown in Figure 9-4. Verify that the Conflicting device list reports no conflicts. If there are no conflicts, proceed to Step 4. If conflicts are reported, you'll need to change the settings of this device to avoid the conflict by proceeding to the section titled "Resolving resource conflicts."
4. If you set jumpers or switches on the adapter, or you ran a separate configuration utility to assign resources to the adapter, verify that those settings exactly match those shown on the Resources tab. If they do, proceed to Step 6. Otherwise, proceed to Step 5.
5. For each resource assignment that doesn't match your manual configuration of the adapter, click the resource type and click Change Setting. In the Edit dialog box, select the value that matches the adapter configuration. Make sure the value you select doesn't conflict with another device. Then click OK. When you've assigned all the resources correctly, proceed to Step 6.
6. In the Driver Properties dialog box, click OK.

Once you've properly assigned system resources to the network adapter, you can proceed to the section titled "Modifying other driver settings."

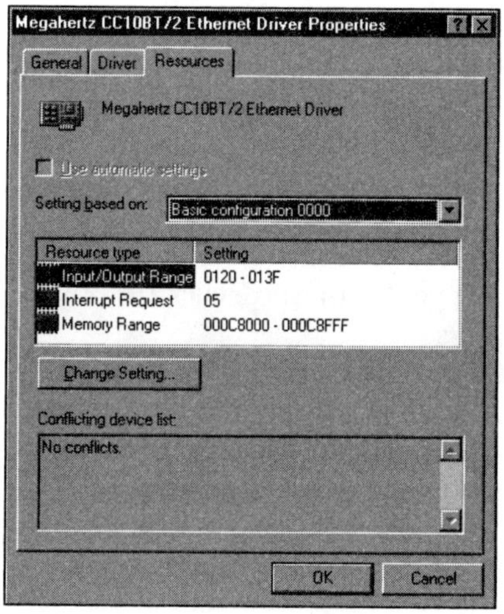

Figure 9-4: The Resources tab in Driver Properties lets you view and modify resource assignments, and identify resource conflicts with other devices.

RESOLVING RESOURCE CONFLICTS The Conflicting device list in the Resources tab usually clues you in on the specific resource and specific device that conflict with your current network adapter settings. When you've identified the conflict, you have two choices: change the network adapter settings, or change the settings of the device with which it's conflicting. Your decision may depend on how many other configuration choices your network adapter provides.

For example, if the conflicting resource is IRQ 5, and your network adapter doesn't allow more than two other IRQ settings – both of which already conflict with other devices – then you may have to change the IRQ configuration of the other device, instead. You can find out what your adapter configuration options are by clicking the resource type and then clicking Change Setting. You can then only choose from the limited set of available values for that resource type. As you scroll through the list in the Edit dialog box, the Conflict information area shows which device, if any, already uses that resource.

Select a resource that isn't used by another device and click OK. Remember that if your network adapter required manual configuration via switches, jumpers, or a software utility, you'll need to change the physical settings on the adapter to match the new settings you've just specified.

MODIFYING OTHER DRIVER SETTINGS After you've configured and verified that the resource assignments are correct and don't conflict with other devices, you can turn your attention to other network adapter settings. Each network adapter offers a different set of options, so you'll need to refer to the documentation that came with your adapter. To access these options, perform the following steps:

1. Click Start → Settings → Control Panel, and double-click the Network icon. In the Network dialog box, click the Configuration tab. Then, click the name of the network adapter driver in the list of installed network components.
2. Click Properties. The tabs in the Driver Properties dialog box provide access to additional adapter configuration options.
3. Make your configuration changes. When you've finished, click OK. If you are prompted to restart the computer, do so.

One important option that's common to most combo adapters is the connector type. If an adapter provides more than one type of network cable connection, you need to set the adapter to match the type of cable you're using. For example, if a combo adapter provides both a coax and a UTP connector, and your network is UTP, set the connector type appropriately. Figure 9-5 illustrates this operation.

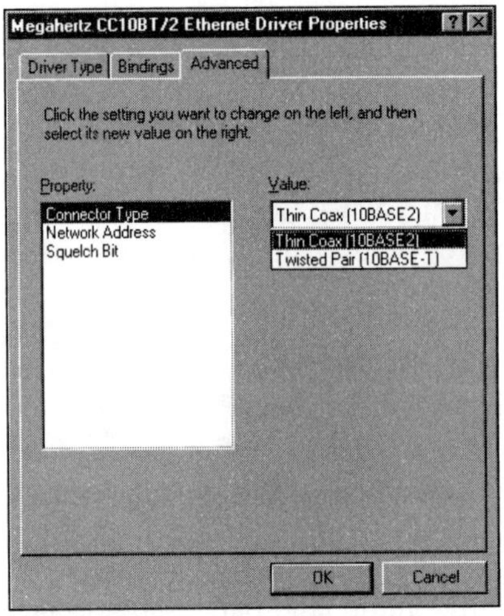

Figure 9-5: You can set the network connector type and other adapter options in the Network application in Control Panel.

IDENTIFYING YOUR COMPUTER

Earlier in this chapter, I mentioned that each computer needs a unique computer name and must be assigned to a workgroup. Here's where you make those assignments, by performing the following steps:

1. In Control Panel, double-click Network. Click the Identification tab.
2. Type the unique computer name in the Computer name box. Then, in the Workgroup box, type the name of the workgroup to which this computer belongs.

3. Optionally, type a description of the computer, its user, or its location in the Computer Description box.
4. Click OK. Then, click Yes to restart the computer with the new identification information.

INSTALLING NETWORK PROTOCOLS

In the following sections, I show you how to install and initially configure the NetBEUI, IPX/SPX, and TCP/IP protocols. I don't cover every configuration option at this point; instead, I focus on installation and the most common configuration requirements for each protocol.

INSTALLING NETBEUI Here are the steps you need to follow to install the NetBEUI protocol, if it isn't already installed:

1. Click Start → Settings → Control Panel. Double-click Network, click the Configuration tab, and then click Add.
2. In the Select Network Component Type dialog box, click Protocol, and then click Add.
3. Under Manufacturers, click Microsoft. Under Network Protocols, click NetBEUI, and then click OK.
4. In the Network dialog box, click OK.
5. You may be prompted for your Windows 98 CD-ROM. After copying files, you'll be prompted to restart your computer.

The remaining NetBEUI configuration settings are automatically established by Windows 98, so no additional configuration is required.

INSTALLING IPX/SPX Here are the steps you need to follow to install the IPX/SPX protocol, if it isn't already installed.

1. Click Start → Settings → Control Panel. Double-click Network, click the Configuration tab, and then click Add.
2. In the Select Network Component Type dialog box, click Protocol, and then click Add.
3. Under Manufacturers, click Microsoft. Under Network Protocols, click IPX/SPX, and then click OK.
4. In the Network dialog box, click OK.
5. You may be prompted for your Windows 98 CD-ROM. After copying files, you'll be prompted to restart your computer.

The remaining IPX/SPX configuration setting defaults are perfectly fine for typical network installation, so no additional configuration is required.

INSTALLING TCP/IP Here's how to install and initially configure the TCP/IP protocol. Make sure you have the IP addressing and other information discussed earlier in this chapter before you begin installing TCP/IP.

1. Click Start → Settings → Control Panel. Double-click Network, click the Configuration tab, and then click Add.
2. In the Select Network Component Type dialog box, click Protocol, and then click Add.
3. Under Manufacturers, click Microsoft. Under Network Protocols, click TCP/IP, and then click OK. Then, in the Network dialog box, click OK.
4. In response to the restart prompt, click No. Double-click Network and click the Configuration tab. Click the TCP/IP protocol, and then click Properties.

NOTE: If you have more than one network adapter on which TCP/IP will run, you need to perform IP address configuration for each adapter individually. You'll select individual adapters here, by clicking the entries that contain both TCP/IP and the adapter name. I discuss the concept of binding protocols to adapters later in this chapter.

5. In the TCP/IP Properties dialog box, click the IP Address tab. If you're using DHCP or automatic IP addressing, click Obtain an IP address automatically, and proceed to Step 7.
6. If you're manually assigning IP addresses, click Specify an IP address and type the IP address of the adapter you're configuring. Type an appropriate subnet mask in the Subnet Mask box. For a Class B IP address, type `255.255.0.0`. For a Class C IP address, type `255.255.255.0`.

NOTE: The subnet mask essentially identifies the network-specific portion of the IP address. You can further subdivide the block of host addresses into multiple networks by specifying a different subnet mask that reduces the number of bits used in the host portion of the address. For example, if you have a Class C IP address, and you want to use the upper two bits of the last byte for an internal network address, and use the remaining six bits for the host address, you can specify a subnet mask of `255.255.255.192`.

7. If you're using DNS to resolve host names to IP addresses, click the DNS Configuration tab and click Enable DNS. Under DNS Server Search Order, type the DNS address specified by your ISP (or the address of your Windows NT Server acting as a DNS server) and click Add. If you have more than one DNS address, type it and click Add.

   To specify a host and domain name for this host, type them in the appropriate Host and Domain boxes. The Host name defaults to the computer name specified earlier in this chapter. The Domain name may be supplied by your ISP.

8. To configure your use of WINS, click the WINS Configuration tab. If you have a Windows NT DHCP server that's configured to provide information on WINS servers, click Use DHCP for WINS Resolution and proceed to Step 10.

9. If a WINS server is available, but a DHCP server isn't, click Enable WINS Resolution. Type the IP address of the primary WINS server and click Add. If you have backup WINS servers available, type their IP addresses and click Add for each address.

10. When you've finished configuring TCP/IP, click OK and follow the prompts to supply the Windows 98 CD-ROM and restart the computer.

If you're using TCP/IP with Dial-Up Networking (DUN) connections, you can configure TCP/IP options for each connection individually. For example, if you have separate connections to two different ISPs, you can set different DNS addresses for each one. You can make these per-connection changes by clicking Start → Programs → Accessories → Communications → Dial-Up Networking. Right-click the icon associated with the dial-up connection you want to configure, click Properties, and click the Server Type tab. Click TCP/IP Settings to set the IP, DNS, and WINS addresses.

CONFIGURING A CLIENT

Client for Microsoft Networks is required on your computer before it can act as a Microsoft networking peer. (This is the redirector network software component I mentioned in Chapter 6.) During installation of your network adapter, Windows 98 may automatically install Client for Microsoft Networks. You can determine whether it's already installed by following these steps:

1. Click Start → Settings → Control Panel. Double-click Network and click the Configuration tab.

2. In the list of network components, look for Client for Microsoft Networks. If it's there, the component is already installed.

Here's how to add the Client for Microsoft Networks if it isn't already installed:

1. Click Start → Settings → Control Panel. Double-click Network, click the Configuration tab, and click the Add button.
2. In the Select Network Component Type dialog box, click Client and click Add.
3. Under Manufacturers, click Microsoft. Under Network Clients, click Client for Microsoft Networks. Then click OK.
4. You may be prompted to insert the Windows 98 CD-ROM. In the Network dialog box, click OK. You'll be prompted to restart your computer.

Once the Client for Microsoft Networks is installed, you can configure it in a couple of ways. First, you can specify whether Windows 98 should reconnect to network resources when it starts, or connect to specific network resources only when they're required. The latter approach is called Quick Logon, because it doesn't take the time to reconnect during the logon process.

Another option available in Client for Microsoft Networks is the capability to use a Windows NT Server domain to validate user accounts and passwords. By default, when you log onto a Windows 98 networked computer, your user name and password are verified on the local computer only. Depending on how you've configured security, you may or may not have access to network resources if you specify an invalid user name or password. (I discuss the topic of security further in Chapter 12.) If you opt to let Windows NT validate security, you need to specify the Windows NT Server domain name. (See Chapter 7 for a discussion of Windows NT domains.)

> If you decide to use Windows NT Server for logon validation, you'll need to create a Windows NT user account on the server before the logon from this computer will work properly.

To configure these options, perform the following steps:

1. Click Start → Settings → Control Panel. Double-click Network and click the Configuration tab.
2. In the list of network components, click Client for Microsoft Networks. Then click Properties.
3. In the Client for Microsoft Networks Properties dialog box, on the General tab, click either Quick logon or Logon and restore network connections, depending on when you want network resource connections to be made.

4. If you want to use Windows NT Server to validate user logons, click to set the Log on to Windows NT domain checkbox. Then, type the name of the Windows NT domain.
5. When you've finished making configuration changes, click OK. In the Network dialog box, click OK. You'll be prompted to restart the computer.

CONFIGURING A SERVER

The capability to share files, drives, and printers over the network is disabled by default when you install Windows 98 networking software. However, enabling peer server capabilities on a Windows 98 network node is very straightforward. You can enable file sharing, printer sharing, or both. Here are the steps to follow:

1. Click Start → Settings → Control Panel. Double-click Network and click the Configuration tab.
2. Click File and Print Sharing.
3. In the File and Print Sharing dialog box, click to set the checkbox that reads I want to be able to give others access to my files, if you want to be able to share files, hard disks, or CD-ROMs from this computer.
4. In the File and Print Sharing dialog box, click to set the checkbox that reads I want to be able to allow others to print to my printer(s), if you want to create print queues on your computer to which other nodes can send print jobs.
5. You may be prompted for the Windows 98 CD-ROM. When you've finished configuring file and print sharing, click OK.
6. In the Network dialog box, click OK. After additional files are copied, you'll be prompted to restart the computer.

Once you enable file and print sharing, the computer can act as both a client computer and a server computer simultaneously.

MANAGING NETWORK BINDINGS

For a network protocol to communicate with a network adapter, the protocol must be *bound* to the adapter driver. For example, even if you install an adapter driver and the NetBEUI protocol, the two won't talk to each other unless there is a *binding* between them.

When you install a protocol, Windows 98 does its best to create the appropriate bindings between adapter drivers and the new protocol, but it doesn't always do exactly what you want it to do. This is especially true if you're running multiple protocols or you've installed more than one network adapter in the computer. You may want one protocol to run on a specific adapter. You can add or remove bindings based on your use of individual network components.

If you look at the list of installed components on the Configuration tab of the Network application in Control Panel, you'll typically see entries that include both a protocol and an adapter. This entry actually represents the binding between them. When you install TCP/IP, for example, and you have both a network adapter and a modem, Windows 98 usually creates two bindings – one between TCP/IP and the network adapter, and one between TCP/IP and the modem (dial-up adapter). If you want to run NetBEUI on your internal network, and use TCP/IP only when dialing to the Internet, remove the binding between TCP/IP and the network adapter.

Here are the steps required to configure bindings between a network adapter and installed protocols:

1. Click Start → Settings → Control Panel. Double-click Network and click the Configuration tab.
2. In the list of network components, click the entry for the network adapter, and then click Properties.
3. In the Properties dialog box for the selected network adapter, click the Bindings tab. Click to set or clear the checkboxes associated with the listed protocols. Clearing the checkbox disables the binding; setting it enables the binding.

> NOTE: If a protocol doesn't appear on the list, it may not be installed correctly or completely. Make sure you restart the computer after protocol installation, before attempting to alter bindings. If the protocol still doesn't show up in the list of potential bindings, reinstall the protocol using the steps outlined in the section titled "Installing network protocols."

4. When you've finished enabling and disabling bindings, click OK. In the Network dialog box, click OK.
5. You may be prompted to restart the computer. Click Yes to restart.

Testing the Hardware and Software

Earlier in this chapter, you used the manufacturer's diagnostic utility to verify basic network adapter functionality. If the manufacturer doesn't provide such a utility, you need to wait until the rest of the network software is installed before testing your new installation.

The first step in testing the hardware and software installation involves determining whether the computers can see each other. This is the most basic acid test for proper network configuration. It tells you whether the hardware, drivers, and protocols are alive and well, and can actually communicate over the network. This approach to testing requires at least two computers with installed network hardware and software. It's a good idea to isolate these newly configured computers from the rest of your production network, but it isn't absolutely necessary. Follow these steps:

1. Make sure at least one other computer is connected to the same network, and that it is up and running. Make sure both computers are configured to be part of the same workgroup.
2. On the desktop, double-click the Network Neighborhood icon.
3. After a few seconds, in the Network Neighborhood window, you'll see at least two entries – Entire Network and the name of the computer you're using. You may also see other names of computers attached to your network.
4. In the Network Neighborhood window, double-click Entire Network. You should see at least one workgroup listed – the workgroup to which this computer belongs. Double-click the workgroup.
5. You should see icons for this computer and other computers in the workgroup that are up and running. Double-click the icon for one of these other computers.

If you don't see this computer or other computers attached to the same network, you'll need to perform some troubleshooting steps. Chapter 14 includes information on how to troubleshoot when your computer can't see other computers on the network. In Chapter 11, I cover the details of sharing resources on the network and connecting to them.

Summary

In this chapter, I've shown you how to install and configure network adapters and Windows 98 network software to establish communications between computers on your network. You've learned how to set up the hardware, drivers, and protocols required to get your network up and running. In Part III, you'll delve into the specific tasks required to administer your network. In Chapter 10, you'll learn about specific network administration responsibilities, tasks, and the tools required to perform them.

Part III

Administering Your Network

Chapter 10

Network Administration Responsibilities and Tools

IN THIS CHAPTER

- Understanding the administrator's role
- Managing and optimizing your network
- Anticipating and troubleshooting problems
- Maximizing your network's potential using administration tools

IN THIS CHAPTER, I fill you in on the requirements, duties, and responsibilities of a successful network administrator. You'll discover that the role reaches far beyond raw technical skills. I also introduce you to some of the key tools that network administrators use to monitor, troubleshoot, manage, and optimize networks and nodes. By the end of this chapter, you'll have a good idea of what's involved in the network administration position.

NOTE: Whether or not you're personally taking on the role of network administrator in your organization, I urge you to read this chapter. Even if you're going to hire someone to do the job, it will give you valuable insights into the duties and responsibilities of a successful network administrator, and uncover valuable insights into the qualities and skills required beyond pure technical savvy. And if you're just trying to learn more about networking, this chapter will give you a better appreciation of what it takes to fill this role.

Understanding the Network Administrator Role

The job of a network administrator is filled with both challenges and rewards. If you're taking on this role, your success depends on understanding the specific duties you'll be expected to perform. Of course, duties and expectations vary from one organization to the next; but whether your title is network administrator, network manager, network engineer, or resident guru, the basic requirements covered in this chapter will apply to you at least in part.

You may find that some of the topics covered in the following sections sound like common sense. If so, great. It means you're probably already on the path to succeeding in this role because some of the skills are already a part of you. And if you find that many of the concepts are new to you, you'll get a pretty good idea of what you need to work on as you grow into a successful network administrator.

Documenting Your Network

As you've seen in previous chapters, quite a few details are involved in planning, designing, installing, and configuring a computer network. You'll see in later chapters that the same holds true for maintaining and growing a network, as the needs and size of your organization change. Although you'll have a variety of responsibilities as a network administrator, one of the most important (and most often overlooked) tasks involves documenting your network.

WHY DOCUMENT?

Thoroughly and consistently documenting your network is critically important to you and your organization for the following reasons:

- When problems crop up and you're under pressure to solve them, you can avoid mistakes and confusion by having the information you need right at your fingertips.
- If you have to be away due to illness, emergencies, or vacations, other people can access the information.
- With up-to-date documentation handy, you'll spend less time searching for details and more time performing more useful tasks. You'll appear more organized and you'll be more organized.
- If you need to deal with technical support personnel to troubleshoot a component, you'll have all the information available. With the industry shift toward charging for technical support, your documentation can save both time and money.
- If you're promoted, move to a different department, or leave the organization, your successors will need your network documentation.

TIP

I've heard many network administrators complain about this aspect of the job — viewing it as an unnecessary or menial task. Some argue that writing down all the information takes away their job security. They're wrong. The way to succeed in this role isn't achieved by holding valuable information hostage so you can't be fired. Success depends on improving an organization's productivity and providing the tools to users so they can be more efficient and succeed at their jobs. To accomplish that goal, you need to be efficient enough at your job to have the time to plan and improve your network to meet the changing needs of your users. That sort of proactive approach to network administration will get you more job security than refusing to write anything down.

WHEN TO DOCUMENT

If you're designing a network from scratch, start keeping track of all the details from day one. Get a notebook and maintain your records in it. Keep it in a safe place. Treat it as a critical component of your network. It's all right to maintain the information electronically as well, but if you're having network or computer problems, you may not be able to access the data when you need it most. Some administrators update their documentation online (for example, if they have poor handwriting, like I do), and then print the information for the physical notebook.

NOTE

Even if you're taking over one or more existing networks, documentation is critical. If your predecessor kept close track of the details and wrote them down — that's the key — your first task should be to study the information and fill in any missing details. Having to study extensive network documentation is a good problem to have. Too often, nothing is ever written down, and you're left with researching and creating the documentation yourself. In this situation, don't skip this step. You and the people who follow in your footsteps will thank you for it.

Your network documentation should never be out of date. Unfortunately, in the day-to-day rush of installing, solving problems, attending meetings, and so forth, it's easy for this task to fall in the "do it tomorrow" category. If time is a problem, set aside a time slot at least once a week to update your documentation. Treat this time as sacred and follow through with it as you would with any important meeting. When the time comes, if you find you have no updating to do, you can turn to your other high priority tasks. The point is to get in the habit and discipline of keeping the material current.

WHAT TO DOCUMENT

What should you include in your network documentation notebook? One of the most obvious elements is the physical layout of your network infrastructure, including locations and types of cables, hubs, network outlets, and other components. If you do the installation yourself, you'll have all the information readily available to write down as you go along. If you hire someone else to do the work, make it your business to watch them, ask questions, and write everything down. If possible, have them include detailed installation documentation as part of their contracted deliverables. See Chapter 5 for details on network infrastructure.

Likewise, it's important to keep track of all the computer and network adapter configuration information you gathered while installing network hardware and software. (See Chapter 9 for details.) It takes time to ferret out these details, so it helps to have them handy when you need them. Keeping this information can also save time and frustration if a user has performed a hardware or software upgrade that has caused a problem with the computer or network. You can use the configuration details as a baseline for a known working system. Your documentation notebook is also a good place to keep the system design objectives you developed in Chapter 8.

Inventories of computers, components, and software packages are also helpful as you maintain and expand your network. Knowing how many 486-based computers you have, how many ISA network adapters you have, and so forth can help you plan purchases for new equipment, pinpoint performance bottlenecks, and quickly answer questions from management about the network. Keeping track of software inventories can also keep you out of legal trouble by giving you the information you need to ensure you have the right number of licenses. In addition, it helps you stay on top of which computers need upgrades when new releases or patches arrive.

The network documentation notebook is a good place to organize and store other information including your disaster recovery plan, backup procedures and schedules, records of problems and their solutions, user requests, maintenance records, and short- and long-term plans for network expansion. You should also include rollout plans for new operating systems or hardware, security policies, and information on training new users. I cover many of these topics later in this chapter.

TIP

Finding ways to communicate with your users can be rewarding for everyone. Consider scheduling periodic meetings with department managers, attending group meetings, providing forums for communicating technology plans, and getting feedback directly from users. Step out from behind your e-mail and deal with users and groups face-to-face. You'll find that you'll serve their needs better, they'll feel more comfortable with you, and you'll learn much more about different aspects of the organization that you didn't know before. This approach really works, and everyone wins.

Administering Your Network Users

Network administration is more about dealing with people and their business needs than it is about dealing with technology. Sure, your technical knowledge and ability to make things work are critically important – but the most important skills you need to exercise and develop are people skills. After all, your users are your customers. Your goal should be to keep both your users and management happy and productive with their investment in technology. That means staying in touch with your organization's goals as well as with the needs of your users.

Building solid relationships with users, departmental managers, and the executive staff is important in creating mutual understanding of the benefits, requirements, and costs of networking technology. Above all, maintain your integrity – admit when you don't know something, and follow through on your commitments. I've seen so much time and effort wasted when administrators start making up answers, making commitments they don't keep, and placing blame where it shouldn't be placed. Integrity is the most valuable virtue you can bring to this role.

Problem-solving and communication skills come next. You need to have or develop the ability to narrow down problems and their causes systematically. Once you know what went wrong, it's also critically important that you be able to communicate the cause, the solution, and how to prevent the problem in the future. Clearly setting user and management expectations about network performance, reliability, and scheduled downtime is also vital. And of course, great communication skills come into play when you're training users and making management presentations.

TIP The role of a network administrator can be hectic and frustrating at times. People who are quick-tempered, defensive, or argumentative don't last long in this role; if they do, everyone can become unhappy and unproductive. Regardless of how much of the world is crumbling around you, stay calm and cool, and help keep others from coming unglued. Focus on the problem and a solution, be as flexible as possible to accommodate your users' needs, and maintain a sense of humor through it all.

Administering Network Resources

In a pure dedicated server network, it's likely that you're responsible for managing the servers and all the network resources they share – printers, files, hard disks, CD-ROMs, and so forth. In this environment, your task is fairly straightforward. Keep all the resources up, running, available, and ready to serve. In a peer-to-peer or mixed network, division of responsibilities can be a bit fuzzier. Each user has the capability (although, perhaps not the knowledge) to share resources on the network. Your involvement may vary, depending on the policies you have in place and the level of user cooperation you enjoy.

Whether it is you or your users who are sharing resources, you'll need to be an expert at sharing, connecting, disconnecting, and managing them. Even if your users do all the sharing and connecting, you'll need to know enough to train them and get them out of trouble if they stray into the woods. I discuss the key elements of administering network resources in Chapter 11.

TIP

If you're implementing a new peer-to-peer network, consider retaining as much control as possible over creating shared resources on the network. Even if some users balk at this prospect, it's always better to start with a very controlled, disciplined approach, and then relax the rules later for some of the more technical users. It's much more difficult to start with no rules and then try to pull in the reigns after the situation is out of control.

Troubleshooting Network Problems

Obviously, one of the most time-critical activities you'll engage in is network troubleshooting. This is where your technical skills and your ability to stay cool and logical meet. As your experience grows, so will your troubleshooting skills. However, it's likely you'll be expected to hit the ground running, with little time for training before your first big network problem. While there's no substitute for experience, knowing where to find the right information quickly can help you reach solutions quickly. Appendix B contains useful pointers to additional resources on Windows 98 and networking.

Rather than waiting for problems to fall on your doorstep, you can take actions that will improve your ability to solve problems when they occur. Develop research skills so you can easily find helpful information when you need it. Become familiar with information resources, to gain a sense of where to turn for various types of problems. Write down observations and recommendations in your network notebook as you go along. Using books, periodicals, and training, educate yourself as much as possible about common problems and solutions. And of course, take steps to prevent problems before they occur. I discuss troubleshooting techniques in Chapter 14.

TIP

Once in a while, you'll encounter a problem with no apparent solution. In fact, sometimes a problem will occur and then simply vanish without any intervention. There are so many hardware, software, cabling, and user variables at play in a network that the occasional mystery is inevitable. But don't just shrug them off. Listen carefully, gather all the information you can, document it in your network notebook, and move on. You'd be surprised at how often another mystery symptom will combine with earlier experiences to reveal the cause of the problem.

Managing Network Security

Good security is absolutely vital to the well-being of your organization's data, software, and hardware. As a network administrator, you're responsible for defining, implementing, managing, and enforcing a network security policy. All the best network hardware, software, and training are worthless if you allow unauthorized people to steal or destroy information. The goals of a software policy include:

- Ensuring that only authorized users gain access to certain restricted network resources. For example, not all employees should have access to sensitive payroll records, but human resources personnel do need access.
- Protecting data, servers, and network equipment from harm due to inadvertent actions or malicious sabotage.
- Preventing unauthorized external access to your network – through RAS or the Internet, for example.

This is one area that's easy to ignore, but it's one you can't afford to ignore. I discuss network security issues in Chapter 12.

Evaluating Software and Hardware

As a network administrator, you're likely to find yourself on the cutting edge of technology, constantly looking for ways to improve the reliability, performance, and usefulness of your network. In looking for upgraded servers, you'll have your eye on the latest CPUs, storage technologies, and network components. When you make a proposal for expanding your network, you'll be expected to know what you're talking about in many areas of new technology. Therefore, it's important to educate yourself through reading, training, and arranging for evaluations of new hardware and software products. Develop good relationships with vendors, and you should be able to try out products for little or no monetary cost.

As your organization installs new applications, it's your job to make sure the hardware you have meets the requirements of the new software. If it doesn't, it's important to include the cost of required hardware upgrades in the overall cost of the applications. In evaluating applications, you'll also want to keep your eye on how well they support networking. Some applications are designed for network installation and use, while others won't work on networks at all. Many applications have networking capabilities added as an afterthought, and this shows in poor performance or low reliability.

CAUTION

I can't stress this often enough: Make sure your application (or operating system) software licenses cover the way you use the software, in terms of either the number of users or the number of computers. Don't be caught in a legal web by violating software license agreements.

Managing Network Change

Organizations rarely stand still. At any given moment, they're either growing, shrinking, or changing the way they do business. Today, change is the one thing people can count on, and it's the primary cause of increased stress and anxiety. As a network administrator, you're also a manager of change. On the technical side, you're involved in researching, planning, designing, and implementing changes. On the people side, you're responsible for communicating, training, and following up to make sure the changes work and are used to everyone's benefit. And at the same time, you're tasked with keeping user stress and anxiety to a minimum.

TIP

In larger organizations, you may want to consider establishing a process that uses change request forms. Users and managers can submit formal requests for specific network or computer changes. The requests can be reviewed by you and other decision makers, prioritized relative to other requests, and delegated to individual network administrators. This is a great way to document changes and decisions as they happen. But regardless of your process, don't forget to document your network changes.

Involve affected departments (managers and users alike) in the process of change. Communicate plans, solicit feedback, and provide the required training to help people feel comfortable with the technology you're putting in front of them. Too often, network administrators provide expanded services and features to their users, but most users never hear about the change – they continue to do things the same old way. This is like having a great product and never marketing it.

TIP

If you have the luxury, make big changes a step at a time. This approach makes diagnosis much easier if a problem occurs, and even lets you back out of a change more easily if you find that something just isn't going to work.

Optimizing Network Performance

Network administrators are responsible for ensuring that the network delivers optimal performance, which translates directly into optimal productivity. Contrary to popular belief, however, optimal performance involves more than just tuning the network to run at its highest possible speed. Reliability is the other half of the equation. If servers, clients, or the network itself are unreliable, productivity for the affected users can drop to zero.

Keeping baseline performance statistics is a good proactive approach to optimizing network performance. Knowing how the network or a particular server behaves under normal conditions (both in terms of speed and reliability) can be invaluable when that behavior starts to change. Whether that new behavior is slower performance or a series of error conditions, your measurements beforehand can pay off during the diagnosis phase. Chapter 1 covers reliability issues, and I discuss network optimization techniques in Chapter 14.

Planning for and Recovering from Disaster

To paraphrase a certain well-known law, whatever can go wrong will go wrong eventually – but if you're unprepared, it will go wrong sooner. Call me a pessimist, realist, fatalist, or sage. (I prefer sage.) The point is that preparation is not only an excellent way to prevent disaster, but also makes recovery from disasters much less painful. As a network administrator, the entire organization will hold you responsible for adequate preparation and quick recovery. Therefore, you need to take steps to avoid loss of data, recover from failed computer and network components, recover from user-induced errors, and prevent damage to hardware and software resulting from viruses, power surges, power failures, and so forth.

In the course of disaster planning, however, you can't limit your thinking to common problems like these. Think much bigger. I don't wish major natural disasters on anyone, but what if an earthquake, hurricane, tornado, fire, flood, or small aircraft completely destroyed your entire network? Would you be able to recover? How quickly? And what specific steps would you take to recover? Do I sound like an insurance salesman? I should, because your best insurance is a solid disaster recovery plan. I discuss this further in lucky Chapter 13.

Reporting on Network Usage and Issues

As a network administrator, it's your responsibility to stay abreast of usage patterns, traffic patterns, and performance and reliability issues affecting your network. Management usually wants a clear picture of how much their investment in the network (and in you) is being used. Also, when it's time to increase network capacity, add new servers, upgrade to new software, buy faster printers, or install more cabling, you can't justify these investments by gut feelings alone. Hard facts and statistics are usually required.

Your job in this area includes obtaining and using the right tools to measure these patterns. Your network documentation notebook, which I discussed earlier in this chapter, is a good starting place – although you may need to gather additional information along the way to help justify an investment in more or better equipment. You'll be introduced to some of these tools in future chapters.

Understanding Administration Tools

Windows 98 includes a broad range of administration tools that deal with managing local computer resources, shared network resources, performance measurement, and troubleshooting. In this section, I point out the most significant tools you need to know about as a network administrator. Some of the tools are designed for use by all users, whereas others should be restricted to administrators like you. In subsequent chapters, I dig into several of the tools in greater detail.

NOTE

Windows 98 is designed so one can easily monitor and manage it remotely. It includes support for established network management protocols such as SNMP (which I discussed in Chapter 6), as well as more recent developments such as *DMI* (*Desktop Management Interface*), *WMI* (*Windows Management Infrastructure*), and others. Moreover, the Windows 98 registry is accessible over the network, enabling utilities to manage system configurations remotely. These design characteristics make it possible for many existing and future third-party network management tools to work well with Windows 98.

System Monitor

System Monitor is a performance measurement tool you can use for measuring the performance of hardware, applications, and software services. This powerful tool can be used for:

- Creating a baseline of normal performance behavior, for comparison with future performance measurements.
- Showing the performance effects of changes you make to hardware and software configurations, by comparing the new behavior with previous measurements.
- Justifying hardware upgrades by identifying performance bottlenecks.
- Diagnosing performance problems on local and remote computers, by comparing with normal performance behavior.

You can use this tool to gather and chart performance information for disks, file systems, CPU, Windows 98 operating system kernel, memory management, and networking. I discuss System Monitor in more detail in Chapter 14.

Net Watcher

Net Watcher is a tool that enables you to easily create, control, and monitor remote shared network resources. With it, you can share a network resource, stop sharing it, and list all shared resources, open files, and connected users. You can also force open files to close and disconnect users, in preparation for removing the shared resource. All of these tasks can be performed remotely over the network. I talk more about Net Watcher in Chapter 11.

System Policy Editor

The System Policy Editor offers two modes of operation: registry mode and policy file mode. In registry mode, you can directly edit the Windows 98 registry of a local or remote computer. In policy edit mode, you can edit system policy files, which don't affect the registry until the policies are downloaded and put into effect.

This tool is very powerful, offering a wide range of control over what a user is and isn't permitted to do. For example, you can hide or disable certain portions of Control Panel applications to prevent users from changing critical settings that may affect reliability or performance. You can also use it to create customized menus, hide certain menu items, run only a restricted set of applications, and disable registry editing tools. You can even prevent users from shutting down, which is especially useful if their computers are acting as servers. All these changes can help users stay out of trouble, and can cut down on support costs. Policies can be set for individual users or computers.

To some extent, the Windows 98 Setup program itself can be used as an administration tool to restrict what the user can do. By configuring client computers so they don't include certain components, you can better control which Windows 98 components exist on a user's computer. However, if users can obtain a copy of the Windows 98 CD-ROM, all bets are off — they can install anything that you may have excluded during Setup.

If you have Windows NT Server in your network, you can create default policies that apply to all users. These defaults are downloaded when the user logs on. In addition, NT gives you the capability to assign policies to groups of users, by setting the policies for Windows NT Server group accounts. This is a convenient way to define classes of users and make the computers within each class behave in a standard way.

The System Policy Editor is a very powerful tool. It's a good idea to keep it out of the hands of average users on your network. Microsoft hides this tool in \TOOLS\RESKIT\NETADMIN\POLEDIT and doesn't install it automatically for this reason. Install it on individual computers only when absolutely necessary, and restrict access to the installation files, to prevent the tool from getting into inexperienced hands.

Microsoft Backup

The Windows 98 Microsoft Backup utility is used to create periodic backups of hard disk or network contents. It's also used to restore backed-up files created under either Windows 95 or Windows 98. You can elect to back up all files, or just the files that have changed or been added since the previous backup. I discuss backup in more detail in Chapter 13.

If you're familiar with Seagate's Backup Exec software, the new version of Microsoft Backup is based on this program. It supports a much broader range of backup devices than does the Windows 95 version.

Scheduled Tasks

The Scheduled Tasks utility lets you arrange to run other utilities periodically at specific times. For example, you might schedule the Disk Defragmenter to run every two weeks, on Thursday at 1:00 am. Tasks can be scheduled to run just once, or on a daily, weekly, or monthly basis. Alternatively, you can arrange for tasks to run at system startup, whenever a user logs on, or whenever the computer is idle for a specified period of time. Whenever tasks are scheduled to run, a schedule icon appears in the task bar.

NOTE: The Windows 98 Tune-Up Wizard automatically schedules the Disk Defragmenter, ScanDisk, Disk Cleanup, and DriveSpace 3 to run at various times. As a network administrator, you should be aware of this and disable these scheduled events, unless you want your users to interact with these utilities.

Registry Editor

As I mentioned in Chapter 3, you can use the Registry Editor to edit values directly in the Windows 98 registry, either on the local computer or over the network. It's used by network administrators to make configuration changes that aren't exposed through other, safer utilities such as Control Panel or System Policy Editor.

CAUTION: If at all possible, use other utilities such as Control Panel applications, the System Policy Editor, or Device Manager to modify the Windows 98 registry indirectly. Registry Editor doesn't perform any validity checking on the information you store in the registry — and a single incorrect value can render the computer unbootable. Be sure you know exactly what you're doing before making any change directly to the registry.

Registry Checker

The Registry Checker utility consists of both a Windows 98 version and an MS-DOS version. It detects and resolves problems in the Windows 98 registry, periodically backs up the registry, and enables you to restore the registry to a previous version.

Microsoft System Information

As you saw in Chapter 8, the Microsoft System Information utility (MSInfo) enables you to collect and view information about your local computer's configuration. In addition to details of system resources such as IRQs and I/O addresses, you can also view information about your Windows 98 software configuration, device drivers, and currently running processes. MSInfo also acts as a launching pad for several other tools discussed in this chapter.

Dr. Watson

Dr. Watson is a utility that automatically creates a detailed record of the state of the system when an application dies due to a fatal error. It creates a file that can be uploaded to technical support personnel to help diagnose the cause and remedy for the application failure.

System File Checker

Windows applications often silently install new versions of Windows 98 system files. While this practice may be good for the application, it may break other applications that were tested against the original Windows 98 system files. The System File Checker, or SFC, verifies your Windows 98 system files, detects whether they've been corrupted, replaced, or deleted, and offers to restore any corrupted files to their original form. When it finds a corrupted system file, you can instruct it to extract the file from your original Windows 98 CD-ROM.

Digital Signature Verification

Drivers that ship with Windows 98 contain embedded digital signatures placed there by Microsoft. These special signatures let Windows 98 know that the drivers have been tested and certified, and that the driver files haven't been modified along the way. Because poorly written, untested drivers can do real damage to the reliability of your computer, this feature takes a giant step toward answering the question "Where has that been?" when loading a new driver.

You can cause Windows 98 to check for these digital signatures as the drivers load, so that attempts to install unsigned drivers will generate a warning or fail to load the driver altogether. You can also use the Signature Verification Tool to view digital signatures on these driver files, search for digitally signed files, and search for unsigned files.

Automatic Skip Driver Agent

If a device driver fails to load during the Windows 98 boot sequence, this could be caused by a hardware failure. You can run the Automatic Skip Driver agent to help determine what went wrong. This utility also turns off the device automatically after two unsuccessful attempts to load the driver.

Windows Update

Windows Update is a Web-based utility that detects whether your computer contains the latest drivers and system files. If Microsoft has any newer files available, it can download and install them on your Windows 98 computer automatically. You can back out of any of these automatic changes using Control Panel's Add/Remove Programs application.

System Configuration Utility

You can use the System Configuration Utility to debug the Windows 98 startup process, thus controlling driver loading, initialization and configuration files, and the Windows 98 Startup Group. This utility also makes it easy to create backup copies of key initialization files.

Hard Disk Tools

Windows 98 includes a number of utilities designed to manage and optimize local hard disks. Except for DriveSpace 3, all of these tools support either the FAT16 or FAT32 file systems:

- **Drive Converter** – If you didn't opt to convert from the FAT16 file system to FAT32 during Windows 98 installation, you can perform a one-way conversion using the Driver Converter tool. Depending on the size of the disk and the number and location of files prior to conversion, the process can take several hours to complete. Once you convert to FAT32, there is no utility provided to convert back to FAT16.

CAUTION

Once you convert to FAT32, either during Windows 98 installation or using this utility, you need to be careful about the older Microsoft disk utilities and any third-party disk utilities you may be used to using. Make sure any utilities you run have been updated to handle FAT32. If they don't, the tools could either fail to run or could corrupt your FAT32 file system. Also, you can't see a FAT32 disk partition when dual-booting to MS-DOS, older versions of Windows, or Windows NT versions prior to 5.0.

- **Disk Defragmenter** – Disk Defragmenter lets you periodically optimize the placement of files on disk to improve the efficiency of disk space usage and to provide quicker access to long files. In Windows 98, this tool uses application log files to rearrange application files, which makes them start more efficiently.
- **DriveSpace 3** – DriveSpace 3, which is compatible with both DoubleSpace and the Windows 95 version of DriveSpace 3 (included with the Microsoft Plus! package), performs disk compression to squeeze more data into less disk space. DriveSpace 3 doesn't compress FAT32 disks.

TIP

Unless you're really pressed for disk space, I don't recommend using DriveSpace 3 on any computer in your network. Although it's reliable and efficient, it imposes a performance penalty because it has to compress and decompress data during hard disk I/O. This is completely unacceptable for servers, and isn't all that desirable for client computers, either. I recommend using it only as a stop-gap measure on client computers — while you wait for a larger hard disk to arrive.

- **ScanDisk** – ScanDisk is a graphical version of the old MS-DOS chkdsk utility. It verifies the integrity of the file system and repairs problems automatically. It can also perform a thorough surface scan of the hard disk to check for potential errors.

TIP

During a thorough disk surface scan, ScanDisk requires uninterrupted access to the hard disk. If a screen saver or other background task kicks in and happens to write to the hard disk at the right time and location, it can cause ScanDisk to start over from scratch. Depending on how your computer is configured, ScanDisk may never finish its job. Disable screen savers and other background tasks before running a thorough ScanDisk.

- **Disk Cleanup** – Disk Cleanup is a utility that lets you easily remove files that are no longer needed – temporary (cached) Internet files, Internet program files such as Java applets, deleted files in the Recycle Bin, and temporary application files. This tool also acts as a launch pad for deleting unused portions of Windows 98 or installed applications, as well as Drive Converter. You can configure Disk Cleanup to run on a user's computer whenever free disk space gets low.

Systems Management Server

Systems Management Server (or SMS) is a tool geared toward medium to large organizations that manage a large number of Windows-based networked computers. It automatically creates hardware and software inventories, enables you to automatically distribute software applications and updates over the network, and performs remote diagnosis of problems. SMS is part of Microsoft BackOffice, and requires Windows NT Server to run. SMS agents run on client computers, and enable the communication of inventory, distribution, and diagnostic information.

NOTE: SMS includes a component called Network Monitor, which can gather and interpret raw data as it travels across the network. If you're familiar with the internal details of network protocols, you can use this tool to monitor and troubleshoot network problems at the byte level. Windows 98 includes a protocol driver and agent software that works with Network Monitor. Debugging network problems at this low level is beyond the scope of this book.

Summary

Now you know what it takes to be a network administrator. Aside from the required technical knowledge and skills, a network administrator needs additional skills that are typical of both management and support roles. You've also been introduced to a number of tools that network administrators use to manage and troubleshoot networks and individual nodes. You'll find more information on many of these utilities in the chapters to come. In Chapter 11, you'll learn all about managing network resources using various techniques provided by Windows 98.

Chapter 11

Managing Network Resources

IN THIS CHAPTER

- Understanding resource naming conventions
- Managing shared files and drives
- Working with shared printers

IN THIS CHAPTER, I show you how to prepare for sharing network resources, how to share them over the network, how to access them from client computers, and how to manage and maintain them. I focus on sharing files and printers, but many of the concepts apply to other resources as well. By the end of this chapter, you'll have a solid set of skills that will let you create and access resources on your network. As a network administrator, you'll need to become an expert in these techniques, because you'll be called upon frequently to share, access, and administer network resources for others. You'll also need to be able to train your users to perform these tasks themselves.

XREF

In this chapter, I show you how to actually share and access resources with Windows 98, using the concepts discussed in Chapter 2. For an overview of the concepts of sharing resources on the network, go back and review Chapter 2.

Referring to Network Resources

Before digging into the nitty gritty details of actually creating and sharing resources in Windows 98, it's important to understand how you name them and refer to them on your network. There are two basic approaches to naming resources: the Uniform Naming Convention and device name assignments. These approaches apply to all Microsoft networking products, and I explain both of them in the following sections.

Uniform Naming Convention

No, this isn't some sort of huge meeting where everyone gives nicknames to articles of clothing. The *Uniform Naming Convention*, or *UNC*, refers to a method of specifying computers and their shared resources on a network. Microsoft operating systems and many applications take this approach to sharing and accessing network resources. The general form of a UNC resource name is *\\computername\sharepoint*. In some applications, and within Windows 98, you can simply specify the UNC name of a resource to access it. See Chapter 2 for a discussion on the concept of a sharepoint. Also, Chapter 9 discusses selecting computer names.

For example, if the name of the computer is BIGSERVER, and it offers a shared directory whose sharepoint is named PICTURES, the UNC name of this shared resource is \\BIGSERVER\PICTURES. Likewise, if the computer name is CHARLIE and it offers a sharepoint named TUNA, then the UNC name of the shared resource is \\CHARLIE\TUNA. The TUNA sharepoint can be a shared directory, drive, printer, or something else. UNC names apply to all types of shared network resources.

Let's say that \\CHARLIE\TUNA is a shared directory containing document files on Charlie's computer. If you want a copy of those document files on your local drive C hard disk, you can simply use the UNC name in your copy command:

```
COPY \\CHARLIE\TUNA\*.DOC C:\MYDOCS
```

This command copies all the files ending with the .DOC extension from the \\CHARLIE\TUNA sharepoint to your local C:\MYDOCS directory. Notice that normal filename and wildcard syntax will work with UNC names. You can even refer to subdirectories within a shared directory or drive resource. For example, if the files that interest you are in the subdirectory called LASTYEAR, you can refer to \\CHARLIE\TUNA\LASTYEAR*.DOC to retrieve the files.

This approach to naming resources enables you to access a network resource without having to establish a connection to it first. You can simply use the UNC name whenever you refer to the shared resource. It's great for one-shot access to a specific resource, but can get cumbersome when you need to access the same resource frequently.

Device Name Assignments

UNC names aren't ideal. For several reasons, which I discuss in this section, they aren't as uniform or as universally accepted as you might hope. First of all, UNC names can be a bit bulky. This is especially true if you need to refer to the same sharepoint repeatedly.

For example, if you want to access a specific set of files on the \\BIGSERVER\PICTURES sharepoint, you may need to retype the name \\BIGSERVER\PICTURES many times. What would be great is some sort of shorthand that would enable you to establish a connection, assign a shorthand name to the resource, and use that shorter name from then on.

TAKING SHORTHAND

There's a simple solution. As I mentioned in Chapter 2, you can assign unused drive letters to sharepoints, and use them as a shorthand way of referring to shared resources. For example, you might assign drive letter G to refer to \\CHARLIE\TUNA. From then on, all you need to do is specify drive G, and Windows 98 or your application will know exactly where to go on the network. To access the LASTYEAR subdirectory on the \\CHARLIE\TUNA sharepoint, simply specify G:\LASTYEAR. A drive letter assigned to a remote resource is sometimes called a *network drive.*

Another advantage of assigning drive letters to resources is that you can use the same time-saving tricks that work with any real drive letter. For example, if you're using a command line to do lots of file copying or other operations on a sharepoint, you can set your current drive to the drive letter assigned to the sharepoint, and you never have to type it again. Making drive G the current drive, for example, lets you perform repeated copy or other operations without even referring to drive G, let alone referring to the bulky UNC name.

DECLARING INDEPENDENCE

Still another advantage of drive letters is their relative independence from the actual location of the resource. Let's face it – over time, for whatever reason, server names change, sharepoint names change, and all the networking infrastructure underneath might change. But if you set up your application to use a drive letter, you can easily decouple the application from the UNC name – and thus from the name of the sharepoint.

For example, if you set up a database on \\BIGSERVER\CORPDATA, and set up client applications to use drive letter F to refer to this location, you can later change the server name, sharepoint name, or both. As long as the client computer assigns drive F to the correct new sharepoint before starting the application, the application and the user never have to know that you changed servers or names.

WORKING WITH THE AGED

Another problem with UNC names is that not all applications understand them. Even though we live in an increasingly networked world, old and even some new applications don't always account for running in a networked environment. But virtually every application understands drive letters. By establishing the assignment of a drive letter to a network resource before starting the application, you can continue to use legacy applications with networked data.

There's still quite a bit of poorly written software out there that doesn't understand network drive letters. For example, some applications only understand drive C, and can't deal with any other drives — even if they're local physical hard disks or CD-ROM drives. Moreover, a few applications can't handle drives disappearing for short periods of time. In a networked environment, when a physical cable breaks, a server gets rebooted, or there's simply a bit of interference on a transmission, some applications are so sensitive that they treat these conditions as fatal errors. Or worse, they just fall over and die — of embarrassment, in my opinion. Check with your application vendor for any special requirements or limitations when running them in a networked environment.

DRIVING BEYOND DRIVES

Drive letters aren't the only shorthand substitutes for UNC names. Recall from Chapter 2 that device names such as LPT1 and LPT2 for parallel printers, COM1 and COM2 for serial devices, and so forth can be assigned as local names that refer to remote network resources. Device names such as LPT1 solve pretty much the same problem as drive letters. They can act as shorthand for UNC names – referring to LPT1 can be much handier than the equivalent UNC name \\PRINTSERV\HPLASERJET2. Likewise, device names shield applications from changes in sharepoint names.

Most importantly, device names enable you to use applications that don't have a built-in understanding of network resources. For example, most MS-DOS applications assume that any printer they might use is attached to either the local LPT1 or LPT2 parallel port. To allow these applications to run under Windows 98, the operating system lets you assign specific device names to specific network resources, and presents those device names to the applications as if they were locally attached devices.

If you already use local printers like LPT1 and LPT2, and you also want to use remote printers with your applications, Windows 98 will let you assign other device names such as LPT3 and LPT4 to the remote printers. Unfortunately, not all applications recognize these higher-numbered devices. Be sure to check with the application vendor to verify which device names the application understands.

If you have a physical parallel port in your computer, but no printer is attached to it, you can assign a remote shared printer to the LPT1 (or LPT2) device name. In this situation, Windows 98 will override the local LPT1 (or LPT2), and send all jobs destined for the port to the remote printer. Once you attach a local printer to your computer, however, you need to assign different device names to remote printers.

Managing Shared Files

In the following sections, I show you how to plan for sharing files, how to share them on the network, and how to access them once they're shared. Then, I show you what you need to do as a network administrator to manage shared directories. Many of the skills you'll acquire here will apply to sharing and accessing other network resources, discussed later in this chapter.

File Sharing Strategies

How you share files – or more specifically, how you share the contents of directories – largely depends on the organization of your servers, your data, and the disciplines you've decided to put in place. In a peer-to-peer network, if you allow each computer to act as both a client and a server, you can end up with a free-for-all file sharing strategy. Actually, it isn't a strategy at all. In this situation, you can quickly end up with many confused users, lost data, and disastrous accidents. Your best bet is to think through where you want to place shared files, how you want to share them, and how you want your users to access them.

In many small workgroups, the bulk of network activity involves simply transferring files from one user to another. One strategy that works well in this environment uses the idea of public directories. On each user's computer, you create a directory called PUBLIC. It can be at the root of drive C, in a subdirectory on drive C, or on some other local hard disk. You then share the PUBLIC directory on the network. Other users can access a specific public directory by specifying the UNC name of the sharepoint, which, for simplicity, you can also call PUBLIC.

NOTE: There's nothing magical about the name PUBLIC. You could name the directory on the hard disk LIONKING, and name the sharepoint SIMBA. If the computer name is GROWL, users would have to connect to \\GROWL\SIMBA. Because users of the shared directory only deal with the UNC name, they never even see that the actual local directory is named LIONKING. Likewise, you could name the directory PUBLIC, but then give the share point a name of SCARESME. On a computer named BARNEY, users would access your public directory as \\BARNEY\SCARESME. Creativity aside, to simplify everyone's life, I recommend that you pick an easy-to-remember naming convention and stick with it throughout the network.

Let's say, for example, that each peer-to-peer computer name is derived from the name of its user. If you have three users – say, Phil, Bobbie, and Matt – you might name their computers after them. If you create a PUBLIC directory on drive C on each of the three computers, and then share that directory with a sharepoint name of PUBLIC, you would end up with three sharepoints: \\PHIL\PUBLIC, \\BOBBIE\ PUBLIC, and \\MATT\PUBLIC. Each sharepoint actually refers to the C:\PUBLIC directory on its respective computer. Naming each computer after its user is not ideal, for reasons discussed in Chapter 9, but many organizations name their computers this way.

If you want to take a more centralized approach, or if you're using a dedicated server network, you might create a shared directory for each user on a centralized server computer. For example, if you have the same three users and your server's computer name is PUBLIC, you might create subdirectories for each user and share them on the network. To avoid clutter at the root level on the server's hard disk, you could put the three subdirectories under a single USERS directory. So, the three directories could be C:\USERS\PHIL, C:\USERS\BOBBIE, and C:\USERS\MATT. You could share them as PHIL, BOBBIE, and MATT, respectively. Then, your users could access the public files of each user by referring to \\PUBLIC\PHIL, \\PUBLIC\BOBBIE, and \\PUBLIC\MATT.

Sharing Files

As an example of how to share files over the network, let's look at what it takes to share files located on a computer whose name is FINANCE. We'll look specifically at the case of creating a directory called MYPUBLIC and sharing its contents over the network as PUBLIC. Every file the user places in this shared directory is immediately accessible by users on the rest of the network. Conversely, other users can place their own files in this shared directory, and everyone can see them. To accomplish this task, perform the following steps on the computer that will share the directory.

NOTE: The computer you're working with in this procedure must be configured with the Windows 98 network server components. If it isn't configured this way, go to the Network application in Control Panel, click the Configuration tab, click File and Print Sharing, and then click to select the checkbox labeled as such: I want to be able to give others access to my files. Then click OK, click OK again, and restart the computer as prompted. After the computer has restarted, you can proceed with the following steps.

1. On the computer that wants to offer the shared directory (that is, the computer acting as a server), create the directory if it doesn't already exist. In this example, the name of the directory is MYPUBLIC, and you'll create it at the root of drive C.

NOTE

You can use any of several methods to create this directory — My Computer, Windows Explorer, or even the MS-DOS Prompt. However, I recommend that you use one of the graphical methods rather than a command line method at this point, so it's easier to follow the next steps.

2. Right-click the folder icon for the directory you just created. On the resulting menu, click Properties.
3. In the Properties dialog box, click the Sharing tab. (If you don't see a Sharing tab in the Properties dialog box, your computer isn't configured to act as a server. See the note earlier in this section for instructions on how to install Windows 98 server components, and begin again with Step 2 above.)

TIP

You can save a step by clicking Sharing in the menu that comes up when you right-click the folder icon. Doing this gets you directly to the Sharing tab in the Properties dialog box.

4. On the Sharing tab, click Shared As. The Share Name (what I've been calling the sharepoint name) is set by default to the name of the local directory you're sharing, as shown in Figure 11-1. In this example, the default is MYPUBLIC, but we want the sharepoint name to be PUBLIC – so type **PUBLIC** in the Share Name box.
5. As shown in Figure 11-1, you can offer different types of user access to your shared directory. Under Access Type, click Read-Only if you want users to be able to see the contents but not modify, delete, or add to the contents of the directory. Click Full if you want to give all users full read, write, delete, modify, and add capabilities. If you'd prefer to control access to the directory via passwords, click Depends on Password, and assign appropriate passwords to the sharepoint.

XREF

If you want to use passwords to control access to the sharepoint, see Chapter 12 for a discussion of security and passwords. For now, I'll simplify the procedure by not using password protection.

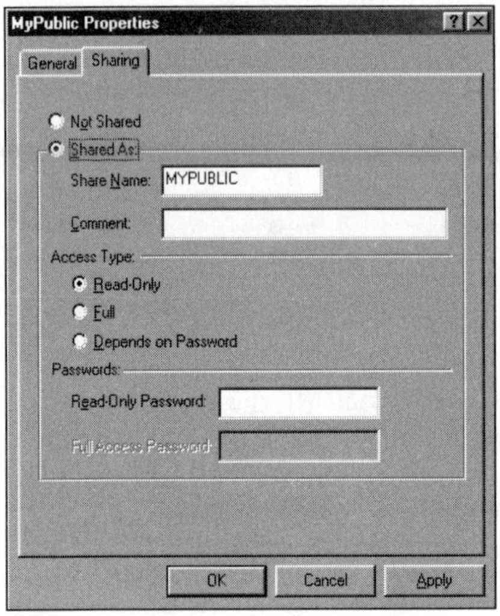

Figure 11-1: The Properties dialog box enables you to share the contents of a directory, assign a sharepoint name, and specify different types of access.

6. When you're done setting the sharing options, click Apply in the Properties dialog box. The sharepoint is created – the directory is now shared on the network. Click OK.
7. Verify that the directory is shared using either Windows Explorer or My Computer to view the icon for the MYPUBLIC directory. You should see a small hand under the folder icon, indicating that it's being shared. Figure 11-2 illustrates this.

Notice that the name displayed under the shared folder icon is the name of the actual directory that resides on the local hard disk – MYPUBLIC. If you want to see the sharepoint name, right-click the icon, click Properties, and click the Sharing tab. In this case, the sharepoint name is what you typed in Step 4 – PUBLIC.

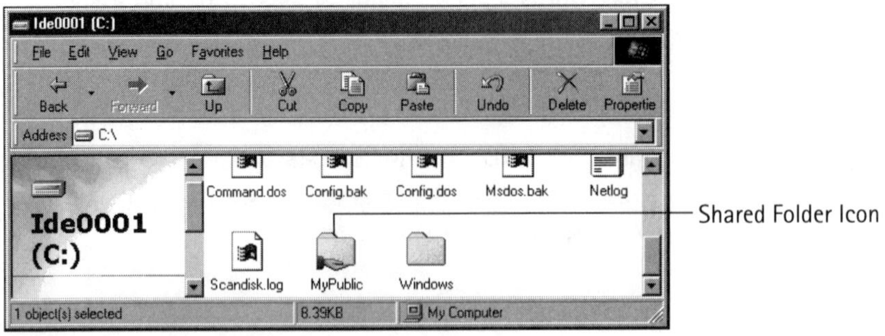

Figure 11-2: Once a directory is shared, its icon changes on the server from a regular folder icon to a shared folder icon.

That's all there is to sharing a directory over the network. In the next section, I show you how to access the shared directory from another computer on the network. Sharepoints survive across system restarts, so this directory will be shared automatically each time you restart the computer or operating system. Later in this chapter, I show you the proper way to stop sharing a directory.

> NOTE: You can also share directories using the Net Watcher utility, which is included with Windows 98. To start Net Watcher, click Start → Programs → Accessories → System Tools → Net Watcher. On the View menu, click by Shared Folders. Then, on the Administer menu, click Add Shared Folder, and type the full pathname of the directory you want to share. Net Watcher has lots of powerful capabilities, many of which I cover in later sections.

Accessing Shared Files

Now, how does a user gain access to this shared data from a computer acting as a client? Let's continue with the same example, this time from the client's point of view. The UNC name of the sharepoint is \\FINANCE\PUBLIC, because the computer name is FINANCE, and you shared the resource using the sharepoint name PUBLIC. (See Step 4 in the previous section.) To gain access to the contents of this shared directory, there are several approaches, outlined in the following sections.

NETWORK NEIGHBORHOOD APPROACH

This is the Network Neighborhood approach:

1. On the computer that wants access to the shared directory (that is, the computer acting as a client), double-click the Network Neighborhood icon on the Windows 98 desktop.
2. In the Network Neighborhood window, find the computer name you're interested in, and double-click it to see which resources it's sharing. In this case, double-click the FINANCE computer to see its one shared resource – the PUBLIC sharepoint, as shown in Figure 11-3.

> NOTE: Notice that the name displayed under the folder icon is the name of the sharepoint (PUBLIC), not the name of the actual directory that resides on the server's hard disk (MYPUBLIC).

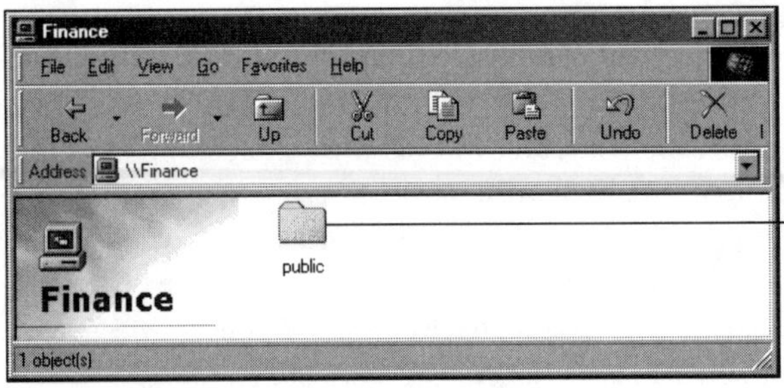

Figure 11-3: On the client computer, Network Neighborhood enables you to view the resources shared by a server.

3. At this point, you can double-click the PUBLIC directory and access files. For example, if the directory contains a Microsoft Word document, and you have Word or the Word Viewer installed on your computer, you can simply double-click the .DOC file and start viewing or editing.
4. Now let's assign a local drive letter to the sharepoint. To assign a local drive letter to \\FINANCE\PUBLIC, right-click the PUBLIC directory icon, shown in Figure 11-3. On the resulting menu, click Map Network Drive.
5. In the Map Network Drive dialog box, shown in Figure 11-4, select a drive letter that you want to assign to the resource. In the example, drive F is the first drive letter available for assignment on the client computer.

Figure 11-4: You can create a temporary or permanent drive letter assignment to a network sharepoint.

6. If you want the drive letter assignment to survive across restarts of the computer, click to select the Reconnect at logon checkbox shown in Figure 11-4. The connection will be reestablished the next time you restart your computer and log on. If you click to clear this checkbox, the connection and drive letter assignment will exist until you log off or shut down the computer.

7. Click OK. You can now use the drive letter to refer to the contents of the sharepoint just as if the drive letter were assigned to a local hard disk or CD-ROM drive. Your access to the contents of the sharepoint is limited by any restrictions placed on it at the server (for example, Read-Only access or password protection).

WINDOWS EXPLORER APPROACH

This approach uses Windows Explorer:

1. On the computer that wants access to the shared directory (that is, the computer acting as a client), click Start → Programs → Windows Explorer.
2. In the left window of Windows Explorer, find Network Neighborhood and click the plus sign (+) next to it. Find the computer name you're interested in, and double-click it to see which resources it's sharing. In this case, double-click the FINANCE computer to see its one shared resource – the PUBLIC sharepoint – in the right half of Windows Explorer.
3. At this point, you can double-click the PUBLIC directory and view and access files. For example, if the directory contains a Microsoft Word document, and you have Word or the Word Viewer installed on your computer, you can simply double-click the .DOC file and start viewing or editing.
4. To assign a drive letter to \\FINANCE\PUBLIC, go to the previous section titled "Network Neighborhood approach" and continue with Step 4 there.

TIP

If you know the UNC name of the sharepoint to which you want to connect, you can assign a drive letter anytime while you're in Windows Explorer. On the Tools menu, click Map Network Drive. Select the drive letter you want to assign, type the UNC name of the sharepoint or select it from the list of recently used UNC names, and click to select or clear the Reconnect at logon checkbox. Then click OK. That's all there is to it!

A World of Changing Icons

Earlier in this chapter, you saw that sharing a directory changes its icon from a regular folder to a folder with a hand under it — symbolizing the act of sharing. Well, when you assign a local drive letter to a sharepoint, that new drive letter has a special icon, as well.

Figure 11-5 shows an icon that represents the connection made in the example. You assigned drive F to the sharepoint \\FINANCE\PUBLIC. In Figure 11-5, the drive shows up as Public on 'Finance' (F:), and the icon looks like a hard disk with a network connection under it. This symbolizes that F: is a drive letter that represents a network connection to a shared directory or hard drive.

COMMAND LINE APPROACH

If you have users that prefer to use the MS-DOS Prompt command line, or you want to write MS-DOS batch files that establish connections to sharepoints, Windows 98 includes a command line utility called NET. This utility has several uses, described when you type NET /? at a command prompt. Perform the following steps to assign a drive letter to the \\FINANCE\PUBLIC sharepoint:

1. To view a list of servers on the network, type **NET VIEW** at a command prompt.
2. To see which resources a particular server is sharing, you can type NET VIEW *computername*. In this example, type **NET VIEW \\FINANCE**.
3. To connect to a sharepoint, you can type NET USE *driveletter*: *computername**sharepoint*. In this example, to connect to \\FINANCE\PUBLIC and assign drive G to it, type **NET USE G: \\FINANCE\PUBLIC**.

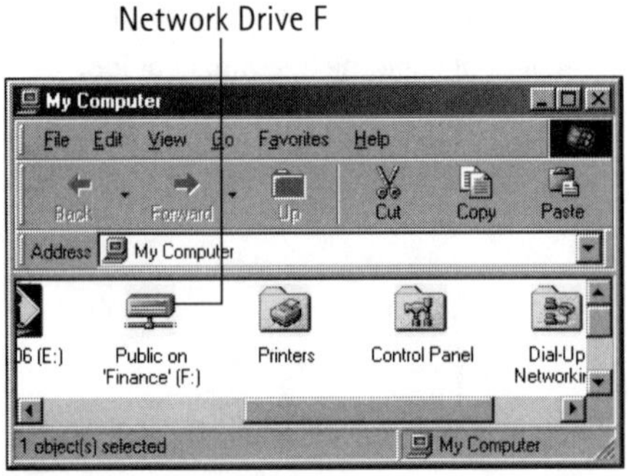

Figure 11-5: A network drive icon shows up on the client computer as a drive connected via the network.

Playing Big (Network) Brother

As a network administrator, you can examine who's connected to your shared resources using the Net Watcher utility. Click Start → Programs → Accessories → System Tools → Net Watcher. Figure 11-6 shows the level of detail available to you.

In the right-hand portion of the Net Watcher window, each shared directory that's currently in use by clients is listed. The left portion of the window shows a list of users, which computer they're connecting from, how many connections they have to the server, how many files they have open, how long they've been connected, and how much of that time has been idle.

Before making drastic changes like removing a sharepoint, it's a good idea to use Net Watcher to verify who, if anyone, is using the sharepoint. That way, you can give them fair warning, and let them shut down their applications or save their data gracefully.

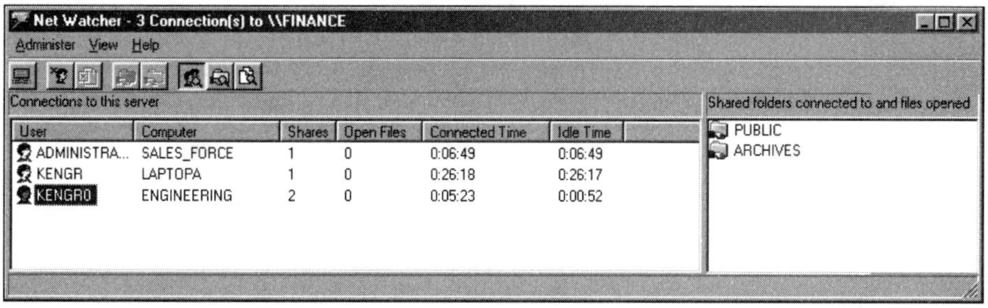

Figure 11-6: Net Watcher enables you to view and manage individual user connections to sharepoints on your server.

Removing a Connection

If you want to disconnect from a sharepoint and remove a drive letter assignment you've established, there are several ways to do it. If you can display the network drive icon, either through My Computer or Windows Explorer, right-click it and click Disconnect. The connection to the sharepoint is immediately terminated, and the drive letter is returned to the pool of unused drive letters.

If you're in Windows Explorer and you want to disconnect from an existing network drive connection, here's how. On the Tools menu, click Disconnect Network Drive. In the Disconnect Network Drive dialog box, click the connection you want to terminate. Then click OK. The connection is terminated, and the drive letter is available for later use in other network connections.

If you prefer a command line approach, or if you need to disconnect a network drive from within an MS-DOS batch file, you can type NET USE *driveletter*: /DELETE. For example, if drive F is assigned to a sharepoint, typing **NET USE F: /DELETE** will terminate the connection and make drive F available for later use.

Removing a Sharepoint

Turning your attention back to the server, it's sometimes necessary to remove a sharepoint on a server. There are several ways to do it. If you can display the shared folder icon, either through My Computer or Windows Explorer, right-click it, and then click Properties → Sharing → Not Shared → Apply. If network users are connected to this sharepoint, Windows 98 warns you and tells you how many users are connected. If you're absolutely sure it's all right to remove the sharepoint, click Yes. The sharepoint is immediately removed, and the directory is no longer shared.

CAUTION: It's critically important to make sure you don't cause users to lose data by taking away a sharepoint while users are connected with files open. If users are actively accessing files on the sharepoint, they could lose data if the sharepoint disappears at the wrong time. As a network administrator, you should get into the habit of checking and warning users before taking drastic measures like this. Using Net Watcher, mentioned in the previous section, is a good approach to heading off disaster in this area.

If you decide to use Net Watcher to check the status of users and open files, you can also stop sharing resources from within the Net Watcher utility. In Net Watcher, click View → by Shared Folders. Then click the directory you want to stop sharing. Check in the right half of the window to make sure no one is connected to the shared directory. If someone is using it, contact them and warn them that the sharepoint will be going away. When you're ready to stop sharing the directory, click Administer → Stop Sharing Folder. Then click Yes.

NOTE: There will come a day when you're forced to close files and disconnect users; in this case, you can use Net Watcher to close an open file or disconnect a user from a sharepoint. To close an open file, click View → by Open Files, click the name of the file you want to close, click Administer → Close File, and click Yes. To disconnect a user from a sharepoint, click View → by Connections, click the name of the user you want to disconnect, and click Administer → Disconnect User. Don't forget to warn users before you close their files or disconnect them, or they could lose data.

Of course, the simplest way to remove a sharepoint – at least temporarily – is to shut down the server. While the server is in use, you should avoid shutting it down at nearly all costs. To clear up certain kinds of problems, however, or to perform scheduled maintenance, an eventual shutdown is a fact of life. If at all possible, it's best to get into the habit of warning users before a shutdown, and giving them adequate time to close their files, save their data, and disconnect from sharepoints.

TIP

You can quickly communicate with users with the WinPopup utility included in Windows 98. It's a good idea to configure each user's computer to run this utility automatically by placing WINPOPUP.EXE in each of their startup directories. You can then use WinPopup to send a message to an individual user or to an entire workgroup — a message such as "FINANCE server going down in 10 minutes. Please close your files and disconnect." Users running WinPopup will see the message, who sent it, and the time and date it was sent.

Managing Shared Drives

Sharing an entire drive over the network is really just a special case of sharing the contents of a directory. When you share a drive, you're simply sharing its root directory with all its contents. In the following sections, I show you how to plan for sharing drives, how to share them on the network, and how to access them once they're shared. Then I show you what you need to do as a network administrator to manage them.

Drive Sharing Strategies

It's generally not a good idea to share an entire hard disk over the network, if all you want to do is share specific files, access a common database, or run shared applications. You don't want to have malicious or inexperienced users viewing, deleting, or changing critical files on your computer. This is especially true of drive C, which contains important operating system files. One exception to this rule is performing backups – if you want to back up an entire hard disk over the network, you need to share the entire drive. I discuss backups further in Chapter 13.

If you do share an entire drive, make it a read-only sharepoint, so no one can modify, delete, or add files to the drive. Of course, doing this will still enable users to read the contents of your hard disk, so it's an even better idea to protect a shared drive with a password. That way, only those with the right password can read or copy the data. I discuss security and passwords in Chapter 12.

CD-ROM drives are good candidates for sharing over the network. If many users need access to the same CD-ROM, if the same CD-ROM remains in the server's drive at all times, and if heavy simultaneous use isn't very frequent, then CD-ROM sharing works well. But if CD-ROMs are swapped frequently (either manually or with a CD-ROM changer), or many users try to access different parts of the CD-ROM simultaneously, then performance and productivity can suffer. If you do share a CD-ROM drive over the network, be sure that your CD-ROM software license agreement covers network access by multiple users.

Sharing Drives

There's really nothing special about sharing drives that's different from sharing directories, as discussed earlier in this chapter. You follow essentially the same steps, but instead of sharing a directory, you share the drive itself. This section includes a set of steps required to share a drive over the network. (If you want more detail, see the section titled "Sharing Files" earlier in this chapter.) In these steps, I use the example of sharing drive D, which can be either a hard disk or CD-ROM drive.

> NOTE: The computer you're working with in this procedure must be configured with the Windows 98 network server components. If it isn't, go to the Network application in Control Panel, click Configuration → File and Print Sharing, and click to select the checkbox labeled as such: I want to be able to give others access to my files. Then click OK, click OK again, and restart the computer as prompted. After the computer has restarted, proceed with the following steps.

1. On the computer that wants to offer the shared drive (that is, the computer acting as a server), display the drive's icon on the screen, either through Windows Explorer or My Computer. In this case, make sure the drive D icon is visible.
2. Right-click the icon of the drive you want to share (drive D), and click Sharing.

> NOTE: If you don't see Sharing on the menu, your computer isn't configured as a server. See the note earlier in this section for instructions on how to install Windows 98 server components, and begin again with Step 1.

3. On the Sharing tab, click Shared As. The Share Name (or sharepoint name) is set by default to the drive letter (D). If you want to share the drive under a different sharepoint name, type the name in the Share Name box.

4. Under Access Type, click Read-Only if you want to prevent users from modifying, deleting, or adding to the contents of the drive. Click Full if you want to grant unrestricted access to everyone. If you'd prefer to control access to the drive via passwords, click Depends on Password, and assign appropriate passwords to the sharepoint. (See Chapter 12 for a discussion of security.)
5. Click Apply, and then click OK.
6. Verify that the drive is shared using either Windows Explorer or My Computer to view the icon for the drive. You should see a small hand under the drive icon, indicating that it's being shared.

NOTE: The name displayed under the shared drive icon is the drive's label and drive letter. If you want to see the sharepoint name, right-click the icon and click Sharing. In this case, the sharepoint name is what you typed in Step 3.

Managing Shared Printers

In the following sections, I show you how to plan for sharing printers, how to share them on the network, and how to access them once they're shared. Then I show you what you need to do as a network administrator to manage shared printers.

Printer Sharing Strategies

Windows 98 computers make excellent print servers, especially in networks where the client computers need to be as efficient as possible. When you configure Windows 98 as a print server, the final rendering (conversion of data to its final output form) is performed on the print server rather than on the client computer. This approach removes much of the printing burden from the client, making the user's application appear to be more responsive. Whether this approach is more or less efficient, in terms of how long it takes to get the job printed, depends on the performance of the print server.

NOTE: Unlike Windows 98, Windows NT and NetWare servers cause the final rendering to take place on the client computer. This approach places a bit more of the processing burden on individual clients, and less of a burden on the print server itself.

When selecting printers to be shared on the network, consider the overall speed of the printer and the frequency of manual intervention required. The faster and more automatic a printer is, the better candidate it is for sharing. The speed issue is obvious – a faster printer cranks out users' jobs more quickly than slower devices. The frequency of manual intervention can be minimized by ensuring large paper tray capacities, multiple paper trays, and a high capacity for ink, toner, and other consumables. If you have to be changing cartridges or toner on a daily basis, printer downtime can really slow down overall printing efficiency.

If your organization does a lot of printing and requires quick turnaround, consider implementing printer pools, which I discussed in Chapter 2. Although Windows 98 doesn't include printer pooling features, Windows NT does. Windows 98 clients can make use of a pool of identical printers whose queue is managed by a Windows NT computer. By sending each job to the next available printer, you can achieve much more efficient printer usage in high volume printing environments such as a publications department.

TIP

If you've dedicated a computer to performing as a print server, it's a good idea to locate the computer near the printer or printers it shares. For example, you might connect three printers to a single computer, and put them all in a small "printer room." It's also helpful to display each print queue on the server's screen, so that it's easy for you and your users to see the status of each printer and the number of jobs in each queue.

Establishing Shared Printers

Before you start to share a printer over the network, be sure to install it and test it locally on the computer that will act as the print server. If you haven't already done so, print a test page to it from the locally attached computer to verify proper driver and hardware installation. To do this, click Start → Settings → Printers, right-click the icon of the printer you want to test, click Properties → General → Print Test Page. Wait for the test page to finish printing, and click Yes if it emerged as expected. If printing didn't go well, click No to start troubleshooting the problem.

Some network printers and standalone print server devices have very specific requirements for network protocols, print queue management, and so forth. For example, some products require that users run either the TCP/IP or DLC protocol on their client computers. (The older HP JetDirect printers typically require DLC.) Consult the device's documentation for specific requirements. Be sure to have all the protocol requirements taken care of before proceeding with the following steps.

The computer you're working with in this procedure must be configured with the Windows 98 network server components. If it isn't, go to the Network application in Control Panel, click Configuration → File and Print Sharing, and click to select the checkbox labeled as such: I want to be able to allow others to print to my printers. Then click OK, click OK again, and restart the computer as prompted. After the computer has restarted, proceed with the following steps.

1. On the computer directly attached to the printer you want to share, click Start → Settings → Printers. Right-click the icon of the printer you want to share. For example, in Figure 11-7 you want to share the local HP DeskJet printer over the network.

In Figure 11-7, the local HP DeskJet printer is the default printer — the check mark indicates this. The Epson Stylus printer is attached to another computer on the network. This is indicated by the printer icon being attached to a network wire.

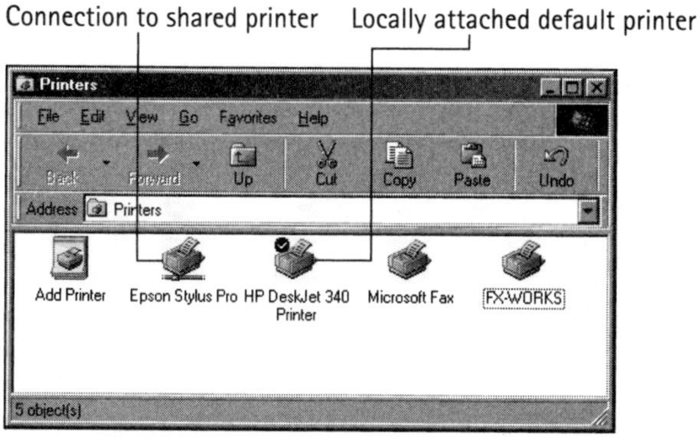

Figure 11-7: The Printers folder differentiates between connections to shared printers, and local printers that can be shared.

2. On the resulting menu, click Sharing.

> **NOTE:** If you don't see Sharing on the menu, your computer isn't configured as a server. See the note earlier in this section for instructions on how to install Windows 98 server components; then, enable the Windows 98 print server, and begin again with Step 1.

3. On the Sharing tab in the Properties dialog box, click Shared As. In the Share Name box, type the sharepoint name you want to use to identify the printer on the network. In this example, type **HP**, as shown in Figure 11-8. Optionally, type a description in the Comment box. If you want to protect access to the printer by means of a password, type it in the Password box. (See Chapter 12 for a discussion of security and passwords.)

> **TIP:** It's a good idea to include a comment when sharing a printer. The most useful piece of information to include is the physical location of the printer. Otherwise, when users send jobs to the printer, they won't know where to go to pick up the output. This comment shows up in the detailed view in Network Neighborhood, and also when you issue the NET VIEW *computer-name* command.

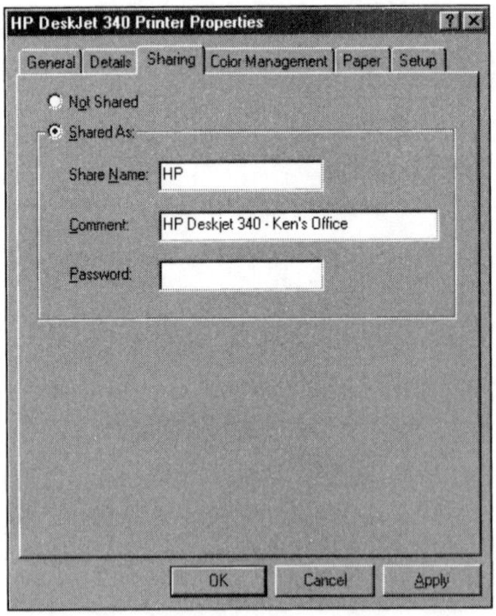

Figure 11-8: The Sharing tab enables you to specify the sharepoint name, an optional comment, and an optional password for the shared printer.

4. Click Apply → OK.
5. Verify that the printer is shared by looking in the Printers folder. Look at the icon for the printer – there should be small hand under the printer, indicating that it's being shared. Figure 11-9 illustrates this.

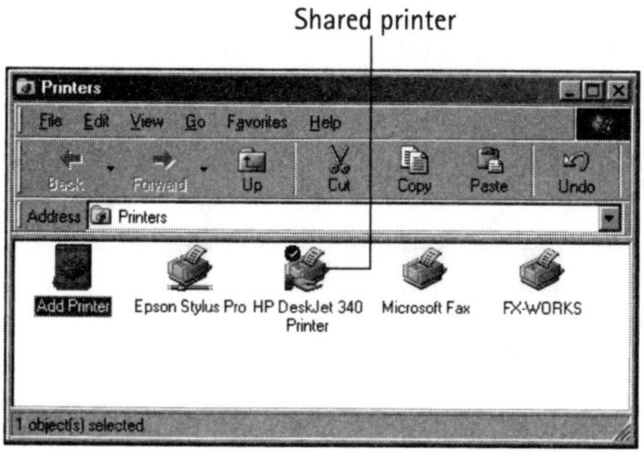

Figure 11-9: The hand added to the printer icon indicates that this computer is sharing the printer on the network.

> **NOTE:** The name displayed under the shared printer icon is the printer driver name, which is typically the make and model of the printer. If you want to see the printer's sharepoint name, right-click the icon and click Sharing. In this case, the sharepoint name is whatever you typed in Step 3.

Now that the printer is shared on the network, you can print to it locally from the computer that's sharing it, and users can print to it from their client computers. Under Windows 98 and Windows 95, a computer sharing a printer requires no additional steps on the server side. The appropriate driver software is stored on the print server, and is copied automatically to the user's client computer when the printer is set up on the client computer. I discuss the client side of network printing in the next section.

Accessing Shared Printers

Using a shared printer is a little more complicated than using a shared drive or directory – at least in terms of the initial work required. Although you can print a file just by dragging its icon and dropping it on a printer icon, a little extra work is required up front when sending the file to a shared printer over the network for the first time. Before printing to a shared printer, the user has to install the appropriate software for it.

Windows 98 (like Windows 95 before it) includes a set of features called *point and print.* These features enable you to drag and drop files onto a printer, or drag and drop printers onto your desktop, and automatically take care of installing the right software for the printer. There are several ways to do this, which I discuss in the following sections.

INSTALLING WHEN PRINTING A DOCUMENT

One point and print feature enables the user to install the appropriate drivers and configure them the first time the shared printer is used from the client computer. Let's say a user wants to print a file to a particular shared printer for the first time. Here are the steps the user would perform on the client computer:

1. Display the icon of the file you want to print, either using Windows Explorer, My Computer, or some other method.
2. Using Network Neighborhood, navigate to the server that's sharing the printer you want to use, and display the icon of that printer.
3. Drag the file icon to the printer icon and drop it.

> **NOTE:** If this is the first time you're printing to the shared printer from this computer, you'll need to proceed with the remaining steps. If you've printed to the printer before from this computer, the file will simply print.

4. When you're asked if you want to set up the printer, click Yes.
5. If you plan to print to this printer from MS-DOS applications, click Yes and proceed to Step 6. Otherwise, click No and proceed to Step 7.
6. Many MS-DOS programs require the assignment of an LPT device name to the shared printer, as discussed earlier in this chapter. Click Capture Printer Port, select an LPT device name, and click OK. (If the shared printer requires a password, you'll be asked for it at this point. Type the appropriate password and click OK.)
7. Click Next. As shown in Figure 11-10, you can change the name of the printer in the Printer Name box, but the default name (make and model) is fine. If this is the only printer you've set up on this computer, it is established as the default printer automatically. If other printers are already installed either locally or over the network, and you want this printer to be the default printer in your applications, click Yes. Otherwise, click No. Then, click Next.

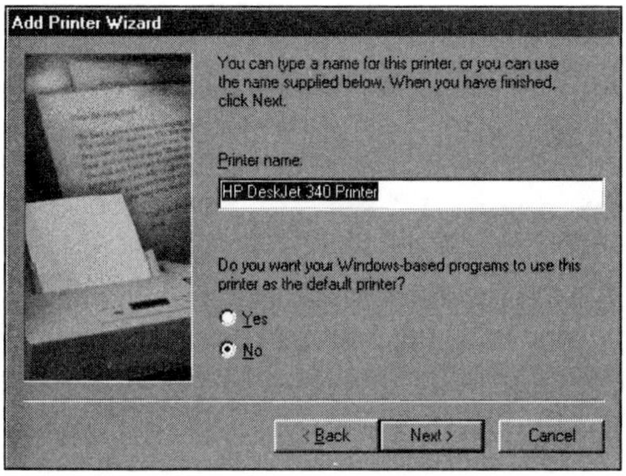

Figure 11-10: You can change the local name of the printer and specify whether applications should use it as the default printer.

8. Click Yes to arrange to print a test page to the printer, then click Finish. The Add Printer Wizard may copy printer driver files across the network from the print server to the client computer.
9. Wait for the test page to finish printing and click Yes if it emerged as expected. If the page doesn't print or doesn't appear to be correct, click No to start troubleshooting the problem.
10. In the Printers folder (reached via Start → Settings → Printers), verify that the printer is set up by examining the newly created printer icon. The icon should have a network wire beneath it, signifying that it's being accessed across the network.

> **NOTE:** If a printer connection icon is ever grayed out, it means that communication could not be established with the printer. For example, if the sharepoint doesn't exist, the server is down, the printer itself has an error, and so forth, the icon may be grayed (or *ghosted*) out.

INSTALLING DURING SHORTCUT CREATION

As a network administrator, you may want to set up connections to shared printers on client computers ahead of time, to shield your users from these extra steps. You can initiate the process by attempting to send a file to a printer, as described in the previous section, or you can explicitly install and configure the driver. There are a couple of ways to do this.

One approach is to drag the printer icon from Network Neighborhood to the client's desktop to create a shortcut to the printer. Then, double-click the new printer icon on the desktop and proceed with Step 4 in the previous section titled "Installing when printing a document." After that, the user can print by simply dragging and dropping files to the printer icon on the desktop. This is another example of Windows 98 point and print features.

INSTALLING THROUGH ADD PRINTER

Another, more manual approach to setting up a printer on a client involves the Add Printer icon in the Printers folder. Let's say that the HP printer shared earlier in this chapter is attached directly to a computer whose name is LAPTOPA – so the UNC name of the sharepoint is \\LAPTOPA\HP. To explicitly set up a connection to this shared printer on a client computer, perform the following steps:

1. On the computer that wants access to the shared printer (that is, the computer is acting as a client), click Start → Settings → Printers, and double-click Add Printer.
2. In the Add Printer Wizard dialog box, click Next. Click Network Printer and click Next.
3. In the Network path or queue name box, type the UNC name of the printer's sharepoint. In this example, type **\\LAPTOPA\HP**, as shown in Figure 11-11.

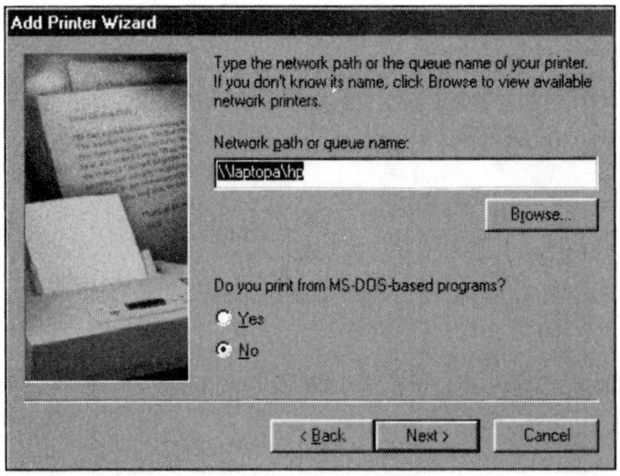

Figure 11-11: When adding a remote printer, you specify the UNC name of the printer's sharepoint, and whether or not MS-DOS will print to it.

NOTE: If you're not sure of the exact sharepoint name, you can browse through the network for available printers. Instead of typing the UNC name, click Browse and double-click the appropriate computer icon to view a list of printer sharepoints. Click the one you want and then click OK. Figure 11-12 illustrates the browsing operation.

Taking Command of Shared Printers

Printers aren't left out of the NET command line approach to accessing shared resources. To see which directories and printers a particular server is sharing, you can type NET VIEW *computername*. To connect to a remote printer, you can type NET USE *devicename*: *computername**sharepoint*. For example, to connect to \\LAPTOPA\HP and assign device name LPT1 to it, you would type:

```
NET USE LPT1: \\LAPTOPA\HP
```

To remove this connection when you're done with it, you would type

```
NET USE LPT1: /DELETE
```

The NET utility has many different uses. Type NET /? for details on its various options.

Figure 11-12: You can browse through the network to look for the computer and sharepoint name of the remote printer you want to install.

4. Proceed with Step 5 in the previous section titled "Installing when printing a document."

Administering Shared Printers

Administration of the print queue for a shared printer is the same as for a local printer. To view and manage the print queue, double-click the printer icon in the Printers folder. Most of the network-specific administration takes place in the Printer Properties dialog box. You can reach it by right-clicking the printer icon in the Printers folder, and then clicking Properties. Or you can reach it from the print queue window by clicking Printer → Properties.

NOTE

If you want to view and administer a print queue from a client computer, but you haven't yet installed the printer driver there, you can use another point and print feature of Windows 98. Simply locate the shared printer on the network and display its icon (using Network Neighborhood, for example), and then double-click the icon. Before you can see the printer queue, you'll go through the steps to set up the printer on the client computer, starting with Step 4 in the previous section titled "Installing when printing a document."

The two tabs that exist for all printers are the General and Details tabs. The existence and contents of other tabs are dependent on the printer make and model. (Consult your printer manufacturer's documentation for details on settings provided in these other tabs.) The General tab includes an option comment that's displayed on the General tab on client computers. It also includes control over separator pages, which let you easily divide output into print jobs from many different users. The General tab's most frequently used feature is the Print Test Page button. It's used to test printing whenever a configuration change is made, and is especially useful to test printing over the network.

The contents of the Details tab vary slightly from printer to printer. From a network printing viewpoint, the most critical element is the box named Print to the following port. On the print server, it contains the name of the physical port to which the printer is attached. On the client, it contains the UNC name of the printer's sharepoint, and perhaps a captured printer port used for MS-DOS printing. If the UNC name ever changes, this is where you'll change the name on the client computers. The Details tab is also the place to capture a printer port for MS-DOS applications, in case you didn't do this during installation of the printer. I discuss some of the other features of the Details tab in future chapters.

TIP

You can use the Net Watcher utility, described earlier in this chapter, to monitor and control the use of shared printers as well. If you need to remove a printer sharepoint, for example, you can use Net Watcher to see which users are connected to it, whether they have open files printing, and so forth.

Summary

In this chapter, you've learned how to plan for, share, access, and manage standard network resources including files, directories, drives, and printers. You've discovered how to set up shared resources on computers acting as servers, and how to gain access to those resources on computers acting as clients. In Chapter 12, you'll learn how to incorporate effective security measures into your network, to protect your resources from unauthorized access.

Chapter 12

Managing Network Security

IN THIS CHAPTER

- Dealing with security responsibilities and threats
- Implementing security policies
- Working with Windows security options

IN THIS CHAPTER, you'll learn about the vitally important area of network security. I explain which threats you should be aware of, what steps to take to prevent them, and which tools are available to help you maintain a secure network environment. You'll learn about the approaches to security available to you, and how to choose among them. By the end of this chapter, you'll understand what it takes to ensure the safety of your network hardware and data, as well as the productivity of your network users. You'll also realize that implementing an effective security policy is a continuous journey – not a final destination.

Understanding Security Responsibilities

Every computer network is vulnerable to unintentional and deliberate damage, theft, or unauthorized use. As a network administrator, you need to take measures to ensure not only the operation of your network, but also the security of the data on the network, to make sure it doesn't fall into the wrong hands. Certainly, information vital to national defense must be safeguarded if you're a defense contractor, but so do payroll and performance review files if you're a human resources department. Unauthorized access to sensitive data of any kind can damage your organization.

As a network administrator, you also need to worry about physical damage to equipment, loss of critical data, network downtime, and theft of equipment and information. All represent real threats to the well-being of your network and your organization. Even if losses are monetarily small, the loss in productivity and the cost of taking preventive measures after the fact can be quite high.

> **NOTE:** Network security is a critically important responsibility. It requires careful planning, continuous education, and constant vigilance. On the other hand, you need to be sure that your network isn't so secure that no one can use it to perform daily tasks. A balanced approach to network security prevents attacks and disasters, but lets users do what they need to do without interference. A key part of achieving this balance is gaining an understanding of what your users need to do or plan to do. The more you know about how they will use the network and their individual computers, the more appropriate and effective your security policies will be.

The primary categories of security threats are damage (whether unintentional or intentional), theft, electronic tampering, and unauthorized access. All of these threats apply to both hardware and data, and all apply to individual computers and the network as a whole. Later in this chapter, I walk you through a list of the major types of threats. Keep in mind, however, that new security threats are appearing all the time. Old threats also reappear, as hackers and researchers discover chinks in the armor of existing preventive measures. Effective network security requires constant education and reeducation to stay one step ahead of new threats.

Creating a Security Policy

The most important step in planning for effective network security is the creation of a security policy. It's just as important as the network documentation I mentioned in Chapter 10. And like that document, your security policy needs to be a living document that's maintained and refined as the needs of your organization and the nature of your network change. A well-planned security policy can also go a long way toward educating both management and users about the importance of network security to individual and organizational productivity.

> **NOTE:** Offering solid training to your users is key to the success of your security policy on two fronts. First, your users become more knowledgeable and are less likely to cause inadvertently destructive errors. Second, by understanding both the hows and whys of security measures, including password protection, physical security, and so forth, your users will have a better appreciation and respect for the policies you put in place.

Focusing on Prevention

The best security policies focus more on prevention, and less on recovery from security breaches. Sure, both are important, and you can't have an effective security policy without elements of both; but good preventive measures can cut way down on your need to recover from disaster, because fewer types of disasters will happen. When problems do occur – and they will – you'll be better equipped to handle the recovery process.

This proactive approach to network security requires that you understand the potential threats and preventive measures up front – security can't be an afterthought. Although this approach takes an up-front investment of time and effort, it costs much less than scrambling to understand what happened and how to fix it when a security breach takes place.

Because people are constantly finding new ways to break through the defenses of network security policies, the landscape of threats, cures, and preventive measures is constantly in flux. The overall problem is analogous to taking a continuous preventive dose of antibiotics, only to find that bacteria have found ways to fool the antibiotics and get around their defenses. As the bacteria change, your preventive measures need to change to match them.

While this analogy applies directly to the computer virus threat, it applies equally well to just about all types of network security threats. Whether they do it for a living or just for fun, people will continue to find open doors tomorrow in networks you thought were securely locked today. So, once again, you need to continuously educate yourself if you want a truly proactive security policy.

NOTE: To be effective, security policies must be applied consistently across the network. Just one computer that's not protected by a password, or that's exposed to unauthorized physical access, can be an open doorway into every computer on your network. While some people may balk at stringent security measures, it's your job to sell everyone on taking the security policies seriously. Management support is an important factor in making this happen.

Reporting Security Issues

Microsoft maintains an e-mail address through which you can report potential security issues with specific Microsoft products. A member of its security response team will provide information on the problem you're reporting, or will gather more information from you to troubleshoot the problem and find a solution. The e-mail address is `secure@microsoft.com`. (Don't use this avenue for general product support or general security questions. Use it to report possible security holes in specific products.)

XREF

A number of *Computer Emergency Response Teams* (*CERTs*) are located throughout the world. Unlike the breath mint of the same name, a CERT's job is to investigate computer security issues and find ways to defend against them. Appendix B includes pointers to some of these response centers.

Dealing with Network Threats

The potential threats to your network are many and real. As a network administrator, you need to know your enemies very well, so you can prevent or quickly recover from the problems they cause. Although connections to the Internet or dial-in RAS access make your network more vulnerable to attack than a completely isolated LAN, no network is immune to these threats. In this section, I discuss the most common perils you need to recognize. Later in this chapter, you'll learn which steps you should take to prevent or minimize their impact.

Hapless Happenings

Most people have the idea that computer security threats always involve malicious hackers bent on destruction, or virulent viruses. The truth is that a large percentage of the electronic data that's lost or damaged these days is lost due to accidental erasure. We've all been there at one time or another. The simple act of accidentally deleting all the files in a directory with a simple DEL *.* command can generate enough weeping, wailing, and gnashing of teeth to rival the most intense images in Revelations. Thank heavens for UNDELETE – when it works.

When turned loose on a network, users can cause the same problems on a much larger scale. For example, deleting a single file or whole directory on a server can cause an entire department to grind to a halt. Then, instead of just one person pulling out his hair, you have an entire group going bald. The point is that accidents can and do happen every day, and anyone can cause them. Your job is to recognize this fact and find ways to keep these accidents from affecting the network and the organization. Later in this chapter, I discuss some steps you can take toward this end.

Viral Infections

An ever-widening array of computer viruses is just waiting to infect and damage your network. While a virus's intentions run the gamut from mild annoyance to severe hardware damage, all viruses are bad and need to be avoided – dare I say – like the plague. Even some supposedly innocuous viruses are poorly written, and their unintentional software bugs can cause serious problems. Many modern viruses are designed to recognize that they're on a network, and make it their business to infect every computer attached to it.

Viruses typically enter a network from two sources – removable disks and the Internet. A well-meaning user may bring an infected disk from home to install his favorite software at work. Or a user may download an infected utility, game, or even a document from the Internet. Either way, the stage is set for an immediate or delayed disaster. Later in this chapter, I discuss some ways to help you prevent or minimize the effect of viruses on your network.

If the life of a virus designer seems exciting and glamorous to you, don't consider a career change just yet. The act of creating and distributing computer viruses is illegal, and folks who get caught are looking at some pretty severe penalties. You can certainly find a more constructive (and legal) way to make use of your computer skills.

A type of virus called a *Trojan horse* masquerades as a useful bit of software, but secretly executes a hidden agenda. Some of these programs go beyond doing direct damage, and actually communicate secretly with the hackers who created them, gathering and sending secured information about accounts and passwords that the hacker can later exploit. Such programs can also open doors to the hacker, allowing direct access to shared network resources. Trojan horses are often run unwittingly by users, but may also be run on purpose by disgruntled employees. There are many other ways in which hackers try to breach your network security. I cover these in the next section.

Hacker Attackers

Armed with a few simple software tools and some technical knowledge, a hacker can mount an offensive against your network that can wreak all sorts of havoc. The first step a hacker must take to make your life miserable is to attempt to gain access to your network, or to specific computers on your network.

An often overlooked technique of hackers, but one that works with alarming frequency, is known as *social engineering*. Hackers either call or e-mail the network administration staff, pretending to be a user in need of assistance. The typical ploy involves asking for a forgotten user account or password. Clever hackers can get a staff member to simply hand over the requested information. Large organizations with many users are especially vulnerable to this type of attack.

A hacker needs either physical access to one of your computers, remote access to your network via a dial-in phone line, or indirect access to your network via the Internet. The hacker might then attack your computer or network with a *brute-force* approach, automatically trying hundreds of thousands of account names and passwords in search of a doorway to your data.

Another technique is *eavesdropping*, which gives the hacker, who has physical access to the network cable and a network monitoring device, the capability to capture and interpret any unencrypted data, account names, or passwords sent over the network. Potentially, this could give the hacker enough information to access your e-mail and even the shared resources on your network. If your passwords are sent over the network in encrypted form, the hacker may be able to play them back and use them if the encryption method always generates the same result.

If your network or individual computers are attached to the Internet, hackers can engage in something called *spoofing* – sending packets from outside your network that look like they came from inside your network. Using this approach, the hacker can issue commands to e-mail out lists of user account names, for example. Armed with this sort of information, the hacker can step up the attack to gain access to specific accounts and data.

Of course, hackers take advantage of any new security holes discovered in NOS software. Known as *trap doors* or *open doors*, these software bugs or features left in the code for debugging purposes are communicated quickly and widely to the hacker community. They're exploited quickly, before the NOS manufacturer can prepare and distribute a patch to close the security door.

Still another approach to attack, which may or may not take advantage of NOS bugs, is known as *denial of service*. In this approach, the hacker focuses on preventing you from using your network or individual computers, rather than on stealing or destroying data or hardware. Hackers can point all sorts of meaningless or redundant network traffic at your servers, effectively soaking up network bandwidth, CPU bandwidth, or disk space. Once this happens, it's impossible to continue normal network operations until the attack is stopped. Some denial of service attacks exploit weaknesses in specific operating systems or routers, causing them to crash or enter a state in which they operate very slowly.

> NOTE: A special case of denial of service involves sending large quantities of unsolicited e-mail — perhaps containing large attachments — to a network, causing degraded performance and wasted disk space. This is sometimes called spamming or bombing, as I mentioned in Chapter 4.

There are other ways in which hackers try to attack your network – I've just presented the most common avenues they take. Because the community of hackers is constantly on the lookout for new ways to access and disrupt your network, and because they quickly communicate specific techniques to use, your constant vigilance is required to keep them at bay.

XREF

Appendix B contains some security-related information resources that can help you stay as informed as the hackers about the latest network security issues.

Natural and Unnatural Disasters

Unless you're able to predict or control the weather, natural disasters probably represent the threat over which you have the least control. Likewise, man-made disasters such as arson, theft, vandalism, and so forth are out of your control. Fires, floods, tornadoes, hurricanes, tidal waves, and other events can quickly destroy your network (and probably other things as well). Although you can't predict these events, you can take specific steps to minimize lost data, downtime, and the pain of getting back in business after a disaster. In Chapter 13, I discuss specific steps you can take to prepare for and recover from such events. At this point, just keep in mind that disaster preparedness is an important element of your security policy.

Implementing Security Policies

There are many concrete steps you can include in your security policy to minimize your vulnerability to security breaches, and to accelerate your recovery time when problems crop up. In this section, I discuss several key issues that your security policy needs to address.

Restricting Physical Access

One network administrator I know had every imaginable software security mechanism in place, including password protection, data encryption, security attributes on individual files, virus protection, and so forth. He thought he'd done all he could to safeguard his organization's valuable data. But he forgot one key element. Anyone with an employee badge could walk up to the main server, pull out the hard disk, and walk away with it. He didn't realize this gaping hole existed in his security policy until someone did exactly that. No amount of software security could compensate for open physical access to the hardware.

It may sound like a very low-tech, trivial approach to security, but one of the single most effective security measures you can take is restricting physical access to the computers on your network. If people can't get to your network, they'll have a tough time foiling its other security measures. If possible, house your servers in a room with restricted access. Because any computer on your network is a potential doorway to all of your network resources, it's best to minimize physical access to clients as well.

Every group of users contains at least one person who wants to show off self-proclaimed computer expertise by "fixing the server" when it's having problems. If the person doesn't really know what he or she is doing, this sort of bravado can result in lost data and added server downtime. The only good preventive measure for avoiding this situation is to lock the servers away from people who aren't fully trained to maintain them.

To prevent eavesdropping, tampering with cable connections, and general disruption of the network, it's best to keep network cables, hubs, routers, bridges, and other devices safely locked away and out of sight. Doing this will make it more difficult for someone to steal information or disrupt network operations through the most vulnerable points in the network. Maintaining network security is an excellent argument for installing network cables inside walls, ceilings, floors, and in locked wiring closets.

There's no way to prevent at least some physical access to computer hardware, but here are a few steps you can take to minimize your risks. However, none are substitutes for restricting physical access to the hardware.

- Enable BIOS passwords
- Disable floppy boot
- Disable floppy drives

In some large networks, administrators provide users with diskless computers that have no floppy drive or hard disk at all. With an appropriately equipped network adapter, these computers can boot an operation system over the network.

- Use internal hard disks

> **CAUTION:** Even without a bootable floppy drive, someone with physical access to a computer can boot Windows 98 in safe mode — which doesn't connect to the network, but does give full access to all local resources without supplying a password. So even with other precautions, it's still important to keep computers containing critical data out of reach of unauthorized people.

Protecting Against Viruses

You can protect your network against viruses through a combination of carefully followed policies and, of course, virus protection software. Because new viruses are cropping up all the time, and because protection software can't typically recover lost data, it's much more effective to prevent viruses than to detect and remove them. Here are several ways to protect against virus attacks:

- **Use virus protection software** – Invest in virus protection software, install it, and use it throughout your network. Don't forget to include a maintenance agreement in your purchase, so you can easily obtain updates to the software as new viruses are identified and handled. If you do have a maintenance agreement, don't forget to actually get the updates.
- **Scan all floppy disks** – Put a strict security policy in place to scan all floppy disks for viruses before copying, opening, or executing any files from the disk. If you have a spare computer available that isn't attached to the network, and you want an extra measure of protection, use this isolated computer to scan floppies for viruses before introducing them into the network.
- **Scan all downloaded files** – Put a strict security policy in place to scan every file downloaded from the Internet for viruses before copying, opening, or executing the files.

> **CAUTION:** Remember that even document files can contain viruses. Word processing and spreadsheet files are notorious for including viruses created using the internal macro language of the application. Be sure to scan all files, not just executable programs, and be sure your virus protection software can detect viruses in all types of files.

◆ **Disable Java execution** – I know this may be an unpopular action to take, but malicious Java programs executed from within Internet browser software can cause trouble. Because Java programs are so easily created, and because it's difficult for virus protection software to detect malicious Java code, it's best to turn off Java support in every browser on your network.

NOTE: If you're implementing an intranet, and the Java programs you want to run are developed internally and are trusted, then enabling Java support in browsers is fine. The danger comes from executing unknown Java code from the Internet.

◆ **Enable BIOS boot sector protection** – Most BIOSs now let you prevent software from tampering with the hard disk's boot sector – a common practice of viruses. It's a good idea to turn on this feature to prevent infection by this class of viruses. Unfortunately, when you install or upgrade an operating system (including Windows 98), the installation program must be allowed to alter the boot sector. On these occasions, you need to disable this protection temporarily. Just don't forget to turn the protection back on after OS installation.

Preventing Other Attacks

Different types of attacks on network security require different types of preventive measures. Here are a few of the most common:

◆ **Staff education** – Each member of the network administration staff needs to be educated about network security issues. This is your best defense against attacks involving social engineering and trap doors or open doors in the operating systems you're using. It's important that staff members recognize the social engineering scams and have a way to verify the identity of the person requesting secured information. It's equally important that they stay on top of new bugs and security holes discovered in the software on your network.

- **Network structure** – There are several ways to structure your network to prevent certain types of spoofing, denial of service, and unauthorized access. For example, you can use a proxy server to connect to the Internet. (A *proxy server*, such as Microsoft Proxy Server, intercepts requests for information and hides the address of the actual location of information from the external Internet.) A proxy server is usually part of a broader solution – a *firewall*. A firewall is a barrier that's typically set up in a bridge, router, or gateway to filter packets between two networks. It prevents certain types of packets from traveling between the internal network on one side and the external Internet on the other.
- **Auditing** – Auditing events plays an important role in recognizing successful or unsuccessful attempts to breach network security. Most dedicated server operating systems, including Windows NT Server, offer auditing features that enable you to record and review security events. Audit logs can include failed logon attempts, password changes, failed attempts to access resources, configuration changes, account creation, and other occurrences that may signify suspicious activity. Moreover, most firewalls can be configured to provide audit reports on the type and origin of packets that it filters out.

NOTE

The usefulness of auditing information reaches beyond security monitoring. It can also let you know how the network is being used, and can help in planning for expansion of capacity and services.

- **Data encryption** – One way to prevent successful eavesdropping or data theft is through data encryption. Software is available that encodes data into an unreadable form for transmission, and then decrypts it back into its original form at the other end. As long as the encryption and decryption keys remain secret, eavesdroppers can't easily make sense of the transmitted data. Some NOSs and add-on utilities let you encrypt data stored on the hard disk – foiling folks who try to steal your data by making off with the drive itself. Windows NT 5.0 offers on-disk data encryption of individual files.
- **Passwords** – The most common security mechanism is the assignment of passwords, which grant users access to the network as a whole or to specific resources on the network. In the remainder of this chapter, I focus on password-based security mechanisms provided by Windows 98 and other Windows products.

TIP

For an added measure of security, you can create hidden sharepoints that don't appear in resource lists when users browse the network. Just add a dollar sign ($) to the end of the name of your sharepoint (for example, PRIVATE$), and it will be invisible. Only users who know of its existence can attempt to connect to it.

Working with Windows 98 Security Options

Over the years, two basic network security models have emerged – namely, share-level and user-level. I briefly introduced these concepts in Chapter 2. In this section, I delve into the details with respect to the Windows 98 environment. Windows 98 fully supports share-level security, and cooperates with Windows NT Server or NetWare to implement network-wide user-level security.

Inside Share-Level Security

Recall from Chapter 2 that share-level access control, or *share-level security,* involves assigning a password to each shared network resource. The operating system grants access to the resource when a user enters the correct password for it – so any user on the network who knows the password assigned to the resource can access it. This is a relatively simple approach to security, but it's prone to the password pandemonium problem I discussed in Chapter 2.

In a share-level security environment, the user account and password that you use to log on to Windows 98 is local to the computer you're accessing. The user account and password are created and stored locally, and aren't authenticated by a central authority. The password you use to log on in this situation is called the *Windows password.* You can change the Windows password using the Passwords application in Control Panel.

Windows 98 supports a single password assigned to a shared printer – it either has a password or it doesn't. To assign a password to a shared printer, right-click the shared printer's icon in the Printers folder, click Sharing, type the password you want to assign, and click Apply. In the Password Confirmation dialog box, retype the same password and click OK. Then click OK in the Properties dialog box. From this point on, any user who tries to connect to the shared printer will be asked for the password. (If you want to remove password protection from the shared printer, simply perform the same operations and specify a blank password.)

The passwords supported on directories and drives are only slightly more complex. Here's a rundown of the three available password options:

- **Read-Only Access** – If you set up a sharepoint with a read-only password, users who know the password are able to view, copy, and print files, but they can't modify files, delete files, or add new files to the shared directory or drive. Users who don't know the password can't access the resource at all.
- **Full Access** – If you set up a sharepoint with a full access password, users who know the password have unrestricted access to read, write, print, delete, modify, and add files. Users who don't know the password can't access the resource at all.
- **Access Depends on Password** – This option enables you to assign two distinct passwords to the sharepoint. One password provides read-only access, and the other provides full access. To use this approach, you must select two different passwords for read-only and full access. Users who don't know either password can't access the resource at all.

To assign passwords to a shared directory or drive, right-click the shared resource's icon (in Windows Explorer or My Computer), click Sharing, and click the type of access you want to provide from the list of three options discussed. Then, type the password (or passwords) you want to assign, and click Apply. In the Password Confirmation dialog box, retype the same password (or passwords) and click OK. Then click OK in the Properties dialog box. (If you want to remove password protection, simply perform the same operations and specify blank passwords.)

> NOTE: Share-level security works only on Microsoft networks. NetWare doesn't support it. You can, however, set a resource to read-only access on a NetWare network.

Figure 12-1 illustrates the Properties dialog box where these passwords are set. Notice that both password boxes are available when you select Depends on Password. If you select either Read-Only or Full under Access Type, only one password box is available.

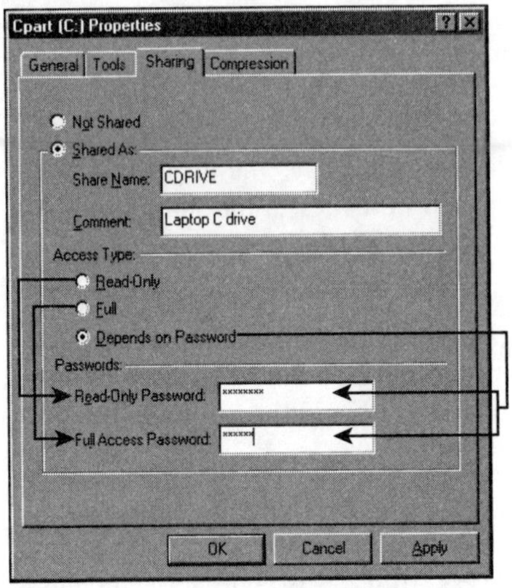

Figure 12-1: You can assign a Read-Only password, and Full access password, or both to a shared drive or directory.

NOTE: If you choose Depends on Password under Access Type, keep in mind that it doesn't make sense to have a password for read-only access but no password for full access. Windows 98 will let you do this, but the implication is that users can gain full access to the resource without a password.

As soon as passwords are assigned, any user who tries to connect to the shared resource is asked for a password. Depending on the access type you specified and the password a user types, the user is granted the appropriate access to the resource. For example, if you assign two passwords (read-only and full access) to the shared drive shown in Figure 12-1, a user attempting to connect to the resource sees the dialog box shown in Figure 12-2.

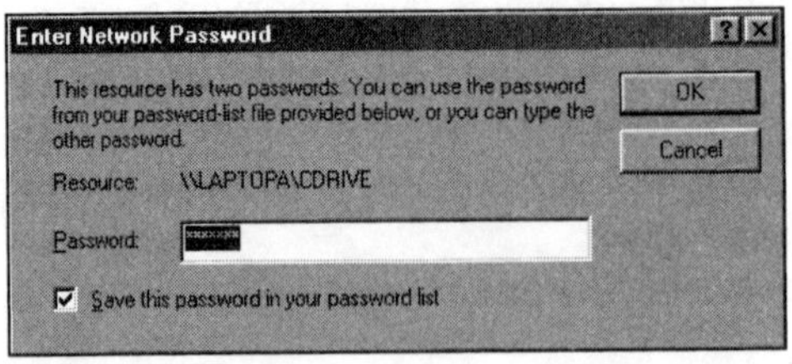

Figure 12-2: When connecting to a password-protected resource, the user must supply the appropriate password.

Figure 12-2 illustrates another important concept in share-level security – *password caching*. By default, Windows 98 keeps an internal list of passwords you've used to connect to resources recently. It stores these in a file for each user who logs on to the computer. (The Windows 98 Resource Kit includes a utility called PWLEDIT, which enables you to edit this list of cached passwords.) When it's time to reconnect to a resource that you've connected to before, Windows 98 automatically supplies the last password you used to gain access to it.

Whether or not you're connecting to a resource for the first time, Windows 98 gives you the option of saving (caching) the password for use the next time you try to connect. The checkbox in Figure 12-2 illustrates this. If you don't want the password saved, click to clear the checkbox. These cached passwords are stored locally in encrypted form in a .PWL password list file. Windows 98 includes a utility called the Password List Editor that lets you view the list of resources for which cached passwords are stored, and lets you delete entries from this list. (You can't actually see the passwords themselves.)

If you cancel the Windows Logon dialog box, the password cache isn't opened for that session – so you won't get any password free rides. Each time you connect to a password-protected resource, you'll be forced to type its password.

Inside User-Level Security

In Chapter 2, I introduced user-level access control, or *user-level security*. In contrast to the share-level approach, user-level security assigns to each user a single account and a single password. The user logs on once to the network, using this one password. The user account determines which resources the user can or can't access. With user-level security, the network administrator assigns permissions to a specific resource by granting or denying resource access to an individual user account, or to a group of user accounts.

A dedicated server NOS is responsible for authenticating the user once at logon time, and then it controls access to individual resources. To implement user-level security, you need either a Windows NT Server computer or a server running NetWare. A server that provides user authentication services is sometimes called a *security provider*. Windows 98 can't perform the user authentication function.

User-level security provides a higher level of security than the share-level approach. Why? It's much more likely that one user will tell another user what the password is to a specific resource – but it's highly unlikely a user would tell another user his personal password to all network resources. (It's up to you, the network administrator, to educate users about the importance of keeping their personal password a secret.)

Dangers of the Password Cache Machine

Although password caching is certainly convenient for users, it's a bit like putting your PIN number on a post-it note on the front of an automatic teller machine. If someone walks up to your logged-on computer when you're not around, that person can easily connect to any network resource you've ever accessed – no password knowledge required.

Disabling password caching adds an extra measure of security, but puts the burden on the user to remember each password. Nevertheless, many network administrators make it a point to disable password caching to tighten up share-level security.

You can disable it using the System Policy Editor, discussed in Chapter 10. Click File → Open Registry and double-click Local Computer. Click the plus sign (+) to expand Windows 98 Network, and then click the plus sign (+) to expand Passwords. Click to select the Disable password caching checkbox. Then click OK → File → Exit → Yes.

User-level security is also more flexible, because it enables the network administrator to give very specific rights to each user. Once users log on and are authenticated via their personal password, access to individual resources is controlled through a set of *access permissions*. These permissions control the access each user has to the resource at a finer level of granularity – beyond just read-only or full access. For example, a user could have some combination of the following access permissions to a shared directory:

- **Read** – The user can read and copy files from the directory.
- **Write** – The user can modify existing files and create new files or subdirectories within the directory.
- **Delete** – The user can delete existing files from the directory.
- **Execute** – The user can run applications or batch files located within the directory.
- **No Access** – The user cannot access the contents of the directory at all.

In large organizations, implementing user-level security can get cumbersome if the network administrator has to assign permissions for individual users to each shared resource or file. To solve this problem, some NOSs, such as Windows NT, provide the capability to define *groups*, or classes of users. The network administrator can assign users to specific groups, and then set group permission on specific resources. If the access needs of a user change, you can simply move the user to a different group with the appropriate permissions.

For example, let's say the members of the sales department need full access to the customer database, so they can make changes and update customer records. The marketing department, on the other hand, needs read-only access to the database in order to generate mailings. If Fred moves from the marketing department to the sales department, and you've implemented groups to describe the two classes of users, all you have to do is move Fred from the marketing group to the sales group. Fred then immediately inherits the permissions granted to the members of the sales group.

> Windows 98 can't place different permissions on different files within a directory, even when user-level security is implemented. FAT16 and FAT32 just don't support the required security information. However, Windows NT does support file-by-file permissions through the NTFS file system. Each file stored on NTFS can have its own set of permissions that grant different levels of access to groups and individual users.

To enable user-level security on Windows 98, you need a Windows NT Server (or NetWare) computer on your network to perform user authentication. On each Windows 98 computer, click Start → Settings → Control Panel, and double-click Network. Click the Access Control tab and click User-level access control. Then, type the name of the Windows NT Server domain that contains the list of network user accounts, and click OK.

Once you do this, Windows 98 automatically enables remote administration, which allows you to perform administration tasks on this computer from other computers attached to the network. All that's required is that you have an account with administrator privileges. (If you're working with NetWare servers, you need to use a supervisor account to perform remote administration.)

Here's how to share a resource with user-level security. From either Windows Explorer or My Computer, right-click the icon of the resource that you want to share on the network. Click the Sharing tab, and click Add. In the Add Users dialog box, click the name of a user or group to whom you want to grant permissions to this resource. The user or group accounts must already exist on a Windows NT Server computer or NetWare server on the network. Proceed to set the access rights for that user (or group) on that resource. Check with your server NOS documentation for details.

Implementing Password Policies

Passwords are useful and valuable commodities if they're managed properly. If they aren't given the appropriate level of respect, however, they're rendered useless. A combination of user training and NOS features can work in concert to maintain an appropriate level of password-based security. Here are some guidelines to implement when dealing with passwords in your organization:

- Train users to remember that their passwords are secret. They should not share them with anyone. If you feel a password has been compromised, change it.
- Avoid writing down any password. Would-be attackers look for passwords in desk drawers, day planners, on post-it notes on the wall or on video displays, at the front or back of desk calendars, and so forth. It's best to train users never to write down a password. Also, don't put passwords into batch files or documents where they can be read electronically.

TIP Many users new to computers or networking are deathly afraid that if they ever forget their password, they'll lose access to all their work forever. Reassure them that as a network administrator, you can arrange for a new password and they won't lose anything.

- Don't use obvious passwords such as names of spouses, children, pets, hometowns, cartoon characters, and so forth.
- Don't type a password while someone else is watching. Even if the typed characters are obscured on the screen, someone can watch the sequence of keystrokes to learn a password.
- Don't let users log on and then leave their computer unattended for long periods of time. Make use of password-protected screen savers that kick in after a few minutes of idle time.
- Never communicate both a user account and its associated password in the same communication. (You never get a bank card and a PIN in the same piece of mail, do you?)
- Require a minimum password length. The longer a password is, the more difficult it is for a hacker to randomly or systematically generate it during an attack. (Windows NT Server and a Windows 98 system policy work together to enforce this rule.)
- Require a mix of numbers and letters in passwords. The better the mixture, the more difficult it is to generate during an attack on the network. (Windows NT Server and a Windows 98 system policy work together to enforce this rule.)
- Impose a minimum and maximum password age. (Windows NT Server is required to enforce this rule.)

Administering Remotely

As a network administrator, you may occasionally need to administer a computer on the network remotely. For example, if a user gets into trouble and you can't personally go to his or her computer, you may want to be able to fix the problem from your desk. Or perhaps you need to monitor the performance of several servers, but you want all the charts to show up on the computer in your office. Windows 98 gives you the capability of remotely administering other nodes on the network using four utilities – System Policy Editor, Registry Editor, System Monitor, and Net Watcher.

> CAUTION: The use of some of these utilities to change the configuration of another computer can be dangerous. As a network administrator, you need to keep these utilities and the associated security measures from falling into the hands of novices or malicious users.

Because this is such a powerful feature and is potentially very destructive, several security prerequisites need to be in place before the feature will work. First, the whole scheme requires implementing user-level security, as described earlier in this chapter. This prerequisite enables you to select exactly which user accounts have the right to perform remote administration. Second, installation of the Microsoft Remote Registry Service is required on all computers that remotely administer or are administered remotely (that is, it's required at both ends of the connection). This service is supplied in the Windows 98 Resource Kit, so it requires an extra step on each participating computer. (See Appendix B for more details on resource kits.) Third, the computer being administered must agree to it – the computer needs to be explicitly enabled for remote administration.

In this section, I walk through the steps required to enable this feature. First, you'll need to create one or more user accounts on the Windows NT Server computer that provides user authentication. Grant these accounts administrative privileges, to allow them to perform remote administrations.

On each computer that will participate in remote administration, perform the following steps:

1. Enable user-level security. Click Start → Settings → Control Panel → Network → Access Control → User-level access control. Type the name of the Windows NT Server domain that contains the list of network user accounts.
2. Click the Configuration tab, then click Add → Service → Add → Have Disk.

3. Type the path of the REMOTREG directory. On the Windows 98 Resource Kit CD-ROM, it's typically \NETADMIN\REMOTREG; on the Windows 98 CD-ROM, it's usually \TOOLS\RESKIT\NETADMIN\REMTOREG. The path may vary depending on the version of CD-ROM you have. Click OK.
4. Click Microsoft Remote Registry, and click OK. You may be prompted for additional files from the Windows 98 CD-ROM.
5. In the Network dialog box, click OK. Restart the computer as prompted.

On each computer that you want to administer remotely, perform the following steps:

1. Click Start → Settings → Control Panel, and double-click the Passwords icon.
2. Click the Remote Administration tab, and then click to select the checkbox named Enable remote administration of this server.
3. Click Add. Add all the user and group accounts you want to allow as remote administrators of this computer. All of these accounts must have administrator privileges.
4. When you've finished adding accounts, click OK in the Passwords Properties dialog box.

Once these steps have been completed, you'll be able to use the remote administration utilities to connect to and administer other computers on the network. For example, you'll be able to monitor the performance of another computer by running System Monitor on your computer. Just click File → Connect in System Monitor, specify the remote computer you want to monitor, and click OK. I discuss System Monitor in more detail in Chapter 14.

Summary

In this chapter, you've been exposed to the many dangers of network security breaches. You've also learned more about the differences between share-level and user-level security, how Windows 98 supports them, and how to manage passwords on your network. In Chapter 13, you'll discover additional steps you can take to ensure the integrity of your data and your network, in case natural disasters or human error come to call.

Chapter 13

Protecting Your Network from Disaster

IN THIS CHAPTER

- Implementing a backup strategy
- Guarding against power problems
- Planning your redundancy strategy

IF YOU'RE AS SUPERSTITIOUS as I am, it seems strangely fitting that Chapter 13 covers disaster planning and recovery. Many of the events you need to plan for are completely out of your control. Whether or not one of these events befalls your site is largely dependent on chance and luck. But by planning for them up front, taking proactive steps to minimize your data loss, and knowing exactly how to recover quickly when disaster strikes, you can replace a reliance on luck with a reliance on sound planning and execution.

Without a disaster recovery plan in place, all your networking efforts can go to waste in a single catastrophic event. However, if you plan and execute well in this area, you'll be a more successful network administrator – one who can turn a major disaster into a minor inconvenience. By the end of this chapter, you'll understand which steps to take to build and execute a sound disaster recovery plan.

Implementing a Backup Strategy

The least expensive and easiest way to prepare for and recover from disaster is to create and implement a plan to back up critical data and store it both on-site and off-site. Tape backup is one of the most economical approaches, although other media can be used for backup storage. Ensuring that the data you back up can be easily restored when needed is a key part of a good backup plan.

In this section, I discuss the key issues and procedures associated with creating and implementing a backup plan. Although the emphasis in this section is on tape backup, the concepts apply to other types of backup media as well. See Chapter 8 for advice on selecting tape backup devices.

Understanding Backup Types

No, I'm not talking about the types of people who perform backups – although you should now count yourself as one of these people. There are several types of backup operations you can perform, each with a slightly different behavior. A good backup plan typically includes a combination of two or more of these backup types.

FULL BACKUP

The two most common types of backup are full and incremental. A *full backup*, sometimes called a *normal backup*, is exactly what it sounds like. It backs up all the files you select, regardless of when they were last backed up or whether they were ever backed up. For example, if you specify that all of drive C should be backed up, and you want a full backup, every file on drive C will be included in the backup. Likewise, if you specify that the contents of a specific directory should be backed up, then every file in that directory and all its subdirectories will be included. A full backup also keeps track of the files included in the backup.

TIP

Full backup is the most thorough and most time-consuming backup type. Although not all backups need to include every file, every good backup plan needs to include a periodic full backup. For example, a full backup every week or every month, depending on the rate of change in your data, is typical in many organizations. Full backups allow for much easier restoration if disaster ever strikes. Other backup types introduce some complexity into the restoration process.

INCREMENTAL BACKUP

An *incremental backup*, on the other hand, will include only files that have changed or been added since the last backup was performed. Incremental backups usually take less time to perform, unless every file has changed since the previous backup. For example, if you specify that all of drive C should be backed up, and you want an incremental backup, only the files on drive C that have changed or been added will be included in the backup. So if you performed a full backup of drive C yesterday, and one file has changed since then, only that file will be included in the incremental backup. Like a full backup, and incremental backup also keeps track of the files it included.

A common approach to backup involves a combination of periodic full backups supplemented by more frequent incremental backups. For example, you may decide that a weekly full backup is appropriate for your organization. To minimize risk, you could also perform an incremental backup each day, to catch all the files that have changed or been created that day. This approach offers the safety of a frequent backup without requiring the time and tape space of a full backup each day.

Digging into the Archives

How does the backup utility know which files have been backed up and which files haven't? How does it sense the presence of new files, or files that have been altered since the last backup was performed? Each file has a set of attributes, including its filename, the date it was last modified, and so forth. One of these attributes is a bit called the *archive bit*.

The operating system turns on this bit when a file is first created and every time it's modified. Most backup utilities turn off the archive bit when the file is backed up to tape or some other media. Using this scheme, the operating system can signal to the backup utility that a particular file hasn't been backed up and needs to be.

In choosing files to include in the backup, a full backup operation ignores the archive bit because it backs up every file you specify. When a full backup is done, however, it turns off the archive bits to indicate that the files have been backed up. An incremental backup examines the archive bits to decide which files will be included in the backup. If a file's archive bit is on, the file is included. If the file's bit is off, the file isn't included. When an incremental backup is completed, it turns off the archive bits to indicate that the files have been backed up.

Setting the archive bit effectively says, "The next time backup runs, this file needs to be included in the backup – it's new or has been modified." Clearing the archive bit says, "This file was included in a backup, and hasn't changed since the backup was performed." All file systems supported by Microsoft operating systems store and maintain the archive bit for this purpose.

To view the status of the archive bit, right-click the icon of the file that interests you (either through Windows Explorer or My Computer). Click Properties → General. In the Attributes section of the General tab, the archive bit is turned on if the Archive checkbox is checked. You can force a file to be included in the next backup (whether or not it has changed) by clicking to select the Archive checkbox.

If you use this approach, and you need to restore files because of lost data, the process requires accessing the most recent full backup and all subsequent incremental backups. Therefore, the restore process in this case is a bit more complex than simply restoring from a full backup – but the time and tape space saved by incremental backups is typically considered worth the tradeoff, because backups (hopefully) occur more frequently than restores.

DIFFERENTIAL BACKUP

Some backup utilities offer additional backup types. For example, a *differential backup* is essentially the same as an incremental backup, but it doesn't turn off the archive bit on the files it backs up. As a result, a differential backup includes all the files that have changed since the last full backup. Each successive differential backup becomes longer and longer, as more and more changed files (that have their archive bit turned on) accumulate.

The advantage of differential backup over incremental backup is that a restore operation requires accessing only the latest full backup and the latest differential backup. None of the interim differential backups are required, because all the changed and created files since the full backup are included in the differential backup. Thus, a combination of full and differential backups is easier to restore than a full/incremental backup combination – but the tradeoff is increased time and tape space for each successive differential backup.

NOTE: Microsoft Backup, which comes with Windows 98, supports the full, incremental, and differential backup types. NT Backup on Windows NT supports these backup types as well.

COPY BACKUP

A *copy backup* is almost identical to a full backup, but the copy backup doesn't turn off the archive bits on the files it backs up. In other words, the copy backup creates a copy of all the files and doesn't do anything to influence the contents of future backups. NT Backup on Windows NT includes this backup type.

DAILY BACKUP

Finally, the least used and most complex of the backup types is called a *daily backup*, or sometimes *daily copy*. It's the only backup type that takes only the file modification date into account when it chooses what to include in the backup. A daily backup includes only files that have been modified or added on the date the backup is performed. For example, if you perform a full backup on Monday and a daily backup on Wednesday, only the files changed or added on Wednesday's date will appear in the backup. Any files changed between the full backup on Monday and the end of Tuesday aren't backed up at all. NT Backup on Windows NT supports this backup type.

Developing a Backup Schedule

Creating and religiously sticking to a backup schedule is vital to the success of your disaster recovery plan. If you skip backups, perform the wrong types of backup, use the wrong tapes, and so forth, you're just asking for trouble. It's important to write down the backup schedule in detail and make it available to everyone who might be involved in the process. Likewise, a log of backups performed is important, to prevent wasted effort and errors when implementing the schedule.

I'd like nothing better than to tell you exactly when and what to back up. Unfortunately, there's no clear-cut answer that applies to all organizations, so I'll fill you in on what you should consider as you develop your backup schedule. The most fundamental question to ask is, "How much data am I willing to lose?" This may sound like a silly question, because the answer is obviously "None." Perhaps that's your answer, but keep in mind that you'll encounter tradeoffs if you decide to continuously back up your data. Files that are open may cause your backups to be incomplete, backup traffic on your network may slow down normal business operations, and you could find yourself with a full-time job just managing backup tapes and storage.

NOTE: There are ways to cut down your risk of lost data due to hardware failure to a very low level. Fault tolerance hardware and software can maintain redundant copies of your data at all times, and automatically recover it when a component fails. I cover fault tolerance techniques later in this chapter.

SELECTING A BACKUP MIX

Let's say that you never want to lose more than a day's worth of file changes. That's a reasonable requirement that applies to many organizations. Does that mean you need to perform a full backup every day? Not necessarily. A backup of just the files that change is typically adequate, with a full backup performed periodically (say, weekly or monthly, depending on the frequency of file changes on your network).

The mix and frequency of backup types you include in your schedule affect the complexity and time required for the restore operation, should you ever need to restore files from your backup tapes. For example, full backups take the longest to create, have the biggest impact on your network, and take up the most tape. But when it's time to restore, the operation is quick and straightforward – just select the files you want to restore, and restore them.

At the other end of the spectrum, an incremental backup takes the least amount of time, the least amount of tape, and has the least impact on your network. But restoring files can be a bit complex, because you may have to sift through more than one incremental backup (which may reside on more than one tape) to find the latest version of the file you're after. Restoring many files using incremental backups may involve multiple restore operations. So like many things in life, you either pay now or pay later.

As I mentioned earlier, one of the most common approaches to backup involves periodic full backups (for example, weekly or monthly) supplemented by daily incremental backups. If a restore is required immediately after a full backup, the restore operation is simple. As you accumulate incremental backups over the course of a week or month, the restore process becomes increasingly more complex. Thus, the longer the time between full backups, the longer a restore process will probably take as you near the end of the cycle.

DECIDING WHAT TO BACK UP

Independent of your decision about the mix of backup types to use, you need to determine exactly what you want to back up. Do you need to back up only the files that reside on a single server, on multiple servers, or do you want to cover all the computers on your network? Do you need to back up operating system files as well as application and data files, or are data files alone sufficient?

Operating systems and applications can be restored relatively easily from the original software packages, but if you have very many of them, you could be in for a long reinstallation process. When deciding on backing up applications and the OS itself, it's best to weigh the relative cost of restoring a configuration from the original installation media (typically CD-ROMs or floppy disks) versus restoring from tape. It might make sense to create a backup of all files once, and then back up data files periodically.

If you're going to perform backups over the network, you should create network connections from the computer with the tape drive to the computers you want to back up. During the backup process, the computer with the tape drive acts as a client, and the remote computers being backed up act as servers. If a computer that you want to include in the backup over the network isn't configured as a server, it needs to be. See Chapter 11 for a discussion of configuring server components and assigning drive letters to network connections.

In practice, you may want to define several distinct subsets of files that you want to back up at different times. The Microsoft Backup utility supplied with Windows 98 enables you to define *backup jobs*, which include information on what to back up, which backup type to use, and so forth. In creating and implementing your backup schedule, you may want to create several different backup jobs to be run at different times. I discuss backup jobs later in this chapter.

SCHEDULING YOUR BACKUPS

The success of your backup plan depends on how you schedule the actual backup operations. As a network administrator, you need to choose the right time of day (or night) to perform backups. You may also need to decide which additional software or hardware you need to make your backups efficient and effective. In this section, I discuss the key issues to consider when scheduling your backups.

Most backup utilities allow themselves to be run unattended, unless a tape change is required during the process to accommodate all of your data. Even then, hardware solutions exist that perform tape changes automatically. Called *autoloaders*, these devices aren't cheap, but they enable you to perform large backups without needing a staff member present.

TIP

It's a good idea to perform a backup just before installing new devices or applications, so you can revert back to a known working configuration if the new hardware or software causes problems. Likewise, once the hardware and software is installed and working, perform a backup so you don't lose the new configuration if the hard disk fails.

MANAGING OPEN FILES Most backup utilities have difficulty backing up files that are currently held open by one or more users. While a file is open, it's nearly impossible to tell what state the data is in, and whether it's safe to back it up. Some older backup software simply terminated the backup operation when it encountered an open file, perhaps leaving many remaining files without a backup. Later utilities simply skipped open files, logged them in a list, and moved on to the next file. Most modern backup utilities will wait briefly for an open file to close, and then skip the file, log it, and move on.

Some applications, such as database servers, are designed to leave their files open constantly. They often include a special backup feature that enables you to generate a safe snapshot of the open files, which you can then back up using your chosen backup utility. Other applications require that you shut them down before you can perform a backup of the data. To minimize the number of files that are skipped during the backup process, it's best to schedule backups during hours when it's less likely the files will be open.

NOTE

The Windows 98 registry (along with the registries on Windows 95 and Windows NT) is always held open by the operating system. Because of this, many backup utilities refuse to back up registry information. It's much easier to skip the registry than to deal with the problem of backing up an open file. Be sure that whatever backup software you choose will handle backing up the registry. Microsoft Backup provides this feature, as does NT Backup in Windows NT.

MANAGING NETWORK TRAFFIC If you're backing up computers over the network, the backup and verify operations can create a significant increase in network traffic. In a production environment, this can lead to reduced performance of your servers and all segments of the network involved in the backup. There are a few of solutions to this problem. One approach involves scheduling your backups at a time when network usage is very low or non-existent. For example, your network may not be used at all during the early morning hours before the start of the business day. If scheduling all your backups during off-hours isn't feasible, you can opt to perform smaller incremental backups during normal hours, and perform your periodic full backups during off-hours.

If you must perform backups during heavy network usage, either for scheduling reasons or because the nature of your business requires more frequent backups, you may want to consider creating an isolated network segment just for backups. This is a costly alternative, but can work well in installations where most of the data to be backed up resides on centralized servers.

If the servers are reasonably close to each other (for example, in the same room, floor, or building), you can add a second network adapter fairly easily to each server, along with an additional hub and wiring to complete an isolated network segment. Then you can run backup to your heart's content without making a significant impact on network performance. Of course, the additional disk and network I/O may affect the performance of individual servers, but your network won't be clogged by backup data.

TIP

If you use one tape drive to perform backups of many computers over the network, it's a good idea to attach the drive to the computer that typically has the most data to back up. That way, you'll reduce the impact of backup data clogging up your network. Because the amount of data may shift to other computers over time, plan on reassessing the placement of your tape drive every few months. If you have several servers with huge amounts of data to back up, consider investing in additional tape drives to keep large amounts of backup traffic off the network.

MANAGING BACKUP MEDIA

Every time you create a backup, regardless of its type, the backup utility writes the files to tape in what's called a *backup set.* If there's room on the tape, you can store multiple backup sets on a single tape. For example, you could store all the incremental backups performed over the course of a week on a single tape. If a backup set exceeds the capacity of available tape, it can span more than one tape. Whenever you add a backup set to a tape that already contains backup sets, you tell the backup utility to *append* the new set to the end of the tape. If you want to erase all backup sets on a tape and start fresh, you tell the software to *overwrite* the contents of the tape.

The sage advice, "Don't put all your eggs in one basket" applies to tape backups. To paraphrase: "Don't put all your backup sets on one tape." Although tape is fairly reliable, it is subject to contamination, magnetic erasure, stretching, and breaking – so you're better off if you cycle through multiple tapes to store your backups. That way, if a tape goes bad for some reason, your data loss is minimized. Also, rotating your backup schedule through multiple tapes evens out the wear and tear on your tapes.

How you decide to place your backup sets on tape is up to you, and should be based on your backup schedule and your tolerance for data loss. Think through what the loss of a single tape – due to disaster or tape failure – would do to your operation. Then work toward minimizing the impact. For example, if you perform a full backup weekly and incremental backups on each succeeding weekday, you might first consider placing one week's worth of backups on a single tape. At the end of the week, your single tape would contain the full backup set, followed by four incremental backup sets. You could then start a new tape for the following week. If you cycled through a set of four tapes, you would always have a month's worth of backups available.

NOTE When you cycle backups through a set of tapes, you pick the one with the oldest backup sets and use that one to perform the next backup. The next time you need another backup tape, pick the oldest one again. That way, you're always overwriting the oldest backup you have, and your entire set of tapes represents the most recent data available. Carefully label your tapes so you always know which one to use next in the cycle.

This scenario works, until you consider what would happen if the tape you're using fails. In the worst case, the tape fails on the last day of the week and your disk fails as well, requiring you to restore files. Your only choice is to revert to the tape from the previous week, which means you've lost a week's worth of changes. If your goal was to lose no more than a day's worth of changes, the use of a single tape is unacceptable.

Another tape management approach to the same backup schedule involves using a different tape each day of the week. The first tape contains the full backup set. Subsequent tapes contain incremental backup sets – one day's worth on each tape. In this case, if a single tape fails, the most you'll lose is one day's changes.

If your backups require multiple tapes because the total amount of data you're backing up exceeds the capacity of a single tape, tape management becomes more complicated. You should try to minimize this condition by using high capacity tapes and opt to compress data on the tape, if your drive supports this feature. For example, many DAT tapes have a 4GB capacity, but can store up to 8GB of data when you enable compression.

STORING BACKUP MEDIA

Once you've put the data on tape and have verified that it's correct, storage of the tape media becomes the next important step. It's amazing how many backup tapes are completely ruined because of improper storage. The network administrator usually doesn't realize there's a problem with the backup until it's time to recover from a disaster – and there's nothing that can be restored. Even with the best tape drive, the highest quality media, and flawless execution of a backup schedule, the whole effort can be utterly wasted if the media is improperly stored.

USING YOUR COMMON SENSE Common sense should prevail when storing backup tapes or any other magnetic media. Avoid storing tapes near magnetic fields generated by video displays, speakers, power supplies, UPS devices, telephones, and so forth. Avoid tape contamination from dust, smoke, and other particles. (Even though the Surgeon General's warning doesn't cover backup tapes, the particles in smoke are indeed hazardous to your data's health.) Extremes of temperature and humidity can also affect stored media. Your best bet is to read the manufacturer's environmental recommendations, and follow them carefully.

STORING IT OFF-SITE Frankly, there's no substitute for off-site storage of backup tapes. In an ideal world, you would create two identical copies of a backup tape – one to store on-site for quick restoration of data, and one to store off-site in the event of a site catastrophe. In you don't have the luxury of making two copies, you can store alternate backups off-site, knowing that you'll have to roll back to an older backup if your site is destroyed.

How far away should off-site storage be? The office or building next door isn't a good choice, since it's more likely that both copies would be destroyed in a disaster. The farther away you store the second copy, the greater the chances it will survive if you lose your site. Storing backups at an employee's home across town is a good choice for some organizations, although security of the data may be an issue. Some firms offer services that include secured storage of backup media – for a fee, they act as your off-site storage site. Your decision about where to store data off-site will involve a tradeoff between convenience, cost, and security.

Safe or Unsafe?

What about storing backup tapes in a fireproof safe? Well, high-quality safes are fine for preventing theft of your tapes, but they usually do little to salvage the data when a fire occurs. A good safe will probably keep the tapes and other contents from actually burning, but the safe's chamber can reach temperatures high enough to destroy the recorded data. Data on backup tapes stored in safes rarely survive a fire.

Some fireproof safes employ special chemicals that release moisture during a fire, helping to prevent the safe's contents from igniting at high temperatures. Unfortunately, if the heat doesn't destroy the data, the resulting moisture can damage the data, too. The bottom line is that safes are great for preventing theft of your backups, but don't rely on them to protect your data from fire.

Even in the best of conditions, tape media will break down over time. The shelf life of data on a tape varies with environmental conditions, tape quality, drive quality, and other factors. It's a good rule of thumb to assume that tapes will lose their data if stored longer than three years. If you need to save data on tape longer than that, restore it somewhere from the original tape and create a new tape. Alternatively, you could record the information on media that lasts longer; for example, some recordable CD-ROMs last for up to 30 years before losing bits. Check with your backup media vendor regarding data shelf life, and be sure to include the refreshing of old archived data in your backup schedule.

Installing Microsoft Backup

Many backup utilities are available for Windows 98, Window 95, and Windows NT. Windows 98 comes with Microsoft Backup, although it isn't installed by default when you install the operating system. It's only installed automatically if you're upgrading a copy of Windows 95 that had Microsoft Backup already installed.

If you're familiar with Backup Exec for Windows 95 from Seagate, the Microsoft Backup utility in Windows 98 will look very familiar to you. This utility is a slightly stripped-down version of Backup Exec.

If Microsoft Backup isn't already installed on the Windows 98 computer containing your tape drive or other backup device, here's how to install it:

1. Install the backup device, if it isn't already installed. If Windows 98 doesn't automatically detect it, click Start → Settings → Control Panel, double-click Add New Hardware, and follow the prompts to detect and configure the device. Restart the computer as prompted.
2. With the backup hardware installed and configured, click Start → Settings → Control Panel, and double-click Add/Remove Programs.
3. Click the Windows Setup tab, and double-click System Tools.
4. Click to select the checkbox next to the Backup icon, and click OK. Then click Apply.
5. Setup copies the appropriate files from your Windows 98 CD-ROM. When it's done, click OK.

The Microsoft Backup utility is added to the System Tools menu. To start it, click Start → Programs → Accessories → System Tools → Backup.

Backing Up Your Data

To perform a backup operation under Windows 98, perform the following steps. If you haven't yet installed your backup device hardware or the Microsoft Backup utility, see the previous section titled "Installing Microsoft Backup."

1. Insert the backup tape into the tape drive. To start Microsoft Backup, click Start → Programs → Accessories → System Tools → Backup.

> NOTE: The first time you start Microsoft Backup, if the utility can't detect a backup device, it asks if you want to start the Add New Hardware application in Control Panel. If you do, click Yes. Otherwise, click No to continue.

2. To create a new backup job, click Create a new backup job, and click OK. The Backup Wizard will guide you through the steps to create a backup job, which describes the files you want to include, what type of backup to perform, and other information.
3. If you want to back up all the files on the local computer (including all local drives), click Back up My Computer, click Next, and proceed to Step 5. If you want to select a subset of local files, or you want to include files from other computers on the network, click Back up selected files, folders and drives. Then click Next and proceed to Step 4.
4. The Backup Wizard asks you to specify which drives, directories, and files to back up, as shown in Figure 13-1. Select items to include by clicking to select the checkbox next to each item. If you select a drive, all files and directories on that drive are included in the backup set. If you want to select specific directories or files, click the plus sign (+) next to the item to expand its details. Then, click to select the checkbox next to the item you want to include.

> NOTE: If you're backing up files that reside on another computer on the network, and you already have a network connection with a drive letter assigned to it, Backup treats this as just another hard disk. For example, in Figure 13-1, Drive H is assigned to a sharepoint on the network. If you want to back up files over the network and you don't have a network connection established, expand the Networks entry and navigate to the sharepoint you want to include in the backup. Click to select the directories or specific files you want to include.

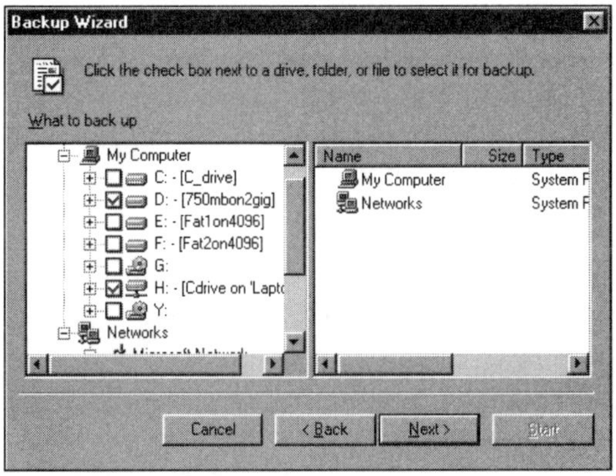

Figure 13-1: Microsoft Backup lets you select specific drives, directories, and files to include in the backup.

5. When you've made all your selections, click Next. If you want to perform a full backup, click All selected files. If you want to perform an incremental or differential backup, click New and changed files. Then click Next.
6. Select a destination for the backup set. If you have a backup device, select it from the list of choices and click Next. If you don't have a backup device, or if you select File from the list of destinations, you can create a file containing the backup set. You'll be asked to supply the destination location of this file before proceeding to the next step.
7. Click to select the checkbox titled as such: Compare original and backup files to verify data was successfully backed up.

Never create a backup set without verifying that the data on the tape matches the data you backed up. Turn on the verify function in your backup utility and just leave it on. Doing this will increase the length of time required to perform a backup, but short of performing an actual restore, it's your best insurance that what you believe you backed up is what you really backed up.

8. Click to select the checkbox titled Compress the backup data to save space. Then click Next. If the tape drive supports data compression in hardware, Backup will instruct the device to compress the data. If the device doesn't support compression, the utility will compress the data before writing it to the device. In general, software compression takes more time than hardware compression.

9. Type a name for the backup job. The name can be up to 53 characters long, including any characters except for `\ / : ? * " < > |`.

10. Verify that the settings for the backup job are correct. If you want to change any of them, click Back to navigate back through the steps. When you're satisfied with the settings, click Start.

11. Backup builds a list of all the files it needs to back up, displaying the Selection Information dialog box to show its progress. If you clicked New and changed files in Step 5, Backup defaults to performing differential backup. If you would rather perform an incremental backup, click Cancel, and then click Job → Options → Type → Incremental backup type → Apply → OK. Then, click Job → Save, click the Backup tab, and click Start.

12. If the tape already contains data, Backup will ask if you want to append the new backup set to the end of the tape or overwrite the existing data. Click either Append or Overwrite. If you clicked Overwrite, Backup asks you to supply a name for the tape. Type one and click OK.

CAUTION

If you click Overwrite, all data currently on the tape will be lost. Make sure you want to erase all existing data before clicking this button. If in doubt, click Append.

---

13. Backup starts the backup operation and reports status in the Backup Progress dialog box, as shown in Figure 13-2. When it's done, click OK. The Report button appears in the Backup Progress dialog box. Click Report to view the results of the backup and verify operations.

14. Backup starts Notepad to let you view the report. When you're done, close Notepad and click OK in the Backup Progress dialog box. You can view the report again later in `\Program Files\Accessories\Backup\Reports\Report.txt`.

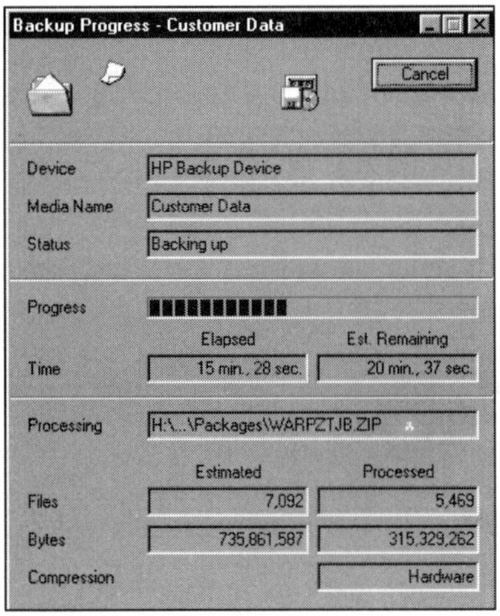

Figure 13-2: Microsoft Backup reports status in the Backup Progress dialog box.

If a computer involved in the backup was in use for other tasks during the backup process, the verify phase may report mismatches between the data on tape and the data on disk. This happens if a file changes between the time it's written to tape and the time it's read during the verify.

Testing and Restoring Your Data

Before you trust any new backup software or hardware, it's best to test the entire process of backup, verification, and restoration of files. Going through all the steps the first time you execute your plan with a new backup component can help point out problems with the process – before you become too reliant on it.

Even if you verify your backups during the backup process, it's a good idea to test periodically to see whether you can restore the data you've backed up. Some network administrators perform this test monthly, just to verify that, in the event of an emergency, they can restore data when they need it. This activity can be used as a training tool for new members of the network administration staff.

When you perform a test restoration of data from tape, make sure you don't restore data on top of your current data. You don't want to overwrite the live data on your computers with stale data from a backup tape. Either use a separate computer for the restore test, or specify a different destination location on the hard disk.

The restore operation is essentially the opposite of the backup operation. You insert a backup tape, specify which files you want to restore and where you want them to go, and start the process. You may elect to restore the entire contents of the tape, or just individual files. (Some backup utilities create a backup of the hard disk image, and don't allow restoration of individual files. This limitation is rare, and is now considered obsolete.)

Here's how to restore the contents of a tape to your hard disk, using Microsoft Backup on Windows 98:

1. Insert the backup tape containing the backup set you want to restore. To start Microsoft Backup, click Start → Programs → Accessories → System Tools → Backup.
2. Click Restore backed up files, and click OK.
3. Select a source for the backup set. If you have a backup device, select it from the list and click Next. If you don't have a backup device, or if you select File from the list of sources, type the source location of the file containing the backup set, and then click Next.
4. Backup reads the list of backup sets stored on the source, and lists them in the Select Backup Sets dialog box. Click to select the checkbox next to the backup set you want to restore. Then click OK.
5. The Restore Wizard asks you to specify which drives, directories, and files to restore from the backup set. Select items to include by clicking to select the checkbox next to each item. If you select a drive, all files and directories from that drive in the backup set are included. If you want to select specific directories or files, click the plus sign (+) next to the item to expand its details. Then, click to select the checkbox next to the item you want to restore.
6. When you've made all your selections for what to include in the restore, click Next.
7. Select a destination for the restored files by clicking either Original Location or Alternate Location. If you select Alternate Location, type the pathname of the location where you want the restored files to go.

NOTE: To restore to a computer other than the one containing the tape drive, you'll need to have a drive letter assigned to a network connection. This enables you to type the pathname of the destination location in this step. If you don't already have a network connection to the destination, create one using Windows Explorer or Network Neighborhood before you proceed to the next step. (See Chapter 11 for details on how to create a network connection.)

8. Click Next. In the Restore Wizard dialog box shown in Figure 13-3, click to select the desired file replacement behavior. Then click Start.

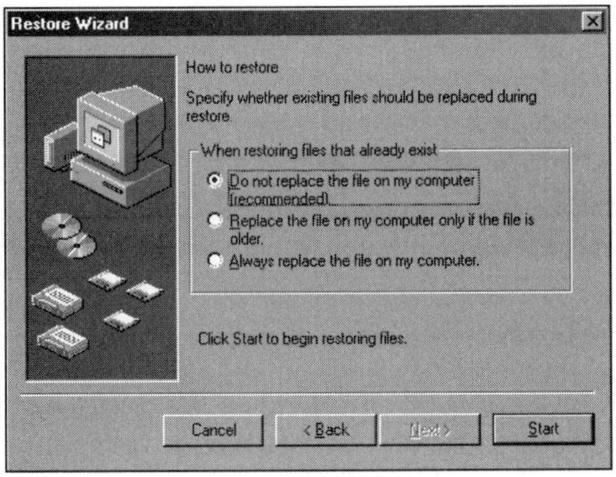

Figure 13-3: Backup enables you to specify whether you want to replace existing files during the restore process.

9. In the Media Required dialog box, click the media that contains the files you want to restore, and then click OK.
10. Backup builds a list of all the files it needs to restore, displaying the Selection Information dialog box to show its progress.
11. Backup starts the restore operation, and reports status in the Restore Progress dialog box. When the restore is done, click OK. The Report button appears in the Restore Progress dialog box. Click Report to view the results of the restore operation. (You can view the report again later in `\Program Files\Accessories\Backup\Reports\Report.txt`.)
12. Backup starts Notepad to let you view the report. When you're done, close Notepad and click OK in the Restore Progress dialog box.

Guarding Against Power Problems

If you can turn on a light switch, consider yourself a "power user" – electrical power, that is. The quality and consistency of your electrical power source depends on your geographic location, the number and quality of redundant systems maintained by your power company, the amount of growth and construction in your area, and many other factors. I've lived and worked in areas where no power problems occurred for months at a time, and also in areas where some sort of *power event* occurred every few hours. Even if you're in an area with relatively clean power, though, isolated power problems can still occur, generating potentially disastrous consequences.

Power Corrupts Absolutely

Power events can cause a wide range of problems – from short interruptions in service to loss of data to physical hardware damage. Your best insurance against these problems is to arm your computers and network equipment with UPS (uninterruptible power supply) devices. As I mentioned in Chapter 8, a UPS is an external power supply that keeps a computer or other equipment running during a power failure. If a power failure lasts very long, some UPS products can initiate an automatic shutdown of the computer, to avoid loss of data.

CAUTION: No UPS device is perfect, and some units fail. When this happens, you must revert to other techniques to restore lost data — your backups, for example. Don't rely on UPS protection as your only defense. It's just one of several components in your disaster recovery plan.

There are four classes of power problems a UPS can help you overcome.

POWER SURGES

Sometimes called a *spike*, a *power surge* is a brief power event that's characterized by a high voltage on the power line. Depending on a number of factors, this type of event can cause a computer to hang, can destroy the computer's power supply, or worse – motherboards, peripherals, and anything else attached to the computer can be permanently destroyed. Power surges can be caused by problems at the power company or by lightning strikes. UPS devices include power surge protection in addition to their standby power source features.

Power surges due to lightning can travel through telephone lines as well. If your computer is connected to both power and phone lines, and you only protect the electrical power source, your equipment is still vulnerable to power surge damage. Everything from your modem to your motherboard to your CPU is at risk. Try to find a UPS that also protects phone lines from power surges, and be sure to use this feature. Alternatively, install a separate surge protector on your phone lines.

Make sure all your computers and external network equipment (such as hubs, and so forth) are protected from power surges. Surges have been known to travel from an unprotected computer through network cabling to other computers – so don't leave your entire network exposed by leaving some equipment unprotected from this danger. Some UPSs also offer network cabling protection.

LOW VOLTAGE PROBLEMS

Low voltage problems, sometimes referred to as brownouts, are less dramatic but can be every bit as damaging. Operating computer equipment at a lower-than-expected voltage can also cause problems ranging from unexplained hangs to permanent hardware damage. Low voltage problems can last for milliseconds, or for days at a time.

For example, one evening I noticed over the course of several hours that lights were a little dimmer than normal and appliances were acting strangely. I called the power company to see what was up (or down, in this case). They came out and verified that the house was consistently getting only 90 volts, while the appliances were expecting 115 volts.

Most UPS devices condition the power coming in and provide a consistent voltage level to the attached devices. The computers attached to the UPS never know that the voltage dropped. If the voltage drops too low for too long, the UPS treats the condition as a power failure, and the battery kicks in to supply power to the attached equipment.

SHORT POWER FAILURES

In some areas, short power failures are very common. For example, in one city where I worked, the power company would switch grids at about 7:10 every morning, causing a power failure that lasted just under a second. Short power failures can cause unprotected computers to restart or hang – either way, this causes a potential loss of data due to improper shutdown. UPS devices are ideal in this environment, because they completely shield the attached equipment from the short power failures.

LONG POWER FAILURES

A power failure that lasts more than a few minutes needs to be handled differently. In this situation, you need to initiate a clean shutdown of the computer before the UPS battery power runs out. To accomplish this, the UPS needs to communicate with the computer to which it's attached – usually via a serial communications (COM) port. With the appropriate cable and UPS software installed on the computer, you can program the UPS to initiate a formal shutdown of the computer whenever a power failure lasts more than a specified number of minutes.

If the computer you're protecting is acting as a network server, some UPS software enables you to notify connected users of the impending server shutdown. You can set up the software to automatically send a message to the users, warning them to save their work and close their connections before the server shuts down. This feature prevents users from losing their data if the server shuts down while they have files open.

Employing UPS Devices

When you select a UPS device, add up the wattage from all the devices you plan to attach, and make sure the UPS is rated to handle the load. Plan to plug the devices that need to stay running into the UPS – at a minimum, this includes the system unit itself and the video monitor. If you have an external modem and you use it frequently, add it to the list of UPS-protected devices so you don't lose your connection when a power event occurs. Network hubs and any other external network devices are also good candidates for UPS protection, unless you want to drop network connections during power events.

Before plugging any device into a UPS, be sure to check both the UPS manual and the device's manual to verify that it's safe to combine the two. Never plug a laser printer into a UPS device, or you could permanently damage both devices. Copy machines and scanners don't do well if they're plugged into UPSs.

If the UPS offers a serial port connection, it's likely to require a special serial cable to communicate power status to the computer and control its shutdown. If you try to use a standard serial cable, you'll probably end up scratching your head when the UPS can't communicate. My advice: purchase the correct cable from the UPS manufacturer, unless they tell you exactly what other cable to use. Once you've connected everything together, install the UPS management software that came with the UPS device. Some manufacturers sell the software as an optional component.

The Windows NT operating system includes its own built-in UPS software that's compatible with many industry standard UPS devices. Check the NT Hardware Compatibility List for information on which UPS devices Windows NT supports.

Planning Your Redundancy Strategy

When a hard disk in a network server fails, you need three elements to recover from it – the most recent backup of the drive's contents, a new hard disk, and the time to install it and restore the data. Unfortunately, any changes made to the drive since the most recent backup will be lost, and you may not have a spare hard disk on hand to replace the failed drive. Even if you do, you still face the tasks of notifying users, shutting down the server, opening the computer case, removing the old drive, installing the new one, and then recovering the data.

In this section, I fill you in on ways to plan for and very quickly recover from hardware failures. First, you'll see how having the right spare components on hand can minimize the downtime of your computers. Then, you'll see how a set of hardware and software components can work together to make your network more *fault tolerant* – better able to recover automatically from specific hardware failures. You'll see how RAID technology, which I introduced in Chapter 7, can prevent data loss and even recover it automatically when a hard disk fails. Finally, you'll learn about a technique for establishing sets of redundant servers called clusters.

Preparing Standby Components

One of the easiest ways to recover quickly from a hardware component failure is to have spare components on hand and ready to install as they're needed. Unless you live right next door to an all-night computer components supplier, you should consider creating your own cache of components.

STORAGE COMPONENTS

As a rule of thumb, the more moving parts a device has, or the more sensitive it is to the environment, the more likely it is to fail. Therefore, hard disks are high on the list of required spare components because they frequently fail – due to mechanical failure and high temperatures. Make sure your spare hard disks are the correct type (IDE, SCSI-2, Ultra2 SCSI, and so forth) and size, so you won't be scrambling to change and configure disk controllers or install two drives to take the place of one larger drive. See Chapter 8 for a discussion of different hard disk technologies.

If your server's hard disks get a lot of use, it may be wise to install them in removable racks, so when you replace one (and you will), server downtime is minimized. With a removable rack, you don't need to open the computer case. Simply turn a key to power the drive down, pull out the old drive, push in the new one, and turn the key to power up the new drive. If the operating system or drivers support it, you may even be able to do this without shutting down the computer.

Hard disk adapters such as SCSI adapters don't fail very often, but when they do, the results can be devastating. In a server, for example, you might have many hard disks connected to a single adapter. My advice is to standardize as much as possible on a make and model of SCSI adapter, and then keep a spare one on hand just in case. Consider stocking spares for other server components that see a lot of use. For example, if you share several CD-ROM drives, it may be wise to have one or two spares, so that a drive failure will have minimal impact on users.

NETWORK COMPONENTS

Network adapters occasionally fail, either by ceasing to work or by chattering gibberish on the network. So, it's a good idea to have a few spare network adapters on hand. Likewise, network cables and connectors sometimes break from abuse or by accident. Keep a set of spare cables of varying lengths and a set of connectors handy for such emergencies. If you have network adapters installed in computers with incompatible system buses, keep a spare network adapter for each bus type on hand. See Chapter 8 for a discussion of system buses and network adapters.

It's debatable whether you need spare hubs in case of a network hub failure. Occasionally, a hub power supply will fail, so it's a good idea to have a spare. If you have a small test network where you try out newly installed network hardware and software, you might get away with using the hub from that environment as a spare, if you ever need one.

SYSTEM UNIT COMPONENTS

Power supplies are often an overlooked candidate for spare parts inventories. Power supplies can and do fail. Depending on the system unit's design, they aren't always easy to replace, either. Nor are they standard across different makes and models of system unit cabinets. Your best bet is to keep at least one spare power supply on hand, and know exactly how to install it if the need should arise.

Some system units include redundant AC power supplies. If one fails, the other takes over and enables you to swap out the failed power supply without having to shut down the computer. On high-end servers, redundant power supplies are becoming a must-have feature to minimize or even eliminate server downtime.

Cooling fans fail more frequently than any other system unit component. If the fan inside a power supply fails, the best approach is to replace the power supply and have the failed fan serviced. If fans mounted in the case or on the CPU fail, however, they're easily replaced. When fans fail, internal heat buildup can cause other components to start failing, so it's not a good idea to run too long without proper air circulation. Products are available that monitor internal temperature and sense whether fans are working or not.

TIP

Every networked organization is different, placing varied demands on your network. Learn from the hardware failures you experience by logging the problems, solutions, and any changes in policy that result. You may find that your organization requires a unique mix of redundant components on hand. If you can learn from your own history, you can approach an optimal inventory of what you need, when you need it.

Understanding RAID Technology

As I mentioned in Chapter 7, you can use a technology called *RAID* (*Redundant Arrays of Inexpensive Disks*) to store redundant copies of your data that can be quickly and automatically restored if one of your hard disks fails. In most cases, you can avoid losing any data as long as only one hardware component fails. (Believe it or not, I had the batteries in two separate cars in my garage fail on the same morning, so multiple component failures are possible, but they're less likely.)

RAID can be implemented in hardware, in software, or in a combination of both. Software RAID lets you use less expensive, off-the shelf components, but it imposes a slight performance penalty due to the extra work performed in software. Hardware RAID solutions don't have the software overhead, but they're also more expensive and often use nonstandard components. Once you invest in a hardware RAID product, you may be locked into that vendor for spare components and upgrades. Combinations of software and hardware RAID usually consist of hardware RAID devices with management software that can control the hardware configuration.

How you decide to implement a RAID solution depends on the capabilities of your operating system, your performance requirements, and the size of your budget. Windows 98 doesn't include any built-in support for software RAID, whereas Windows NT Workstation and Server products do. Hardware RAID devices are available for both operating systems, and require the installation of appropriate driver and management software.

TIP When shopping for a hardware RAID solution, look for additional features that can increase reliability and reduce downtime. For example, look for redundant, hot-swappable power supplies in the RAID cabinet. Hot-swappable hard disks are another key feature. Also, be sure that the product in which you invest is fully compatible with the operating system on which you intend to run it.

Whether you choose a hardware or software RAID solution, they all implement the same concepts – simultaneously writing redundant data to multiple hard disks, and allowing data recovery if a disk should fail. Different approaches to RAID have been assigned numbers, or levels, which loosely correlate to the level of fault tolerance they provide. In addition to fault tolerance, some RAID levels offer performance advantages over conventional storage. In the sections that follow, I review the most popular RAID levels available today.

RAID 0 – DISK STRIPING

RAID 0, also called *disk striping* or *Level 0 RAID*, breaks up data into equal-sized chunks and writes sequential chunks across multiple hard disks. Two or more hard disks are required to implement a RAID 0 array. The array appears to the operating system like one large disk whose total capacity equals the combined capacities of the individual hard disks in the array. For example, if you combine five 4GB hard disks in a RAID 0 array, the operating system sees it as one 20GB hard disk. Figure 13-4 illustrates a RAID 0 array containing five hard disks.

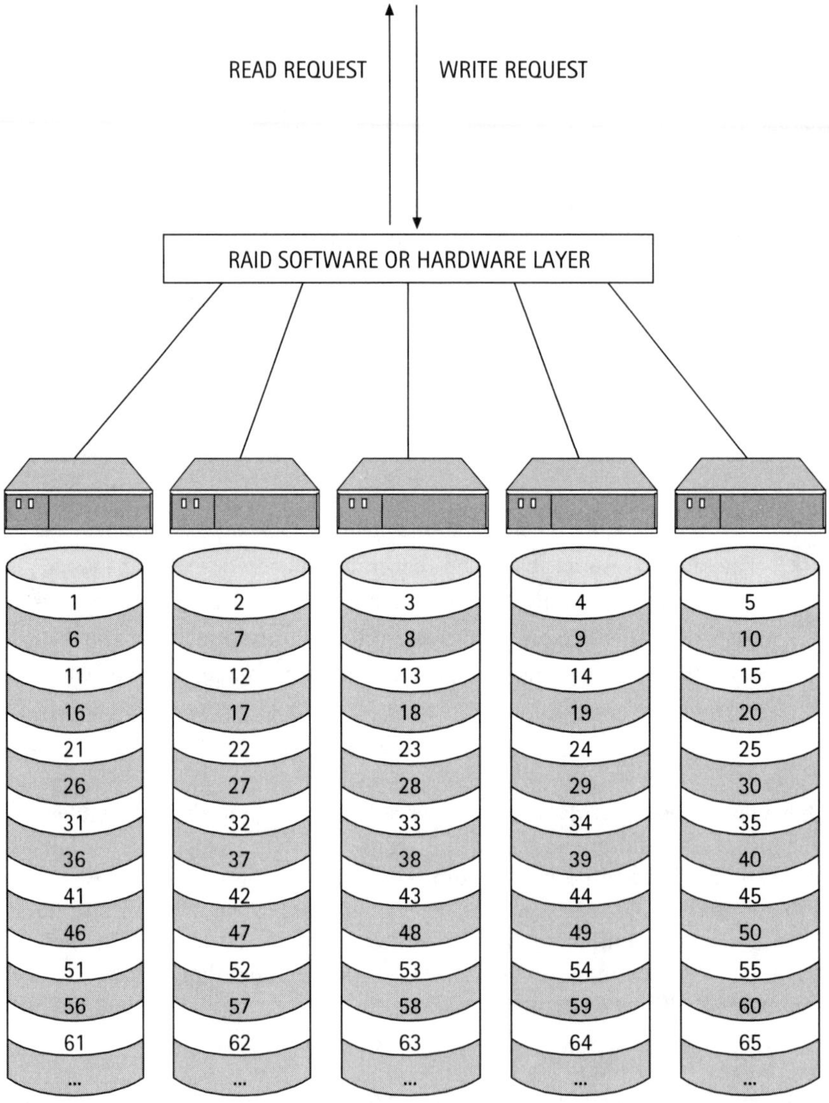

Figure 13-4: A RAID 0 disk array "stripes" sequential data chunks across multiple hard disks.

As you can see in Figure 13-4, data is spread out evenly across the five drives. The numbers represent sequential chunks of data, which generally range from 4K to 64K per chunk. If the chunks are 64K long, and an application writes 194K of data to the array, the first three 64K chunks are written across three separate disks, and the remaining 2K is written to a fourth disk. Similarly, data is read from multiple drives and is reassembled before being presented to the application.

RAID 0 offers absolutely no fault tolerance. (This is an easy fact to remember: "RAID zero offers zero fault tolerance.") No redundant information is written to any of the hard disks, so there's no way to recover any data if one of the disks fails. In fact, from a fault tolerance perspective, RAID 0 is more vulnerable to a disk failure than a standard disk configuration, because the data is scattered across multiple hard disks.

So why bother with RAID 0 at all? In a word, performance. By spreading the write and read operations equally across multiple hard disks, you can achieve much better performance than is possible by reading and writing a single hard disk. As long as the storage technology is capable of performing simultaneous I/O to multiple drives, as with SCSI technology, RAID 0 can offer a significant performance advantage.

CAUTION: Don't even think about using IDE, EIDE, or even Ultra DMA/33 technology hard disks in any RAID implementation. Because only one hard disk can be accessed at a time, you'll see horrible I/O performance in a disk array. Use SCSI or one of the emerging technologies discussed in Chapter 8.

RAID 0 has a home in applications where performance is vitally important, but reliability isn't absolutely critical. Because of its vulnerability to disk failures, it's not a good choice for network servers. For specialized workstation applications, however, it might be just the ticket. For example, if you need to digitize video information to your hard disk, a RAID 0 array can offer the performance needed to keep up with the stream of data without dropping frames. Likewise, if you run 3-D animation software, the time to render scenes to disk can be greatly reduced using this RAID scheme.

NOTE: Windows NT Workstation and Windows NT Server both support RAID 0 disk striping in software. You can connect up to 32 hard disks in a single RAID 0 array and manage it with the tools provided with the NT operating system.

I'll revisit the disk striping concept, because RAID 0 is closely related to RAID 5, which I discuss later in this chapter. RAID 5 uses almost the same approach as RAID 0, but adds redundant information that makes it fault tolerant.

RAID 1 – DISK MIRRORING

RAID 1, also called *disk mirroring* or *Level 1 RAID*, writes identical data to two separate hard disks. As you might guess, exactly two hard disks of identical size are required to implement a RAID 1 array. One drive acts as the *primary* hard disk, and the other acts as its *mirror*. The array appears to the operating system like a single hard disk whose total capacity equals the capacity of one of the hard disks. The data on the second hard disk is completely redundant. For example, if you place two 4GB hard disks in a RAID 1 array, the operating system sees it as one 4GB drive. Figure 13-5 illustrates a RAID 1 array combining two hard disks in a primary-mirror relationship.

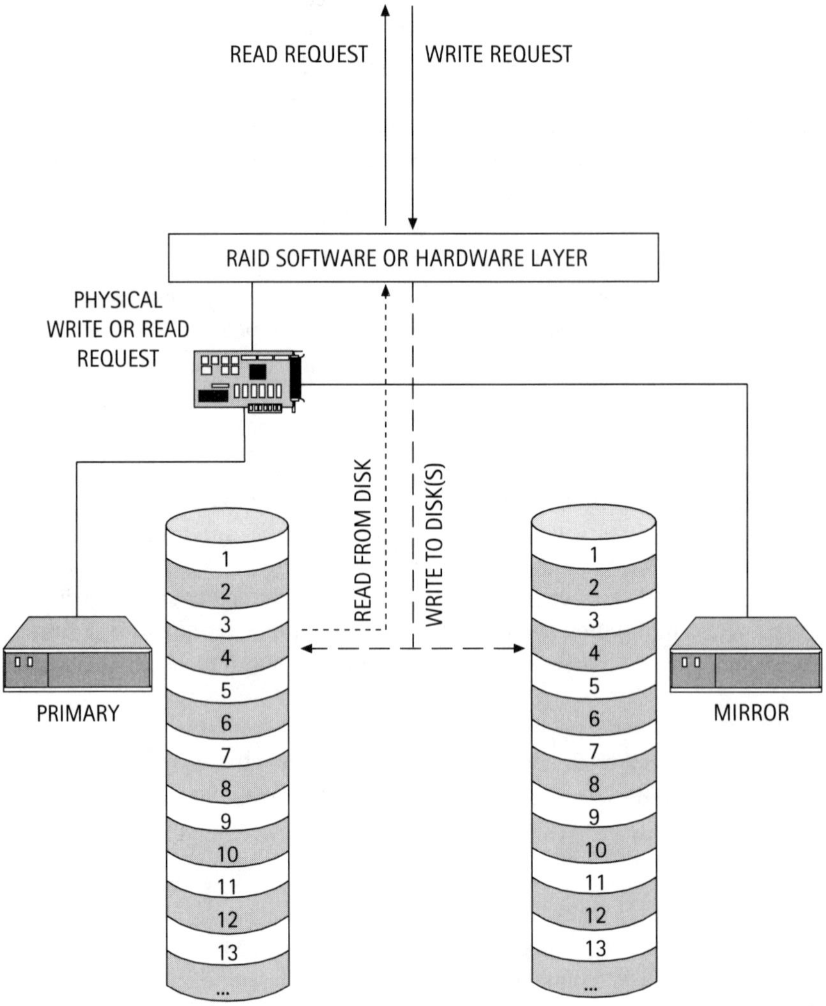

Figure 13-5: A RAID 1 disk array "mirrors" data between two hard disks, writing identical information to both drives.

As you can see in Figure 13-5, when data is written, the two hard disks are treated as equals – what one drive gets, the other gets as well. The primary-mirror relationship comes into play only during a read operation. When the operating system reads from the array, the hard disk playing the role of the primary delivers the data. The mirror doesn't get involved at all.

RAID 1 offers a high degree of fault tolerance by keeping a complete redundant copy of the primary hard disk. If the primary hard disk fails, the mirror immediately takes over to deliver data when read requests are made. Essentially, the mirror takes on the role of the primary, and the failed primary drive is ignored. When you replace a failed hard disk with a new one, the contents of the existing drive are automatically copied to the new drive, to get the two drives in sync. At that point, all writes are again performed to both hard disks, and the primary responds to all read requests.

NOTE: If the hard disk acting as the primary is in good health, but the mirror drive fails, the primary-mirror relationship is said to be *broken*. Until the mirror drive is replaced with working hardware, the primary hard disk handles all read and write requests by itself. When a new mirror drive is installed, all data from the primary is copied to the mirror, and the primary-mirror relationship is reestablished automatically. You don't even have to suffer through seven years of bad luck.

RAID 1 is a costly approach to fault tolerance, because it requires that you invest in exactly twice the amount of hard disk space you actually need for data. In RAID 1, you must chalk up 50 percent of your storage costs to redundant information. On the other hand, recovery is quick, painless, and automatic. The mirror takes over without skipping a beat, and without any decrease in performance. So, although RAID 1 is a relatively expensive approach to fault tolerance, it's ideal for use on network servers. Windows NT Server supports RAID 1 disk mirroring in software.

RAID 1 – DISK DUPLEXING

There's another flavor of RAID 1 that's worth mentioning. It's called *disk duplexing*. This technique is identical in every way to disk mirroring, except that a separate hard disk adapter is attached to each hard disk. Consider the disk mirroring illustration in Figure 13-5. What if the hard disk adapter failed? Both hard disks would be down for the count. Not only would you have no fault tolerance – you'd have no access to the data at all. The single disk adapter in disk mirroring is sometimes called a *single point of failure*. If that one component fails, the entire storage subsystem is out of business.

By introducing redundant hard disk adapters, RAID 1 removes the single point of failure issue. If one of the adapters fails, the other one can still operate. Figure 13-6 illustrates the concept of disk duplexing.

Disk duplexing is slightly more expensive than disk mirroring, because it requires the addition of a second hard disk adapter. However, the added level of fault tolerance is usually considered worth the extra expense, especially on a server.

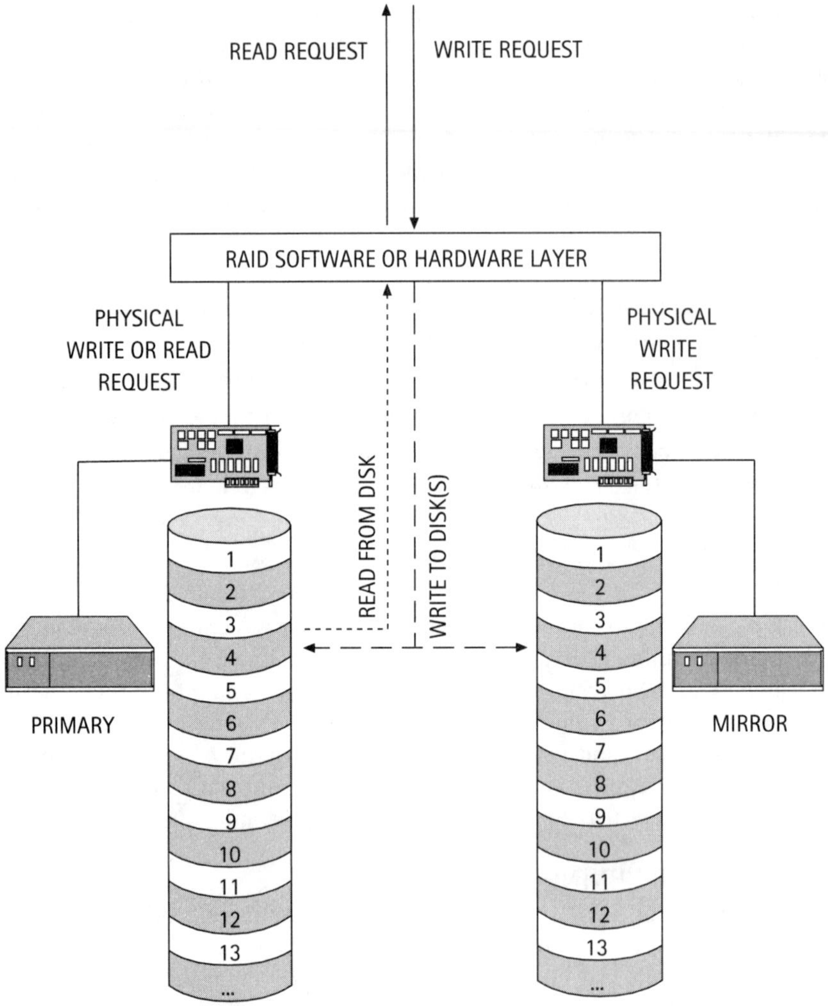

Figure 13-6: RAID 1 disk duplexing uses two separate hard disk adapters to allow survival if one of the adapters fails.

RAID 5 – DISK STRIPING WITH PARITY

RAID 5, also called *disk striping with parity, stripes with parity,* or simply *Level 5 RAID*, uses a concept similar to RAID 0, discussed earlier in this chapter. It adds the concept of *parity* to the basic disk striping scheme. In addition to spreading chunks of data evenly across multiple hard disks, a RAID 5 array also writes parity information that is used to reconstruct lost data if one of the hard disks fails. Because of the space consumed by this redundant information, the equivalent of one hard disk is unavailable for data storage. Therefore, three or more hard disks are required to implement a RAID 5 array.

The array appears to the operating system like one large disk whose total capacity equals the combined capacities of the individual hard disks in the array, minus one drive for parity information. For example, if you combine five 4GB hard disks in a RAID 5 array, the operating system sees it as one 16GB hard disk. Effectively, only four drives are available for data storage, and the fifth is used for parity information. Figure 13-7 illustrates a RAID 5 array containing five hard disks.

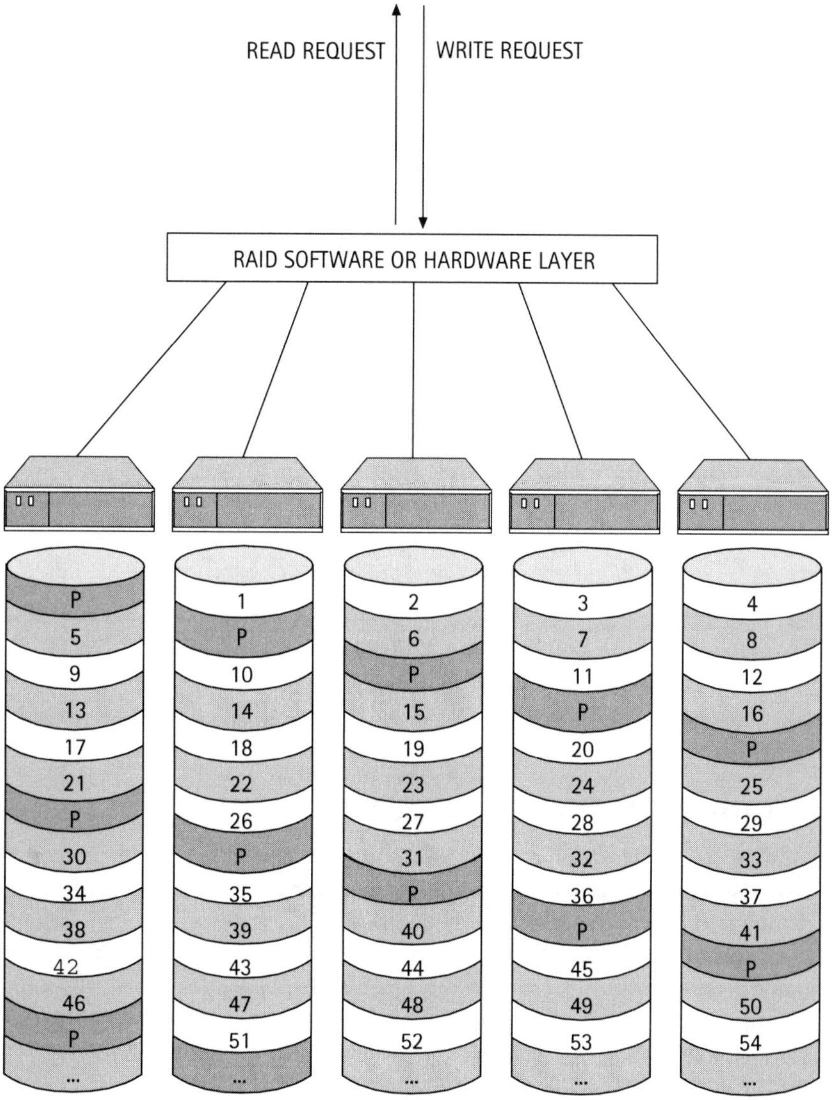

Figure 13-7: A RAID 5 disk array "stripes" sequential data chunks across multiple hard disks, and adds redundant parity information to allow data reconstruction.

As shown in Figure 13-7, data and parity information is spread out evenly across the five drives. The numbers represent sequential chunks of data, which usually range from 4K to 64K per chunk. Parity chunks are labeled with a "P." If the chunks are 64K long, and an application writes 194K of data to the array, the first three 64K chunks are written across three separate disks, and the remaining 2K is written to a fourth disk. Redundant parity information is written to a fifth disk. Similarly, data is read from multiple drives and is reassembled before being presented to the application. Notice that the parity information itself is spread across all drives in the array.

If all hard disks in the array are healthy, the parity information is never read. If one hard disk fails, however, the parity information is used to automatically reconstruct the missing data. This technique provides continuous availability of the data after a drive failure, but can significantly degrade performance due to the CPU overhead of data reconstruction. The array continues to function this way until the failed drive is replaced.

RAID 5 is one of the most popular approaches to fault tolerance. For very small arrays, it's more costly than mirroring, because it requires a minimum of three hard disks; as the number of drives in the array increases, however, the cost overhead per unit of storage decreases. In a RAID 5 array containing three hard disks, 33 percent is used up by parity information. In a five-drive array, 20 percent is consumed by parity. In a 32-drive array, just over 3 percent overhead is required for parity information. In contrast, 50 percent of all storage is used up by redundant data in a disk mirror (RAID 1) approach.

NOTE

Windows NT Workstation and Windows NT Server both support RAID 5 disk striping in software. You can connect between three and 32 hard disks in a single RAID 5 array, and manage it with the tools provided with the NT operating system.

Understanding Server Clustering

The concept of *server clustering* takes the redundancy idea one step further. A server cluster is a group of two or more independent servers that are interconnected with each other so they work together as a single unit. The individual servers are typically connected to each other on their own private network, which they use to communicate status and control information. If one server within the cluster fails, the others automatically take on the load of the failed server. To client computers, a server cluster appears to be one powerful server, and clients never know when one member of the cluster has failed.

Clusters offer both a high degree of fault tolerance and the potential for greatly improved performance. *Availability clustering* refers to the fault tolerance features, through which surviving servers transparently and automatically take over the work of a failed server in the cluster. (In a cluster containing two servers, one server is said to fail-over to the other when it fails.) *Scalability clustering* refers to the performance improvements achieved as work is distributed evenly across multiple servers in the cluster, and as performance is improved further by adding more servers to the cluster.

Some clusters include shared hard disk storage that's physically attached to more than one computer in the cluster. In this arrangement, the shared disk storage is typically some flavor of a hardware RAID product, and it's interconnected to the servers through SCSI or another storage technology architecture.

NOTE: Windows NT Server Enterprise Edition includes the Microsoft Cluster Server (MSCS), which at the time of writing enables you to connect two Windows NT Server computers together in a cluster.

Summary

In this chapter, you learned about the importance of disaster planning and recovery. You also learned about several key areas of disaster planning – backups, UPSs, RAID, and clustering. These technologies provide a foundation on which to build a solid disaster recovery plan for your organization. In Chapter 14, you'll learn techniques for optimizing and troubleshooting your network.

Chapter 14

Troubleshooting and Optimizing Your Network

IN THIS CHAPTER

- Troubleshooting your Windows 98 network
- Troubleshooting system components
- Optimizing your Windows 98 network

IN THIS CHAPTER, you'll learn several useful techniques and tools you can use to troubleshoot and optimize your Windows 98 network. First, I show you some general techniques for dealing with network problems. Then, you'll delve into network troubleshooting techniques at several different levels – from cabling and adapters to protocols and high-level operations. Next, you'll find out how to troubleshoot other components that can affect the operation of your network. Finally, I fill you in on the tools and techniques you'll need if you want to make your network perform at maximum efficiency. By the end of this chapter, you'll have a solid foundation of troubleshooting and optimization techniques to make the most of your network.

Troubleshooting Your Windows 98 Network

Troubleshooting network problems involves asking key questions and listening carefully to the answers. As a network administrator, you'll often be faced with a short, vague description of a problem. You'll need to know the right questions to ask and what clues to look for in the answers. In this section, I discuss this aspect of network troubleshooting by providing some key questions you should ask users who report problems.

TIP

Windows 98 includes a Network Troubleshooter that walks you through several of the most common causes of network problems. To use it, click Start → Help → Contents → Troubleshooting → Windows 98 Troubleshooters → Networking, and follow the prompts. The Network Troubleshooter doesn't solve every type of network problem, but it's a good online tool to help you think about what might be causing trouble. I recommend that you try it out on a couple of network problems. Over time, however, your expanded knowledge and experience will make it less useful to you.

Identify the Symptoms

Users often begin by reporting symptoms in vague terms, or in terms of how a problem affects the behavior of their application. It's then up to you to ask specific questions and listen to the answers to gather clues about the true nature, impact, and potential causes of the problem. In the initial problem report, a user may offer no more detail than the following:

- "The network is down. I'm going home."
- "The network is dog slow. What have you done to it?"
- "My computer is broken."
- "I can't print anything."
- "I can't connect to the server."
- "Nothing works at all. I hate computers."
- "I must have hit the wrong key again."

Smile if you will, but these are exactly the sorts of complaints that network administration help desks receive. It's your job to remain objective and calm, and take a systematic approach to finding and fixing the real problem.

TIP

Never dismiss a problem report completely. Even if you can't determine the cause after a reasonable amount of investigation, be sure to log the problem. It may surface again as a clue when you investigate a more serious network problem in the future.

The first step in this process is to ask enough questions to narrow down the exact set of symptoms. From those symptoms, you need to assess the level of impact the problem has on the user and on the business.

Prioritize the Problem

You and your network administration staff can't handle every problem immediately, unless your staff outnumbers your network users. Since that's pretty unlikely, your reality becomes one of prioritization. If a single user can't print, but can do everything else, that issue has less impact than if the sales database is inaccessible and users can't record customer orders. Likewise, if a user is having trouble playing audio CDs, while another is experiencing extremely slow network performance, your attention needs to turn to the issue that has the larger impact on business.

Users want their problems solved immediately, but this isn't realistic unless you have nothing else to do. Assign a priority to the problem, and set the users' expectations for how long it may be before the problem is addressed. You may not please everyone, but at least everyone will know what to expect.

Isolate the Problem

Your approach to isolating the problem as you search for a cause and solution will vary depending on the nature of the problem, your experience, and the degree of cooperation you receive from your users. As you ask specific questions with the intent of isolating the problem, you'll find that the priority of the problem may change based on new information you gather:

- Is only one user affected by the problem, are all users affected, or does the problem seem to affect a random set of users? The answer to this question helps you further assess the impact and determine how localized the problem is.
- Is there an easy way to demonstrate the problem consistently? Does the problem occur constantly, only at certain times of the day, only when certain other events occur, or at seemingly random intervals? Has this exact problem occurred before, or is it similar to another problem that has occurred before? These questions help you determine how easy it is to reproduce the symptoms, and to a degree, how difficult the problem will be to diagnose. Also, if a similar problem occurred before, you may have records of it in your network documentation.
- Does the computer operate normally when it's disconnected from the network, or does the problem persist even when the network isn't involved? This is a key question from a network administration perspective, because it helps you determine whether the problem lies primarily with a specific computer, or with the interaction between computers over the network.

Once you've isolated the problem, go back and reassess its priority, relative to other problems that need to be addressed. More often than not, the problem's priority will change after this round of questions.

Identify What Has Changed

At this point, you move into the diagnosis portion of the process. The first key question to ask is whether the feature ever worked correctly. If it never worked, you can start from scratch to install, properly configure, and diagnose the feature. If it did work before, the next task is an investigation of any software, hardware, or configuration changes made since the feature last worked. As a network administrator responsible for installing, configuring, and maintaining at least some of the network components, you may be able to answer some of these questions yourself:

- If the operating system or an application was upgraded since the feature last worked, consider trying to uninstall the upgrade and revert back to the old version. Was a new application added? If so, consider trying to uninstall it to determine if it's a contributing cause. Does the problem happen only with one application, or with all applications?
- Does the problem occur only with MS-DOS applications, and not with Windows applications? For example, is the user unable to print from MS-DOS applications, but Windows printing works fine? The problem may be caused by the need to capture a printer port that MS-DOS can use.
- Has any of the affected equipment been moved recently? Moving equipment can loosen cable connections, or in rare cases, damage the equipment. Have any of the cables been changed recently (including network, printer, modem, or telephone lines)? New cables could be bad cables, or may not be properly connected at both ends. If coax or SCSI cables were changed, they may not have been terminated properly.
- Has any new equipment been added to the network (for example, a network printer, hub, bridge, router, or computer node)? If so, was it cabled and configured properly? Does removing the new piece of equipment make the problem go away?
- Has anyone taken some action to "fix" the network? Well-meaning but untrained individuals sometimes take it upon themselves to help you out by trying to diagnose and fix network problems themselves. You may need to step in to undo the hardware and software configurations changes they make.

TIP

If you're making a series of hardware and software changes to the network, try to make only one change at a time, test it, and then make the next change. Likewise, if you've made several changes and something appears to have broken, undo each change you made until the problem disappears. This isn't always practical, but it's a useful habit to get into.

Know When and Where to Ask for Help

Don't let pride get in the way of knowing when to ask for assistance. These days, no one can keep all the details in their head. There are just too many issues to keep track of. Your best defense and your best shot at success come from knowing when and how to get the help you need. When you've exhausted the diagnosis possibilities you're aware of, switch into the mode of finding someone else who can help. If you take this approach, you'll waste less time.

Consult hardware and software documentation, manufacturers' technical support, vendors' technical support, and diagnostic research tools. As you gain knowledge and experience, you'll become an increasingly valuable technical resource for your organization – not because you know everything off the top of your head, but because you know exactly how to get the right answers. I discuss many of these technical resources in Appendix B.

Diagnosing Network Cable Problems

Problems with network cables account for a large percentage of network behavior glitches. You may have a cabling problem if one node is having problems seeing other nodes, and your attempts to search for other computers via Network Neighborhood result in errors. In a physical bus topology, network problems involving a few nodes or the entire network can also point to cabling problems. (To refresh your memory about topologies and types of network cabling, see Chapter 5.)

TIP

You can save yourself time — and grief, later on — by taking preventive steps during the installation of your network infrastructure. Invest in cable test equipment, or borrow it from your network installer. Test each length of cable before installation, and make sure the connectors on each end are wired properly. Verify that the cable is of the proper grade (for example, Category 5 UTP), and that it doesn't exceed the length restrictions imposed by the type of network you're installing. Don't use any cables or connectors that have the slightest hint of damage, even if they pass the electrical tests.

CHECK THE CONNECTION

Believe it or not, the most common problem encountered with network cabling is that the network cable isn't physically connected to the computer or device. This is the first thing you should check. You'll be amazed at how often this is the root of the problem.

Cables may sometimes fall out, be accidentally pulled out, or be disconnected by a well-meaning user. If you find a loose or damaged connection, replace the defective component to ensure a tight fit – or you'll be back to fix it again.

CHECK THE CABLE

If the connection appears to be in good shape, check the cable that attaches the computer to the network wall socket, hub, or adjacent computer. Look for breaks, frayed sections, and crimps or very sharp bends. Verify that the cable is the right type, and check to make sure it falls within the documented length restrictions.

In a physical star topology, if the cable between the hub and the computer (or device) is in good shape, try connecting it to a different port on the hub. Occasionally, a specific port can fail in an otherwise healthy hub. In a bus topology, check all the remaining cables between devices to verify that there are no breaks, frays, crimps, bends, or length problems anywhere along the bus.

CHECK FOR PROPER TERMINATION

In a bus topology, improper termination at one or both ends of the bus is a common problem. If both ends aren't terminated, the behavior can range from one or two nodes having problems seeing others, to the entire network being down. Make sure that appropriate terminators are installed at both ends of the bus, and that both terminators are properly attached to an electrical ground.

If the cable isn't properly terminated, the Windows 98 networking components may not start correctly during startup. Even if you discover the termination problem and fix it, you'll probably need to restart all the computers attached to the affected network segment before the network software components will properly recognize the network.

CHECK FOR INTERFERENCE

Sometimes, network cables are installed too close to sources of interference such as large electric motors, fans, air conditioning units, or large transformers. In other cases, these interference generators are installed after the network cabling is in place. Either way, if the interference is bad enough, it can cause a virtual break in the network connection. If you suspect this is a problem, try turning off these devices, test the network, and then turn the devices on again to verify that they're causing the problem. The solution to the problem requires either rerouting the network cables or moving the source of interference.

TIP

Make sure you supply a map of your network wiring to anyone who's planning to install large electrical equipment at your site. Doing this will help avoid interference with your network infrastructure. It's much easier to prevent these problems than to diagnose and fix them later.

Diagnosing Network Adapter Problems

Once you've ruled out cabling problems, the next step is to check the network adapter on the node that's experiencing problems. Your goal is to determine whether the adapter is functioning at all, and if it's configured correctly.

CHECK THE LEDS

Most modern network adapters include one or more status LEDs (light-emitting diodes), which provide visual cues about the adapter's behavior and health. Each manufacturer uses these LEDs in slightly different ways, so check your network adapter documentation for details on what each solid or flashing LED represents. Try removing the network cable and then reattaching it to the adapter to observe the LED behavior and compare it with the description in the manual.

CHECK THE HARDWARE CONFIGURATION

Use Device Manager (by clicking Start → Settings → Control Panel → System → Device Manager) to examine the network adapter's hardware settings. Make sure none of them conflict with other installed devices. Also, make sure the settings shown in Device Manager are identical to any manual switch or jumper settings you configured on the adapter before installing it.

Verify all the hardware resource settings for correctness and conflicts, including the IRQ, I/O address ranges, memory mapped address ranges, and DMA channels. If your motherboard has a built-in network adapter, check its settings as well to be sure it doesn't conflict with an adapter you've installed. (See Chapter 9 for more detailed information on finding and resolving hardware conflicts.)

CHECK THE CONNECTION TYPE

If the network adapter is a combo card (with more than one type of network cable connection), make sure the adapter is configured to use the connection that's actually being used to attach to your network. Attempting to use the wrong connector is the most common error made when installing and configuring combo cards.

This setting is specified either through a hardware switch or jumper, or through software via the Network application in Control Panel. If it's a software setting, click Start → Settings → Control Panel → Network → Configuration, click the network adapter, and then click Properties → Advanced. Some network adapters use other approaches to configure the connector. See your adapter documentation for details.

CHECK THE SPEED SETTING

If you have a dual-speed network adapter, check to make sure that the speed setting of the adapter matches your network. Typical Ethernet adapters can operate at either 10Mbps or 100Mbps, and most Token Ring adapters can run at either 4Mbps or 16Mbps. Some adapters automatically sense the prevailing network speed, but if they allow you to set the speed through hardware or software, be sure the speed is set correctly.

Even if all your network adapters are capable of 100Mbps operation, don't forget that you need hubs or switches capable of this speed, as well. Check the specifications of your hubs and other external devices before attempting to set adapter speeds.

CHECK THE DEVICE DRIVER

Even if the make and model of your network adapter matches the installed device driver, they may not work well together. For example, if the driver version is significantly newer than the hardware, the driver may not account for hardware bugs in the older hardware. The opposite problem can also occur – an old driver running on a newer adapter may not behave correctly. It's best to check with the manufacturer to verify that the driver you're using matches the hardware exactly – especially if you've downloaded an updated driver and you've installed it on an older adapter.

Diagnosing Network Communication Problems

Assuming that your network cabling, adapters, and device drivers are in good working order, the next steps involve checking the network software that runs on top of the drivers. You'll need to verify that your nodes are running the correct set of protocols, the correct client component (redirector), and the server component (file and printer sharing), if applicable.

If you can't see a recently added computer on the network by looking in Network Neighborhood on another node, you may need to wait for up to 36 minutes and look again. It can sometimes take this long for the node to show up in the list. Likewise, if you've removed a computer from the network, it may take up to 36 minutes for it to be removed from the Network Neighborhood list.

CHECK THE PROTOCOLS

To communicate with each other over the network, all nodes need to be running the same network protocol. You can run multiple protocols at the same time, but any two nodes that talk to each other need to be running the same protocol. Verify this through the Network application in Control Panel. Click Start → Settings → Control Panel → Network → Configuration, and make sure the protocol you should be running appears in the list and is bound to the network adapter.

> **NOTE:** If the desired network protocol shows up in the list, you know it's installed. But if it doesn't show up as being bound to the network adapter you're trying to troubleshoot, it's not going to work. (See Chapter 9 for a discussion of protocol bindings.)

NETWORK PRINTER PROTOCOL REQUIREMENTS If you're using network printers (directly attached to the network) or other specialized devices, verify that you're running the correct network protocol required by the device. For example, some older network printers require installation of the DLC protocol on all computers that communicate with the printer. Others require the TCP/IP protocol, and may require manual configuration of a unique IP address for the print server.

APPLICATION PROTOCOL REQUIREMENTS To operate correctly, some applications require that you use specific network protocols. For example, there's an accounting package that requires IPX/SPX protocol installation on all nodes that use the application. (There's no technical reason for this – the developers of the application require this configuration because it matches the environment in which they develop and test the product.) Moreover, an application may require changes to the default protocol configuration settings. Check with the application documentation for any special requirements, and configure the network protocol accordingly.

NAME AND ADDRESS CONFLICTS Check for computer name or address conflicts. Each computer requires a unique computer name, which is specified on the Identification tab of the Network application in Control Panel. If you're running TCP/IP and you've assigned a static IP address to each adapter, double-check that each IP address is indeed unique.

IPX/SPX FRAME TYPES If you're using the IPX/SPX protocol, make sure the frame type matches the frame types specified for all other computers on the network running IPX/SPX. (Just as protocols need to match on the network, so do the frame types.) In the Control Panel Network application, click the IPX/SPX protocol binding that interests you, click Properties → Advanced, and check the setting for the frame type. See Chapter 6 for a discussion of network protocols, and look at Chapter 9 for information on installing them on Windows 98.

CHECK THE CLIENT COMPONENT

In most cases, when you install a network adapter and protocol, Windows 98 will automatically install the redirector, Client for Microsoft Networks. If the client isn't automatically installed, go to the Configuration tab of the Network application in Control Panel. Click Add → Client → Add → Microsoft → Client for Microsoft Networks → OK. Then, configure the client component as discussed in Chapter 9.

> NOTE: If you're using the IPX/SPX protocol and you want to communicate with Novell NetWare servers, you'll need the Microsoft equivalent of the NetWare *requester*, called Client for NetWare Networks. Alternatively, you'll need Windows 98 client software supplied by Novell. Check with your NetWare server documentation for specific recommendations for configuring client computers in this environment.

CHECK THE SERVER COMPONENT

If the computer you're troubleshooting is supposed to act as a server, as well as a client, verify that the server software components are installed. On the Configuration tab of the Network application in Control Panel, look for an entry in the list of components called File and printer sharing for Microsoft Networks.

If the component isn't listed, click File and Print Sharing, click to select the appropriate file and printer sharing checkboxes, and then click OK. Restart the computer if prompted to do so. When Windows 98 restarts, you should see the component listed on the Configuration tab.

CHECK THE BINDINGS

After verifying that the correct protocols are running, that they're bound to the correct network adapter, and that the appropriate client and server components are installed, verify that the protocol is also bound to the client and server components. If the client (redirector) and server components aren't bound to the protocol, the node won't be able to communicate.

In the Network application in Control Panel, click the Configuration tab, click the appropriate protocol-adapter entry in the list, and click Properties. On the Bindings tab, verify that the Client for Microsoft Networks entry has a check mark next to it. If the computer is also acting as a server, verify that there's a check mark next to File and printer sharing for Microsoft Networks.

CHECK BASIC COMMUNICATION

If all the components appear to be configured correctly, you can attempt basic communication using the diagnostic software that comes with Windows 98. The most basic test uses the `NET DIAG` command. To use this utility, perform the following steps:

1. On one of your Windows 98 computers that has networking installed, click Start → Programs → MS-DOS Prompt.
2. At the command prompt, type **NET DIAG**.
3. If you have more than one network protocol running, specify the protocol you want to test by pressing the appropriate letter as prompted.
4. When you're asked if a diagnostic server exists, press the N key.
5. At this point, the computer plays the role of the diagnostic server, listening to the network for other computers to communicate with it. It will remain in this state until you press a key to stop it. For now, leave the diagnostic server running.
6. On a different computer that has networking installed (one you're trying to troubleshoot), click Start → Programs → MS-DOS Prompt.
7. At the command prompt, type **NET DIAG**.
8. If you have more than one network protocol running, specify the protocol you want to test by pressing the appropriate letter as prompted.
9. If the diagnostic server is located, this computer will take on the role of the client, and you'll see the following messages in the command prompt window:

```
The diagnostic server has been located on the network.

Communicating with diagnostic server. This may take several
seconds.

Validating reply from diagnostic server.

The diagnostic server's reply is correct.

This indicates that network information is being sent and
received properly.

The command was completed successfully.
```

On the diagnostic server, you should see a message indicating that the server replied to a workstation (client). The test passed. If these aren't the messages you see, proceed to Step 10.

10. If instead you see the question about whether a diagnostic server exists, this means the two computers weren't able to communicate. One of the network components discussed earlier in this chapter (cables, adapters, drivers, protocols, and so forth) is causing a communication problem.

If you're running the TCP/IP protocol on your network, Windows 98 includes additional tools that enable you to diagnose communication problems. Perform the following steps to verify basic TCP/IP communication:

1. On each Windows 98 computer you want to diagnose, click Start → Run, type **WINIPCFG**, and click OK.
2. Click More Info. Take note of the TCP/IP configuration information displayed. Specifically, copy down the IP address and the host name (which should be the same as the computer name).
3. Use the special loopback diagnostic IP address to check local TCP/IP operation. To do this, type **PING 127.0.0.1** at a command prompt and press ENTER. (*Loopback* refers to the capability to communicate locally without another computer being involved.)
4. The computer should respond with several successful attempts to send a packet to itself. At the same command prompt, type **PING** followed by the IP address you wrote down in Step 2, and then press Enter.
5. The computer should again respond with several successful attempts to send a packet to itself.
6. Repeat Steps 1 through 5 on another computer attached to the network. When you've done this, proceed to Step 7.
7. On the first computer you tested, type **PING** followed by the IP address of the second computer you tested, and then press Enter.
8. The first computer should respond with several successful attempts to send a packet to the remote (second) computer.
9. Repeat Steps 7 and 8 on other computers you want to test, using a known working IP address as the remote computer address.

If at any point the ping operation fails, verify the following items:

- Both computers involved in the communication have TCP/IP installed and are up and running.
- Both computers were restarted after TCP/IP was installed. This is required to properly configure TCP/IP.
- The IP addresses you used are correct.
- Both computers are physically connected to the network.

NOTE: Windows 98 includes the following TCP/IP diagnostic utilities: ping, ipconfig, netstat, nbstat, tracert, and arp. To find out more about the syntax and capabilities of these utilities, type the command at a command prompt, followed by **/?**.

Diagnosing Network Operation Problems

At this point, you've verified that all the lower-level components are installed and configured correctly, and you can perform basic communication tests. If you're still experiencing problems, there are a few other things you can check. In this section, I cover the most common problems that occur at the higher levels of networking.

CHECK THE SHAREPOINT NAME

If a shared resource doesn't appear in the list of shared resources on a specific server, verify that the server is running the server software component, and that the desired resources are in fact shared correctly. Then, check to make sure the sharepoint name assigned to the resource on the server is identical to the sharepoint name to which the client is attempting to connect. Also, verify that the client is pointing to the correct computer name assigned to the server. Occasionally, in a peer-to-peer network, users change their computer name without realizing the impact on other users connecting to their resources. See Chapter 11 for a discussion of sharing resources.

If the resource appears to be shared correctly, but doesn't show up in the list when a client node views the server's resources, check the sharepoint name on the Sharing tab of the Properties dialog box associated with the resource. (Right-click the drive, directory, or printer icon, and click Sharing.) If the sharepoint name ends with a dollar sign ($), it's invisible by definition. If the client attempts to map a drive to it explicitly, via Windows Explorer → Tools → Map Network Drive or via the NET command, it should be able to access the resource.

CHECK THE RESOURCE STATUS

Verify that the shared device is in fact attached to the server (or directly to the network), and that it's powered up. Also verify that the server is up and running. One of the most common problems encountered when attempting to print to a shared printer, for example, is that the printer isn't turned on, or that the printer cable is detached.

> **NOTE:** There are several reasons why a shared printer may not print when sent a job. The printer may be offline, out of paper, out of ink or toner, or powered off. It may be physically detached from the server or network, or it may be logically detached via a printer switchbox. The entire print queue may be paused, or specific documents may be paused. (Click Start → Settings → Printers, double-click the printer in question, and check the Pause Printing status on the Printer menu.) If it's a network printer, it may not be configured with the correct network type, protocol, or IP address.

If the resource is a hard disk or directory, verify that the hard disk is installed and powered up. If the drive is installed in a removable bay unit, it may be physically present but may not be powered up. If the resource is a CD-ROM drive or directory on a CD-ROM, verify that the appropriate CD-ROM disc is installed, that the drive door is closed, and that the disc can be accessed locally on the server computer. It's common for someone to inadvertently remove a CD-ROM from the drive, not realizing it's being shared by other users.

CHECK THE PRINTER DRIVER

If a print job comes out looking subtly incorrect or completely garbled, one of the most common causes is an incorrect printer driver. Windows 98 won't stop you from installing a driver that's incompatible with the printer you're using. The problem can occur with a locally attached printer or a printer on the network.

Make sure the driver on the print server and the driver on each client are all in sync with each other and with the printer itself. On the server, click Start → Settings → Printers. Right-click the shared printer you're investigating, and click Properties → Details. Under Print using the following driver, verify that the make and model of the driver matches the physical printer.

If it doesn't match, click New Driver and install the correct driver. Test the new driver by printing a test page from the General tab in the Properties dialog box. After making sure the server is using the correct driver and can print correctly, perform the same steps on the client computers. Verify printing from each client by printing a test page using the correct driver.

CHECK THE RESOURCE PERMISSIONS

If you've configured your network for user-level security, check the permissions on the shared resource to verify that the user who's trying to access the resource has the right to perform the desired operations. If the user account isn't listed in the resource's permissions list, check the user's membership in any groups that aren't listed. Refer to your Windows NT Server documentation for information on creating user accounts, groups, and assigning permission to specific shared resources.

Troubleshooting System Components

Earlier in this chapter, I gave you some pointers on troubleshooting your network adapter. However, many components within the computers on your network can have a significant impact on other users, if the components don't work as expected. In this section, I zoom in on a few key areas of network and non-network device issues that may have an impact on your network.

Handling Device Driver Problems

Windows 98 introduced a new driver model called WDM, or Windows Driver Model. It enables hardware manufacturers to write a single device driver that will work under both Windows 98 and Windows NT. This represents a huge cost savings, in terms of developing device drivers. Microsoft supplies a number of generic WDM drivers that can be used on a wide range of devices under both operating systems. However, some older devices can't operate with these generic WDM drivers. Here are some tips on diagnosing WDM-related problems:

- To determine whether a device is using a WDM driver, click Start → Settings → Control Panel → System → Device Manager, and double-click the device that interests you. Click the Driver tab, and then click Driver File Details. If the driver filename ends with a `.SYS` extension, it's a WDM driver.
- If you receive a fatal exception error after installing a WDM driver, it's likely that the device hardware just doesn't play well in the WDM sandbox. If the device came with its own driver diskette, install it instead. If the device didn't come with a driver, contact the device manufacturer to obtain a device driver that matches the hardware you have.
- If a device driver fails to load, due to a hardware or software conflict or for some other reason, run the Automatic Skip Driver utility. Click Start → Run, type ASD.EXE, and click OK. Click the load operation that failed, click Details, and follow the recommendations in the Enumerating Device Details dialog box.

TIP

If the computer is stalling during the Windows 98 startup sequence, and you have no idea what's causing the problem, use the Windows 98 boot log. Restart the computer, press Ctrl (or F8 on some computers) when the Starting Windows 98 message first appears, and select Logged (\BOOTLOG.TXT) from the menu. Then examine the \BOOTLOG.TXT file to determine where the problem occurred.

Handling Power Management Problems

If you set up a Windows 98 computer to turn off specific devices after periods of idleness, and the devices don't turn off when you expect them to, there are a few possible causes:

- The system BIOS settings may be overriding the Windows 98 settings, either by disabling power management or by imposing a different set of timeout values.
- An application may be periodically accessing the device, preventing the power-down timer from expiring. To determine whether this is the cause, press Ctrl+Alt+Del, and close all tasks listed in the Close Program dialog box except for the tasks labeled Explorer and Systray. Wait for the specified power-down period. If the device powers down, this means one of the previously running tasks was accessing the device.
- If the devices power down when you don't expect them to (for example, when the timers in Windows 98 are set to Never), the BIOS is probably the culprit. In the BIOS, turn off power management, and then contact your BIOS or motherboard manufacturer for an updated BIOS that doesn't override Windows 98 settings.

If the computer stops responding after one if its devices powers down automatically, you're probably dealing with hardware that doesn't fully support Windows 98 power management functions. Try to narrow down which component is causing the problem (CPU, hard disk, or video display) by setting two of the three timers to Never, and letting the third device power down. When you've figured out which component doesn't like power management, set its timer to Never and contact your hardware manufacturer for further information.

CAUTION

Your best bet is to disable CPU and hard disk power management on any computer that's acting as a server (peer server or dedicated server). If something goes wrong with the power management function, the PC may not awaken when it's needed by a network client. Even if it does wake up, the client will have a long wait before receiving a response. The latter condition can potentially cause timeouts, retries, increased network traffic, and lower network performance.

Handling Hard Disk Problems

All sorts of odd things can happen when you start to run low on hard disk space. Depending on the application or utility you're running, and the action it's trying to perform, it might hang, crash, or report an error.

FREEING HARD DISK SPACE

If you're lucky enough to get an error message that somehow implies you're out of disk space, try one or more of the following to regain space:

- Empty the Recycle Bin to free up space occupied by deleted files.
- Verify that Windows 98 has control over where it's placing the swap file by clicking Start → Settings → Control Panel → System → Performance → Virtual Memory. Be sure to click the option labeled Let Windows manage my virtual memory settings.
- Run Disk Defragmenter (click Start → Programs → Accessories → System Tools → Disk Defragmenter) to reclaim disk space occupied by disk fragmentation.

CHECKING THE TEMP VARIABLE

Some applications assume that the TEMP environment variable is always set to a valid path name. If it isn't, the application may act as though you're out of disk space. Verify that the TEMP variable is set to a valid path name by clicking Start → Programs → MS-DOS Prompt and then typing **SET**. If an application tries writing to the TEMP path, and you truly are running out of hard disk space, consider pointing the TEMP variable to another drive that contains more free space.

DEALING WITH LOST HARD DISK SPACE

To detect and recover lost hard disk space, perform the following steps:

1. Restart Windows 98, press Ctrl (or F8 on some computers) as soon as the Starting Windows 98 message appears, and select Safe Mode Command Prompt Only from the menu.
2. In the C:\WINDOWS\COMMAND directory, run SCANDISK and follow the prompts. (If you installed Windows 98 in a directory other than C:\WINDOWS, substitute that directory.)

Never run a disk utility on Windows 98 that isn't specifically designed for Windows 98. For example, don't run utilities that came with MS-DOS, Windows 3.1, or Windows 95. Because of differences in file naming and file system structures, you could end up corrupting files on your hard disk and rendering the computer unbootable.

DEALING WITH INCOMPATIBLE SYSTEM FILES

If you experience problems after installing an application, it may be caused by installation of a system file that's either obsolete or incompatible with the version of Windows 98 you're running. On the Tools menu of the System Information utility, click System File Checker → Scan for altered files → Start. You can then use the same utility to replace corrupted files from your Windows 98 CD-ROM.

Handling Network Problems

A number of tools are available that enable you to perform preventive and diagnostic analysis of your network components. They range from pure hardware tools such as cable testers to software tools that let you view packets on the network. In this section, I discuss some of the options available to you.

NETWORK CABLE TESTERS

The simplest type of tool is a cable tester, which lets you test a network cable by verifying electrical continuity, checking for shorts, and ensuring proper resistance. Some cable testers support different types of cabling, including coax, UTP, and even fiber-optic. Some units require that you have both ends of the cable close by, whereas others let you test cable runs from one room to the next using a transmitter that communicates between two tester devices. As you might imagine, the two-piece tester approach is much more useful in real-world situations, but it's more expensive.

The next step up in network cable testing is the *time-domain reflectometer*, or *TDR*. This device sends a sonar-like signal along a network cable, and can detect major and minor imperfections that could affect network performance. A TDR can usually find a problem within a few feet of the actual cable problem, cutting way down on the time you need to spend searching in walls, floors, and plenum areas.

Moving up the chain of testing intelligence, you can use more advanced cable testers that actually send and receive data over the cable and analyze the results. They generally operate at layers 2 and 3 of the OSI reference model, and can also be used to test network adapters. (See Chapter 6 for a discussion of the OSI reference model.)

NETWORK ANALYZERS

Network analyzers, sometimes called *protocol analyzers* or *sniffers*, consist of a combination of hardware and software that can perform network traffic analysis in real-time. Most of these products can capture packets, decode and display them, and create and transmit packets to other nodes. A sniffer can look inside network transmissions at the byte level to help diagnose transmission problems, failing network adapters, and other conditions. Some can produce detailed traffic reports and maps of the network they're sniffing. You can use this information to take specific actions that improve your network's performance and reliability. Sniffers from Network General, HP Network Advisor, and Novell LANalyzer are examples of popular sniffer products in use today.

MICROSOFT NETWORK MONITOR

Microsoft Network Monitor is a software implementation of a sniffer. (The original code name for Network Monitor was "Bloodhound," because it was such a great sniffer.) Microsoft Systems Management Server (SMS) includes the full version of Network Monitor, whereas Windows NT Server includes a slightly stripped-down version of it. Windows 98 doesn't include Network Monitor, but the Windows 98 Resource Kit does include support files that enable you to view a Windows 98 computer's network traffic through Network Monitor.

To capture network traffic to and from a Windows 98 computer using Network Monitor, you need to install the Network Monitor Agent and Network Monitor Protocol. Doing this essentially grants permission to Network Monitor to capture and analyze network traffic – sort of a consensual form of eavesdropping. It also provides the required client software needed to communicate control information between Network Monitor and the computer it's monitoring.

NOTE: Effective use of Network Monitor requires some knowledge of the internals of the network protocols you're running. Analyzing the specific contents of network packets is beyond the scope of this book. Network Monitor's online help provides pointers to references on protocol analysis. In Network Monitor, click Help → Contents, double-click Reference, and double-click Reference Guide to Books on Networking. Also, take a look at Appendix B for additional reference pointers.

Here's how to install the Network Monitor Agent and Network Monitor Protocol:

1. Click Start → Settings → Control Panel, and double-click Network.
2. Click Configuration → Add → Service → Add → Have Disk.
3. In the Install From Disk dialog box, type the path to the Windows 98 Network Monitor components. This path is normally \NETADMIN\NETMON on your Windows 98 Resource Kit CD-ROM or \TOOLS\RESKIT\NETADMIN\NETMON on your Windows 98 CD-ROM. (The path may vary depending on the version of CD-ROM you have.)

4. Click OK. Then, in the Select Network Service dialog box, click Microsoft Network Monitor Agent, and click OK.
5. In the Network dialog box, click OK and restart the computer as prompted.

In the Configuration tab in the Control Panel Network application, you should see Microsoft Network Monitor Agent listed as a service, and Microsoft Network Monitor Driver bound as a protocol to your network adapter. Once these components are installed, you can use Network Monitor from another computer to monitor the traffic on this computer. Repeat these steps for each computer you want Network Monitor to analyze. (See your Network Monitor documentation for additional information on configuring these components.)

Optimizing Your Windows 98 Network

If you took my advice in Chapter 8 and you selected hardware that will provide the best performance for the computers on your network, you've won a large part of the performance battle. However, the way in which you and your users put each computer to use will vary widely, and there's no magic formula for an optimal configuration that applies to all situations.

Optimizing the individual nodes on the network goes a long way toward optimizing the entire network, but it isn't the complete solution. Depending on traffic patterns on your network, there are concrete steps you can take to make your network run more efficiently – independent of optimizing the nodes themselves. In this section, I fill you in on the tools and techniques you can use to measure performance and optimize your network for maximum efficiency.

Performance optimization is utterly useless without reliability optimization. Don't cut corners or press equipment beyond its specifications in order to squeeze extra performance out of your equipment. For example, don't run CPUs at a higher speed than they're intended to go (a practice called *overclocking*). Also, don't use lower-grade network cabling or hubs to implement a high-speed network. If you do, you'll spend your time just trying to make everything work, rather than trying to make everything work efficiently.

Introducing System Monitor

Windows 98 includes a powerful performance monitoring utility called System Monitor. You can use it to track various aspects of the performance of a local or remote computer, create performance charts, and log performance information to a text file.

You can use System Monitor to take baseline performance measurements when the computer or network appear to be operating normally. In fact, to make the best use of this tool, you need to run it frequently in a variety of situations so you become familiar with what typical situations look like. As you change configurations, upgrade hardware and software, and take other steps to optimize performance, you can measure performance before and after the changes to determine the effect of your efforts. In addition, System Monitor offers a great way to identify system bottlenecks and candidates for performance improvement upgrades.

XREF

If you want to use System Monitor to track performance on a remote computer over the network, you need set up remote administration. See the section in Chapter 12 called "Administering Remotely" for instructions on how to enable this feature.

CREATING PERFORMANCE CHARTS

To create a real-time performance chart using System Monitor, follow these steps:

1. Click Start → Programs → Accessories → System Tools → System Monitor. By default, the System Monitor chart is configured to show the percentage of CPU usage, which is updated every five seconds. Watch the chart for a bit, while performing various tasks, to see the effect of those tasks on the percentage of CPU bandwidth used. For example, Figure 15-1 shows the percentage of CPU usage while the computer is idle, while it's running a 3-D screen saver, and while it's launching various applications.
2. Click Edit → Add Item. Under Category, click the category of the item you want to monitor. The list of categories that appears will vary depending on the computer's configuration.
3. Under Item, click the item you want to monitor. If you want an explanation of the item, click Explain.
4. Select one or more items from the list. If you want to select more than one item, press Ctrl while clicking to select the items.

5. When you've finished selecting items, click OK. The new item(s) will appear in the chart as soon as it's updated (typically, in five seconds).
6. To change the frequency of chart updates, click Options → Chart, move the slider to adjust the update interval, and click OK.
7. To change the appearance of a charted item, click Edit → Edit Item, click the item, and click OK.
8. Under Color, click Change, click the color you want, and click OK.
9. Under Scale, click Automatic if you want System Monitor to choose an appropriate vertical scale for the item in the chart. Otherwise, click Fixed and type the maximum value to be used on the vertical scale.
10. When you're done making changes to an item, click OK. If you want to change the appearance of other charted items, go back to Step 7. Figure 15-2 contains an example of a performance chart tracking six items.

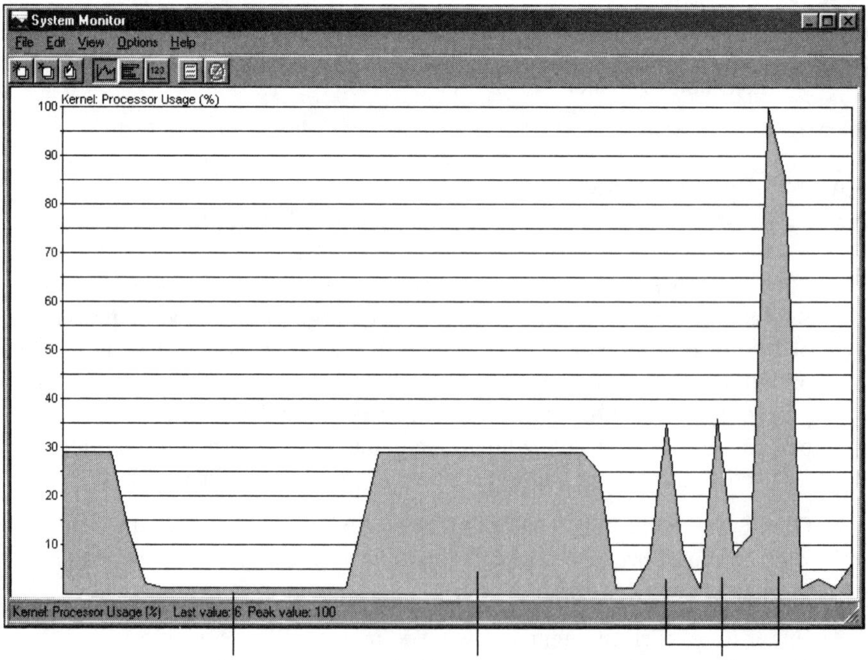

Figure 15-1: System Monitor enables you to chart specific performance items over time — in this case, the percentage of CPU usage.

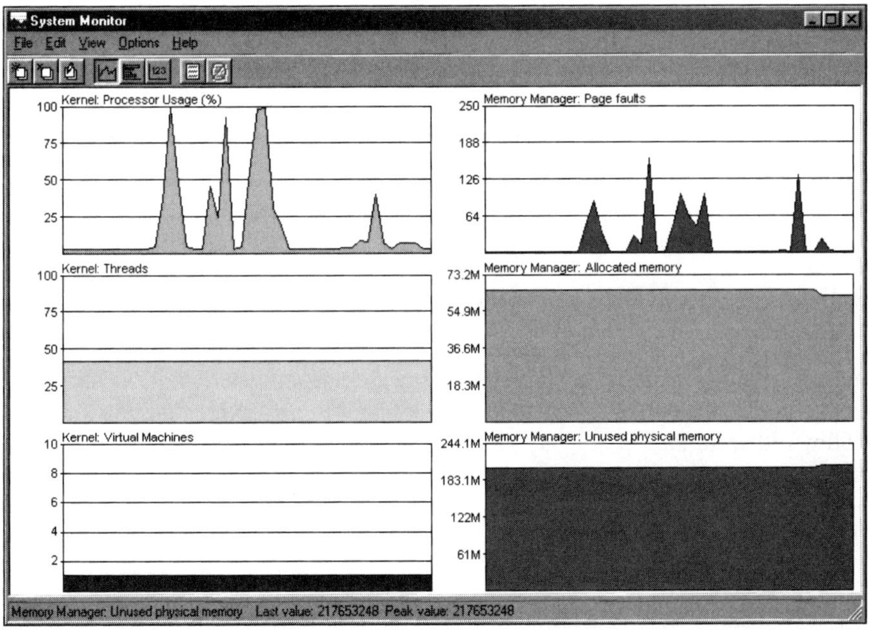

Figure 15-2: System Monitor can track multiple performance items simultaneously.

CREATING PERFORMANCE LOGS

System Monitor can generate a comma-delimited log file of performance data, which you can use as input to spreadsheets, analysis software, and so forth. To create a System Monitor log file, perform the following steps:

1. Specify the set of items you want logged by adding items to the chart in System Monitor, as described in the previous section.
2. Click Options → Chart, move the slider to adjust the update interval to 15 seconds or more, and click OK.

Be careful not to make the update interval so small that the act of monitoring significantly affects the performance numbers and uses up your hard disk space. This situation is similar to the electron microscope that affects the behavior of the particles it's trying to observe. A performance logging operation can generate a huge amount of data and disk I/O. In most cases, an update interval of 15 seconds is just fine.

3. Click File → Start Logging.

4. In the Save As dialog box, specify the filename and location where you want the data stored, and click Save. The default filename is SYSMON.LOG.
5. When you've collected the data you want, click File → Stop Logging.
6. Use Notepad or WordPad to view the resulting file, or import it into another application (such as Excel) for further analysis.

Managing System Performance

You can track dozens of items using System Monitor. It's a good idea to look through each item to understand what it's measuring and see what a chart of it looks like under normal load. But there are so many items – where do you start? In the following sections, I point out some key items that will help you evaluate the most common performance issues. Along the way, I also show you some other techniques for optimizing performance in specific areas of the system.

> CAUTION: Don't waste time taking performance measurements on a computer that's idle. Make sure you monitor the computer under what you consider to be its typical load. Only then will the numbers be meaningful as you investigate where the bottlenecks are and how to overcome them.

MANAGING CPU PERFORMANCE

If a CPU performance bottleneck exists, investing in a faster CPU and faster motherboard is a straightforward solution. Before you spend money this way, however, it's important to find out if a CPU bottleneck really exists. If it doesn't, the money might be more effectively spent on improving performance in another area of the system.

MEASURING PROCESSOR USAGE As you may have already guessed, the Kernel: Processor Usage (%) item is the key to measuring CPU bottlenecks. Just viewing a few common situations can speak volumes about how much bandwidth a particular task requires. For example, notice in Figure 15-1 that the 3-D screen saver on this particular computer takes nearly 30 percent of the CPU bandwidth. If the CPU is needed for other background tasks (for example, running the server portion of a client-server application), the screen saver's drain on the CPU can be devastating to performance. That's why I offered the advice in Chapter 8 about avoiding complex screen savers – especially on computers acting as servers.

The red flag to watch for (or cyan flag, depending on which chart colors you've selected) is a consistent level near 100 percent. This can actually mean one of two things: either you truly have a CPU bottleneck, or you're running a set of applications that are so CPU-intensive that they'll soak up all the CPU power they can get, no matter how fast your processor is.

INCREASING PROCESSOR SPEED If you find that you do have a CPU bottleneck, the best approach is to end up with a motherboard than runs no slower than 100MHz and a Pentium II processor that's compatible with it. Large Level 1 and Level 2 caches, fast bus speed, and high clock speed all contribute to solving a CPU bandwidth problem.

USING MULTIPLE SERVERS If increasing the speed of the hardware isn't an option for you, but you have multiple servers available, consider spreading the workload across multiple servers. For example, if you have a server that's CPU-bound when it's acting as a database server, application server, e-mail server, file server, and print server, try moving one of the CPU-bound tasks to a different computer. In this case, the database, application, or e-mail server components are likely candidates.

NOTE: If your CPU bandwidth problem is severe, and the application you're running is designed to run on Windows NT as well, check with the application manufacturer to determine whether it can take advantage of multiple CPUs. If it can, consider moving the application to a multiprocessor computer running Windows NT. Before you invest in a second processor, though, it's a good idea to use NT's Performance Monitor to verify that the application is CPU-bound on NT as well. If it is, it may benefit from a second (or third, or fourth) CPU.

MANAGING MEMORY PERFORMANCE

A key indicator of memory usage is the Memory Manager: Page Faults item, which measures the number of page faults per second. (A *page fault* occurs when a needed chunk, or *page*, of memory isn't in physical RAM, but must be retrieved from the hard disk.) In a computer with enough physical RAM for the load you're placing on it, the number should hover below five page faults per second, with occasional peaks as you launch applications, for example. If the number stays consistently at five or above, you may have found a memory bottleneck. If the number is consistently at ten or more, the computer is in serious need of more physical RAM. It's probably spending more time paging than performing useful work.

If the items Memory Manager: Discards and Memory Manager: Page-outs are consistently high (ten or more), this means Windows 98 is spending a lot of time making room in RAM by throwing things out of memory. The Discards item measures the number of pages thrown away each second, while the Page-outs item measures the number of pages written to disk each second. Consistently high numbers here usually accompany a high page fault rate. (The Memory Manager: Page-ins item doesn't provide useful performance information, because everything that's ever loaded into memory must be paged in, even if there's plenty of RAM available.)

ADDING MORE RAM The best approach to solving this problem is to add more physical RAM to the computer. If your computer is consistently taking between five and ten or more page faults per second, it's most definitely time to add more RAM to the computer. (See Chapter 8 for a discussion of RAM types and sizes.) Keep in mind that the optimal RAM size should be based on actual performance analysis under the load you're placing on the computer – not on an arbitrary size recommendation.

NOTE: Adding more RAM is now the cheapest and easiest way to improve performance in other areas as well. For example, hard disk I/O performance can benefit by using larger amounts of memory to cache blocks of disk data. Network I/O performance can be similarly affected, again due to larger data cache areas in RAM. So, when you consider adding RAM, keep in mind that you may be improving performance in other areas as well. I discuss disk and network performance later in this chapter.

TRACKING MEMORY LEAKS If an application (or Windows 98, for that matter) allocates memory and then never frees it, system performance can suffer. This condition is known as a *memory leak*. Memory leaks are somewhat difficult to trace, and the solution once you find a leak isn't always straightforward.

There are a couple of ways to detect memory leaks. One approach is to monitor Memory Manager: Allocated Memory and Memory Manager: Disk Cache Size. To see how much memory the applications and the operating system are actually using, you need to subtract Allocated Memory from Disk Cache Size. If the allocated memory changes during a period of no activity on the computer, it means the disk cache is resizing itself. Therefore, it's important to subtract out the disk cache, or your measurements will be meaningless.

Look for relatively large numbers in this value that tend to grow over a period of time. The growth trend is the key to catching this type of problem. Likewise, you can monitor Kernel: Threads to see if an application is starting threads and never reclaiming their resources. This is a common form of memory leak bug in multithreaded applications. On the flip side, you can watch for decreasing trends in Memory Manager: Unused Physical Memory.

TIP

When you're looking for longer-term trends in performance measurement, it's a good idea to set the update interval to a much longer period. You'll have less data to sift through, and it becomes much easier to spot trends. System Monitor lets you crank up the update interval as high as one hour between samples.

The solution to a memory leak problem isn't typically cut-and-dried. Some memory leaks can be cured temporarily by exiting the offending application and restarting it. Of course, for critical server applications, this solution is far from acceptable. The only complete solution is to fix the bug in the application that's causing the memory leak, and that may mean waiting for an upgrade or patch from the software manufacturer.

NOTE

This is one class of problem that won't go away if you throw more or faster hardware at it. In fact, using faster hardware components can actually cause the problem to accelerate.

The Leaking Locks

Another type of memory leak that can affect performance involves *locked memory,* which is memory that cannot be paged out to disk. A device driver or application can lock a chunk of memory, and it's guaranteed never to be paged out until the memory is unlocked. This approach can improve performance of the application, but can significantly degrade performance of the computer overall.

To examine this problem, use System Monitor to view both Memory Manager: Locked Memory and Memory Manager: Allocated Memory. If the former consistently represents a large percentage of the latter, say greater than 75 percent, the locked memory may be degrading the performance of the rest of the system. The driver or application that locks memory may be locking it unnecessarily, or may be locking it for too long a time period.

MANAGING VIRTUAL MEMORY SWAPPING Windows 98 is a virtual memory operating system; it keeps some memory contents in physical RAM and moves the rest to the hard disk. It pulls in chunks (pages) of memory as needed, and throws out pages that aren't needed right away. Where does Windows 98 store the contents of virtual memory? It uses a file referred to as the *virtual memory swap file, paging file*, or simply *swap file*. Windows 98 grows and shrinks the swap file dynamically, depending on how much virtual memory is required for the tasks at hand.

Here are the most significant actions you can take to optimize the Windows 98 swap file:

- Ensure that the hard disk on which the swap file resides has plenty of free space, so the file can grow as needed. If the hard disk doesn't have much room to spare, consider moving the swap file to another hard disk.
- Don't place the swap file on a compressed drive. Even though Windows 98 doesn't compress this file, the added overhead of accessing it on a compressed drive can degrade performance.
- If you have multiple physical hard disks, place the swap file on the drive with the highest performance, unless that drive is already heavily used for other things.

Don't confuse multiple physical hard disks with multiple partitions on a single hard disk. One of the worst virtual memory performance mistakes you can make is placing the swap file on a hard disk partition when the other partitions on the same hard disk are heavily used. In this situation, the hard disk heads have to move wildly between partitions to satisfy all the I/O requests. This configuration can have a huge negative impact on disk I/O performance and overall system performance.

- If you have multiple physical hard disks, place the swap file on the drive with the least activity, unless that drive is a slow performer.

To specify a different hard disk destination for the swap file, click Start → Settings → Control Panel, double-click System, and click Performance → Virtual Memory. Click to select the option labeled Let me specify my own virtual memory settings. In the Hard Disk box, click the hard disk where you want the swap file to reside, and click OK → Close. Restart the computer as prompted.

CAUTION

Never disable virtual memory, even though the System application in Control Panel lets you do this. You may end up with a computer that won't boot to Windows 98 anymore. The only time you should consider disabling virtual memory is when a product support engineer tells you to do so.

MANAGING FILE I/O PERFORMANCE

System Monitor provides performance data for basic hard disk I/O operations and other useful data. However, there's no clear way to identify disk performance bottlenecks using System Monitor. The performance measurements it offers are great for comparative analysis – comparing disk I/O performance before and after you install a faster hard disk or SCSI adapter, for example. The two categories System Monitor provides are File System and Disk Cache. Because the hard disk cache is dynamic in Windows 98, there's not much you can do to control it; however, you can tune disk caching based on the role your computer plays on the network. See the section titled "Optimizing hard disk performance" later in this chapter.

If you carefully measure one disk-intensive application or operation at a time, you can combine the file system performance items with CPU utilization to draw conclusions about the impact of disk I/O on the system's performance. For example, you can discover that IDE hard disks use up more CPU bandwidth than SCSI disks, and that faster SCSI technologies allow greater data throughput than slower ones. While these conclusions may seem obvious, System Monitor lets you quantify them to see the actual performance effects of making these sorts of changes in configuration. Over time, you can deduce the average sizes of reads and writes by taking the number of bytes read or written per second and dividing by the reads or writes per second. This gives you an idea of the amount of data you're reading and writing to disk.

HARD DISK/FILE SYSTEM TIPS Here are a few tips for optimizing Windows 98 hard disk and file system performance:

- Optimize the computer for maximum performance. Provide sufficient RAM to allow the disk caches to grow as needed. Use high-performance SCSI adapters and drives – avoid IDE, EIDE, and Ultra DMA/33 drives. Use a 32-bit PCI adapter, if possible. (See Chapter 8 for details on hardware choices.)
- Minimize data signal interference, errors, and retries by using high-quality data cables and active terminators. One of the most common SCSI disk performance problems results from retries due to poor quality cables and terminators. Reducing the number of errors can dramatically improve performance. (See Chapter 8 for a discussion of SCSI cabling and termination.)

- Separate heavily used files on individual physical hard disks. For example, place the Windows 98 swap file on one hard disk and a busy database on a separate drive. See the section titled "Managing virtual memory swapping" earlier in this chapter.
- Consider converting to the FAT32 file system to improve overall file system performance under Windows 98. Keep in mind that if you dual-boot to another operating system on the same computer, only Windows 95 OSR2 and Windows NT 5.0 or later can access a FAT32 disk partition.
- Avoid using DriveSpace, DoubleSpace, or other disk compression schemes. The compression and expansion of files takes a significant amount of CPU bandwidth, and typically results in slower disk performance. But even if the disk I/O throughput is the same, compression steals CPU cycles away from other activities, which can affect overall system performance. Invest in more hard disk space, instead of using compression.
- Consider using RAID arrays to improve both performance and reliability. Hardware RAID solutions are available for Windows 98. Windows NT supports RAID implementations in both software and hardware.
- Use hard drives with fast I/O transfer rates, fast seek times (8 milliseconds or less), and high rotation speeds (5,600 to 10,000 RPM and up). Use AV-tuned drives to avoid time-consuming pauses. (See Chapter 8 for a discussion of hard disk technologies.)
- Configure your SCSI adapter to take full advantage of the maximum available SCSI speeds and asynchronous I/O. Doing this will enable high-speed I/O in parallel to multiple hard disks. See your SCSI adapter documentation for details.
- Periodically check your hard disks for fragmentation using the Windows 98 Defragmenter utility. This is especially important on servers, because fragmented files can slow I/O performance in behalf of multiple users. If you need to defragment, schedule the operation during off hours. Otherwise, the process will significantly slow down other operations, both locally and over the network.

OPTIMIZING HARD DISK PERFORMANCE The System application in Control Panel provides a simple way to optimize hard disk performance, depending on the typical role the computer performs. It gives a mechanism for controlling how Windows 98 sizes the disk cache, and how frequently the cache is written to the hard disk. You can select from among the following profiles:

- **Mobile or docking system** – This profile instructs Windows 98 to assume that the amount of physical memory is limited. It also assumes that the computer has the potential to be running on batteries at any moment.

Consequently, Windows 98 writes (or *flushes*) the disk cache to the hard disk more frequently, to minimize RAM usage and to lower the chance of lost data.

- **Desktop computer** – This profile tells Windows 98 that the computer is primarily used as a standalone system or as a client computer on the network. An adequate amount of RAM is assumed, and the computer always runs on AC power. With this profile in place, Windows 98 flushes the disk cache less frequently, enabling the disk cache to grow larger than it does under the mobile system profile.
- **Network server** – This profile informs Windows 98 that the computer is primarily performing network and disk I/O operations. It assumes that the computer has plenty of RAM available, and that disk I/O activity is high. The disk cache is flushed much less often, and the disk cache size is allowed to grow even larger than under the desktop computer profile.

NOTE: Unfortunately, a computer participating in a peer-to-peer network muddies the waters a bit when it comes to deciding whether to select Desktop computer or Network server. In this case, you have to use your judgement. Your final decision may depend on the number of users accessing the computer's shared resources. It could also depend on the requirements of the computer's user, who may want quicker interactive application response. The needs of the many outweigh the needs of the one — unless the one is very vocal or the one is your boss.

Here's how to set the appropriate file system profile:

1. In Control Panel, double-click the System icon.
2. Click Performance → File System → Hard Disk.
3. Move the Read-ahead optimization slider all the way to the right.
4. In the list titled Typical role of this computer, click the appropriate profile, as discussed earlier in this section.
5. Then click Apply → OK → Close. Restart the computer as prompted.

OPTIMIZING CD-ROM PERFORMANCE Obviously, the faster your CD-ROM drive, the better performance you'll get. Moving from an EIDE to a SCSI CD-ROM drive can improve overall performance as well, because it removes some of the I/O burden from the CPU. A CD-ROM drive with a large internal cache can also boost performance.

Windows 98 maintains its own cache for CD-ROM drives. The size of this cache ranges from 64K to 1238K bytes. You can and should specify the largest cache setting. Here's how to do this: In Control Panel, double-click the System icon. Click Performance → File System → CD-ROM. Move the Supplemental cache size slider all the way to the right. In the list titled Optimize access pattern for, click Quad-speed or higher, and then click Apply → OK → Close. Restart the computer as prompted.

MANAGING NETWORK I/O PERFORMANCE

System Monitor provides performance data for basic network I/O operations and other useful data. However, there's no clear way to identify network performance bottlenecks using System Monitor. The performance measurements it offers are great for comparative analysis – comparing network I/O performance before and after you install a faster network adapter, for example. If you carefully measure one application or operation at a time, you can combine the network items and CPU utilization to draw conclusions about the impact of network I/O on the system's performance.

WORKING WITH SYSTEM MONITOR System Monitor provides information for both the client (redirector) and server components. On both sides, you can measure bytes read and written per second, among other things. On the server side, you can view the amount of memory used by the server component and the number of threads running in the server. By taking periodic measurements, you can identify trends that may require server or network upgrades to keep up with an increasing load. Moreover, these numbers, when compared with the memory and CPU items I discussed earlier in this chapter, can help you draw conclusions about the server component's contribution to the overall load on the computer.

> **NOTE:** If you install the Microsoft Network Monitor Protocol driver, discussed earlier in this chapter, it adds another category called Network Monitor Performance Data, which lets you track I/O performance on specific network adapters at the byte and frame level. Some other network protocols and network management tools install their own performance monitoring items, which can be accessed by System Monitor. Check with the manufacturer to determine if there are additional items you can monitor after installing their products. Some of these products require installation of the Microsoft SNMP Agent. (*SNMP* stands for *Simple Network Management Protocol.*) You install this as a network service from the Windows 98 CD-ROM, in TOOLS\RESKIT\NETADMIN\SNMP.

NETWORK PERFORMANCE TIPS Here are a few tips on how you can optimize Windows 98 network performance.

- Optimize the computer for maximum performance. Faster servers have the greatest impact on network performance, but clients have an effect as well. Provide sufficient physical memory for network caches to grow as needed. Use high-performance hard disks and controllers in the computer. Use 32-bit, bus-mastering PCI network adapters in your servers – dedicated servers or high-traffic peer servers. (See Chapter 8 for a discussion of hardware choices.)
- Minimize network signal interference, errors, and retries by using high-quality cabling, hubs, adapters, and other components. One of the most insidious network performance drains is the additional traffic caused by packets being resent when errors occur. Reducing the errors reduces the traffic. (See Chapter 5 for a discussion of network cabling and infrastructure.)
- Avoid installing any network protocols you don't use. Install only the protocols you actually use. Unused protocols consume disk space, memory, CPU bandwidth, and even network bandwidth. Having unnecessary protocols loaded drags down the performance of the protocol (or protocols) you need. (See Chapter 6 for a discussion of network protocols.)
- Upgrade slower network adapters. A fast adapter attempting to send data to a slow one can impede overall network performance. In a high-traffic network, your goal should be to get the data off the wire and to its destination as quickly as possible, freeing up the cable for other network traffic. Move away from ISA adapters in favor of PCI, if possible. (See Chapter 8 for details on the ISA and PCI buses.)
- Consider installing network switches in place of hubs. Depending on your network traffic patterns, switches can offer significant performance gains. (See Chapter 5 for a discussion of hubs and switches.)
- Use NDIS drivers for your network adapters, rather than ODI drivers. In general, NDIS drivers will perform more efficiently and reliably.
- If your computer doesn't have a modem, or you don't use the modem, remove Dial-Up Networking components from the computer. These components occupy disk space and memory.
- Disconnect rarely used nodes. If you have nodes on your network that are rarely used to access it, disconnect them from the network. This reduces broadcast traffic and increases network performance.

- Use the read-only bit on files and sharepoints whenever possible. Network clients and servers can make more efficient use of cached data when the files are known to be read-only, thereby improving network performance.
- Break your network into multiple segments to isolate traffic and spread the network load. Spread heavy traffic across multiple segments, and use powerful servers to connect the segments together.

CAUTION

Segmenting the network requires adding at least one network adapter to a server. If the server's CPU and I/O bandwidth are already fully consumed, adding another network adapter won't help performance, and may actually slow down overall data throughput. Be sure the server you select has the additional capacity to handle the second network segment.

- Move to a higher-speed network technology. For example, move from 10Mbps Ethernet to 100Mbps, or from 4Mbps Token Ring to 16Mbps. This upgrade implies the possible need to upgrade adapters, hubs, and cabling.

NOTE

Data errors on the network — whether they're due to external interference, poor quality or damaged cabling, failing network adapters, or other component problems — can have a negative effect on performance. Windows 98 System Monitor doesn't provide network error statistics, but Windows NT Performance Monitor does. You can also get network error information from Network Monitor, which I described earlier in this chapter.

MANAGING PRINTING PERFORMANCE

Windows 98 makes every effort to return control to an application as quickly as possible after submitting a print job. It does this by quickly creating a device-independent version of the print job (called an *enhanced metafile format file*, or *EMF file*). As soon as control is returned to the application, Windows 98 converts the EMF file into the form required by the target printer. Meanwhile, the user can continue using the application while this conversion and the printing itself proceed in the background.

Printing from a Windows 98 computer to a shared printer on the network results in varying behaviors depending on the print server's operating system. If the server is running Windows 98 or Windows NT 5.0, the conversion from EMF to the printer-specific format takes place on the server. This behavior reduces the burden on the client computer, creating slightly better application performance for the user. If the print server is running Windows NT (4.0 or earlier) or NetWare, the client computer has to perform the conversion from EMF.

You have some control over the behavior of this EMF creation and conversion process. Your decision involves tradeoffs between disk space, time to return control to the application, and overall printing time. Here are your choices:

- **Start printing after first page is spooled** – If you select this option, the creation of the EMF file and its conversion to the printer-specific format take place simultaneously. This option uses less disk space for the print job, reduces the total time required to print the job, and increases the time it takes to return control to the application. Because the printer-specific data is ready sooner, the job begins to print sooner.
- **Start printing after last page is spooled** – If you select this option, the EMF file is completely created before the conversion begins. This returns control to the application more quickly, but it increases the amount of disk space used by the job, and increases the total time it takes to print the job. Most network administrators prefer this setting for shared printers.

To make this selection, perform the following steps on each client computer that prints to a shared printer:

1. Click Start → Settings → Printers, right-click the printer you want to configure, and click Properties.
2. Click Details → Spool Settings.
3. Click Spool print jobs so program finishes printing faster.
4. Click one of the two options described earlier in this section.
5. In the Spool data format box, make sure EMF is selected, then click OK → Apply → OK.
6. Repeat the previous steps (1 through 5) for each remote printer you want to configure.

If you select RAW as the spool data format, Windows 98 skips the EMF step and creates a printer-specific job directly from the application on the client. This usually takes longer than creating an EMF file, so it takes longer for the user to regain control of the application. Resort to using RAW format only if you're experiencing problems with EMF.

Summary

In this chapter, you've been exposed to network troubleshooting and optimization at many different levels. You've learned how to troubleshoot problems encountered on the network, as well as in other system components that can affect network operation. You've also seen how to analyze the performance of your computers and your network, along with techniques for making your network operate at peak efficiency. I showed you how you can use System Monitor to identify performance bottlenecks, evaluate performance improvements, and identify performance trends. In Appendix B, you'll find additional troubleshooting and optimization resources that you can add to your networking arsenal.

Appendix A

Installing Networking on Microsoft Operating Systems

IN THIS APPENDIX, you'll learn how to install networking software for several Microsoft operating systems, including Windows 95, Windows for Workgroups 3.11, Windows 3.1, and MS-DOS. See Chapter 9 for information on installing network hardware and software for Windows 98.

Installing Windows 95 Networking

Installing networking software on Windows 95 is similar to Windows 98 network software installation, which is covered in Chapter 9. Most of the concepts covered there apply to both products. In this section, I present a step-by-step approach to installing Microsoft networking software on a Windows 95 computer. This section assumes that the Windows 95 operating system is already installed. See Chapter 9 for details on network hardware installation.

> NOTE: Because Windows 95 supports Plug and Play hardware, it may automatically detect, install, and configure some of the network software components for you, depending on your network hardware and the current configuration of your computer. Therefore, some of the steps outlined in this section may already be done for you.

Perform the following steps to install Windows 95 networking software:

1. On the Windows 95 computer, click Start → Settings → Control Panel. Double-click the Network icon.
2. In the Network dialog box, examine the list of installed network components. If an entry for your network adapter hardware already exists, proceed to Step 6. Otherwise, continue to Step 3.

Installing the Driver

3. In the Network dialog box, click Configuration → Add.
4. In the Select Network Component dialog box, click Adapter → Add.
5. In the Select Network Adapters dialog box, under Manufacturers, click the manufacturer of your network adapter hardware. Under Network Adapters, click the model name of your network adapter hardware, and then click OK.

If your network adapter's manufacturer or model doesn't appear, and you have a floppy disk or CD-ROM containing Windows 95 drivers, click Have Disk and follow the prompts to install the network adapter driver. If you don't have a driver for the adapter, contact the adapter manufacturer.

Installing and Configuring Protocols

6. Once your adapter driver is successfully located and installed, Windows 95 installs other networking components automatically. These include the NetBEUI and IPX/SPX protocols, and the Client for Microsoft Networks (redirector) and Client for NetWare Networks (requester). If you are satisfied with this set of components, proceed to Step 9. Otherwise, continue to Step 7.

The components that Windows 95 installs by default may vary, depending on the version of Windows 95 you have. If you don't have NetWare servers in your network, you don't need the IPX/SPX protocol or Client for NetWare Networks. Removing IPX/SPX automatically removes Client for NetWare Networks. (See Chapter 6 for a discussion of network protocols.)

---

7. To remove a protocol, click the protocol in the list of network components, and click Remove → OK.
8. To add a protocol, click Add → Protocol → Add. In the Select Protocols dialog box, under Manufacturers, click the manufacturer of the network protocol you want to install. Under Protocols, click the specific protocol you want to install, and click OK. To configure the new protocols, on the Configuration tab click the protocol in the list of network components, click Properties, and proceed with configuration. (See Chapter 9 for a discussion of protocol configuration.)

Configuring the Driver

9. In the Network dialog box, on the Configuration tab, click the network adapter in the list of installed components. (If more than one network adapter is listed, click the one you've just installed.) Then click Properties.
10. Click the Driver Type tab and verify that the driver type is set to Enhanced mode NDIS driver. If it isn't, click to select this setting.
11. Click the Resources tab and verify that the hardware resource settings match your actual network adapter settings. The resource options vary from one adapter to another, but can include IRQ, I/O address, memory mapped address, and DMA channel.

If an asterisk (*) appears before a hardware resource setting, that setting conflicts with another hardware device installed in the computer. See Chapter 9 for a discussion of how to resolve resource conflicts. If a pound sign (#) appears before a resource setting, that setting was read directly from the device itself.

12. Click the Bindings tab and verify that the adapter has the correct protocols bound to it. If not, add and remove bindings as necessary. See Chapter 9 for a discussion of network bindings.

Unlike Windows 98, Windows 95 bindings between network adapters and protocols don't appear in the list of components on the Configuration tab. To find out which protocols are bound to a specific adapter, you need to click the network adapter, click Properties, and then click the Bindings tab.

13. When you've finished configuring the network adapter, click Close.

Configuring the Node

14. In the Network dialog box, click the Identification tab. Type a unique computer name assigned to this computer. Then type the name of the workgroup in which this computer will participate. Optionally, type a description for the computer. (See Chapter 9 for details on how to select computer names and workgroup names.)

By default, Windows 95 configures the computer to use share-level security. If you want user-level security, click the Access Control tab in the Network dialog box. Then, click User-level access control, type the Windows NT Server domain name that contains the list of network user accounts, and click OK. See Chapter 12 for a discussion of share-level and user-level security.

15. In the Network dialog box, click Configuration → File and Print Sharing. In the File and Print Sharing dialog box, click to select the checkbox that reads I want to be able to give others access to my files, click to select the checkbox that reads I want to be able to allow others to print to my printer(s), or click to select both. Then click OK. If you don't select either one, the computer will act only as a network client.

Installing and Configuring the Client

16. On the Configuration tab in the Network dialog box, verify that Client for Microsoft Networks appears in the list of installed components. If it does appear, proceed to Step 18. Otherwise, continue to Step 17.

If you're using Client for NetWare Networks instead of Client for Microsoft Networks, then verify that the client you need is already installed. The remainder of these steps will assume you want to install and configure Client for Microsoft Networks.

17. On the Configuration tab, click Add → Client → Add. In the Select Clients dialog box, under Manufacturers, click the manufacturer of the network client you want to install (in this case, Microsoft). Under Clients, click the specific client you want to install (in this case, Client for Microsoft Networks). Then click OK.
18. On the Configuration tab, click Client for Microsoft Networks, and then click Properties.
19. In the Client for Microsoft Networks Properties dialog box, on the General tab, under Logon validation, click to clear the checkbox titled Log on to Windows NT domain, unless you're using a Windows NT Server computer for user account validation. See Chapter 12 for a discussion of user-level security.

20. On the General tab, click to select either Quick logon or Logon and restore network connections, depending on when you want network resource connections to be made. Then click OK.

21. In the Network dialog box, click OK. Files are copied, and you may be asked to supply your Windows 95 installation CD-ROM. Follow the prompts to copy the files and restart the computer.

Installing Windows NT Networking

You can install Windows NT Workstation networking either during operating system setup or after operating system setup. In this section, I focus on installing network software after the NT Workstation operating system is already installed and running. By definition, Windows NT Server network software must be installed during operating system installation. A working network adapter is required during this process. You can, however, configure network components after the operating system is installed. For details on network hardware installation, see Chapter 9.

NOTE: In this section, I assume you're using Windows NT version 4.0. If you want to install networking software on an earlier version of Windows NT (3.1, 3.5, or 3.51), consult the documentation supplied with your operating system. I highly recommend that you upgrade to Windows NT 4.0 from earlier versions. NT 4.0 performs significantly better and is more reliable than previous versions.

Installing Windows NT Workstation Networking

Perform the following steps to install Windows NT Workstation networking software:

TIP: If you're implementing user-level security via a Windows NT Server domain, you'll need to create a *computer account* for each Windows NT Workstation computer that joins the domain. Before installing Windows NT Workstation networking, establish an account in your Windows NT Server domain that has the right to add workstations. Note the domain name, the name of this account, and the password of this account before proceeding. You'll need them in Steps 9 through 11.

1. On the Windows NT Workstation computer, click Start → Settings → Control Panel. Double-click the Network icon.
2. In the Network Setup Wizard dialog box, click Yes.
3. Follow the prompts from the Network Setup Wizard to select protocols. (See Chapter 6 for a discussion of network protocols, and Chapter 9 for a discussion on configuring protocols.)
4. Allow NT to scan for network adapters. If your network adapter is automatically detected, proceed to Step 6. Otherwise, continue with Step 5.
5. In the Select Network Adapter dialog box, click the make and model of your network adapter hardware, and then click OK.

NOTE: If your network adapter doesn't appear on the list, and you have a floppy disk or CD-ROM containing a Windows NT driver, click Have Disk and follow the prompts to install the network adapter driver. If you don't have an NT driver for the adapter, contact the adapter manufacturer.

---

6. Verify, modify, or enter the adapter configuration information as appropriate. The configuration parameters vary from one adapter to another, but can include IRQ, I/O address, memory-mapped address, and DMA channel. When you've finished configuring the adapter, click OK. (See Chapter 9 for details on configuring network adapters.)
7. The Network Setup Wizard asks for a workgroup or domain name. If you're attaching this computer to a peer-to-peer network, click Workgroup, type the workgroup name, click Next, and proceed to Step 12. If you're attaching this computer to a Windows NT Server domain, proceed to Step 8.
8. Verify that your computer is physically attached to the network, and that the Windows NT Server domain controller computer is up and running. (See Chapter 12 for a discussion of user-level security.)
9. Click Domain and type the domain name of the Windows NT Server domain you want this computer to join.
10. Click to select the Create a Computer Account in this Domain checkbox. Then click Next.
11. In the Create Computer Account dialog box, type the user account name and password of an account that has rights to add workstations to the domain. Then click OK.

If the creation of the computer account fails for some reason, the computer will default to joining a workgroup. You can later troubleshoot the network or server problem that caused the failure, and then attempt to create an account again using the Network application in Control Panel. Simply click Change on the Identification tab to make the change.

12. Restart the computer as prompted.

Installing Windows NT Server Networking

Perform the following steps to install Windows NT Server networking software:

If you're implementing user-level security via a Windows NT Server domain, and you're installing this copy of Windows NT Server as a standalone server, you'll need to create a *computer account* for the computer to join the domain. Before installing Windows NT Server as a standalone server, establish an account in your Windows NT Server domain that has the right to add workstations. Note the domain name, the name of this account, and the password of this account before proceeding. You'll need them in Steps 21 through 23.

1. Perform all the steps required to install the Windows NT Server operating system, up to the point where the graphical Setup Wizard asks you to enter a computer name. Type the name you've chosen for this computer and click Next. (See Chapter 9 for a discussion of computer name selection.)
2. When asked for the server type, click to select Primary Domain Controller, Backup Domain Controller, or Stand-Alone Server, depending on the role you want this computer to play. Then click Next.

Select PDC if you're using this computer to create a new Windows NT Server domain. Select BDC if you already have a PDC running and you want to use this computer as a backup for user authentication. Be sure the PDC is up and running when you attempt to create the BDC. If you don't want the computer to be any kind of domain controller, select Stand-Alone Server. (A Windows NT Stand-Alone Server is sometimes called a *member server*, because it's a member of the domain, but it doesn't act as a domain controller.)

3. Type the password you want to assign to the administrator account, press TAB, retype the password to confirm it, and click Next.

Don't forget this password. If you do, you'll have to reinstall Windows NT Server on this computer.

4. When asked if you want to create an Emergency Repair Disk, click Yes → Next.
5. Select the optional components you want to install. When you're done, click Next.
6. When the Setup Wizard indicates that it's about to install networking, click Next.
7. Click to select the checkbox named Wired to the network.

If you elected to install as a standalone server in Step 2, you'll have the choice of setting up networking later. If you'd prefer to install networking at a later time, click Do not connect the computer to the network at this time.

8. Click Next. Click to clear the Install Microsoft Internet Information Server checkbox, and then click Next. (I don't recommend installing IIS until Windows NT Server is already up and running. You'll have an opportunity to install it later, along with the TCP/IP network protocol it requires.)
9. Click Start Search to begin the automatic search for your network adapter hardware. If it finds an adapter, proceed to Step 11. Otherwise, continue with Step 10.
10. Click Select from list → Have Disk, insert the disk or CD-ROM containing the NT network adapter driver, and follow the prompts to install the driver. When you're done, proceed to Step 12.
11. The Setup Wizard lists the first adapter it finds. If the adapter is correct, and you've installed only one adapter, click Next. If there are more network adapters installed, click Find Next. When all adapters have been found, click Next.

12. Click to select the network protocols you want to install. Click to clear the protocols you don't want to install. Then click Next. (You'll be able to add or delete protocols later, after Setup is complete. See Chapter 6 for a discussion of network protocols.)

> NOTE: If the protocol you want to install isn't in the list, click Select from list and follow the prompts to install the protocol you want.

13. When asked which services you want to install, click Next. (You'll have a chance to add and delete services after Setup is complete.)
14. When the Setup Wizard tells you it's about to install network components, click Next.
15. Verify, modify, or enter the adapter configuration information as appropriate. The configuration parameters vary from one adapter to another, but can include IRQ, I/O address, memory-mapped address, and DMA channel. When you've finished configuring the adapter, click OK. (See Chapter 9 for details on configuring network adapters.)
16. When asked to review or change network bindings, click Next. (You'll have a chance to modify network bindings after Setup is complete.)
17. When the Setup Wizard tells you it's about to start the network, click Next.
18. If you're setting up a Stand-Alone Server, proceed to Step 19. If you're setting up a PDC or BDC, press TAB, type the Windows NT Server domain name, and click Next. Then proceed to Step 24.
19. The Setup Wizard asks for a workgroup or domain name. If you're attaching this computer to a peer-to-peer network, click Workgroup, type the workgroup name, click Next, and proceed to Step 24. If you're attaching this computer to a Windows NT Server domain, proceed to Step 20.
20. Verify that your computer is physically attached to the network, and that the Windows NT Server domain controller (PDC or BDC) computer is up and running. (See Chapter 12 for a discussion of user-level security.)
21. Click Domain and type the domain name of the Windows NT Server domain you want this computer to join.

22. Click to select the Create a Computer Account in this Domain checkbox. Then click Next.
23. In the Create Computer Account dialog box, type the user account name and password of an account that has rights to add workstations to the domain. Then click OK.

If the creation of the computer account fails for some reason, the computer will default to joining a workgroup. You can later troubleshoot the network or server problem that caused the failure, and then attempt to create an account again using the Network application in Control Panel. Simply click Change on the Identification tab to make the change.

24. Continue through the remainder of the Setup Wizard by following the prompts.

If you're installing a standalone server and the PDC isn't available to allow it to join the domain, you can opt to join a workgroup, troubleshoot the problem, and join the domain later. If you're installing a BDC, and you can't join the domain for some reason, you'll need to troubleshoot the problem before proceeding with the Setup Wizard. Otherwise, you may have to reinstall Windows NT Server from scratch.

You can later add, remove, or configure network protocols using the Protocols tab in the Control Panel Network application. You can also view and modify the bindings between network components using the Bindings tab. Chapter 9 discusses protocol configuration and bindings in more detail.

Installing Windows for Workgroups Networking

If you have Windows for Workgroups 3.11 installed, but haven't yet installed the networking features, you're in the right place. I present a step-by-step approach to installing the Microsoft networking software on Windows for Workgroups computers. Only software installation is covered here. For details on network hardware installation, see Chapter 9.

If your network adapter is a Plug and Play device, you may need to disable Plug and Play, and then perform manual configuration of the adapter to get it working under Windows for Workgroups. Or, you may need to assign specific resources to the adapter using your computer's BIOS configuration utility. Refer to your network adapter manufacturer's documentation on configuring the adapter to work in a Windows for Workgroups environment.

To install Windows for Workgroups network software, after you've installed the network hardware, perform the following steps:

1. Go to the Main group in Program Manager and double-click Windows Setup.
2. In the Windows Setup window, the Network entry should read No Network Installed – unless networking is already installed. You can use Windows Setup to change the configuration of your network software.
3. Click Options → Change Network Settings. Setup displays the Network Setup dialog box.
4. Under Network Settings, click Networks. Click Install Microsoft Windows Network, and click OK.
5. Click Sharing. If you want the computer to act as a peer server, click to select the appropriate checkboxes for file and printer sharing, and click OK.
6. Click Drivers → Add Adapter. From the list of network adapters, click the name of your network adapter and click OK.
7. Setup displays a network adapter configuration dialog box, requesting settings for IRQ, I/O Address, and so forth. The actual content of the dialog box varies depending on the make and model of your adapter. Type the settings that match your installed network adapter, and click OK.
8. Click Close in the Network Drivers dialog box. Then click OK in the Network Setup dialog box.
9. In the Microsoft Windows Network Names dialog box, review and correct the user name, workgroup name, and computer name. When you're satisfied that all three names are correct, click OK.
10. Setup copies files from your installation disks to your hard disk. It then modifies your configuration files, and informs you where it has stored backup versions of these files.
11. Click OK and restart the computer as prompted.

Installing MS-DOS and Windows 3.1 Networking

In this section, I present a step-by-step approach to installing the Microsoft networking software on MS-DOS and Windows 3.1 computers. The process of installing the network is performed under MS-DOS, and Windows 3.1 uses the underlying network components once they're installed. Only software installation is covered here. For details on network hardware installation, see Chapter 9.

NOTE: If your network adapter is a Plug and Play device, you may need to disable Plug and Play and perform manual configuration of the adapter to get it working under MS-DOS. Or, you may need to assign specific resources to the adapter using your computer's BIOS configuration utility. Refer to your network adapter manufacturer's documentation on configuring the adapter to work in an MS-DOS environment.

If you don't already have the Microsoft Network Client software floppy disks, here are two ways to obtain them:

- **Microsoft FTP Site** – You can download the Network Client for MS-DOS free of charge from `ftp://ftp.microsoft.com/bussys/clients/msclient`. There are two self-extracting executable files, each of which creates one floppy disk in the two-floppy set.

  Copy the first downloaded file to an empty temporary hard disk directory and run it. The compressed files will be extracted. Delete the original file, and move all the remaining extracted files to a floppy disk. Repeat this procedure for each downloaded file.

- **Windows NT Server CD-ROM** – NT Server includes all of the Microsoft network clients, along with tools that let you create installation diskettes and install network software over an existing network. If you have Windows NT Server in your network, this is the more convenient approach.

  Simply copy the contents of \CLIENTS\MSCLIENT\DISKS\DISK1 on the CD-ROM to a floppy disk. Then, copy the contents of \CLIENTS\MSCLIENT\DISKS\DISK2 to another floppy.

Microsoft also offers a product called Workgroup Add-On for MS-DOS 3.11 (WGAO for MS-DOS). It contains the same network client code as Microsoft Network Client, but doesn't include the TCP/IP, IPX/SPX, or DLC network protocols. WGAO lets the MS-DOS computer function as a peer server, whereas Microsoft Network Client doesn't. Because I don't recommend using MS-DOS as a server, and because the network protocols missing from WGAO are important, I recommend that you stick with the Microsoft Network Client software.

Installing the Network Client

Perform the following steps to install the Microsoft Network Client 3.0 for MS-DOS:

1. Insert Disk 1 of the Microsoft Network Client floppy disk set into drive A. From drive A, type **SETUP** and press Enter.
2. On the Welcome screen, press Enter to set up the Network Client software.

If a particular screen or option isn't clear to you during the Setup process, you can always get more information about a particular screen by pressing F1.

3. When Setup asks for the destination directory, type the full path of the directory where you want to store the network client software on your hard disk. Then press Enter.

Make sure you check the default destination path before using it. Depending on how your floppies were created, the default path may point to drive A — which is not very helpful. I recommend using C:\NETWORK or something equally meaningful.

Specifying Names

4. Setup may ask if you want to set network buffers for optimal performance by using more memory. Press Enter. (If you're extremely tight on memory, press C. But I recommend optimizing for best performance.)

5. Setup may ask for a user name. Type the user name of the person who typically uses this computer. Then press Enter. User names can be up to 20 characters long, consisting of letters, numbers, and any of the following characters: `! # $ % & ( ) ^ _ ' { } ~`. (See Chapter 12 for a discussion of user names and security.)
6. Setup asks you to review names, setup options, and network configuration settings. Use the arrow keys to select Change Names and press Enter.
7. Setup asks you to review the user name, computer name, workgroup name, and domain name. Use the arrow keys to select an item to change, and press Enter. Type the new name and press Enter. When you've finished making changes to these names, use the arrow keys to select The listed names are correct, and press Enter.

NOTE

If Setup already asked for a user name, it sets the computer name to be the same as the user name. It typically defaults to a workgroup name of WORKGROUP and a domain name of WORKGROUP. You need to select a unique computer name for this computer, and a workgroup name that matches the actual name of the workgroup. See Chapter 9 for details on choosing these names. See Chapter 12 for a discussion of user names and domain names.

Configuring Client Behavior

8. Use the arrow keys to select Change Setup Options and press Enter.
9. Redir Options should be set to Use the Full Redirector. If it isn't, use the arrow keys to select Change Redir Options, press Enter, and modify the setting.

TIP

The full redirector takes up a bit more memory and disk space than the basic redirector, but it lets you log on to Windows NT domains and provides advanced networking features used by some network-aware MS-DOS applications. Your best bet is to install the full redirector, and back off to the basic redirector only if you're running out of memory. I've seen network administrators beat their heads against the wall trying to get something to work, only to discover that the problem was caused by running the basic instead of the full redirector on the MS-DOS client computer.

10. Startup Options should be set to Run Network Client. If it isn't, use the arrow keys to select Change Startup Options, press Enter, and modify the setting.

> NOTE: In addition to automatically starting the network client software, you can load a pop-up interface to the network that lets you press Ctrl+Alt+N (or some other character) to gain instant access to network functions. However, this feature takes nearly 30K of memory, and some MS-DOS applications use this key sequence for other operations. (You can change the key sequence, if it does conflict.)

11. Logon Validation should be set to Do Not Logon to Domain, unless you're logging on to a Windows NT Server domain. If you need to change this setting, use the arrow keys to select Logon Validation, press Enter, and modify the setting. (See Chapter 12 for a discussion of Windows NT Server domains.)
12. When you're satisfied with the Setup Options, use the arrow keys to select The listed options are correct. Then press Enter.

Configuring Drivers and Protocols

13. Use the arrow keys to select Change Network Configuration and press Enter.

> NOTE: The screen is divided into two boxes. The upper box contains a list of installed network adapters and protocols. The lower box, the Options box, contains a list of actions you can perform. Use Tab to switch between the boxes. Use the arrow keys to select individual items within a box.

14. To add your network adapter, move to the Options box. Select Add Adapter and press Enter. Use the arrow keys to scroll through the list of adapters. If you find your network adapter in the list, proceed to Step 15. If your adapter isn't listed, proceed to Step 16.
15. Select your network adapter from the list, press Enter, and proceed to Step 17.

16. Select Network adapter not shown on list below, and press Enter. Type the path to the driver files supplied by the network adapter manufacturer. For example, if the drivers are supplied on a floppy disk, the path might simply be A:\. Follow the prompts in Setup and the instructions provided by your network adapter manufacturer.

17. Select your network adapter in the upper box on the screen. Select Change Settings in the lower box on the screen. Verify that your network adapter hardware settings are correct, and that they match the current physical settings on the adapter. If they don't, follow the prompts to modify them to match the hardware.

18. Select your network adapter in the upper box on the screen. Select Add Protocol and press Enter. Use the arrow keys to scroll through the list of protocols. Select the protocol you want to install and press Enter.

19. Repeat Steps 14 through 18 to add more network adapters and/or protocols. When you've finished making changes, select Network configuration is correct, and press Enter.

20. Setup copies the appropriate files from the Network Client floppy disks to your hard disk. Follow the prompts to insert and remove floppy disks. Setup then modifies your CONFIG.SYS and AUTOEXEC.BAT files to load the appropriate network software according to the configuration you've specified.

> NOTE: Setup makes a backup copy of these files in the root directory of drive C. The file extension on the backup copies is replaced by a three-digit number. For example, the files might be saved to CONFIG.001 and AUTOEXEC.001, unless those files already exist.

21. Remove the floppy from drive A and press Enter to restart the computer automatically. When your computer restarts, the network software you installed should load and run.

22. The first time your password is requested by the network client software, it will ask you if you want to create a password file. Press Y and Enter to create the local password file.

If you ever want to change your network configuration (for example, to add adapters, protocols, and so forth), you can run Setup again from within the directory where you installed the network files in Step 3.

Appendix B

Windows 98 and Networking Resources

KNOWING HOW AND where to find more information quickly is one key to your success as a network administrator. In this appendix, I point to several additional resources on networking, Windows 98, and related topics and products.

Microsoft Information Resources

Microsoft provides several ways to obtain information. They include product support, documents by mail and fax, a Web site, a bulletin board service, product resource kits, and CD-ROM subscription services. In this section, I discuss each of these areas, and give you a flavor of what you can expect from them.

Using Product Support Services (PSS)

Microsoft Product Support Services (PSS) may be the most expensive source of information, because calling them typically results in phone charges, incident charges, and a significant chunk of your time on hold. Contact PSS only after you've exhausted all the other information resources discussed in this section.

To make the most efficient use of time, make sure you have all your hardware and software configuration information in front of you. If possible, be in a position to reproduce the problem while on the phone with the PSS engineer. Have any serial numbers or other data required to prove you're a legal, registered user of the product. If you have a support contract, have that information handy as well. Keep track of the date, time, person, problem resolution, and any confirmation or incident numbers you're given. You'll need all of this information later, if you need to follow up on the same issue. Having all this information handy when you call will save time and money.

As Microsoft's support policies change for different products and different classes of problems, your best bet in finding the right PSS phone number is in the materials that came with the product. Alternatively, you can visit the Microsoft Web site and look under Support for the latest information. If the software products came preinstalled and you didn't receive any support materials, contact your hardware vendor for information on obtaining support.

Using the Fast Tips Service

Microsoft maintains a telephone-based service called Fast Tips. With it, you can order information by phone and have it mailed or faxed to you. The first thing you should order is the Fast Tips catalog, which lists all the available documents with their document numbers. You'll need the document numbers to order additional documents:

Personal Systems (Windows 98, Windows 95, Windows, MS-DOS)	(800) 936-4200
Business Systems (Windows NT, BackOffice products)	(800) 936-4400
Desktop Applications (Office applications)	(800) 936-4100
Development Tools (Visual tools)	(800) 936-4300

Using the Web Site

Microsoft maintains a comprehensive Web site at `www.microsoft.com`. It includes detailed product information, notes from technical conferences, whitepapers on many technical issues, real-world case studies of network installations, and access to their product support knowledge base. A comprehensive search engine lets you look for material in just one area or across the entire site. You can also use it to download drivers, patches, add-on utilities, and workarounds.

If you're creating a Windows-based network, I highly recommend becoming familiar with the Microsoft Web site. If you know what's available out there, you'll be better equipped to answer questions and solve problems.

Using the Bulletin Board Service (BBS)

Microsoft maintains a bulletin board service that covers networking products. Microsoft Download Library, or MSDL, as it's called, offers the latest drivers and other network-related software for download. Other than the cost of the phone call, the service is free.

To access it, you can use the HyperTerminal utility included with Windows 98 and Windows 95. Click Start → Programs → Accessories → Communications → HyperTerminal and double-click HYPERTRM.EXE. Set your modem to 8 data bits, 1 stop bit, no parity, and no flow control. Then dial (425) 936-6735.

All of the material available in MSDL is also available from Microsoft via the Internet. If you have Internet access, you're better off downloading what you need from their site. But if you don't have Internet access, MSDL can be a cost-effective alternative.

Using Microsoft Resource Kits

Microsoft Press publishes a set of book and software combinations known as resource kits. They're typically targeted at the network administrator who's responsible for deploying and supporting Microsoft operating systems and applications within an organization. The kits typically include a large amount of printed documentation, in the form of one or more books, that goes far beyond user manuals to discuss specific configuration and troubleshooting techniques. They also include either a CD-ROM or floppy disks containing software utilities useful to the administrator.

Some of the kits are available in beta form before the operating system is released. For example, the Windows 98 Resource Kit was available several months before the Windows 98 product release. Microsoft also periodically updates some of the kits with supplemental books and updates to software.

The software included in these kits isn't officially supported by Microsoft. Over time, however, the best utilities find their way into the product itself, so eventually most of these utilities are supported.

WINDOWS 98 AND WINDOWS 95 RESOURCE KITS

The Windows 98 Resource Kit includes a 1,700+ page book and a CD-ROM chock full of utilities and additional documentation. One of the key utilities in the kit is called Batch98, which greatly simplifies setting up automated installation scripts, if you need to install Windows 98 on a large number of computers. The kit costs approximately $70. I highly recommend this kit if you're going to have more than a handful of Windows 98 computers in your network. (The resource kit software is included on the Windows 98 CD-ROM in \TOOLS\RESKIT.)

The Windows 95 Resource Kit includes a 1,300+ page book and either a set of floppy disks or a CD-ROM containing administration utilities and additional documentation. It includes detailed information on setting up an internal e-mail system using the post office software included in Windows 95. The cost of the kit is approximately $50. If you plan to have Windows 95 computers in your network for very long, this resource kit can be a worthwhile source of information. But if you plan to migrate everyone to Windows 98 or Windows NT, stick with the other resource kits.

WINDOWS NT WORKSTATION RESOURCE KIT

The Windows NT Workstation Resource Kit is a single 1,300+ page book and a CD-ROM containing utilities. While some coverage of networking is included, the most comprehensive sections of the book are dedicated to performance optimization using the Performance Monitor utility, and registry editing using the Registry Editor. At the time of writing, the resource kit costs about $70.

WINDOWS NT SERVER RESOURCE KIT

The Windows NT Server Resource Kit consists of anywhere from three to five volumes and a CD-ROM containing utilities. As you might expect, the focus of this kit is on enterprise networking, including detailed information on connecting safely to the Internet. Microsoft typically updates this kit by adding books and utilities to the package once or twice a year. You can purchase the updates separately, whether or not you already own the basic kit. At the time of writing, the resource kit costs about $150, and updates cost between $40 and $50 each.

If you're using both Windows NT Server and Windows NT Workstation in your network, I recommend having both resource kits on hand. While there is some overlap between them, each focuses on different areas in terms of deployment and optimization issues.

TIP

Before you purchase a resource kit update, check whether the update is for software only, or for both a book and software. If it's just a new CD, you may be able to pick up the software free from the Microsoft Web site. Also, if you want all the latest resource kits in completely electronic form, consider a subscription to Microsoft TechNet, which I describe in the next section.

Using Technical Information Network (TechNet)

If you're supporting multiple operating systems and applications, and you need to stay abreast of the latest bugs, workarounds, and patches, a subscription to Microsoft TechNet may be just what you need. I consider it a must for any organization that runs an internal helpdesk for solving problems encountered with Microsoft products.

When you subscribe, Microsoft sends you a monthly package of CD-ROMs that includes, but isn't limited to, the following:

- **Microsoft Product Support Knowledge Base** – Tens of thousands of indexed knowledge base articles cover known bugs, workarounds, troubleshooting tips, time-saving techniques, and solutions. This is the same database used by Microsoft product support personnel. For a helpdesk environment, this component alone is worth the subscription price.
- **Books, manuals, and articles** – Entire product manuals, Microsoft Press books, journal articles, and whitepapers are included. Topic categories include BackOffice, Internet, personal systems, Office applications, development tools, PC hardware, Year 2000 product status, and others. All are fully indexed for searching.
- **Drivers, patches, and service packs** – The package includes the latest device drivers, patch files, and entire service packs for Microsoft operating systems, BackOffice applications, and desktop applications.
- **Resource kits** – The resource kit manuals and software are included in the package. All Microsoft operating systems are covered, as well as BackOffice, Internet Information Server, and several other Microsoft applications.
- **Technology evaluations** – Microsoft throws in an occasional sampler of specific technologies or applications not typically included in the standard TechNet subscription.

Much of this information is available on the Microsoft Web site or through separately purchased products (such as the resource kits, for example). But having all of this material in one place, instantly accessible, is a better way to go. At the time of writing, a single-user TechNet subscription costs $299 per year. An unlimited network version runs $699 per year.

> Now that Microsoft charges for technical support on network-related issues, the cost saving realized from avoiding support calls can more than pay for the subscription in no time at all.

To order TechNet, you can call (800) 344-2121 during Microsoft business hours, which are 6:30 a.m. to 5:30 p.m. PST.

Using Microsoft Developer Network (MSDN)

Microsoft used to be criticized for withholding technical information from the development community. But now they're selling this technical information – more of it that any one person could ever possibly digest. If you think TechNet represents information overload, here's the next step up. If your organization develops software for Microsoft operating systems, has Microsoft got a deal for you: the Microsoft Developer Network, or MSDN.

MSDN offers a quarterly subscription to detailed technical information primarily targeted at software developers. Available at various subscription levels, it offers a developer knowledge base that includes electronic versions of books, periodicals, whitepapers, and articles. At higher subscription levels, MSDN includes operating systems, software development kits (SDKs), device driver development kits (DDKs), development tools such as Visual C++, BackOffice applications such as SQL Server, and applications such as Office Professional and Project. Table B-1 summarizes the costs and benefits of the three available MSDN subscription levels.

Pay attention to the licensing restrictions on MSDN software. You're allowed to use it for development and testing purposes only. If you use the software in a production environment on your network, you're expected to purchase the individual software packages or licenses.

TABLE B-1 MSDN SUBSCRIPTION LEVELS

Feature	Library Subscription	Professional Subscription	Universal Subscription
MSDN Library CD-ROM, with quarterly updates	Yes	Yes	Yes
MSDN Newsletter, sent bimonthly	Yes	Yes	Yes
Full access to online member forums	Yes	Yes	Yes
20% discount on Microsoft Press books	Yes	Yes	Yes
Free telephone support	Setup and configuration support	Setup, configuration, and two priority support incidents	Setup, configuration, and four priority support incidents

Feature	Library Subscription	Professional Subscription	Universal Subscription
Microsoft operating systems (Win98, Win95, NT Workstation, NT Server), option packs, service packs, SDKs, and DDKs, updated quarterly, U.S. and localized versions (Licensed for single user development and testing purposes)	No	Yes	Yes
Interim updates to operating systems, option packs, service packs, SDKs, DDKs, and beta releases	No	Yes	Yes
Windows NT HCT and Device Driver Tests	No	Yes	Yes
BackOffice Test Platform, updated quarterly, U.S. and localized versions (Licensed for testing purposes, limited to 10 simultaneous users)	No	No	Yes
Interim updates to BackOffice applications and beta releases	No	No	Yes
Microsoft Office Professional, Developer Edition	No	No	Yes
FrontPage	No	No	Yes
Microsoft Project, Microsoft Team Manager	No	No	Yes

Continued

Table B-1 MSDN SUBSCRIPTION LEVELS *(Continued)*

Feature	Library Subscription	Professional Subscription	Universal Subscription
Visual Studio, Enterprise Edition (Visual InterDev, Visual J++, Visual C++, Visual SourceSafe, Macro Assembler)	No	No	Yes
Visual Basic Enterprise Edition	No	No	Yes
Visual FoxPro Professional Edition	No	No	Yes
Microsoft Access Developer's Toolkit	No	No	Yes
Windows CE Toolkits	No	No	Yes
Annual subscription cost	$199	$499	$1999

A number of other subscription benefits are available, and they change from time to time. Visit `www.microsoft.com/msdn/services/subscription/benefits.htm` for more information.

Using Training and Certification Resources

As I mentioned in Chapter 14, there are several training and certification programs you can go through to receive training on Microsoft operating system products and networking them together. The Microsoft Web site includes an area that outlines the curriculum for each certification level, including topic outlines and sample exams that you can download. Visit `www.microsoft.com/train_cert` for more information.

You can be trained for certification exams anywhere, but if you're interested in receiving Microsoft authorized training, look for a facility that's designated as an Authorized Technical Education Center (ATEC). If you call (800) 999-5505, Microsoft can help you locate the nearest ATEC.

Sylvan Prometric is the only testing agent authorized by Microsoft to deliver MCSE exams. You can find out where the nearest testing center is or schedule a time to take an exam by calling (800) 755-3926. All exams are given electronically.

Windows and Networking Reference Books

In this section, I've listed several books covering Microsoft Windows operating systems and networking. You may find these additional references useful as you continue your networking education.

Windows Networking References

Windows NT Server 4.0 Administrator's Bible. Cowart and Gregg, IDG Books Worldwide, 1996.

Windows NT Workstation 4.0 Bible. Wyatt, IDG Books Worldwide, 1996.

Networking Essentials (Second Edition). Microsoft Press, 1997.

Networking Essentials MCSE Study Guide. Nash, IDG Books Worldwide, 1998.

MCSE Test Prep: Networking Essentials. Barry et al., New Riders Publishing, 1997.

TCP/IP MCSE Study Guide. Bulette, IDG Books Worldwide, 1998.

TCP/IP: A Survival Guide for Users. Derfler and Rigney, IDG Books Worldwide, 1997.

General Networking References

TCP/IP Administration. Zacker, IDG Books Worldwide, 1998.

Network Protocol Handbook. Naugle, McGraw-Hill, 1994.

Networking for Dummies. Lowe, IDG Books Worldwide, 1994.

Computer Networks. Tanenbaum, Prentice-Hall, 1981.

Distributed Systems (Second Edition). Mullender, ACM Press, 1993.

The RAIDbook – A Source Book for Disk Array Technology (Sixth Edition). Massiglia, Peer to Peer Communications, 1997.

High-Performance Networking. Sportack et al., Sams.net Publishing, 1997.

General Windows References

Alan Simpson's Windows 98 Bible. Simpson, IDG Books Worldwide, 1998.

Windows 98 Secrets. Livingston and Straub, IDG Books Worldwide, 1998.

Windows 95 Secrets. Livingston and Straub, IDG Books Worldwide, 1995.

Windows Annoyances. Karp, O'Reilly & Associates, 1997.

Inside Windows NT (Second Edition). Solomon, Microsoft Press, 1998.

Useful Contacts for Network Administrators

In this section, I provide contact information (by phone, Web, and e-mail) for a number of manufacturers, vendors, and organizations. These aren't comprehensive lists, but the contacts included here have proven useful to network administrators in the real world.

National Internet Service Providers

Thousands of ISPs are operating throughout the country, but Table B-2 provides a short list of ISPs that have a national presence and a reasonably good reputation for service.

TABLE B-2 CONTACT INFORMATION FOR NATIONAL ISPS

Internet Service Provider	Web Address	Phone
AT&T WorldNet	`www.att.com/worldnet`	(800) 746-7846
Concentric	`www.concentric.net`	(800) 745-2747
EarthLink	`www.earthlink.com`	(800) 395-8425
NETCOM	`www.netcom.com`	(800) 251-6708
PSINet	`www.psinet.com`	(518) 283-8860
Sprint	`www.sprint.com`	(800) 747-9428

If you're outside the U.S., you can find information on worldwide Internet connections at the International Telecommunications Union Web site in Geneva at `www.itu.ch`.

Hardware Information

In this section, I provide contact information for hardware manufacturers and other hardware-related organizations. Table B-3 presents a list of contacts for manufacturers of components and devices.

TABLE B-3 HARDWARE DEVICE MANUFACTURER CONTACTS

Manufacturer	Web Site	Phone
Adaptec (and Trantor)	www.adaptec.com	(800) 959-7274
AMD	www.amd.com	(408) 732-2400
BusLogic (and Bustek, Mylex)	www.mylex.com	(800) 707-7274
Corel	www.corel.ca	(800) 772-6735
Cyrix	www.cyrix.com	(972) 968-8388
DPT	www.dpt.com	(407) 830-5522
Emulex	www.emulex.com	(714) 662-5600
Fujitsu	www.fcpa.com	(408) 894-3627
Intel	www.intel.com	(800) 628-8686
Maxtor (fax-back service)	www.maxtor.com	(800) 262-9867
Microsoft	www.microsoft.com	(425) 882-8080
Philips	www.philips.com	(615) 521-4316
Quantum	www.quantum.com	(800) 826-8022
S3	www.s3.com	(408) 588-8000
Seagate (and Conner)	www.seagate.com	(408) 438-5382
Symbios Logic (and NCR Microelectronics)	www.symbios.com	(800) 334-5454
Tecmar (and Wangtek, WangDAT, Sytron, Rexon)	www.tecmar.com	(303) 682-3700
Tyan Computer	www.tyan.com	(408) 956-8000
Western Digital	www.wdc.com	(800) 275-4932

Table B-4 presents a list of vendors who specialize in SCSI repeaters, converters, active terminators, high-quality cables, diagnostic tools, and so forth. See Chapter 8 for a discussion of SCSI technologies.

Table B-4 VENDORS OF SCSI-RELATED ACCESSORIES

Organization	Web Address	Phone/E-mail
Adaptec (and Trantor)	www.adaptec.com	(800) 959-7274
Ancot Corporation	www.ancot.com	(415) 322-5322
Apcon Inc.	www.apcon.com	(503) 639-6700
Digi-Key Electronics	www.digikey.com	(800) 344-4539
Granite Digital	www.scsipro.com	(510) 471-6442
Paralan Corporation	www.paralan.com	(619) 560-7266
Peripheral Test Instruments	www.scsitools.com	(800) 829-SCSI
Rancho Technology	www.rancho.com	(909) 987-3966

Here are several other useful Web sites that can provide additional hardware-related information:

- **Accelerated Graphics Port (AGP)** – To follow the latest developments in AGP technology and adoption, visit www.agpforum.org.
- **Fibre Channel** – You can keep up with the news on Fibre Channel technology by visiting the Fibre Channel Association (FCA) Web site at www.fibrechannel.com.
- **FireWire (IEEE 1394)** – You can find out about the latest developments in FireWire technology by visiting the IEEE-1394 Trade Association site at www.firewire.org.
- **Intel OverDrive** – You can find details on Intel's OverDrive CPU upgrades at www.intel.com/overdrive/odpfaq.htm. OverDrive BIOS upgrade requirements are available at www.intel.com/overdrive/upgrade/bios.
- **Microsoft HCL** – You can find information on Microsoft's hardware compatibility testing program at www.microsoft.com/hwtest, and updates of the hardware compatibility list (HCL) at www.microsoft.com/hwtest/hcl.
- **Network Scanners** – HP provides useful information on network scanners (scanners that attach directly to the network) at www.sender.hp.com.

- **Plug and Play (PnP)** – Microsoft Hardware Vendor Relations Group (HVRG) maintains a mailing list dedicated to Plug and Play information. It includes specifications, announcements, information on hardware-related workshops, details of the Windows Hardware Engineering Conference (WinHEC), and so forth. Contact `playlist@microsoft.com`. The Compuserve PLUGPLAY forum includes similar information.
- **Serial Storage Architecture (SSA)** – The SSA Industry Association (SSA-IA) maintains a Web site with the latest news on SSA technology at `www.ssaia.org`.
- **Universal Serial Bus (USB)** – Keep up with the latest USB developments by visiting `www.usb.org`.

ISDN Information

Your local telecommunications carrier should be your first stop in finding out about ISDN service in your area. Costs, installation lead times, and services offered vary widely from one region to another. Table B-5 provides pointers to a few of these carriers, as well as additional sources of information on ISDN.

TIP

Microsoft offers an online service that lets you investigate and even order ISDN service in your area. Visit `www.microsoft.com/windows/getisdn` for more information.

TABLE B-5 ISDN INFORMATION RESOURCES

Organization	Web Address	Phone/E-mail
Ameritech ISDN	`www.ameritech.com/products/data/teamdata/isdn/index.html`	(800) 832-6328
Bell Atlantic ISDN	`www.bell-atl.com/about/isdn.htm`	(800) 570-4736
BellSouth ISDN	`bsonline.bellsouth.net/cgi-bin/WebObjects/ISDN`	(800) 428-4736
Cincinnati Bell ISDN	`www.cinbelltel.com/business/isdninfo.html`	(513) 566-3282

Continued

Table B-5 ISDN INFORMATION RESOURCES *(Continued)*

Organization	Web Address	Phone/E-mail
Bellcore National ISDN Hotline	www.bellcore.com/ISDN	(800) 992-ISDN isdn@cc.bellcore.com
Pacific Bell ISDN	www.pacbell.com/products/business/fastrak/networking/isdn/info/index.html	(800) 472-4736 (800) 995-0346
Southwestern Bell ISDN	www.sbc.com/swbell/shortsub/isdn_services.html www.swbell.com/Catalog/Product_Detail/ISDN_User/	(800) 792-4736
SNET ISDN	www.snet.com	(800) 430-4736
Stentor ISDN	www.stentor.ca	(800) 578-4736
US West ISDN	www.uswest.com/isdn/index.html	(800) 728-4929

ADSL Information

At the time of writing, ADSL (Asymmetric Digital Subscriber Line) service is available only in selected markets, but is expected to broaden its scope quickly. Here are a few Web sites you may want to visit to keep up with the ADSL wave:

- www.aware.com/products
- www.adsl.com
- www.gte.com/adsl
- www.mot.com/SPS/MCTG/MDAD/adsl/index.html
- www.pairgain.com
- www.telechoice.com
- www.uawg.org
- www.westell.com
- www.zdnet.com/intweek/print/960408/infra/doc5.html

Other Information Resources

As a network administrator, you'll want to explore all the roads to timely information you can. In this section, I outline a few other possible sources for up-to-date networking material. Here are a few places to start looking:

- **Periodicals** – Books on Windows and networking can become outdated fairly quickly, as new product versions and new technologies emerge. As a network administrator, you should supplement your knowledge with up-to-date information found in periodicals. LAN Magazine, Network Magazine, InfoWorld, PC Week, Windows NT Magazine, and BackOffice Magazine all cover topics relevant to Windows-based networking.
- **User groups** – You can probably find a user group that focuses on just about any product you use. User groups tend to be highly specialized, but can be a good source of information through shared experiences and commiseration between users. Check with your product vendors, manufacturers, and local trade publications for information on user groups in your area.
- **Internet searches** – Searching the Internet for specific information on topics or products can yield some good (and not so good) information that you might not find in other sources. I've listed a few of the more popular Internet search engines later in this section.
- **Online newsgroups** – Several Windows newsgroups are active, at the time of writing. Newsgroups are often overlooked as an information resource, but can sometimes be the catalyst in figuring out the solution to a nagging problem. I've listed a few of the more active newsgroups later in this section.

Here are pointers to a few of the more popular search engines:

- AltaVista – `www.altavista.digital.com`
- Excite – `www.excite.com`
- HotBot – `www.hotbot.com`
- InfoSeek – `www.infoseek.com`
- Lycos – `www.lycos.com`
- Magellan – `www.mckinley.com`
- Webcrawler – `www.webcrawler.com`
- Yahoo! – `www.yahoo.com`

Here are some USENET newsgroups that deal with Windows 98, Windows 95, Windows NT, and networking:

- microsoft.public.win98.pre-release
- microsoft.public.win98
- comp.os.ms-windows.pre-release
- comp.os.ms-windows
- comp.os.ms-windows.misc
- alt.windows95
- comp.os.ms-windows.nt.admin.misc
- comp.os.ms-windows.nt.admin.networking
- comp.os.ms-windows.nt.misc
- comp.os.ms-windows.nt.setup.misc
- comp.os.ms-windows.nt.setup.hardware
- comp.os.ms-windows.nt.software.backoffice

Internet Background Information

Here are a few Web sites that contain some useful background information on the Internet and how it's being used:

- **Ethics and the Internet** – Visit `ei.cs.vt.edu/~cs3604/lib/WorldCodes/IAB.html` and `www-frd.fsl.noaa.gov/~moninger/STPP.html`.
- **Internet user demographics** – To explore the GVU WWW User Surveys, mentioned in Chapter 4, visit `www.gvu.gatech.edu/user_surveys/`.
- **General background** – Visit `wwwbacc.ift.ulaval.ca/~ift20327/notes/histoire/nsfmci.html`.

Web Site Testing Resources

Here are some pointers to Web sites related to testing the validity and usability of your Web site in various browser environments:

- `www.testnow.com`
- `www.research.digital.com/nsl/formtest`

- www.delorie.com/web/wpbcv.html
- www.avnet.co.uk/tesseract/webtesters
- www.tsdesign.com/tsdesign/audit/audit.html
- www.uark.edu/~wrg
- www-dsed.llnl.gov/documents/WWWtest.html

Network Security Resources

In the following sections, I point you to a number of resources relevant to computer and network security. See Chapter 12 for a discussion of the most typical security problems and solutions.

Computer Emergency Response Teams (CERTs)

A number of *Computer Emergency Response Teams* (*CERTs*) are located throughout the world. CERTs investigate computer security issues and find ways to defend against them. Table B-6 includes pointers to some of these response centers.

TABLE B-6 COMPUTER EMERGENCY RESPONSE TEAMS

Response Team	Web Site	Phone/E-mail
Australian CERT (AusCERT)	www.auscert.org.au	(61) 7 3365-4417 aucert@auscert.org.au
Automated System Security Incident Support Team (ASSIST)	www.assist.mil	(800) 357-4231 assist@assist.mil
CERT Coordination Center	www.cert.org	(412) 268-7090 cert@cert.org
Computer Incident Advisory Capability (CIAC)	ciac.llnl.gov	(510) 422-8193 ciac@llnl.gov
Federal Computer Incident Response Capability (FedCIRC)	fedcirc.llnl.gov	(412) 268-6321 fedcirc@fedcirc.nist.gov
Forum of Incident Response Security Teams (FIRST)	www.first.org	first-sec@first.org

Continued

TABLE B-6 COMPUTER EMERGENCY RESPONSE TEAMS *(Continued)*

Response Team	Web Site	Phone/E-mail
German Research Network CERT (DFN-CERT)	www.cert.dfn.de/eng/dfncert	(49) 40 5494-2262 dfncert@cert.dfn.de
NASA Incident Response Center (NASIRC)	www-nasirc.nasa.gov/nasa	(800) 762-7472 nasirc@nasirc.nasa.gov

You can find a complete list of CERTs in Europe at www.cert.dfn.de/eng/csir/europe/certs.html.

Security Web Sites

Below is a list of Web sites that disseminate and track information on computer and network security issues:

- cs-www.ncsl.nist.gov
- java.sun.com/security
- spam.abuse.net
- www.cert.org
- www.cs.purdue.edu/coast/coast.html
- www.cs.purdue.edu/coast/hotlist
- www.iss.net/vd/library.html
- www.ncsa.com
- www.nsi.org
- www.ntbugtraq.com
- www.ntsecurity.net
- www.telstra.com.au/info/security.html
- www.tno.nl/instit/fel/intern/wkinfsec.html

Index

A

B

D

E

G

H

I

J

K

L

N

O

P

Q

R

S

T

U

V

W

X

my2cents.idgbooks.com

Register This Book — And Win!

Visit **http://my2cents.idgbooks.com** to register this book and we'll automatically enter you in our fantastic monthly prize giveaway. It's also your opportunity to give us feedback: let us know what you thought of this book and how you would like to see other topics covered.

Discover IDG Books Online!

The IDG Books Online Web site is your online resource for tackling technology — at home and at the office. Frequently updated, the IDG Books Online Web site features exclusive software, insider information, online books, and live events!

10 Productive & Career-Enhancing Things You Can Do at www.idgbooks.com

- Nab source code for your own programming projects.
- Download software.
- Read Web exclusives: special articles and book excerpts by IDG Books Worldwide authors.
- Take advantage of resources to help you advance your career as a Novell or Microsoft professional.
- Buy IDG Books Worldwide titles or find a convenient bookstore that carries them.
- Register your book and win a prize.
- Chat live online with authors.
- Sign up for regular e-mail updates about our latest books.
- Suggest a book you'd like to read or write.
- Give us your 2¢ about our books and about our Web site.

You say you're not on the Web yet? It's easy to get started with IDG Books' *Discover the Internet*, available at local retailers everywhere.